Philosophical Studies Series

Volume 156

Series Editor
Massimo Durante, Dipartimento di Giurisprudenza, Università degli studi di Torino, TORINO, Torino, Italy

Editorial Board
Phyllis Illari, University College London, London, UK
Patrick Allo, Vrije Universiteit Brussel, Brussel, Belgium
Shannon Vallor, Santa Clara University, Santa Clara, USA

Advisory Editors
Lynne Baker, Department of Philosophy, University of Massachusetts, Amherst, USA
Stewart Cohen, Arizona State University, Tempe, Israel
Radu Bogdan, Department of Philosophy, Tulane University, New Orleans, USA
Marian David, Karl-Franzens-Universität, Graz, Vatican City State
John Fischer, University of California, Riverside, Riverside, USA
Keith Lehrer, University Of Arizona, Tucson, USA
Denise Meyerson, Macquarie University, Sydney, Australia
Francois Recanati, Ecole Normale Supérieure, Institut Jean Nicod, Paris, France
Mark Sainsbury, University of Texas at Austin, Austin, USA
Barry Smith, State University of New York at Buffalo, Buffalo, USA
Linda Zagzebski, Department of Philosophy, University of Oklahoma, Norman, USA

Philosophical Studies Series aims to provide a forum for the best current research in contemporary philosophy broadly conceived, its methodologies, and applications. Since Wilfrid Sellars and Keith Lehrer founded the series in 1974, the book series has welcomed a wide variety of different approaches, and every effort is made to maintain this pluralism, not for its own sake, but in order to represent the many fruitful and illuminating ways of addressing philosophical questions and investigating related applications and disciplines.

The book series is interested in classical topics of all branches of philosophy including, but not limited to:

- Ethics
- Epistemology
- Logic
- Metaphysics
- Philosophy of language
- Philosophy of logic
- Philosophy of mind
- Philosophy of religion
- Philosophy of science

Special attention is paid to studies that focus on:

- the interplay of empirical and philosophical viewpoints
- the implications and consequences of conceptual phenomena for research as well as for society
- philosophies of specific sciences, such as philosophy of biology, philosophy of chemistry, philosophy of computer science, philosophy of information, philosophy of neuroscience, philosophy of physics, or philosophy of technology; and
- contributions to the formal (logical, set-theoretical, mathematical, information-theoretical, decision-theoretical, etc.) methodology of sciences.

Likewise, the applications of conceptual and methodological investigations to applied sciences as well as social and technological phenomena are strongly encouraged.

Philosophical Studies Series welcomes historically informed research, but privileges philosophical theories and the discussion of contemporary issues rather than purely scholarly investigations into the history of ideas or authors. Besides monographs, *Philosophical Studies Series* publishes thematically unified anthologies, selected papers from relevant conferences, and edited volumes with a well-defined topical focus inside the aim and scope of the book series. The contributions in the volumes are expected to be focused and structurally organized in accordance with the central theme(s), and are tied together by an editorial introduction. Volumes are completed by extensive bibliographies.

The series discourages the submission of manuscripts that contain reprints of previous published material and/or manuscripts that are below 160 pages/88,000 words.

For inquiries and submission of proposals authors can contact the editor-in-chief Mariarosaria Taddeo via: massimo.durante@unito.it

Waldomiro J. Silva-Filho
Editor

The Epistemology of Conversation

First Essays

Springer

Editor
Waldomiro J. Silva-Filho
Department of Philosophy
Universidade Federal da Bahia
Salvador, Bahia, Brazil

ISSN 0921-8599   ISSN 2542-8349 (electronic)
Philosophical Studies Series
ISBN 978-3-031-74068-8   ISBN 978-3-031-74069-5 (eBook)
https://doi.org/10.1007/978-3-031-74069-5

© The Editor(s) (if applicable) and The Author(s), under exclusive license to Springer Nature Switzerland AG 2024

This work is subject to copyright. All rights are solely and exclusively licensed by the Publisher, whether the whole or part of the material is concerned, specifically the rights of translation, reprinting, reuse of illustrations, recitation, broadcasting, reproduction on microfilms or in any other physical way, and transmission or information storage and retrieval, electronic adaptation, computer software, or by similar or dissimilar methodology now known or hereafter developed.
The use of general descriptive names, registered names, trademarks, service marks, etc. in this publication does not imply, even in the absence of a specific statement, that such names are exempt from the relevant protective laws and regulations and therefore free for general use.
The publisher, the authors and the editors are safe to assume that the advice and information in this book are believed to be true and accurate at the date of publication. Neither the publisher nor the authors or the editors give a warranty, expressed or implied, with respect to the material contained herein or for any errors or omissions that may have been made. The publisher remains neutral with regard to jurisdictional claims in published maps and institutional affiliations.

This Springer imprint is published by the registered company Springer Nature Switzerland AG
The registered company address is: Gewerbestrasse 11, 6330 Cham, Switzerland

If disposing of this product, please recycle the paper.

This book is dedicated to all the victims of intolerance and the cruel absence of dialog. Dedicated to the memory of Alvin I. Goldman. His rigorous, revolutionary, and generous work inaugurated a new path for epistemology.

Contents

Introduction. Conversation: Epistemological Investigations 1
Waldomiro J. Silva-Filho

Conversation and Joint Agency:
Why Addressees Are Epistemically Special 13
John Greco

On the Contours of a Conversation 29
Sanford C. Goldberg

Virtuous Arguing 49
Duncan Pritchard

Wit, Pomposity, Curiosity, and Justice:
Some Virtues and Vices of Conversationalists 65
Alessandra Tanesini

Conversation and Joint Commitment 85
Margaret Gilbert and Maura Priest

Group Belief and the Role of Conversation 109
Fernando Broncano-Berrocal

Knowledge Norms and Conversation 127
J. Adam Carter

Norms of Inquiry Conversations: An Essay 149
Florencia Rimoldi

Deception Detection Research: Some Lessons
for the Epistemology of Testimony 173
Peter J. Graham

Twisted Ways to Speak Our Minds, or Ways to Speak
Our Twisted Minds? 207
Luis Rosa

Aesthetic Disagreement, Aesthetic Testimony, and Defeat 223
Mona Simion and Christoph Kelp

Critical Social Epistemology and the Liberating Power of Dialogue..... 239
Solmu Anttila and Catarina Dutilh Novaes

Epistemology of Conversation: General References 263

References 265

About the Authors

Solmu Anttila is completing a PhD project on political epistemology and the political theory of epistemic injustice at Vrije Universiteit Amsterdam. Her project is a subpart of the consolidating project funded by the European Research Council "The Social Epistemology of Argumentation."

Fernando Broncano-Berrocal is a Ramón y Cajal Research Fellow at the University of Barcelona and a Senior Member of the LOGOS Research Group and the Barcelona Institute of Analytic Philosophy. He is author of *The Philosophy of Group Polarization. Epistemology, Metaphysics, Psychology* (with J. Adam Carter, Routledge, 2021) and co-editor of *The Epistemology of Group Disagreement* (Routledge, 2021).

J. Adam Carter is a Professor of Philosophy at the University of Glasgow. He is the author, among others, of *Stratified Virtue Epistemology: A Defence* (Cambridge University Press, 2024), *A Telic Theory of Trust* (OUP, 2024), *Autonomous Knowledge* (OUP, 2022), and *Digital Knowledge* (Routledge, 2021) and co-editor of *The Philosophy of Group Polarization. Epistemology, Metaphysics, Psychology* (Routledge, 2021).

Catarina Dutilh Novaes is a Professor and University Research Chair at the Department of Philosophy of the VU Amsterdam and a Professorial Fellow at Arché in St Andrews (2019–2024). She is the author of *The Dialogical Roots of Deduction* (Cambridge University Press, 2020; winner of the 2022 Lakatos Award).

Margaret Gilbert is an Abraham I. Melden Chair in Moral Philosophy and Distinguished Professor in the Philosophy School of Humanities at the University of California, Irvine. She is the author, among others, of *Life in Groups* (OUP, 2023), *Rights and Demands* (OUP, 2018), and *Joint Commitment* (OUP, 2013).

Sanford C. Goldberg is a Chester D. Tripp Professor in the Humanities at the Northwestern University. A good sample of his work can be found in his books,

Anti-Individualism (Cambridge University Press, 2007), *Relying on Others* (OUP, 2010), *Assertion* (OUP, 2015), *To the Best of Our Knowledge* (OUP, 2018), *Conversational Pressure* (OUP, 2020), and *Foundations and Applications of Social Epistemology* (OUP, 2021).

Peter J. Graham is a Professor in the Department of Philosophy and the Program in Linguistics at the University of California, Riverside. He is the co-editor of *Routledge Handbook of Social Epistemology* (Routledge, 2021) and *Epistemic Entitlement* (Oxford University Press, 2019).

John Greco is a Robert L. McDevitt, K.S.G., K.C.H.S., and Catherine H. McDevitt L.C.H.S. Professor of Philosophy. His publications include *The Transmission of Knowledge* (Cambridge University Press, 2020), *Virtue Theoretic Epistemology* (co-editor; Cambridge University Press, 2020), *Epistemic Evaluation: Purposeful Epistemology* (co-editor; OUP, 2015), *Achieving Knowledge* (Cambridge University Press, 2010), *Putting Skeptics in Their Place* (Cambridge University Press, 2000), and *The Oxford Handbook of Skepticism* (editor; OUP, 2008).

Christoph Kelp is a Professor of Philosophy at the University of Glasgow, Vice Director of Cogito Epistemology Research Centre, and Director of The British Society for the Theory of Knowledge. He is the author of *The Nature and Normativity of Defeat* (Cambridge University Press, 2023), *Sharing Knowledge: A Functionalist Account of Assertion* (with M Simion, Cambridge University Press, 2021), *Inquiry, Knowledge, and Understanding* (OUP, 2021), and *Good Thinking: A Knowledge First Virtue Epistemology* (Routledge, 2018).

Maura Priest is an Associate Professor of Philosophy and Bioethicist at Arizona State University. She is the author of numerous articles in the most important philosophy journals in the fields of Epistemology, Moral Philosophy, and Medical Ethics.

Duncan Pritchard is a Distinguished Professor of Philosophy at the University of California, Irvine. He is the author, among others, of *Skepticism* (with A. Coliva, Routledge, 2022), *Scepticism: A Very Short Introduction* (OUP, 2019), *Epistemic Angst: Radical Skepticism and the Groundlessness of Our Believing* (Princeton University Press, 2015), *Epistemological Disjunctivism* (OPU, 2012), and *Epistemic Luck* (OUP 2005).

Florencia Rimoldi is an Associate Research Fellow at the National Council for Scientific and Technical Research (CONICET, Argentina) and Philosophy Professor at Universidad de Buenos Aires.

About the Authors

Luis Rosa is a Lecturer at CONCEPT, University of Cologne and Visiting Professor at the Federal University of Bahia. He is the author of numerous articles in the most important philosophy journals in the fields of Epistemology and Logic.

Waldomiro J. Silva-Filho is a Full Professor of Philosophy at the Federal University of Bahia. He is the author, among others, of *Inquiring Reasons* (Springer, forthcoming) and co-editor of *Thinking About Oneself: The Place and Value of Reflection in Philosophy and Psychology* (Springer, 2019)

Mona Simion is a Professor of Philosophy and Deputy Director of the COGITO Epistemology Research Centre at the University of Glasgow. She is the author of *Resistance to Evidence* (Cambridge University Press, 2024), *Shifty Speech and Independent Thought* (OUP 2021), and *Sharing Knowledge* (with C. Kelp Cambridge University Press, 2021).

Alessandra Tanesini is a Professor of Philosophy at Cardiff University. He is the author of *The Mismeasure of the Self: A Study in Vice Epistemology* (OUP, 2021), co-editor of *Polarisation, Arrogance, and Dogmatism: Philosophical Perspectives* (Routledge, 2020), and co-editor of *The Routledge Handbook of the Philosophy of Humility* (Routledge, 2020), *Philosophy of Language A-Z* (Edinburgh University Press, 2007), and *Wittgenstein: A Feminist Interpretation* (Cambridge: Polity Press, 2004).

Introduction. Conversation: Epistemological Investigations

Waldomiro J. Silva-Filho

> *Yes, meaning something is like going toward someone.*
> L. Wittgenstein, *Philosophical Investigations*, § 457.

> *In my opinion, the most fruitful and natural exercise of our mind is the conversation.*
> Michel de Montaigne, De l'art de conferer, Les Essais III.8.

1 Opening a New Path

Conversation, dialogue, reasonable disagreement, and the acquisition of knowledge through the words of others, all of this has always been at the center of philosophers' concerns since the emergence of philosophy in Ancient Greece. It is also important to recognize that in contemporary philosophy, marked by the linguistic turn, there is a wealth of intellectual production on ethical (e.g. McKenna, 2012), psycho-linguistic (e.g. Clark, 1996), logical-linguistic (e.g. Grice, 1989) and pragmatic (e.g. Walton, 1992) aspects of the conversation. Despite all this, this is the first collection of texts dedicated exclusively to the strictly epistemic aspects of this phenomenon which is so decisive for the very constitution of our humanity. This book brings together the contributions of 15 leading philosophers on some of the most relevant issues of what we could call the Epistemology of Conversation.

The recent publications of *Conversational Pressure* by Sandford Goldberg (2020) and *The Transmission of Knowledge* by John Greco (2021), each in their way, mark a movement of growing convergence of interest around epistemological

W. J. Silva-Filho (✉)
Universidade Federal da Bahia, CNPq, CONCEPT, Salvador, Brazil
e-mail: waldojsf@ufba.br

© The Author(s), under exclusive license to Springer Nature Switzerland AG 2024
W. J. Silva-Filho (ed.), *The Epistemology of Conversation*, Philosophical Studies Series 156, https://doi.org/10.1007/978-3-031-74069-5_1

investigations into conversation. On the one hand, Goldberg (2020, 2) deals with the *constrictions* and *regulations* that are generated by the very performances of some linguistic acts, such as assertions, declarations, testimonies, reports, and other similar acts that involve "saying something" to someone. Goldberg (2020, *passim*) understands conversation as involving two aspects: an *interpersonal* aspect and an *epistemic* aspect. By interpersonal aspect he considers the fact that conversation is a rational and cooperative act; when someone performs some linguistic acts, such as declaring, reporting, affirming, this generates rational expectations and demands in the participants. By epistemic aspect, he considers that these acts imply the exchange of the speaker's representations and beliefs about how the world is. Greco (2021, viii) explores the nature of the epistemic relationship between speakers and listeners in testimonial exchanges, the nature and extent of epistemic dependence, the importance of an epistemic division of labor, and the role of trust in testimonial justification and knowledge.

For Greco, Social Epistemology seeks to understand how the quality of a person's epistemic position depends not only on their individual cognitive resources and capacities but on the good health and proper functioning of interactions in a wider epistemic community. Also for Goldberg, Social Epistemology has the basic assumption that the various people who make up an epistemic community are important cognitive agents precisely because there is a characteristic feature of human experience based on the distribution of epistemic tasks. This practice emerges in real-time conversation, both in its good and bad forms, and when it does, it reflects the cooperative norms of the conversation itself.

That's what this book is about. About how the participation of people as agents of conversational acts is a rich horizon of themes for epistemology.

2 Towards an Epistemology of Conversation

Like everything else in philosophy, there is always a long history and countless paths that lead us today to return to an old and persistent question about the technique, value, and possibility of conversation. On the occasion of receiving the Hegel Prize from the city of Stuttgart, Germany, Donald Davidson gave a lecture entitled "Dialectic and dialogue" (Davidson, 1994). On this occasion, Davidson, on the one hand, suggested that the Platonic dialogues in which Socrates plays a central role establish a common heritage that intertwines the traditions of analytic and continental philosophy and, on the other hand, summarized one of his most important contributions to philosophy: it is in the effective practice of linguistic communication, dialogue and disagreement that our metaphysics, the notions of truth, knowledge, justice, make sense.

The conference "Dialectic and Dialogue" is part of a short series of articles by Davidson (1985, 1992a, 1994, 1997) on Plato's work. They are short texts that are different from the typical style of analytical philosophers: they deal with the dialectical method, the role of Socrates, the philosophical meaning of dialogue, conversation, and the problem of linguistic comprehension. Davidson (1992a) discusses, for example, Plato's reflections on the difference between the spoken word and the written word and why Socrates keeps all this philosophical work in the form of dialectical conversation. The spoken word would be superior to the written form for several reasons: firstly, the written word would be a mere simulation of the *episteme*, which induces the reader to believe that they know something when in reality they only have a *doxa*. In Plato's metaphor, written words are like a painting: its image appears to be alive, but it is completely devoid of vitality, remaining completely silent, unable to interact and respond to any challenge made to it, limiting itself to a monotonous and endless repetition of itself. Without discerning with whom it is convenient and possible to communicate, the written word wanders from hand to hand and can reach both the person competent enough to understand its message and the one who is not prepared to understand it and has no interest in it. In addition, the written word seems to depend on the spoken word, i.e. to defend itself against criticism and challenges from interlocutors, it needs the help of its author's voice. In the end, written words serve as a remedy for memory (Davidson, 1990).

Speech, on the other hand, involves both moral and epistemic commitments on the part of those taking part in a conversation. It is for this reason that participants must be aware that *sincerity* is not an arbitrary imposition, but a *condition*. A person's agency as a speaker is related to their intention to address another person and to be correctly interpreted—and, of course, to exchange positions with their interlocutor. In dialogue, as conducted by Socrates—but which could be present in all forms of linguistic communication—speaking meaningfully does not depend on the fact that speakers and listeners are supported by previously known grammatical rules and conventions (Davidson, 1992b); roughly speaking, what is needed is for people to be willing both to assume the provisional position of a speaker who wants to be interpreted and that of a listener, both of whom attribute to their interlocutor the legitimate right to be treated as a rational agent. Above all, people must intend to cooperate with each other in pursuit of something they can only achieve together. Something trivial in a conversation between men and women becomes a central point in philosophy: the mutual desire to act together toward understanding, knowledge, and enlightenment through language.

The word 'conversation' covers a broad spectrum of episodes that have certain *family resemblances*. Roughly speaking, we can talk about conversation as *an exchange of words* as well as conversation as *dialog* in the philosophical and argumentative sense of the term. Conversation as an exchange of words refers to the fact that many conversations, such as everyday conversations, have diverse and asymmetrical objectives: they are exchanges of words aimed at entertainment, flirting, intimidation, manipulation, gossip, jokes, etc. Conversation as dialog, on the other hand, implies that certain conversations can involve the transmission and generation of knowledge, can be motivated by disagreements and disputes over the justification of beliefs, but can also be guided by epistemic cooperation on a subject, curiosity, doubt, etc. and have epistemic objectives.

Our conversations, even the most trivial ones, are not just a succession of disconnected fragments. For Paul Grice (1989), conversations are characteristically joint agencies and cooperative efforts; each person taking part in a conversation recognizes a common purpose or set of purposes, or at least a mutually accepted direction—even though there may be corrections and calibrations along the way. Grice (1989, 26) then suggests a "Cooperative Principle" that participants should observe: "Make your conversational contribution such as is required, at the stage at which it occurs, by the accepted purpose or direction of the talk Exchange in which you are engaged." Similarly, for Herbert Clark (1996), conversation arises when people use linguistic exchange to coordinate the joint activities in which they are involved. In this peculiar type of *language use*, people cooperate to reach local agreements in the course of each section and subsection, including the opening and closing of the conversation itself.

One of the intuitions we can explore is the idea that an Epistemology of Conversation could be a field of investigation for Social Epistemology.

Such an Epistemology of Conversation should consider at least six points (there may be others or perhaps not those listed below):

(a) *norms of conversation*: it is necessary to investigate whether the norm of conversation should be reducible to the norm of speaker-audience interaction when the speaker must intend to speak something true and the listener must understand this intention, and whether the theoretical field of the Epistemology of Conversation is contained in the set of problems and concepts of the Epistemology of Testimony.

(b) *motivations for conversation*: people can feel stimulated in a relevant way to start a conversation because of legitimate disagreements, curiosity about an interlocutor's beliefs, and doubts about a topic they share with the interlocutor;

(c) *competences required for conversation*: since conversation is a joint agency, it involves a performance with many intellectual demands, we must investigate which virtues facilitate and which vices hinder its epistemic achievements;

(d) *conversation as a means of inquiry*: conversation can be a means or method of inquiry in cases of the intentional pursuit of epistemic goods when the interlocutors believe that *joint agency* can lead them to achieve, understanding, knowledge, or another epistemic good;

(e) *goals of the conversation*: since disagreement, curiosity, and doubt are among the motivations of conversation and the interlocutors must have intellectual virtues and avoid vices, any outcome of a conversation will fulfill an epistemic good, whatever it may be, such as knowledge, justification, keeping an open mind, etc. and;[1]

(f) *benefits of an Epistemology of Conversation*: considering the new scenarios of liberal democracies and the processes of corrosion of public space, an

---

[1] It could be argued that reaching a state of doubt or impasse, recognizing a cognitive difficulty and even suspending judgment can be considered epidemic goods. Thanks to Plínio Smith for pointing this out.

Epistemology of Conversation could contribute to shedding some light on events such as polarization (total impossibility of conversations), disintegration of epistemic communities, silencing and epistemic injustices and so on.[2]

The chapters of this book sail on the waves of these and other subjects.

3 Contributions to the Volume

As will be seen in the chapters of this book, there is a crucial epistemic proximity and difference between *testimony* and *conversation*. Similar to testimony, when a person forms a belief *from* the words of others (Lackey, 2008; Goldberg, 2010; McMyler, 2011), the conversation is a cooperative means of forming and transmitting epistemic states. However, unlike testimony, conversation is characterized by a dynamic (often adversarial) in which people continually switch positions as speaker and listener in the same event. In addition, the position of conversation participants (as speakers and addressee) and overhearers can have some crucial differences. This is the starting point of this book.

In the first chapter of this book, "Conversation and joint agency: Why addressees are epistemically special", John Greco explores the idea that the category of conversation is both *broader* and *narrower* than the category of testimony. For him, the epistemologies of conversation and testimony overlap in ways that need to be investigated. Drawing on Herbert H. Clark's (1996) description of conversation as a structure, Greco claims that both conversation and testimony essentially involve *joint agency*.[3] Furthermore, he argues that an appreciation of this point resolves an important dispute in the Epistemology of Testimony: whether addressees have a special epistemic position in relation to eavesdroppers or mere observers. The claim defended by Greco in this chapter is that the participants have a special position and that the etiologies of the beliefs of the recipients and those the non-recipients are different. This difference makes the testimonial beliefs of addressees epistemically superior because the model of cooperation between speakers and addressees usually

---

[2] More recently, more specifically in Social Epistemology, there has been a rich growth of studies on the *epistemology of politics* and the *epistemology of democracy* that deal with the formation and distribution of beliefs in the political environment, especially the processes of epistemic formation of *deliberation*, the central pillar of liberal democracies (Johnson, 2018; Broncano-Berrocal & Carter, 2021; Edenberg & Hannon, 2021; Tanesini & Lynch, 2021). This is because it seems that one of the necessary characteristics of the democratic way of life is associated with the fact that political agents cannot renounce the power of words and the open and indeterminate game of disputing reasons in the environment of dialog, of conversation based on arguments.

[3] Elsewhere, John Greco (2021, 47) understands "joint agency" in these terms: "... recent action theory recognizes a special kind of action, one that can be characterized as 'acting together.' It is now standard that joint agency involves a network of shared intentions and common understanding between the participating actors, as well as specific kinds of interdependence."

has the consequence of making the testimonial belief more reliable, more secure, better supported by evidence, etc.

Around the same problem, the second chapter, "On the contours of a conversation" was written by Sanford C. Goldberg. As I said earlier, Goldberg is the author of an important and influential monograph on the epistemology of conversation, *Conversational Pressure* (Goldberg, 2020). In the chapter that integrates this book, Goldberg states that conversations are normatively structured exchanges: to be a participant in a conversation is to be subject to certain normative expectations. At the same time, the information that speakers offer in a conversation seems to be available also to those people to whom the statements are not directly addressed. This suggests that the contours of a conversation are not epistemically significant. In the chapter, Goldberg argues that the contours of a conversation have a broad normative significance because the participants will be within the conversation under distinct forms of constrictions and obligations. However, he claims that these norms that underpin a conversation are non-epistemic in nature and that epistemic norms themselves go beyond the contours of a conversation.

Once we accept that conversation is a joint agency, we must imagine that this requires certain specific skills and competences from the participants. Some requirements for the participants in a conversation are linguistic competences and others are epistemic virtues. *What are the intellectual virtues required for conversation?*

Duncan Pritchard's "Virtuous Arguing" explores this problem. For him, an important type of conversation is essentially adversarial in nature, when two parties engage in a debate on a subject of common interest and can hold different opinions. How should these conversations be conducted properly from a specifically epistemic point of view? Pritchard argues that intellectual virtues are of crucial importance in answering this question. In particular, he argues that a conception of good argumentation based on intellectual virtues is preferable to alternative ways of thinking about good argumentation in purely formal or strategic terms (although it may capture what is attractive about these formal conceptions while avoiding some fundamental problems they face). Considering the contemporary social and political scenario, we should seek the cultivation of a virtuous intellectual character and, therefore, the development of individuals who embody the virtuous way of disputing their opinions and beliefs.

Alessandra Tanesini, in her "Wit, pomposity, curiosity, and justice: some virtues and vices of conversationalists," faces the same problem. Her text has two main aims. The first is to defend a virtue-theoretical characterization of what makes a conversation good as a conversation. In Tanesini's view, excellent conversations are conversations that are carried out in the way in which virtuous conversationalists would execute them. The second aim of the chapter is to outline some character traits that may have a distinct contribution to the epistemology of conversation. Two of these traits, 'wit' and 'justice' are virtues that contribute to the success of conversations as vehicles for exchanging information and strengthening bonds of trust. Another trait, 'pomposity,' is an obstacle to these types of conversational success. Finally, Tanesini argues that 'curiosity' can be a very important component in conversation, promoting both the failures and successes of conversations.

A common point in this collection is that conversations are cooperative communicative acts in which the participants assume common purposes and make a commitment to contribute relevant statements. Margaret Gilbert (1996, 2014, 2023) has an influential philosophical contribution on joint commitments and has defended a specific description of collective belief. In "Conversation and joint commitment," Margaret Gilbert and Maura Priest propose that paradigmatic conversations involve the negotiation of a series of collective beliefs. According to the authors, *collective beliefs* are constituted by commitments that are *joint* in a sense that is explained in the chapter. The parties to any joint commitment have associated rights and obligations. This helps to consolidate a given collective belief once it has been established. Even when interlocutors fail to negotiate a collective belief whose content has been explicitly specified, they are likely to establish one or more associated implicit collective beliefs. They call this the *negotiation of collective belief* thesis—the NCB thesis, for short. The NCB thesis holds that conversation, as described in the chapter, consists of the development of a *collective cognitive profile*. This is collective and not summed, in the sense of being attributable to each of the participants as individuals.

Building on the ideas of Gilbert and Priest (2013), the chapter "Group Belief and the Role of Conversation" by Fernando Broncano-Berrocal examines the role of conversation in the formation of group beliefs in the context of the summativism/non-summativism debate, i.e. the debate about whether group beliefs are a function of the beliefs of individual group members. Broncano-Berrocal investigates whether it is possible for groups to form collective beliefs without communication between their members and, in doing so, seeks to explain how this relates to the summative and non-summative views and Margaret Gilbert's (2014) idea of *joint commitment*. He analyzes the *negotiation of collective belief* thesis originally presented by Gilbert and Priest (2013), according to which the process of everyday conversation is structured around the negotiation of collective beliefs. For Broncano Berrocal, this thesis only makes sense in a non-summative framework, but when specific non-summative views are combined with it, the relevant non-summative views either become inapplicable or yield the wrong results. The chapter closes by concluding that summativism offers a simpler, more neutral, and theoretically less loaded picture of the role of conversation in the formation of group beliefs.

The seventh chapter was written by J. Adam Carter. "Knowledge Norms and Conversation" poses the following question: Might knowledge normatively govern conversations and not just their discrete constituent thoughts and (assertoric) actions? Adam Carter answers yes, at least for a restricted class of conversations that he calls "*aimed* conversations." In the view defended in the chapter, aimed conversations are governed by participatory know-how—viz., knowledge how to do what each interlocutor to the conversation shares a participatory intention to do by means of that conversation. In the specific case of conversations that are in the service of joint inquiry, the view defended is that interlocutors (A, B, ... n) must intentionally inquire together into whether p, by means of an aimed conversation X, only if A, B, ... n *know how* to use X to find out *together* whether p. The view is supported by considerations about instrumental rationality, shared intentionality, the epistemology of intentional action, as well as linguistic data.

Florencia Rimoldi's "Norms of Inquiring Conversations" explores the epistemic aspects of what she calls *Inquiry Conversations* (ICs), i.e. conversations that have epistemic goals. Although the existence of this sub-class of conversations has been acknowledged since the beginning of philosophy, they seem to have been under the radar by contemporary epistemologists. Thus, she argues that there is a fertile area of research, within the epistemology of conversation, that has, as its object of study, the epistemic norms of Inquiry Conversations. To give plausibility to this hypothesis, Rimoldi follows a two-step strategy. The first step tries to motivate the project of recognizing ICs and studying their epistemic norms. To do so, the first section provides a general characterization of ICs, motivated by some examples from ordinary life. The second section tries to motivate the idea that they are proper inquiries. For this, It takes into account a broad understanding of the notion of research which, not surprisingly, is what interests research epistemologists. This chapter proposes a way of addressing the specific epistemic aspects of ICs: non-ideal inquiry epistemology; it is therefore suggested that the conversational pressure that participants of ICs are subject to cannot be reduced to epistemic norms of assertion or of uptake of testimonial beliefs. The second step is to dig deeper into the theoretical steps and resources needed to study the epistemic norms of Inquiry Conversations. The third section focuses on the nature of these conversations, and their identity conditions, with the explicit intention of not idealizing aspects that might be epistemically relevant. The chapter's argument is based on Grice and post-gricean literature for the first task, and Walton's Theory of Type Dialogues for the second. The last section discusses the epistemic import of certain factors that in section three I have identified as relevant for identifying ICs: (i) environment, (ii) participants and (iii) epistemic goals.

"Deception detection research: Some lessons for the epistemology of testimony" by Peter J. Graham explores a fundamental topic of conversation, the possibility of lying in linguistic exchanges. According to the author, in the *folk-theory of lying*, liars let slip observable clues to their insincerity, observable clues that make it easier to detect a liar in real time. Several social epistemologists rely on the explanatory accuracy of this folk-theory as empirically well-confirmed when constructing their normative accounts of the epistemology of testimony. However, research into fraud detection in communication studies has shown that our folk theory is mistaken.

Graham draws on a wealth of empirical research material. From this point of view, popular theory is not empirically well confirmed, but empirically refuted. Graham confronts arguments from epistemologists who object to this empirical research and who question whether experiments in the laboratory can be transferred to real life. The chapter then presents the methodology of the research, defends its ecological validity, and discusses further research into the nature and frequency of lies in everyday life. For Graham, social epistemologists stand to gain from understanding the details of fraud detection research and its findings. The chapter concludes with a detailed examination of Elizabeth Fricker's (1994, 2024) reliance on folk theory in her "local reductionist" epistemology of testimony.

"Twisted Ways to Speak our Minds, or Ways to Speak our Twisted Minds?" by Luis Rosa is the ninth chapter. The central problem of the chapter revolves around a problem similar to Peter Graham's chapter: there are many ways in which a speaker can confuse his audience. In this chapter, Luis Rosa focuses on one of these ways, namely a way of speaking that seems to manifest a kind of cognitive dissonance on several levels on the part of the speaker. The chapter aims to explain why these ways of speaking sound so distorted. The explanation is twofold, since their distorted nature can come from the very mental states that the speaker manifests or from how they choose to express themselves (even if there is nothing wrong with their mental states). So-called 'Moore-paradoxical' utterances are but one example of the phenomenon, and the explanation of what is wrong about them is subsumed under a more general explanation here—one that captures also the twisted-ness of utterances whereby questions are raised or intentions expressed.

Mona Simion and Christoph Kelp are the authors of "Aesthetic Disagreement, Aesthetic Testimony, and Defeat". The chapter investigates the relationship between the epistemology of conversation on aesthetic issues, aesthetic disagreement, defeat, and the semantics of aesthetic discourse. For the authors, the phenomenon of the epistemic defeat of testimony on aesthetic issues has received little or no attention in the literature. This chapter makes up for this lack: it argues that the existence of the defeat of testimony on aesthetic issues gives us reason to prefer a realistic view of the semantics of aesthetic discourse, together with optimism about the epistemology of aesthetic testimony. The epistemology of aesthetic testimony has mainly focused on whether it is possible to gain knowledge about aesthetic issues based on the mere opinion of others. The *optimism* of aesthetic testimony answers 'yes,' but *pessimism* disagrees. The type of pessimism that Simion and Kelp discuss is known as *unavailability pessimism*. The authors finally defend a conditional claim: that aesthetic defeat supports realism about aesthetic discourse. This is because rival views, such as contextualism and invariantism, cannot accommodate the phenomenon of aesthetic defeat. Furthermore, aesthetic defeat also supports optimism about aesthetic testimony. The reason for this is that testimony about aesthetic claims can only defeat aesthetic beliefs if it can also justify those beliefs. In short, if we accept aesthetic defeat, there are reasons to be realistic about aesthetic discourse and optimistic about aesthetic testimony.

The last chapter is by Solmu Anttila and Catarina Dutilh-Novaes, "Critical social epistemology and the liberating power of dialogue." For the authors, in recent years, epistemologists have extensively discussed how epistemic injustices can occur in conversational situations, for example, when a speaker is given less credibility than is appropriate given their actual experience of the topic in question (injustice of testimony). But conversation and dialog can also be the site for resistance and liberation from oppression, not just injustice. For the authors, this is one of the main insights of the work of Brazilian educator, philosopher, and academic Paulo Freire (1921–1997), who investigated the role of dialogical forms of education in empowering traditionally oppressed groups. This chapter presents some important aspects of Freire's (2000) thinking, in particular, the centrality of dialogue for the theory and practice of critical pedagogy and for liberation from oppression. The connections between Freire's views and a selection of recent critical social epistemology topics are also discussed: epistemic injustice, the epistemology of resistance, and epistemic oppression.

4 A Praise of Conversation

Just as the ability to make and receive statements is basic for someone to be a speaker, the ability to take part in a civic conversation concerns a basic ability of the game of a form of life like democracy: to replace all force and violence with the power of speech and thus be able to debate in front of a human audience, sustain deliberations in the light of the best reasons, conceive of rivals as equals, investigate the sources of epistemic disagreements and seek virtuous means of resolving these epistemic conflicts.

Arguably, the philosopher who best captured the meaning of conversation was Michel de Montaigne. Montaigne speaks of conversation (*conférence*) in a peculiar sense, even though it is not a sense foreign to tradition: he speaks of conversation both as a confrontation, a dispute between two people about a common subject, and as a movement that *teaches* certain virtues and skills to enhance the free and autonomous spirit and, likewise, *exercises* these virtues in the pursuit of the good life and truth. He writes:

> The study of books is a languid and weak movement that doesn't warm you up, whereas conversation [*conférence*] teaches and exercises you in one fell swoop. If I converse [*Se je confère*] with a strong soul and a tough fighter, he assaults my flanks, pokes me left and right, his ideas sharpen mine. Rivalry, ambition, contention drive me on and lift me above myself (Montaigne, 1988, , 203).

This accommodates a type of conversation that can't just be described as a meeting between speakers who share the same language to deal with the trivialities of life, more like an episode that happens to us in social life—such as events at the table or work relationships. In this conversation, for example, there is the unavoidable rivalry that goes beyond disagreement, the irreconcilable confrontation that drags us either into violence or resentment. This is a rivalry that challenges us, showing us something (perhaps) surprising: more often than not, we hide our intellectual weaknesses and, refugees in the safety of our own home, we almost always "flee from correction." Montaigne suggests, on the contrary, that we need to "offer and expose ourselves [to correction], especially when it comes in the form of conversation [*conférence*] and not in the form of a lesson [*régence*]" (Montaigne, III.8, 205). Of course, adherence to conversation is voluntary; there is no external, heteronomous constraint that forces someone to join and remain in the conversation, only the commitments that the speakers make to each other have this power. The tension at the root of the conversation causes a kind of flowering in the person, lucidity about oneself, about one's own vices that are obstacles to a healthy social life, and about the ways to gain the best information to lead a good private and public life.

I sincerely hope that this book is just a starting point for an intense debate.

Acknowledgements This book is the result of research funded by the National Council for Technological and Scientific Development (CNPq) (process no. 308967/2022-4). The idea for this book came about during my time as a Visiting Researcher at CONCEPT (Cologne Center for Contemporary Epistemology and the Kantian Tradition) at the Universität zu Köln, Germany, in the biennium 2021–2022. I gratefully acknowledge the support of Sven Bernecker, director of CONCEPT, and the Coordination for the Improvement of Higher Education Personnel, Brazil (CAPES-PRINT) (process 88887.568338/2020-00). I would also like to thank the Philosophy Department of the Federal University of Bahia (UFBA) for allowing me the time and resources to carry out my research and cooperative work with colleagues from various universities in Europe, the United States, and Latin America. I would also like to thank my friend Plínio Smith for his support and encouragement.

References

Broncano-Berrocal, F., & Carter, J. A. (Eds.). (2021). *The epistemology of group disagreement*. Routledge.
Clark, H. H. (1996). *Using language*. Cambridge University Press.
Davidson, D. (1985). Plato's philosopher. In *Truth, language, and history* (pp. 223–240). Clarendon Press, 2005.
Davidson, D. (1990). *Plato's Philebus*. Garland Publishing.
Davidson, D. (1992a). The socratic concept of truth. In *Truth, language, and history* (pp. 241–250). Clarendon Press, 2005.
Davidson, D. (1992b). The second person. In *Subjective, intersubjective, objective* (pp. 107–121). Oxford University Press, 2001.
Davidson, D. (1994). Dialectic and dialogue. In G. Preyer et al. (Eds.), *Language, mind, and epistemology* (pp. 429–437). Kluwer Academic Publishers.
Davidson, D. (1997). Gadamer and Plato's *Philebus*. In *Truth, language, and history* (pp. 261–275). Clarendon Press, 2005.
de Montaigne, M. (1988). In P. Villey (Ed.), *Les Essais. Livre III*. PUF.
Edenberg, E., & Hannon, M. (Eds.). (2021). *Political epistemology*. Oxford University Press.
Freire, P. (2000). *Pedagogy of the oppressed* (M. B. Ramos, Trans.). Bloomsbury.
Fricker, E. (1994). Against gullibility. In A. Chakrabarti & B. K. Matilal (Eds.), *Knowing from words* (pp. 125–161). Kluwer Academic Publishers.
Fricker, E. (2024). A defense of local reductionism about testimony. In M. Steup, B. Roeber, J. Turri, & E. Sosa (Eds.), *Contemporary debates in epistemology* (Third ed., pp. 279–289). Wiley.
Gilbert, M. (1996). *Living together: Rationality, sociality and obligation*. Rowman and Littlefield.
Gilbert, M. (2014). *Joint commitment: How we make the social world*. Oxford University Press.
Gilbert, M. (2023). *Life in groups: How we think, feel, and act together*. Oxford University Press.
Gilbert, M., & Priest, M. (2013). Conversation and collective belief. In A. Capone, F. Lo Piparo, & M. Carapezza (Eds.), *Perspectives on pragmatics and philosophy*. Springer.
Goldberg, S. C. (2010). *Relying on others: Essay in epistemology*. Oxford University Press.
Goldberg, S. C. (2020). *Conversational pressure: Normativity in speech exchanges*. Oxford University Press.
Greco, J. (2021). *The transmission of knowledge*. Cambridge University Press.
Grice, H. P. (1989). *Studies in the way of words*. Harvard University Press.
Johnson, C. R. (Ed.). (2018). *Voicing dissent: The ethics and epistemology of making disagreement public*. Routledge.

Lackey, J. (2008). *Learning from words: Testimony as a source of knowledge*. Oxford University Press.
McKenna, M. (2012). *Conversation and responsibility*. Oxford University Press.
McMyler, B. (2011). *Testimony, trust, and authority*. Oxford University Press.
Tanesini, A., & Lynch, M. P. (Eds.). (2021). *Polarisation, arrogance, and dogmatism: Philosophical perspectives*. Routledge.
Walton, D. N. (1992). *Plausible argument in everyday conversation*. SUNY Press.

Conversation and Joint Agency: Why Addressees Are Epistemically Special

John Greco

The category of conversation is both broader and narrower than the category of testimony. It is broader because conversations involve more than testimony. It is narrower because not all testimony takes place within conversation. Nevertheless, the epistemologies of conversation and testimony overlap in interesting ways. On the account to be defended here, both conversation and testimony essentially involve joint agency and joint achievement, including epistemic joint agency and achievement. Moreover, it will be argued, appreciation of this point resolves an important dispute in the epistemology of testimony: whether addressees have a special epistemic standing over eavesdroppers and other overhearers of testimony. The claim defended here is that they do, and precisely in virtue of their participation in joint agency.

Section 1 reviews a joint agency account of testimonial knowledge, including a joint agency account of *telling*, considered as a dedicated speech act for transmitting knowledge. Section 2 reviews Herbert H. Clark's joint agency account of language use in general and conversation in particular (Clark, 1996). Here we focus on Clark's "levels" of joint agency in conversation, and how these imply several epistemic dimensions of conversation. Section 3 takes a closer look at the epistemic dimensions of conversation implied by Clark's account, and how these set a rich agenda for the epistemology of conversation. Section 4 explores the implications of Clark's account for an important point of dispute in the epistemology of testimony: whether addressees have a special epistemic standing, in contrast to eavesdroppers and other overhearers of testimony. Here it is argued that they do, in virtue of their participation in joint agency. For example, participants in a conversation exploit "common ground" in ways that mere observers of the conversation do not. More generally, participants in a conversation cooperate epistemically in ways that mere observers of the conversation do not, and in ways that underwrite differences in epistemic standing.

J. Greco (✉)
Georgetown University, Washington, DC, USA
e-mail: john.greco@georgetown.edu

© The Author(s), under exclusive license to Springer Nature Switzerland AG 2024
W. J. Silva-Filho (ed.), *The Epistemology of Conversation*, Philosophical Studies Series 156, https://doi.org/10.1007/978-3-031-74069-5_2

1 Joint Agency and Testimonial Knowledge

In previous work I have defended a joint agency account of the transmission of knowledge via testimony (Greco, 2020). On this account, not all testimonial knowledge involves knowledge transmission. Rather, knowledge transmission is a special phenomenon in which speakers and hearers intentionally cooperate to share knowledge. The account therefore allows that testimonial knowledge sometimes occurs in a noncooperative context, in which cases it is perhaps better analyzed in more individualist terms, as in reductionist and inductivist accounts. Nevertheless, testimonial knowledge is typically the result of intentional cooperation between speaker and hearer for the purpose of sharing knowledge.

Featured in this account is a joint agency account of *telling*, understood as a speech act dedicated to the purpose of sharing knowledge, or "letting know," or "giving to know." This explains one of the most common answers to the question, "How do you know?". Namely, "So and so told me". Similarly, it predicts common excuses for not knowing: "No one told me that"; "You should have told me that!". And predicts common rebukes: "I told you that!"; "I tried to tell you, but you wouldn't listen." This last phrase suggests a stronger point: that successful telling requires cooperation on the part of the hearer. In that sense, telling someone that p is like passing someone a ball—you can do your part, but success requires the other person's cooperation, that they do their part as well.[1]

This simple idea—that the transmission of knowledge involves joint agency—yields several attractive results. First, it offers a specific take on the idea that testimonial knowledge, at least in typical cases, involves an important kind of social epistemic dependence, or dependence on other persons for one's epistemic standing. More specifically, it vindicates the idea that epistemic dependence is often *vulnerable* dependence; that one's epistemic standing often depends on other persons doing their part epistemically, and in a way that is not guaranteed by one's doing one's own part well.[2] In related fashion, the account vindicates anti-reductionism and anti-inductivism about testimonial knowledge. Insofar as the transmission of knowledge essentially involves joint agency, it cannot be reduced to good inductive reasoning on the part of the hearer. Finally, the account integrates nicely with positions in epistemology that emphasize the importance of intellectual agency and that see knowledge in general as a kind of achievement. The twist is that knowledge can involve joint agency as well as individual agency, and that knowledge is sometimes a joint achievement.

---

[1] This stronger point will be complicated and defended below.

[2] Nor guaranteed by anything else on the hearer's part, such as the hearer's evidence for speaker reliability. For a defense of epistemic dependence as vulnerable dependence, see Greco (2021).

2 Joint Agency and Conversation

The account of knowledge transmission reviewed above fits nicely with Clark's account of language use in general and conversation in particular (Clark, 1996). On Clark's view, language use in general is characterized by joint agency among language users. More importantly for present purposes, conversations emerge as the result of joint agency among conversational participants, and in such a way that knowledge transmission is a common occurrence among participants in a conversation. On Clark's picture, this happens in two ways. First, knowledge transmission commonly occurs within conversational dynamics *per se*. Second, the transmission of knowledge is sometimes the external goal of a conversation, even its "dominant goal." (Clark, 1996, 33) That is, at times the primary purpose of a conversation is to transmit knowledge.

As the notion of *dominant goal* suggests, Clark sees conversations as organized by a hierarchy of goals. Furthermore, at each level of the hierarchy, participants in the conversation act jointly to achieve their joint goals, many of which are epistemic in nature. The result is an epistemically rich picture of conversation, framing a rich agenda for the epistemology of conversation. To better see this picture, the next two sections consider (a) Clark's notion of conversation, and (b) the several levels of joint activity that on his view constitute any conversation.

2.1 Clark's Notion of Conversation

Following Charles Fillmore (1981), Clark thinks that face-to-face conversation is "the basic and primary use of language." (Clark, 1996, 8) Conversation in general is characterized by "the free exchange of turns among the two or more participants." (Clark, 1996, 4) In addition, face-to-face conversations are characterized by the following features.[3]

1. *Copresence*. The participants share the same physical environment.
2. *Visibility*. The participants can see each other.
3. *Audibility*. The participants can hear each other.
4. *Instantaneity*. The participants perceive each other's actions at no perceptible delay.
5. *Evanescence*. The medium is evanescent—it fades quickly.
6. *Recordlessness*. The participants' actions leave no record or artifact.
7. *Simultaneity*. The participants can produce and receive at once and simultaneously.
8. *Extemporaneity*. The participants formulate and execute their actions extemporaneously, in realtime.

---
[3] Cf. Clark (1996, 9–10). Following Clark and Brennan (1991).

9. *Self-determination.* The participants determine for themselves what actions to take when.
10. *Self-expression.* The participants take actions as themselves.

One sense in which face-to-face conversation is "basic" for Clark is that it is universal to human societies (Clark, 1996, 8). Another is that other forms of language use deviate from the features of face-to-face conversation in one way or another. For example, conversations over the telephone lack Visibility. Non-conversational uses of language deviate in any number of ways (Clark, 1996, 8, 11).

2.2 Levels of Joint Activity in Conversation

Clark thinks that conversation involves joint agency at various levels of activity. Here is a statement of that central idea.

> What people do in arenas of language use is take actions. At a high level of abstraction, they negotiate deals, gossip, get to know each other. At a lower level, they make assertions, requests, promises, apologies to each other... At yet a lower level, they produce utterances for each other to identify. And at the lowest level, they produce sounds, gestures, writing for each other to attend to, hear, see. ... Strikingly, all these actions appear to be joint actions—an ensemble of people doing things in coordination. (Clark, 1996, 17–18)

Here Clark identifies several levels of joint agency. At the highest level, joint activities employ conversation as a means. As such, these activities are external to conversation *per se*, but may constitute a goal of the conversation, including its "dominant goal." For example, two people might engage in conversation with the goal of exchanging gossip, catching up on the latest news, or making plans for dinner. At the next level down, participants in conversation employ communicative acts such as assertions, requests and promises. At the next level down, they present and identify "signals," including linguistic utterances using sentences, phrases and words. At the lowest level, participants in conversation produce sounds, gestures and other physical behaviors for others to hear or see.

On Clark's view, all of these levels involve joint actions rather than mere individual actions, or what Clark calls "autonomous" actions. To see what he means, let's consider each level in turn.

Level 1. Executing and attending to physical behaviors.

Making a sound, nodding one's head, or executing some other physical behavior is certainly an individual action. What Clark has in mind is not the individual vocalization or gesture, but the joint action of *vocalizing or gesturing for someone to attend to*. On Clark's model, the individual's vocalization or gesture and the other person's attending to it are each "participatory actions" that together constitute a joint action. For Clark, this is the general structure of joint actions. Consider Clark's example of playing a duet.

> In Ann and Ben's flute and piano duet, there are three distinct actions:

> 0. the ensemble Ann-and-Ben plays the duet (a joint action)
> 1. Ann plays the flute part as part of 0 (an individual action by Ann)
> 2. Ben plays the piano part as part of 0 (an individual action by Ben)
> The joint action in 0 is performed by means of the individual actions in 1 and 2. (…) Joint actions can only be performed by means of participatory actions—by the individual participants each doing their parts. So we can denote a joint action by A and B as a joining of two participatory actions, $part_1(A)$ and $part_2(B)$, as here:
> Joint[$part_1(A)$; $part_2(B)$]. (Clark, 1996, 60)

Clark applies the point to making sounds or gestures for someone else to attend to.

> I present a signal for you to identify… by executing a bit of behavior specifically for you to perceive—by articulating "Please sit down" in your hearing or by moving my arm within your vision. I cannot get you to perceive my behavior without your coordination. In conversation, you must be attending to and perceiving it precisely as I am executing it. This too results in a joint action:
> Joint [A executes behavior t for B to perceive; B attends perceptually to behavior t from A] (Clark, 1996, 149–150)

Importantly, participatory actions are not the same as autonomous actions strung together in the right way. Rather, participatory actions have their identity and meaning only in the context of the joint actions that they constitute. As Margaret Gilbert (1990) has famously argued, walking to the restaurant alone is not the same act as walking to the restaurant together with someone else, even if one's physical movements are the same in the two cases. Clark illustrates that same point here:

> Suppose I play my part of the Mozart duet on an electronic keyboard twice — once solo and once with Michael playing his part. If you listened to my part through earphones, you might not notice any difference, yet what I did was very different. In the solo performance I took every action on my own. In the duet I coordinated every action with Michael, and as anyone who has played duets knows, that is no small feat…
> We must therefore distinguish two types of individual actions. When I play the piano solo, I am performing an *autonomous action*. When Michael and I play the piano duet, we are also performing individual actions, but as parts of the duet. These actions are what I will call *participatory actions*: They are individual acts performed only as parts of joint actions. (Clark, 1996, 19)

Accordingly, at level 1 we have more than pairs of autonomous actions. Rather, we have coordinated participatory actions constituting a joint action. "Executing behaviors to be attended to and attending to those behaviors, then, are participatory acts: Roger cannot do his part without Nina doing hers, and vice versa," (Clark, 1996, 275)

Again, for Clark this is the general structure of joint actions. Among other things, it requires that the speaker execute her behavior *with the intention of the hearer attending to it*. Moreover, it involves the hearer *understanding* that this is the speaker's intention, and *coordinating* his own intentions and actions accordingly. We thus have all the hallmarks of joint agency: shared intention, understanding of shared intention, and coordination of actions so as to fulfill shared intention.

Level 2. Presenting and identifying signals.

The physical behaviors noted in level 1 are not mere physical behaviors — they are signals, or actions "by which one person means something for another person." (Clark, 1996, 13) These include utterances using words and sentences, but on

Clark's views not all signals are linguistic objects in the standard sense. Moreover, on his view non-linguistic signals (such as smiles and gestures) play important roles in coordinating joint agency within a conversation. For example, facial expressions can signal understanding, confusion, agreement, permission to keep speaking, etc.

At level 2, speakers and hearers act jointly to present and identify such signals. As with all joint actions, this requires participatory actions on the part of each.

> I signal something to you... by getting you to identify my behavior as a particular signal—as an act by which I mean a specific thing for you. I do this by presenting the signal (an instance of the sentence *Please sit down*, or a gesture toward the chair) for you to identify. I cannot get you to identify the signal without your help. You and I must coordinate what I present with what you identify, and that too is a joint action:
> Joint[A presents signal *s* to B, B identifies signal *s* from A] (Clark, 1996, 149)

On Clark's view, then, even the presentation and identification of speech involves significant joint agency. That is, it does so even before speech is interpreted. This is because even here language requires extensive and extended coordination between speakers and addressees.

> Utterances are often viewed as the prerogative of speakers — products that speakers formulate and produce on their own. Nothing could be further from the truth. Uttering things involves two levels of joint actions. At level 1, speakers execute certain behaviors — vocalizations and gesticulations — for addressees to attend to. At level 2, speakers present signals for addressees to identify. There can be no communication without tight coordination at both levels.
>
> Speakers and addressees have a battery of strategies for coordinating at these two levels of action... Utterances are truly products of speakers and addressees acting jointly. (Clark, 1996, 285–286)

Clark offers significant empirical evidence in support of this view, including the analysis of various speech patterns and other behaviors in the context of real-life conversations. The presentation of that evidence is beyond the scope of this chapter. Nevertheless, we have enough here to conclude that Clark presents a compelling picture.

Level 3. Meaning and understanding.

The notion of speaker's meaning is, roughly, what a speaker intends to mean by their utterance. On the traditional view, a speaker's intending to mean something is an autonomous act. For Clark, it is only one element of activity at level 3, of "getting one to construe what one is to be taken to mean." The latter is a joint action, only partly constituted by the speaker's intending to mean something as a participatory action. According to Clark, the idea that communicative acts are joint actions is already implicit in Grice's framework (cf. Grice, 1957).

Here is Clark's take on Grice's notion of speaker's meaning:

> *Speaker's meaning (reflexive)*
> In presenting *s* to audience A, a speaker S means for A that *p* if and only if: (*i*) S intends in presenting *s* to A that A recognize that *p* in part by recognizing that *i*. (Clark, 1996, 130)

Grice's "m-intention" (or meaning intention) *i* is reflexive in the sense that it refers to itself. More specifically, part of the intention is that the addressee recognize it for the intention that it is. This has the result, Clark argues, that the intention cannot be fulfilled without the addressee's cooperation.

> Grice's m-intention — the heart of speaker's meaning — is a curious type of intention: It is one the speaker cannot discharge without the audience's participation. When I say "Please sit down" and mean you are to sit down, I rely on you doing your part by recognizing what I mean. In Grice's formulation, my intention depends directly on your recognition of that intention. (Clark, 1996, 130)

The result is that communicative acts, rightly understood, are joint actions.

> Suppose Ann presents signal s to Ben (e.g., she utters "Please sit down") meaning that p (e.g., that he is to sit down). Again we have a joint act r and participatory acts (1) and (2):
> Speaker's meaning (joint)
> In presenting s to A, speaker S means for A that p if and only if:

0. the communicative act r includes 1 and 2;
1. S presents s to A intending that p as part of r;
2. A recognizes that p as part of r. (Clark, 1996, 131)

Clark argues that this same idea — that communicative acts are joint actions—is also implicit in John Austin.

> It is obviously necessary that to have promised I must normally (A) have been *heard* by someone, perhaps the promisee; (B) have been understood by him as promising. If one or another of these conditions isn't satisfied, doubts arise as to whether I have really promised, and it might be held that my act was only attempted or was void. (Austin, 1962, 22; quoted at Clark, 1996, 138)

Austin's idea in the passage is that promises require recognition by the promisee. Without that, it is plausible to say that nothing has been promised. Austin's point here is not that the *perlocutionary* act can fail—that promises can go unaccepted. Rather, it is that even the *illocutionary* act fails if the hearer does not do his part. In support of this, consider how natural it would be to say the following: "I tried to promise her, but she didn't hear me." Or: "I tried to promise, but he didn't understand what I was saying." This implies that the illocutionary act of promising requires coordination between speaker and addressee.

Here is Austin again:

> I cannot be said to have warned an audience unless it hears what I say and takes what I say in a certain sense. An effect must be achieved on the audience if the illocutionary act is to be carried out... Generally the effect amounts to bringing about the understanding of the meaning and of the force of the locution. (Austin, 1962, 115–116)

Clark concludes that Austinian illocutionary acts such as promising and warning are in fact joint actions.

> If illocutionary acts require actions from both speakers and addressees, as Austin argued, that makes [the latter] participatory acts. Most investigators dropped Austin's requirement that illocutionary acts include "bringing about the understanding of the meaning and of the force of the locution" simply because they refused to treat illocutionary acts within a framework of joint actions. The view championed here might have suited Austin very well. (Clark, 1996, 219)

These considerations are sufficient to establish that actions at level 3 are joint actions. Clark argues for an additional dimension of joint action at level 3, however. Namely, speakers and addressees work together to *assign meaning* to speakers' utterances.

> In the view I will argue for, the notion "what the speaker means" is replaced by "what the speaker is to be taken to mean." The change is small, but radical. The idea is that speakers and addressees try to create a joint construal of what the speaker is to be taken to mean. Such a construal represents not what the speaker means per se — which can change in the very process of communicating — but what the participants *mutually take* the speaker as meaning, what they *deem* the speaker to mean. (Clark, 1996, 212)

Essential to the present point is the notion of *joint construal*. Clark's insight is that what a speaker intends to mean is often ambiguous, vague, or otherwise left open to interpretation. Crucially, the interpretation that is eventually hit upon is a joint interpretation—something jointly agreed to by the speaker and addressee.

To illustrate, consider one of Clark's examples—Jack says "Sit here" to Kate. As Clark points out, this utterance might be a request, an offer, a piece of advice, a command, or something else. The mere form of words does not determine which. What the utterance ends up meaning is determined by (a) what Jack initially intends, (b) what Kate initially understands, and ultimately (c) what Jack and Kate agree on. What they agree on is something that they work out together.

For example, suppose that Kate responds with "Thank you." This signals to Jack that she is taking his utterance as an offer. It also signals that she is not taking it as a command. Suppose Jack continues without remark. This signals to Kate that he has accepted her construal. In other words, he has accepted that his utterance will be construed by the two of them as an offer, and that their conversation will proceed accordingly. Importantly, this might be the case even if Jack did not originally intend his utterance as an offer. For example, suppose he intended it as a command. But if Kate construes it as an offer, and he accepts that construal, they now jointly construe his utterance as an offer.

Here is another possibility: Kate correctly understands that Jack intends a command, but she has no intention of complying with a command. If she replies with "Thank you" and Jack accepts this reply, she has effectively turned a command into an offer.

> By this principle, Kate isn't trying simply to identify what Jack means by 'Sit down.' She is trying to create a construction that the two of them are willing to accept as what he meant by it. She will usually try to infer his initial intentions, but the joint construal they arrive at will often be different from those intentions. (Clark, 1996, 212)

The notion of joint construal is importantly related to the notion of "common ground" — roughly, the set of assumptions, beliefs, and knowledge that participants mutually take for granted as background in a conversation. Following Robert C. Stalnaker (1978) and D. K. Lewis (1979), common ground accumulates as a conversation proceeds. The main vehicle for this is standardly understood to be assertion: assertions in a conversation add and/or change common ground unless rejected. But other communicative acts also contribute to the accumulation of common ground, as participants mutually update to accommodate them.

But how are we to understand the accumulation of common ground, which is by nature the updating of *mutual* assumptions, beliefs, and knowledge among participants of a conversation? The answer must be in terms of *mutual* construals of communicative acts. To put the point differently: a communicative act will fail to contribute to the common ground of a conversation unless it is construed in the same way by the conversation's participants. If Jack construes his utterance one way and Kate construes it another, their common ground will not be updated successfully. Understanding communicative acts in terms of joint agency explains how common ground gets updated successfully.

All this is further consideration in favor of the conclusion that activity at level 3—the level of communicative acts—involves joint agency between speaker and addressee.

Level 4 and beyond. Proposing, considering and executing joint projects

Clark's "action ladders" detail various levels of joint activity in conversation. Here is a version including Clark's level 4 (Clark, 1996, 152).

Level	Speaker A's actions	Addressee B's actions
4	A is *proposing* joint project *w* to B	B is *considering* A's proposal of *w*
3	A is *signaling* that *p* for B	B is *recognizing* that *p* from A
2	A is *presenting* signal *s* to B	B is *identifying* signal *s* from A
1	A is *executing* behavior *t* for B	B is *attending* to behavior *t* from A

At level 4, the speaker *proposes* a joint project and the addressee *considers* it. For example, Arthur proposes that Beth answer his question and Beth considers whether to do so. Clark argues that this activity is different from the *signaling* and *recognizing* at level 3. To see this, consider a conversation with more than two participants. In Clark's example, Arthur's question is directed at Beth, and not at a third participant, Charles. But notice: Arthur's question was intended to be understood by *all* the participants in the conversation. Accordingly, we have to distinguish *signaling* and *recognizing* (level 3) from *proposing* and *considering* (level 4).

Nevertheless, Clark certainly recognizes a further distinction between *considering* a joint project and *taking it up*. Accordingly, we can add an additional level of joint action to the four that are explicitly represented on Clark's action ladders. I will call this level *executing joint projects*. Here is Clark acknowledging the point.

> What am I doing by asking you to sit down — by performing an illocutionary act? I am proposing, suggesting, posing, or putting forward a project for us to carry out jointly — namely, that I get you to sit down. Now, getting you to sit down is another thing I can't do by myself. It is a joint action that I am projecting for the two of us to do, and that requires us to coordinate our actions. I will call this joint action a *joint project*. (Clark, 1996, 150)

Here again, Clark sees the point to be at least implicit in Austin.

> Recall that Austin argued that "My attempt to make a bet by saying 'I bet you sixpence' is abortive unless you say 'I take you on' or words to that effect," and that marrying, bequeath-

ing, and appointing also require uptake. That makes betting, marrying, bequeathing, and appointing joint projects. (Clark, 1996, 150)

Next, recall Clark's point that conversations are organized by a hierarchy of goals, including one or more dominant goals. We may now make a distinction between (a) joint activities that are part of the internal dynamics of a conversation and (b) joint activities that are an external goal of the conversation. For example, asking questions and answering them can be part of the internal dynamics of a conversation. More generally, the joint activities at levels 1–3 are constitutive of conversation and in that sense internal to it. On the other hand, transacting business can be an external goal of conversation. That is, it can be the purpose of engaging in conversation, as can playing a game or interrogating a witness. External goals of conversation can be further divided between sub-goals and dominant goals. For example, conducting a business transaction might be the dominant goal of a conversation, and describing a service or product one of its sub-goals. Finally, conversations can be parts of broader joint activities. For example, conversations might be part of broader joint projects such as running a business, or teaching a course, or conducting research. All this suggests the following levels of joint activity.

Level 8. Executing broader joint projects in which conversations are a part.
Level 7. Executing joint projects that are a dominant goal of a conversation.
Level 6. Executing joint projects that are a sub-goal of a conversation.
Level 5. Executing proposed joint projects that are internal to a conversation.
Level 4. Proposing and considering joint projects.
Level 3. Signaling and recognizing meaning.
Level 2. Presenting and identifying signals.
Level 1. Executing and attending to behavior.

Each of these levels of joint activity are related to conversation in one way or another. At the lower end, joint activity is constitutive of conversational dynamics and of conversation *per se*. At the higher end, joint activities employ conversation as a means.[4] In next two sections, we explore some implications of this view for the epistemology of conversation.

3 The Epistemic Dimensions of Conversation

The broad picture defended by Clark implies that conversation is rich in epistemic dimensions, thereby implying a rich agenda for the epistemology of conversation.

---

[4] It is interesting to note, although not essential to present purposes, that our extended action ladder retains Clark's properties of upward causality and downward evidence. That is, actions at higher levels are completed "by means" of actions at lower levels; and evidence that actions at higher levels have been completed is evidence that actions at lower levels have been completed (Clark, 1996, 147–148).

First, joint agency in general involves several epistemic dimensions. For one, joint agency as such involves common understanding of shared intentions among participants. Different accounts theorize *shared intention* and *common understanding* of shared intention in different ways, but virtually all accounts of joint agency recognize these as elements of the target phenomenon.[5] But how is common understanding of shared intention to be understood detail? What is the nature of such understanding and what is its source? Since joint agency is an essential element of conversation, these questions must be included in an epistemology of conversation.

Second, the notion of *common ground* is central to Clark's account of joint agency in general and therefore conversation in particular. "Common ground is the foundation for all joint actions, and that makes it essential to the creation of speaker's meaning and addressee's understanding as well." (Clark, 1996, 14) The notion of common ground also figures prominently in theories of conversation more broadly, as we have seen above. As Clark notes, it traces back to similar notions of common knowledge (Lewis, 1969), mutual knowledge (Schiffer, 1972) and joint knowledge (McCarthy, 1990). On Clark's view, "Two people's common ground is, in effect, the sum of their mutual, common, or joint knowledge, beliefs, and suppositions." (Clark, 1996, 93) But even if the notion of common ground appropriate to conversation includes more than knowledge, it certainly includes epistemic dimensions. As such, the nature and workings of common ground is also a topic for the epistemology of conversation.

Third, there are several epistemic dimensions to the joint activity that occurs at Clark's levels 1–3 specifically. At level 3, participants in a conversation must *recognize* the intended meaning of signals. At level 2, they must *identify* signals, and at level 1 they must *attend* to behaviors. These are all epistemic notions, or at least plausibly so. Also plausibly, these various activities recruit different cognitive processes and thereby require different epistemic treatment. An epistemology of conversation should include an epistemology of these various processes.

A number of philosophers have argued that the speech act of *assertion* has an essential role in the updating of common ground or common knowledge in the context of conversation (Stalnaker, 1978; Lewis, 1969, 1979). Others have argued that assertion plays a special role in testimony and therefore testimonial knowledge (Williamson, 2000; Goldberg, 2015; Graham, 2016; Kelp & Simion, 2022). Others have argued that the speech act of *telling*, a species of assertion, is essential to testimonial knowledge in general (Hinchman, 2005; Moran, 2005; Fricker, 2006). While others have argued that telling is essential to the transmission of knowledge (Greco, 2020). Since assertion and telling play essential roles in conversation, understanding the epistemic functions of these speech acts is essential to the epistemology of conversation.

In this regard, consider the following passage from Clark:

---

[5] For example, Margaret Gilbert (1990); Michael Bratman (2014), John Searle (1990),

> When Jane asks Kate "Who is it?" she is trying to get Kate to tell her who she is. She is proposing a joint project — a transfer of information. If Kate is willing and able, she will complete it and tell Jane who she is. Let me stress that Kate's answer ("oh it's Professor Worth's secretary, from Pan American College") is not just any perlocutionary effect of Jane's utterance. She might have been surprised, outraged, or pleased by Jane's question. Rather, it is the perlocutionary effect projected by Jane's illocutionary point. It is an uptake of the particular joint project Jane proposed. Such joint projects become complete only through uptake, so completion at level 4 requires not only Jane's question but Kate's answer. (Clark, 1996, 198)

In the quoted passage, Clark treats telling as an illocutionary act (at level 3) and as a perlocutionary effect (at level 4). According to Clark, telling is a participatory act in the joint project of transferring information. From my own point of view, the joint project at issue is not merely the transferring of information but the transferring of knowledge. If the case that Clark is describing is typical, Jane asks Kate "Who is it?" because she thinks Kate knows, and she wants Kate to tell her what she knows. If I am right, then telling often effects a transmission of knowledge that is internal to a conversation — it is part of the conversational dynamics that move a conversation forward.

But the transmission of knowledge can also be the external goal of a conversation, including its dominant goal. That is, sometimes the very purpose of a conversation is to execute a transmission of knowledge. For example, one stops a stranger to get directions to the train station. Or one visits a colleague to find out what time the meeting is. Other examples include conversations that are more extended. For example, you want to know about family history, and so you ask your grandmother. At other times, the dominant goal of a conversation is to generate knowledge rather than to transmit it. That is, generating knowledge can also be a joint project executed by conversation, as when two people consider a question together and mutually work out an answer.[6]

These are only some of the epistemological issues raised by Clark's joint agency account of conversation. There are others as well.[7] Together these set a rich agenda for the epistemology of conversation.

4 The Special Epistemic Standing of Addressees

In this final section we consider a dispute in the epistemology of testimony — whether addressees of testimony have special epistemic standing over eavesdroppers and other overhearers of conversations. With the forgoing in place, the dispute can be resolved fairly straightforwardly. In sum, addressees of testimony are participants in joint agency in ways that eavesdroppers and other overhearers of a

---

[6] Cf. Greco (2020, 100). Sweet (2022) argues that joint knowledge generation is ubiquitous.

[7] For example, Clark's book contains discussions about types of evidence for common ground, and about the quality of evidence necessary for establishing common ground.

conversation are not, and are thereby engaged in different cognitive processes. For example, utterances addressed to hearers as testimony are designed with those hearers in mind. In related fashion, addressees exploit common ground differently from eavesdroppers and other overhearers. Accordingly, any epistemology on which these differences make an epistemic difference will thereby entail that addressees have special epistemic standing in virtue of their role as addressees. And that turns out to be any plausible epistemology.

The issue in dispute is nicely articulated by Benjamin McMyler.

> If a hearer comes to believe that p on the basis of a speaker's testimony that p, does the fact that the speaker's testimony is actually addressed to the hearer make any salient difference to the epistemic credentials of the hearer's belief? Do the other-directed intentions embodied in a speaker's addressing her testimony to a hearer have any distinctive epistemological significance? (McMyler, 2013, 1059)

According to McMyler, the "overwhelming consensus" in epistemology is that the answer is no. Here is his articulation of this negative position:

> That a speaker's testimony is actually addressed to a hearer makes no salient difference to the epistemic credentials of the hearer's testimonial belief. Hence, if we divide a hearer's testimonial beliefs into beliefs based on testimony that is addressed to the hearer — call these *address-based beliefs* — and beliefs based on testimony that is not addressed to the hearer — call these *non-address-based beliefs* — there is no salient epistemological difference between these two classes of beliefs. From an epistemological perspective, address-based and non-address-based beliefs are of a piece. (McMyler, 2013, 1059–1060)

McMyler cites Fricker (2006) and Lackey (2008) as explicitly endorsing the so-called consensus position. McMyler rejects it, citing Hinchman (2005) and Moran (2005) as allies.

As suggested above, Clark gives us ample resources for rejecting the position as well. The most central point that we get from Clark in this regard is that participants in joint agency benefit epistemically from cooperation with speakers in ways that non-participants do not. One way to see this is at the level of determining speaker's meaning. For example, speakers intentionally design their utterances for the benefit of addressees:

> As an addressee, Barbara can count on Alan having designed his utterance for her to understand, but as an overhearer, Damon cannot. As a result, the two of them go about trying to interpret what Alan says by different means, by different processes. (Clark, 1996, 15)

A related point is that addressees are in a position to exploit common ground in ways that overhearers of conversation are not.

> When Ann tells Ben 'Bob went out with Monique last night,' she expects to be understood by Ben, but not by just any overhearer. Most overhearers wouldn't know who Bob and Monique were. If Ann said 'You-know-who did you-know-what with you-know-who last night,' she would be posing a coordination problem unsolvable by anyone not privy to the special common ground she shares with Ben (Clark, 1996, 74)

The preceding points are made in regard to recognizing speaker's meaning: speakers cooperate differently with addressees than with eavesdroppers and other overhearers, and this gives addressees an epistemic advantage in interpreting the meaning of speakers' utterances. This is at level 3, which includes illocutionary acts such as asserting, testifying and telling. But the same points can be generalized to apply to other levels of joint activity, both lower and higher on the action ladder.

> What makes an action a joint one, ultimately, is the coordination of individual actions by two or more people. There is coordination of both *content*, what the participants intend to do, and *processes*, the physical and mental systems they recruit in carrying out those intentions. (…)
> Joint actions with language are no different. (Clark, 1996, 59–60)

At lower levels, speakers cooperate with addressees so that they can better attend to speakers' behavior and better identify speakers' signals. At higher levels, speakers cooperate with addressees to execute their joint projects, including asking and answering questions, managing testimonial exchanges, and transmitting knowledge. All of this includes the various ways that speakers and addressees exploit common ground to further those joint projects. "Common ground is a *sine qua non* for everything we do with others—from the broadest joint activities to the smallest joint actions that comprise them." (Clark, 1996, 92)

In sum, addressees of testimony are participants in joint agency in ways that non-addressees are not, and this makes an epistemic difference—addressees of testimony (at least often) benefit epistemically in virtue of their cooperation with speakers.

The forgoing conclusion fits nicely with the joint agency account of knowledge transmission reviewed in Sect. 1. It also fits nicely with the virtue-theoretic account of knowledge that I have defended elsewhere (Greco, 2010). From that point of view, knowledge in general is an achievement attributable to virtuous agency. Transmitted knowledge is a joint achievement attributable to virtuous joint agency. However, neither of these positions is necessary to draw the conclusion that addressees of testimony enjoy special epistemic standing. That is because the present considerations from Clark are more general. So long as conversation involves joint agency in the ways that the above action ladders suggest, addressees form their testimonial beliefs in ways that overhearers of conversation do not. That is, they engage in different cognitive processes and even recruit different cognitive systems. Accordingly, this entails differential epistemic standing on any epistemology for which these differences make an epistemic difference. Put differently, this entails differential epistemic standing on any epistemology for which the etiology of belief matters (cf. Goldman, 1979). This includes reliabilist theories, proper functionalist theories, safety theories, and sensitivity theories, among others. In fact, it even includes evidentialist theories, insofar as participants in joint activity have access to and base their beliefs on different evidence than do non-participants. This too is entailed by differential access to and exploitation of common ground.

Here is a summary of the argument:

1. Addressees receive and assess testimony differently (by engaging in different cognitive processes and recruiting different cognitive systems) than do non-addressees. Moreover, they do so necessarily, in virtue of their participation in joint agency with speakers.

2. These differences make an epistemic difference on any plausible epistemology (roughly, on any for which "etiology matters").

Therefore,

3. Addressees necessarily have special (i.e. differential) epistemic standing in virtue of their participation in joint agency with speakers.

That is not to say that addressees always have *better* epistemic standing than non-addressees. We can imagine cases where the reverse is true. Nevertheless, the distinctive relationship between addressees and speakers entails a distinctive epistemic standing. Moreover, this difference will often be epistemically beneficial. That is, the relevant kinds of cooperation between speakers and addressees will often have the consequence of making testimonial belief more reliable, more safe, better supported evidentially, etc.

Accordingly, we may draw the following conclusion: On any plausible epistemology, the etiologies of belief of addressees and non-addressees are different, in ways that often make the testimonial beliefs of addressees epistemically superior, and *in virtue* of their role as addressees. All plausible epistemologies that we know of entail this. Moreover, they do so in virtue of features that would be retained by any plausible epistemology whatsoever.[8]

References

Austin, J. L. (1962). *How to do things with words*. Oxford University Press.
Bratman, M. (2014). *Shared agency: A planning theory of acting together*. OUP.
Clark, H. H. (1996). *Using language*. Cambridge University Press. Kindle Edition.
Clark, H. H., & Brennan, S. A. (1991). Grounding in communication. In L. B. Resnick, J. M. Levine, & S. D. Teasley (Eds.), *Perspectives on socially shared cognition* (pp. 127–149). APA Books.
Filmore, C. (1981). Pragmatics and the description of discourse. In P. Cole (Ed.), *Radical pragmatics* (pp. 143–166). Academic.
Fricker, E. (2006). Second-hand knowledge. *Philosophy and Phenomenological Research, 73*, 592–618.
Gilbert, M. (1990). Walking together: A paradigmatic social phenomenon. *Midwest Studies in Philosophy, 15*(1), 1–14.
Goldberg, S. C. (2015). *Assertion: On the philosophical significance of assertoric speech*. Oxford University Press.
Goldman, A. I. (1979). What is justified belief? In G. Pappas (Ed.), *Justification and knowledge* (pp. 1–25). R. Reidel.
Graham, P. (2016). Testimonial knowledge: A unified account. *Philosophical Issues, 26*(1), 172–186.
Greco, J. (2010). *Achieving knowledge: A virtue-theoretic account of epistemic normativity*. Cambridge University Press.
Greco, J. (2020). *The transmission of knowledge*. Cambridge University Press.
Greco, J. (2021). What is social epistemic dependence? *Philosophical Topics, 49*(2), 113–132.

---

[8] I am grateful for helpful comments from Sandy Goldberg, Peter Graham, Waldomiro J. Silva Filho, and Katherine Sweet. Thanks also to Deborah Tollefsen, who pointed me to Clark's work.

Grice, H. P. (1957). Meaning. *Philosophical Review, 66*, 377–388.
Hinchman, E. (2005). Telling as inviting to trust. *Philosophy and Phenomenological Research, 70*, 562–587.
Kelp, C., & Simion, M. (2022). *Sharing knowledge: A functionalist account of assertion.* Cambridge University Press.
Lackey, J. (2008). *Learning from words: Testimony as a source of knowledge.* Oxford University Press.
Lewis, D. K. (1969). *Convention: A philosophical study.* Harvard University Press.
Lewis, D. K. (1979). Scorekeeping in a language game. *Journal of Philosophical Logic, 8*, 339–359.
McCarthy, J. (1990). Formalization of two puzzles involving knowledge. In V. Lifschitz (Ed.), *Formalizing common sense: Papers by John McCarthy* (pp. 158–166). Ablex Publishing.
McMyler, B. (2013). The epistemic significance of address. *Synthese, 190*, 1059–1078.
Moran, R. (2005). Getting told and being believed. *Philosopher's Imprint, 5*, 1–29.
Schiffer, S. R. (1972). *Meaning.* Oxford University Press.
Searle, J. (1990). Collective intentions and actions. In P. Cohen, J. Morgan, & M. Pollack (Eds.), *Intentions in communication* (pp. 401–415). MIT Press.
Stalnaker, R. C. (1978). Assertion. In *Syntax and semantics*, 9 (pp. 315–332). Academic Press.
Sweet, K. (2022). *Collaborative inquiry: An epistemological account of inquiring together.* Dissertation, Saint Louis University, St. Louis.
Williamson, T. (2000). *Knowledge and its limits.* Oxford University Press.

On the Contours of a Conversation

Sanford C. Goldberg

1 Introduction

There are various things one ought to do if one is a participant in a conversation. Some of these are familiar from the work of Paul Grice. For example, participants ought to be brief, informative, and relevant, and we ought not to make claims for which we lack adequate evidence. But there are things beyond these that a conversational participant ought to do: we ought to pay attention to the contributions of other participants, acknowledge these contributions (as appropriate), and respond when called upon to do so. We should take turns, and we should not delay when initiating our response. There are proper ways to change the subject, and ways that seem improper; there is regular feedback that ought to be given to indicate attentiveness and comprehension, and ways to repair flaws when these arise in a conversational exchange. No doubt, there is much else besides.[1]

To be a participant in a conversation, then, is to be subject to a distinctive set of norms to which those who are not participants are not subject. I will call these *within-conversation* norms. This chapter addresses these norms and our being bound by them: under what conditions does one count as a participant in a conversation, and so as subject to these norms? In virtue of what does one so count? In addition, I will also be addressing how these norms interact with other norms that bear on conversations: how do within-conversation norms interact with other norms? Are within-conversation norms a species of ethical norm (and if not, what is the source of their normativity)? How do they relate to the norms of epistemology?

---

[1] For a popular overview, see Enfield (2017).

S. C. Goldberg (✉)
Northwestern University, Evanston, IL, USA
e-mail: s-goldberg@northwestern.edu

These questions point to the importance of a general question that (I think) has not received the attention that it deserves: how do we draw the boundaries of a conversation, marking those within and those without?

2 Conversational Boundaries

Before addressing this question, I'd like to put down some constraints on an adequate answer. These are facts about conversations—about who is in them, who is not—that will be more or less obvious to people. I introduce this range of facts as adequacy constraints: an adequate answer to our question about the determination of conversational boundaries ought to be consistent with these facts, and answers are better to the extent that they (are not merely consistent but actually) *explain* them.

The range of facts I wish to highlight are these. First, it is usually and paradigmatically the case that *one knows when one oneself is a participant, as well as when one oneself is not a participant, in a conversation*. Second, it is often enough the case that in face-to-face settings *one knows who the other conversational participants are*. Third, it is usually and paradigmatically the case that *competence in speaking a language involves familiarity with the various within-conversation norms to which one is subject when in a conversation*—although of course people vary quite a bit in how sensitive they are to those norms (as well as how well they conform to them). Fourth, it is usually and paradigmatically the case that *participants in a conversation know when the conversation has ended*.

Is there an account of the contours of a conversation that not only is compatible with, but actually explain, these facts? While I am not confident, I believe that a good deal of what is to be explained can be explained by appeal to two core features of a conversation: the phenomenon of *address*, and what I will call the *Gricean nature* of paradigmatic speech exchanges (as rational and cooperative). I will take these up in turn before moving on to try to assemble an account with these as components.

Consider first address.[2] To a rough first approximation, this is the act wherein one subject (i) calls for the attention of another or others (the 'target') and (ii) directs some communicative act at the target. In Goldberg (2020, chapter 2) I argued that, at least in typical (non-defective) cases, the act of addressing a target puts the target under normative pressure to give the speaker—the one addressing the target—their attention. My thought there was that, given certain conditions regarding the intelligibility and the cooperativity of the act of address, to address another is to make their attention something that is owed to you. I will refer to this idea as the *attention-demandingness* of address. My present point is that the attention-demandingness of address can be used to explain how conversations are initiated—and by extension,

---
[2] This was a topic I first addressed (so to speak) in Chapter 2 of Goldberg (2020).

how one comes to be in the grip of within-conversation norms. The key hypothesis is this:

Hypothesis 1: All conversations are initiated by an act of address.

This hypothesis may not be particularly controversial. But I think Hypothesis 1 is more interesting than might first be apparent: if we combine it with the attention-demandingness of address, we have the basis for a potential explanation of some of the facts listed above.

To begin, Hypothesis 1 and the attention-demandingness of address put us in a position to be able to explain what I will call the *non-participant-to-participant transition*. This is the transition from *not* being a participant in a conversation, and hence not subject to any of the within-conversation norms, to *being* a participant, and hence potentially[3] subject to those norms. The claim on the table is that this transition is always explained by one or another act of address—either by one's addressing another subject, or by one's being addressed by another subject.

I submit that this gives us the basis for explaining how one is rendered subject to within-conversation norms in the first instance. My thought is this. Suppose we have two people, A and B, who are such that A has addressed B under conditions in which A's address succeeds at placing a normative demand on B to give A their attention. Then not only is it the case that B is subject to a norm requiring them to give A their attention, it is also true that once A has B's attention, A can communicate further with B, and in particular A can try to communicate whatever joint activity A proposes to do with B. Insofar as A communicates with B by way of performing one or another speech act, A's performance of that act will itself place *additional* normative demands on B—demands not only to attend to the act, but also to (try to) comprehend it, and to respond as appropriate. And insofar as B responds to A's act by performing a speech act in their turn, B's performance will generate similar normative demands on A, to attend to B's act, (try to) comprehend it, and respond as appropriate. This sequence can continue for as long as A and B mutually desire, ensuring that they are in a context rich with normative demands on each. In this way we see how the act of address creates a context which is potentially rich with normative demands—*potentially*, because whether further demands obtain, and if so which ones, depend on what A, having captured B's attention with the act of address, does with that attention, how B responds in turn, and so forth.

The foregoing account makes it seem as if A, in their act of address, freely (and without normative constraint) initiates a potentially normatively rich exchange with B. But this is misleading. Because acts of address purport to place audiences under an obligation to attend to the speaker—of owing it to the speaker to give her their attention—acts of address themselves are governed by norms (Goldberg, 2020, chapter 2). If I address you, I ought to have something in mind that justifies my claim on your attention. Perhaps I need your help and am justified in thinking that I am entitled to your attention as a way to request that help. Perhaps I plan to propose

---

[3] To be explained below.

a joint activity regarding which there is good reason to think that this activity will be of interest to you, and I need to get your attention to make this proposal. Perhaps I aim merely to acknowledge your presence—to greet you in passing, as it were—where the prevailing norms of politeness condone calling for you attention for the brief moment it takes to express such a greeting. Or perhaps there are other things that might justify my claim on your attention. However, if I lack any such justification, I have addressed you *improperly*. This suggests that norms are in play even *prior to* the non-participant-to-participant transition: there are proper and improper acts of address, and so there are norms governing acts of this type.

This raises a question: are the norms of address themselves to be understood as within-conversation norms, or rather as falling *outside* that class? On the one hand, they are norms that govern the transition *into* a conversation, and so appear to be outside of the domain of within-conversation norms. On the other hand, we do address one another even when we are already conversing with one another,[4] so they appear to be inside the domain of within-conversation norms. In the end, I want the category of within-conversation norms to include *all of the norms related to the initiation, sustainment, and conclusion of conversations*, so I will include norms of address in the category as well.

The second hypothesis I want to introduce in this connection will be familiar from the work of Paul Grice (1975). It is this:

Hypothesis 2: Conversations are rational, cooperative activities.

Again, this hypothesis is not novel. My claim will be that it can explain a good deal of the normative demands that take place in conversation. I submit that if Hypothesis 2 is true, then we would expect conversations to be full of (i) the normative demands of cooperation as well as (ii) the normative demands of both (ii.a) practical rationality and (ii.b) epistemic rationality. This is precisely what we find.

I should acknowledge that Hypothesis 2 has been contested by many recent writers who worry that it assumes an overly-idealized account of the contexts in which conversations take place.[5] This is a fair worry to have. At the same time, I will be arguing below that we can use the hypothesis so as to explain the results I want to explain without running afoul of worries of this sort. So let me get to the explanation I want to offer, and then show how a version of that explanation is invariant across concerns about over-idealization of conversational context.

I first want to begin by noting how I understand the key terms in Hypothesis 2.

By 'cooperative' I understand the kind of mutuality that is associated with a common goal. At a concrete level, the goals of a conversation are many and varied. They can be oriented around the exchange of information, the addition of tasks on a to-do list, the entertainment of the participants, the exchange of the sorts of social niceties that are considered proper and fitting in the community, and so forth. I will

---

[4] Imagine a conversation with multiple participants, where I want to address my next comment to you in particular. Then I will address you in the course of this ongoing conversation.

[5] See Camp (2018), Saul (2018), Lackey (2020), Khoo and Sterken (2021), Ellefsen (2021), Mühlebach (2022), Stanley and Beaver (2023).

want to generalize over this list. I want to say that at a high level of generalization, the shared goal of a conversation is simply to *communicate information through linguistic means*. I understand this shared goal broadly: such communication involves the conveying by linguistic means of any of the sorts of contents associated with the various kinds of illocutionary acts performed in the course of a conversation. Included among these acts are not only assertions, but also requests, demands, queries, proposals, and so forth.

By 'rational' I understand in the first instance practical rationality, the sort of rationality associated with means-ends reasoning.[6] To say that conversations are rational in this sense is to say (among other things) that proposed acts within a conversation can be evaluated for how likely they are to advance the various aims in play in a conversation. While some of these aims will be the private aims of the various participants (what they privately desire or hope to achieve by participating in the conversation), a good many others will be the shared aims of the conversation itself. These were the ones described above, which I lumped under the generic category *communicating information through linguistic means* (broadly understood). In a very rough way, then, we might thus distinguish between the *broad* practical rationality of a contribution to a conversation—how well the contribution serves (or is likely to serve) all of the interests of a given participant, where these include both her private interests as well as the interests deriving from the shared aims of the conversation itself—and the *narrow* practical rationality of a contribution to a conversation—how well the contribution serves (or is likely to serve) the shared interests of all of the conversational participants *qua* conversational participants. I surmise that when Grice speaks of conversations as rational activities, he has mainly the latter in mind, but it will be important to have the former in mind as well. (I will return to this below.)

I say that the sort of rationality involved in conversation is practical rationality, but there can be little doubt that epistemic rationality also comes into play. At the same time, I submit that epistemic rationality and epistemic norms play what I would describe as either *subsidiary* or *derivative* functions in conversation. The *subsidiary* functions played by epistemic norms come into play in connection with the judgments that have to be made in the course of a conversation: since what it is practically rational to do at any point in a conversation depends on what came previously, discerning what came previously is relevant to what it is practically rational to do now, and epistemic norms govern the relevant set of judgments (deciphering aspects of the context, recovering of the illocutionary act performed by the speaker, etc.). The *derivative* functions played by epistemic norms in conversation come into play in connection with certain speech acts, paradigmatically, those from the assertoric category of illocutionary acts: when one observes that another has asserted something, for example, one is then in a situation in which one's doxastic response is governed by epistemic norms. (Roughly speaking, this is the subject-matter of the

---

[6]Alternatively, we might say that practical rationality is the sort that is in play in decision theory, and the sort for which one might do a cost-benefit analysis.

epistemology of testimony.) To be sure, much recent work suggests that one's doxastic response may also be subject to non-epistemic norms as well;[7] I will get to this in a moment. But for now my point is only that there is a derivative role played by epistemic norms in conversation, in those scenarios in which one observes another speaker presents something as true.

Where Hypothesis 1 can explain how one enters into a conversation—and so how one becomes subject with within-conversation norms at the outset—Hypothesis 2 (together with familiar auxiliary facts) can explain how, once one is in a conversation, one continues to be subject to a variety of different normative demands. At the most general level, these normative demands derive from (i) the rationality and cooperativity of conversations together with (ii) facts about the conversational context, including the speech act most recently performed. To see this, suppose that I am correct to think that participants to a conversation have a shared interest in communicating information through linguistic means (in the sense characterized above). Insofar as they share this interest, they will be subject to norms of cooperation and of (practical and epistemic) rationality as these bear on the actions they take in the course of their attempts to communicate with one another. Various things might be explained in this general fashion.

For example, we might explain in this way why, after one has been addressed by another speaker in the course of a conversation, one is under normative pressure to respond appropriately. The explanation is this: illocutionary acts call for uptake, and some forms of uptake require a response, so insofar as an audience who observes an illocutionary act is cooperative, the audience is thereby under normative pressure to respond appropriately to the act observed. Precisely what this involves will depend on the type of illocutionary act one observed. And insofar as all acts of illocution call for uptake (and possibly further response), the audience who responds with an illocutionary act of her own thereby puts normative pressure on the original speaker, and so forth, until the conversation is brought to a close. By contrast, note that those who are not being addressed by a speaker are (typically[8]) under no such obligation to respond. This is so even if they happen to overhear the exchange, and indeed even if they begin to follow the exchange as a non-participant.

In addition, we might also explain why, when one is a participant in a conversation, there is added pressure on one to give periodic indications of one's attentiveness and comprehension of the speech acts being performed. A good deal of empirical work makes clear how speakers can be thrown off when they do not receive such periodic signals. Schlegloff (1982) notes that indications like nodding or vocalizing "Uh huh" are ways in which an audience member signals to the

---

[7] I think here not only of the literature on epistemic injustice (initiated by Fricker (2007)) but also that on epistemic partiality in friendship (see e.g. Baker (1987), Keller (2004), Stroud (2006), Hawley (2014), and Goldberg (2019)) as well as the literature in moral encroachment (see e.g. Basu (2018, 2019), Basu and Schroeder (2018), and Moss (2018)). Goldberg (2022) aims to suggest how these literatures are connected (or not) in the phenomenon of (our responses to) testimony.

[8] I will return to this below, as the speech act of assertion raises some specific questions in this regard.

speaker that she is following along adequately. Work on conversations involving a speaker who is narrating a story offers further confirmation of this point. Having reviewed thousands of exchanges involving spoken narratives, Bavelas et al. (2000) found that when audiences fail to respond with the anticipated acknowledgement of the narrative at relevant junctures this affects the fluency and quality of the narrated speech itself. They found further that on average audience members give such indications *every 27 seconds* while listening to a narrative. These results are explicable insofar as we think of conversations as rational, cooperative activities whose shared aim is the linguistic communication of information: given the mutual knowledge of the ways in which conversations can go wrong, it is important for participants to give regular indications to the speaker that one is still appropriately attentive (so that it is OK to continue). Doing so is both cooperative, in the sense that it serves the mutual aim of successful communication, and practically rational, in the sense that it serves to enable participants to avoid situations in which misunderstanding is permitted to continue for some time, by which time it will have become costly to correct.

By contrast, consider someone who starts off a conversation as a mere overhearer, but who gives these sorts of periodic indications of attentiveness and comprehension to the speaker. I submit that this sort of act constitutes a signal indicating a desire to be included among participants—a request of sorts *to be counted among those being addressed*. This request can be accommodated (as when a speaker, recognizing this request, begins to address herself to the person in question) or else repudiated (as when a speaker, recognizing this request, says something to the effect "I am not speaking to you," or perhaps some less hostile version of this). At the same time, my sense is that such "requests" are hard simply to ignore: the longer a person continues to make these periodic indications of attentiveness and comprehension without being told to "butt out," the more claim she has to being a participant in the conversation—a kind of accommodation, as it were. This can be explained by treating these indications of attentiveness and comprehension, when directed at a speaker by someone who started out as a non-participant, as a way of *addressing* the speaker—the address being part of the implicit request that is being made. This would explain why there is some normative pressure on a speaker to respond in one of the ways indicated.

More familiarly, Hypothesis 2 (together with auxiliary information about context) might also explain a good number of the observations that Grice (1975) brought to our attention. Grice (1975) aimed to show how the presumed rationality and cooperativity of conversation underwrites various maxims, which in turn (he argued) can explain the pragmatic inferences that we draw in conversation. To be sure, the resulting "Gricean" account of pragmatic inferences is not uncontroversial.[9] Happily, as I am interested only in the normative demands generated in conversation, I need not resolve that controversy here. Rather, focusing on normative

---

[9] Some deny that Grice's maxims offer the best explanation of pragmatic inference; others deny that it is any explanation at all. See e.g. Davis (1988), Gauker (2001), Saul (2002, 2010), and Lepore and Stone (2015).

demands in conversation, it seems that Grice's maxims earn their keep—whatever their explanatory power regarding pragmatic inference might be. Simply put, the maxims appear to capture norms whose (apparent) violation is noteworthy: when a speaker (apparently) violates them an audience seeks an explanation, where the failure to find an explanation leaves one with a distinct impression that the exchange is normatively deficient. (For my purposes here I can leave it open how these sorts of normative demands in conversation relate to the basis of pragmatic inference.)

We might also try to appeal to the cooperativity and rationality of conversation to account for the norms on turn-taking. Assume that participants in a conversation share the aim of communicating information through linguistic means. Since linguistic communication requires uptake (otherwise there is no communication), we will have a normative demand on a minimal kind of turn-taking: after a speaker has spoken, an audience must apprehend the speech act performed. What is wanted, though, is (an account of) a more robust turn-taking demand. Here the appeal to cooperativity and rationality provide for various complimentary explanations.

To begin, for any type of speech act which itself calls for a manifest response—acknowledgements and greetings, requests, questions, and many others—cooperation requires that the audience offer a manifest response. Here we might suppose that the norms of (practical) rationality, operating in conjunction with the norms of cooperation, place time constraints on the time interval in which a response is to be given.[10] This would appear to put normative pressure both on the audience (to offer an appropriate response in the relevant interval) but also on the speaker (to give the audience the opportunity to do so).

So far I have been appealing to conversational participants sharing an interest merely in communicating information through linguistic means. But the shared interest is often much more detailed than this. It may involve an interest in informing an audience on some subject, or jointly constructing a plan, and so forth. (Presumably, in most cases it will be even more detailed than this.). One thought is that, in the same way that planning (*qua* cooperative rational activity) places normative demands on those involved (Gilbert, 2009, 2017; Bratman, 2013), so too will conversations with these more specific ends. This is perhaps obvious: conversations that aim to inform ought to give space to those who are to-be-informed to respond in ways that confirm their understanding, allow them to ask questions, and so forth; conversations that aim to eventuate in a jointly-created plan ought to give opportunities for all to participate in the planning itself; and so forth. Of course, precisely what sort of "turns" this provides for the audience will be highly context-sensitive; but the point is that there is a basis for some sort of turn-taking, deriving from the nature of the conversational aims together with the general cooperativity and rationality of conversations.

Although I have only explored Hypothesis 2 in connection with a few kinds of within-conversation norms, I hope to have given some sense of how this hypothesis

---

[10] See Roberts and Francis (2013) for empirical work on how conversational participants interpret silences differently, depending on the duration of time that passes prior to a manifest response to a speech act.

might be employed to explain various other within-conversation norms. At the same time, I have been assuming that conversation is a cooperative endeavor, and a good number of authors have called this into question.[11] Here I want to suggest why my present argument is less susceptible to this sort of worry than one might suppose—and arguably bypasses it altogether. My point is simply that linguistic communication cannot hope to succeed without some level of cooperation. It may be that the degree of cooperativity required for successful communication is less than is typically assumed, but it is not nothing either. Let me explain.

Let us use the term "successful communication" to refer to whatever it is that constitutes the sort of "meeting of minds" at which linguistic communication aims. To ensure that I do not beg the question against those who argue that communication need not be cooperative, let this condition be as minimal as possible, consistent with the claim that there has been the relevant sort of "meeting of the minds". Perhaps this condition can be satisfied even if the audience fails to recover the very content of the speaker's illocutionary act (Pollock, 2015, 2023), or even if the audience is mistaken as to the speaker's communicative intentions, or even if the audience doesn't even so much as form an opinion about the speaker's communicative intentions.[12] Still, it will require that the speaker succeeded in getting *something* across, where the "message" recovered by the audience is close enough (along some plausible, if perhaps multi-dimensional, scale of closeness) to count the attempt at communication as successful.

On the assumption that all linguistic communication aims at success in this sense, any two or more participants who hope to communicate with one another through language must ensure that their contributions are intelligible. And insofar as participants have not agreed ahead of their conversation regarding how their contributions are to be interpreted, they must make do with what is already at hand. My suggestion is that there are a variety of norms—semantic and pragmatic norms to be sure, but also mutually salient social norms—which are non-negotiable in this endeavor. Failure to conform to these norms is tantamount to failure to communicate.

It is important not to overstate the significance of the foregoing points. Successful communication is possible under a wide variety of conditions, including conditions of oppression and other contexts of conflict (or competition) in which a significant number of participants' interests fail to align with one another. This is precisely why I distinguished above between the wide rationality of conversation, having to do with *all* of the interests a participant might have in connection with an ongoing conversation, and the narrow rationality of conversation, having to do only with the interests connected to the aim of communicating information through language. Since in the first instance I am talking only about the latter here, I am in a position

---

[11] See e.g. Elletsen (2021). For an overview of the philosophy, linguistics, and cognitive psychology literature that has questioned Grice's Cooperative Principle, as well as an attempted defense of the CP itself against these criticisms, see Ke and Li (2017).

[12] Schiffer (1987) argues that successful communication cannot depend on the audience's recovery of the speaker's communicative intentions.

to grant that a good many conversations take place under conditions of misaligned interests. This is to say that participants cannot presume that there is any normative pressure of the wide rationality sort in play. But this says nothing about the normative pressure that comes from the shared interest in communication itself. Note, too, that even in contexts in which one has interests that would be better served if one were to refrain from communicating, even so, insofar as one has any interest in communication, one will be subject to these minimal norms. It may be that a worker would be better served not to respond to queries from their imperious and oppressive boss, but insofar as they aim to be understood by the boss, they will be under normative pressure e.g. to proffer intelligible responses, to respond in the relevant time frame, and so forth. Of course, in contexts in which there is a more robust form of cooperativity amongst conversational participants, there will potentially be more norms in play, and more normative demands on participants. But this is as it should be. My present point is only that even under conditions of the greatest conflict, if communication is to be successful, certain norms will need to be followed.[13] At a minimal, Hypothesis 2 is apt to account for these kinds of normative pressures.

3 Epistemological Dimensions of Conversation

So far, I have had very little to say about the epistemic norms in play in conversation. For those interested in the distinctively epistemological dimensions of conversation, this is a lacuna. In this section I aim to address this. My main objectives are two-fold. First, I want to suggest that, while the distinction between being a conversational participant and being a mere overhearer is of substantial normative significance, this significance is (mostly) non-epistemic in nature. Second, I want to argue that epistemic norms transcend the contours of a conversation, making the distinction between within-conversation norms and without-conversation norms inapt in connection with the epistemic dimension of conversations.

Suppose you witness an ongoing conversation among a group of people who are discussing the daily routines of beavers. You hear them discuss many things: their sleeping and eating patterns, their mating season, their habitat, and so forth. Even if you are not a participant in the conversation—say, you are just listening in—even so you are in a position to learn a good deal about the daily routine of beavers. In particular, it is plausible to suppose that you are (close to) as well-positioned as any of the conversation's participants to acquire knowledge about beavers by accepting what the speakers are saying. This is not to say that you will acquire such knowledge: perhaps the speakers don't know what they are talking about. But it is to say that you are (close to) *as well-positioned as* the conversation's participants are. I qualify this with "close to," since it may be that the conversation's participants know

---

[13] An instructive illustration of this concerns the respect for the white flag under conditions of war. See e.g. Shiffrin (2014).

each other, and know other details of the context as well, and so have better grounds to determine how reliable each speaker is. But this difference, while certainly common, has nothing to do with the distinction between their status as participants and your status as an outside observer. The contour of the conversation, it would appear, has no distinctly *epistemic* significance. In this respect the epistemic dimensions of a conversation are unlike the other normative dimensions mentioned above, where there did appear to be important differences between being a participant and being a mere overhearer.

Not everyone accepts this point. Some theorists have argued that there is an epistemic difference between being the addressee of another's telling, and being a mere overhearer.[14] My own view is that it is better to see the difference between being an addressee and being an overhearer as a normative difference, albeit one in which the norms in question are of the (non-epistemic) types discussed in the previous section. This is what I will try to defend here. I will do so by considering and rejecting two arguments that might be offered in support of the claim that there is an *in-kind* epistemic difference between being an addressee and being a mere overhearer.

Before doing so, however, I want to be clear on the commitments of such a position. It is uncontroversial—and all parties to this dispute should allow—that there are many contingent epistemic differences between addressees and overhearers in actual cases. For example, addressees can be predicted to know more than overhearers know about the speaker and about various aspects of the context. I would allow, further, that there may even be true generalizations about these contingent epistemic differences between addressees and overhearers. What I am contesting, rather, is a view on which

> in virtue of being addressed by a speaker who tells you something, you have access to epistemic goodies from which an overhearer is excluded *in principle*.

Call this the *Principled Epistemic Difference* thesis. And consider a version of the thesis that holds not only for addressees but for conversational participants as well: such a thesis holds that participants and addresses alike enjoy this sort of epistemic access from tellings when these take place in conversations in which they are participants. Call this the *Generalized Principle Epistemic Difference* thesis. My aim is to target both of these theses. I will do so by targeting the Principled Epistemic Difference thesis; since this thesis is entailed by the Generalized Principled Epistemic Difference thesis, if I can show that the arguments for the former fail, I will thereby have shown that the same arguments fail to establish the latter.

As I survey the literature, there are two arguments that might be offered for the Principled Epistemic Difference thesis.

One familiar argument appeals to the claim that tellings involve second-personal normative relations that affect the epistemology involved. Such arguments, which is associated with the position that has come to be known as the 'assurance view of

---

[14] This difference has been emphasized by Hinchman (2005), Moran (2006), and McMyler (2011, 2013). I should acknowledge, however, that both Hinchman and Moran appear to have modified their views. See e.g. Hinchman (2013) and Moran (2018).

testimony,' see tellings as analogous to, or perhaps even involving, other verifiably second-personal speech acts. Thus Hinchman (2005) construes tellings as 'invitations to trust,' and Moran (2006) characterizes tellings as offering a kind of 'guarantee' or 'promise' to one's addressee. On the plausible assumption that extending an invitation to another person, like offering them a guarantee or a promise, changes one's normative relations to that person, we are then invited to conclude that this difference underwrites an epistemological difference.

Without going into details about why such proposals face serious epistemological challenges,[15] I note that the intuitions driving accounts of this sort can be accommodated without conceding the Principled Epistemic Difference thesis. I will illustrate this with the proposal that construes tellings as invitations to trust, but what I have to say holds, *mutatis mutandis*, for the other versions of the assurance view.

Suppose that tellings involve invitations to trust. And let us grant for the sake of argument that, if tellings involve invitations to trust, the addressee *but not an overhearer* would have an entitlement to feel a bit angry or resentful if (having believed the speaker) it turns out that the speaker's say-so wasn't warranted or wasn't true. Even if we grant this, the claim itself would appear to have nothing to do with epistemology. For one thing, an addressee has grounds to feel angry or resentful when she receives a faulty invitation *of any sort*. Compare: you would have an entitlement to feel a bit angry or resentful if (having tried to go to a party to which you were invited) you discover that the party never happened, or if you found out that the person who invited you did not have the authority to invite you. In response perhaps it will be said that it is not the invitation alone, but the fact that it is an invitation *to trust*, that renders this an epistemic phenomenon. This brings me to a second point.

While invitations to trust do appear to carry presuppositions to the effect that the speaker has the authority to invite such trust—which is to say, that the speaker is relevantly trustworthy—such presuppositions are also available to be presupposed or believed by overhearers, with no principled *epistemic* difference between them and the addressee. To see this, suppose that speaker S invites addressee A to trust her, where overhearer O observes the whole scene. Is A in an in-principle different epistemic position than O with respect to the presuppositions that are generated by S's having invited A to trust her (S)? Perhaps it will be thought that A, but not O, is justified in believing S trustworthy merely in virtue of S's invitation (to A) to trust. But this is not so. In particular, it is incorrect to think that A is justified in believing S trustworthy merely in virtue of S's invitation. On the contrary: it is a familiar point that, even when a speaker invites your trust, we will criticize you as unreasonable or irrational for believing them trustworthy when the speaker is known to be untrustworthy. ("Why did you believe Sam to be trustworthy? You know he's not reliable.") To be sure, we may quibble over when it is reasonable—epistemically reasonable—to believe a person to be trustworthy when they have invited your trust. It may well

---

[15] This has been forcefully argued elsewhere. See e.g. Owens (2006), Lackey (2008), Schmitt (2010), Goldberg (2015, 2020), and Leonard (2016).

be that, when it comes to a speaker who invites you to trust her, you are presumptively entitled to believe her to be trustworthy. But even if we grant this point (as I am inclined to do), it does not illustrate an in-principle epistemic difference between addressee and overhearer. Rather, it sanctions a rather ordinary version of a kind of *anti-reductionism* regarding invitations-to-trust, according to which audiences are (presumptively but defeasibly) entitled to believe, of a speaker S who invites an addressee A to trust her (S), that S is trustworthy in the relevant way with respect to A. Once again, this epistemic principle holds for *everyone*, not just the addressee.

Indeed, our present point holds not only of invitations to trust, but of invitations more generally. Invitations carry presuppositions. To see this, suppose S invites A to X (where 'X' can be anything that one can be invited to do). S's doing so generates presuppositions in connection with X: invitations to a party presuppose that the party will take place (and that the speaker has the authority to grant permission to S to attend), invitations to dine together presuppose that that the speaker will show up (and, in some cultures, that the speaker will pay), etc. (There may be other presuppositions as well, but these will do for now.). That invitations to trust carry the presupposition that the speaker is trustworthy is simply a special case of this. The presuppositions in this class are available to the addressee for presupposition and belief; but in moving to presuppose or believe them, the addressee enjoys no principled epistemic difference over an overhearer. To repeat what was said above: we might well favor an anti-reductionist view of *invitation-beliefs*, according to which audiences are entitled to believe the presuppositions of a proffered invitation unless they have reasons for doubt. But once again, this principle would hold for *everyone*, not just the person invited: if I hear you inviting Makwa to the party, and I have no reasons for doubt, I would (on this version of anti-reductionism) be justified in believing that there will be a party at the location you specified. The only difference between Makwa and me is that I haven't thereby been invited. This explains why Makwa now enjoys certain *non*-epistemic entitlements and responsibilities that I lack: she now is under some obligation to respond to the invitation, she has permission to go to the party, etc. Similarly: if I observe you *tell* Makwa that there is a party, and I have no reasons for doubt, I would (on anti-reductionism about testimony) be justified in believing that there is a party at the location you specified. It's just that I haven't been invited to rely on your say-so, and so am not entitled to the reactive attitudes associated with feelings of betrayal.[16]

Similar things can be said, *mutatis mutandis*, about the proposals that tellings involve guarantees or promises. The speaker who contracts with an addressee, like the person who makes another person a promise, does indeed change the normative relationship between themselves and their addressee: there are new obligations and entitlements that hold between them, which were not in place before. But these are non-epistemic matters; the epistemology is in principle available to anyone who is apprized of the relevant speech exchange.

---

[16] But see Goldberg (2015) for the idea that if testimony involves assertion, then *some* reactive attitudes are open to any observer who comprehends the assertion.

I have just argued against a first attempt to establish the Principle Epistemic Difference thesis. A variant on this argument highlights the unique sort of care and concern a teller has, or ought to have, towards their addressee.[17] If I tell you something, I should take care to ensure that I am sensitive to your epistemic needs. This involves knowing your practical situation: if I know you are deathly allergic to nuts, then I ought to be particularly careful when I tell you whether some food item contains nuts. By contrast, if I know you are merely curious whether food items contain nuts, I need not be as careful in the nut tellings I direct at you. This is a way in which I am responsible *to you*, as the person I am addressing. I am typically not (and am under no obligation to be) similarly sensitive to an overhearer. Perhaps then we can say that tellings ought to satisfy an epistemic standard that is tailored in this way to the specific needs of the addressee, putting her in a better position to appreciate the epistemic significance of the telling.

In response, I want to concede all of the points made, but deny that this establishes the Principled Epistemic Difference thesis. On the contrary, the sort of factors just mentioned might all be known by a third party overhearer, in which case the overhearer who observed your testimony would be in as good a position to discern its epistemic significance as the addressee herself. It is true that the third party would not stand in the same normative relationship to the speaker as the addressee, at least as far as feelings of resentment might arise if the testimony proved false: the addressee might resent the fact that the speaker, who aimed to be meeting *her* epistemic needs, failed in this way. But this point is no different from the point above: it has no epistemic significance *per se*.

Indeed, we can generalize our point here. It is obvious that different people are typically differently situated (epistemically speaking) to respond to another's assertion. Some know the speaker well, others have a good deal of background knowledge on the topic of the assertion, still others have special knowledge of the contextual features that tell in favor or against the speaker's reliability on this occasion. But none of this has anything to do with their standing in the conversation. In effect, Hinchman's point, that responsible speakers try to inform their assertions with a sensitivity to their addressee's epistemic needs (and that these needs might be common knowledge between speaker and addressee), is simply a special case of this idea that people come to conversations with different background knowledge. And we might make the very same point more general by speaking of the speaker's sensitivity (not only to the addressee, but) to the conversational participants more generally. Even if Hinchman is correct about all of this, it still fails to mark an important epistemic distinction between participants and overhearers.

I conclude, then, that neither of these two attempts to establish the Principled Epistemic Difference thesis succeeds. Still, I think epistemic norms have a wider (if still derivative) role to play in conversation, and perhaps it is worth bringing this out.

---

[17] This point is emphasized in Hinchman (2014). (Hinchman also uses the allergy example I borrow below.) I should note, however, that my criticism here is not directed against Hinchman, but rather against those who would use these considerations to argue for the conclusion I am criticizing. Hinchman himself would appear not to do so.

To this end, in the section that follows I want to offer a model for how epistemic norms come to bear in conversation. The result will offer further confirmation of my main contention: while participants (unlike overhearers) are under normative pressure to attend to the exchanged speech acts (and to respond to them as appropriate) merely in virtue of being a participant in the conversation, overhearers who attend to the speech exchange are in a situation in which their doxastic responses are governed by precisely the same epistemic norms. In fact, this very point may suggest that there are some *non*-epistemic ways in which mere overhearers are under the very same normative pressure as addressees when they observe a speaker tell an addressee that p.

4 Participant Versus Overhearer

Let me reiterate what I take to be the key difference between being a participant in a conversation and being a mere overhearer. To be a participant is to be subject to a variety of within-conversation norms in virtue of one's role (as a participant), whereas overhearers *as such* are not subject to these norms.[18] Among other within-conversation norms to which participants are subject is a norm of attention. Participants owe their attention to the other members of a conversation: they ought to distribute that attention, as appropriate, across those who are actively contributing to the conversation (and ought to contribute in their own manner as appropriate). Insofar as one is under a normative obligation to attend to another's speech contribution, one is under normative pressure to comprehend that contribution. This suggests at least two ways in which epistemic norms can bear on participants in a conversation. Epistemic norms clearly govern acts of would-be comprehension: the way in which an audience has comprehended a speaker can be assessed as more or less reasonable. (This is so whether or not we regard states of comprehension as explicit judgments regarding the observed speech act.[19]). What is more, comprehension ought to be sensitive not only to the words produced by the speaker and the manner in which they were produced; it also involves attending to relevant aspects of the context. This points to a second dimension in which epistemic norms are relevant in conversation: one's "take" on these aspects of context is also susceptible to epistemic assessment, as an audience's assumptions about the context can be more or less reasonable as well.

---

[18] I say 'as such': clearly overhearers can be subject to these norms, but when this is so it is not in virtue of their status *as* overhearers. Suppose S and T are involved in a heated discussion amongst themselves, and V comes along and starts listening in. It may be that S, noting that V is listening in, starts "playing to the crowd" as it were. If it is manifest between S and V that this is what is going on, arguably V is then under some additional obligations to attend to the discussion, even though V remains an overhearer. Here it is in virtue of an implicit kind of address that is involved in "playing to the crowd." (There can be other cases as well, no doubt.)

[19] See e.g. Fricker (2003) and Graham (2010).

Now it is easy to see that in both of these respects, there would appear to be no difference in one's susceptibility to epistemic norms whether one is a participant in the conversation itself or a mere overhearer who happened to observe the speech act in question. It may be that the overhearer is in a worse position to comprehend an observed speech act—she may not be privy to relevant aspects of the context, perhaps she didn't quite catch the utterance itself, she knows less about the speaker, she has less background knowledge on the topic of conversation, etc. But this is not a principled difference between participant and overhearer.

What I now want to argue is that, in at least one very significant respect, an overhearer may face the very same *non*-epistemic normative pressures as an addressee or participant. If I am correct about this, it indicates a point on which the distinction between being a participant and being an overhearer is less normatively significant than is the distinction between those who observe (and understand) a conversational exchange and those who do not. This makes clear that while the distinction between participant and non-participant marks a normatively significant divide in conversations, it is not the end of the story.

Take a case in which S tells A that it is 2:35 pm, where observer O is manifestly listening in. If what I have said in the previous section is correct, there is nothing in principle which prevents O from being in the same epistemic position to benefit from S's say-so as A is. In this way O might come to be in a position to know that it is 2:35 (assuming that S's testimony was knowledgeable, and that O was entitled to accept it). Now suppose that O is immediately asked by Q (another person) what time it is, and O responds, "I have no idea." And suppose further that it is not that O harbors any doubts about S or her testimony; it's just that O gives S no credence whatsoever.[20] Here it can seem that S, were she to learn of this (having observed that O was listening in on what she said), might be justifiably upset at this. This is so, I submit, *whether or not* O was the addressee. S might well say: "But you just heard me tell A that it is 2:35 pm!" Here, I don't think O gets himself off the hook merely by pointing out that he was not being addressed by S.

Indeed, this scenario is related to a phenomenon that is by now very familiar: the phenomenon of *testimonial injustice* (Fricker, 2007). Consider a variant of the case above in which S is a woman, and O is a man who disbelieves S out of identity prejudice (O being an inveterate sexist). Clearly, this is a case of testimonial injustice; and it will not do for O to defend himself on the grounds that he wasn't being addressed. This should clinch the case for thinking that overhears may be under the same normative pressure as they respond doxastically to others' assertions.

Keeping our focus on the case of testimonial injustice, we can ask: what type of normative pressure is this? If we trust the analysis of Fricker (2007), this normative pressure derives from the normativity *of justice*. Justice demands that we not downgrade the credibility we assign to a speaker's say-so on the basis of identity prejudice. As I have put it elsewhere (Goldberg, 2022), we are under a justice-based

---

[20] This case is modeled on one from Hinchman (2005). Hinchman used it to make a point about being invited to trust; my point is about assertions more generally.

demand not to respond to another's say-so in a way wherein identity prejudice leads us to violate the norms of epistemology. If this is correct, then the demands of justice can generate normative pressure in a way that *does not respect the borders of the conversation itself*.

Why might this be? Actually, I think the explanation is near-to hand. It derives from my previous claim (that the contours of a conversation have no distinctive epistemic significance) together with a claim that captures the nature of the act of assertion itself. Suppose that we think of a speaker S's asserting that p as involving S's presenting the proposition that p as true in a way that implicates S's relevant epistemic authority, where the standard for proper assertion is having an 'adequate' epistemic position regarding whether p.[21] And suppose that pragmatically competent speakers implicitly grasp this. In that case it will be common knowledge among competent language users that a speaker S who asserts that p does something that is proper only if she occupies an adequate epistemic position regarding whether p. Assuming that S is pragmatically competent and minimally reflective, S knows that her audience knows this, and so (by asserting that p) can be taken to present herself to her audience as occupying such an epistemic position. As a result, any audience who rejects S's assertion (without calling S's sincerity into question) is implicitly questioning S's competence at assessing her own epistemic authority. Since our status as epistemic subjects is a core part of our value as human beings, one whose epistemic competence is questioned in this way is thereby diminished. And justice requires that one not be diminished in this way on the basis of e.g. identity-prejudice.

One point to note about this explanation is that it nowhere makes use of the notion of addressee, conversational participant, or the contours of the conversation. And this, I submit, is fitting. While the distinction between those who are, and those who are not, participants in a conversation is of great significance from the perspective of speech act normativity and the norms of attention, it is of little or no significance from the epistemic point of view. So if justice demands something of us insofar as we observe another's assertion, its demands will transcend the contours of the conversation itself.

5 Conclusion

In this chapter I have argued that the contours of a conversation have extensive normative significance, in that those who are participants will be under distinctive forms of within-conversation normative pressure. But I argued that within-conversation normative pressure is non-epistemic in nature, and that the norms of epistemology proper transcend the boundaries of a conversation. I concluded by

---

[21] One of the core questions pursued in the norm of assertion debate concerns the content of the adequacy requirement. I leave this open here. But see Goldberg (2015), where I defend the foregoing characterization and spell out what I see as the content of the norm.

noting that this point appears to explain why one can commit an epistemic injustice against a speaker even if the speaker wasn't speaking to one, and even if one wasn't in the conversation at all.

References

Baker, J. (1987). Trust and rationality. *Pacific Philosophical Quarterly, 68*, 1–13.
Basu, R. (2018). Can beliefs wrong? *Philosophical Topics, 46*(1), 1–18.
Basu, R. (2019). Radical moral encroachment: The moral stakes of racist beliefs. *Philosophical Issues, 29*(1), 9–23.
Basu, R., & Schroeder, M. (2018). Doxastic wronging. In B. Kim & M. McGrath (Eds.), *Pragmatic encroachment in epistemology* (pp. 181–205). Routledge.
Bavelas, J., Coates, L., & Johnson, T. (2000). Listeners as co-narrators. *Journal of Personality and Social Psychology, 78*(6), 941–952.
Bratman, M. (2013). *Shared agency: A planning theory of acting together.* Oxford University Press.
Camp, W. (2018). Insinuation, common ground, and the conversational record. In D. Fogal, D. Harris, & M. Moss (Eds.), *New work on speech acts* (pp. 360–384). Oxford University Press.
Davis, W. (1988). *Implicature: Intention, convention, and principle in the failure of Gricean theory.* Cambridge University Press.
Ellefsen, G. (2021). Conversational cooperation revisited. *The Southern Journal of Philosophy, 59*(4), 545–571.
Enfield, N. (2017). *How we talk: The inner workings of conversation.* Basic Books.
Fricker, E. (2003). Understanding and knowledge of what is said. In A. Barber (Ed.), *The epistemology of language* (pp. 325–366). Oxford University Press.
Fricker, M. (2007). *Epistemic injustice: Power and the ethics of knowing.* Oxford University Press.
Gauker, C. (2001). Situated inference versus conversational implicature. *Noûs, 35*(2), 163–189.
Gilbert, M. (2009). Shared intention and personal intentions. *Philosophical Studies, 144*, 167–187.
Gilbert, M. (2017). Joint commitment. In M. Jankovic & K. Ludwig (Eds.), *The Routledge handbook of collective intentionality* (pp. 130–139). Routledge.
Goldberg, S. (2015). *Assertion: On the philosophical significance of assertoric speech.* Oxford University Press.
Goldberg, S. (2019). Against epistemic partiality in friendship: Value-reflecting reasons. *Philosophical Studies, 176*(8), 2221–2242.
Goldberg, S. (2020). *Conversational pressure.* Oxford University Press.
Goldberg, S. (2022). What is a speaker owed? *Philosophy and Public Affairs, 50*(3), 375–407.
Graham, P. (2010). Testimonial entitlement and the function of comprehension. In D. Pritchard, A. Millar, & A. Haddock (Eds.), *Social epistemology* (pp. 148–174). Oxford University Press.
Grice, P. (1975). Logic and conversation. In *Syntax and semantics* (Vol. 3: Speech arts, pp. 41–58). Academic.
Hawley, K. (2014). Partiality and prejudice in trusting. *Synthese, 191*, 2029–2045.
Hinchman, E. (2005). Telling as inviting to trust. *Philosophy and Phenomenological Research, 70*(3), 562–587.
Hinchman, E. S. (2013). Assertion, sincerity, and knowledge. *Noûs, 47*(4), 613–646.
Hinchman, E. S. (2014). Assurance and warrant. *Philosopher's Imprint, 14*, 17.
Ke, W., & Li, Z. (2017). Critical voices against the cooperative principle. *Canadian Social Science, 13*(10), 15–21.
Keller, S. (2004). Friendship and belief. *Philosophical Papers, 33*(3), 329–351.
Khoo, J., & Sterken, R. (Eds.). (2021). *The Routledge handbook of social and political philosophy of language.* Routledge.
Lackey, J. (2008). *Learning from words.* Oxford University Press.

Lackey, J. (2020). The duty to object. *Philosophy and Phenomenological Research, 101*(1), 35–60.
Leonard, N. (2016). Testimony, evidence and interpersonal reasons. *Philosophical Studies, 173*(9), 2333–2352.
Lepore, E., & Stone, M. (2015). *Imagination and convention: Distinguishing grammar and inference in language*. Oxford University Press.
McMyler, B. (2011). *Testimony, trust, and authority*. Oxford University Press.
McMyler, B. (2013). The epistemic significance of address. *Synthese, 190*, 1059–1078.
Moran, R. (2006). Getting told and being believed. In J. Lackey & E. Sosa (Eds.), *The epistemology of testimony* (pp. 272–306). Oxford University Press.
Moran, R. (2018). *The exchange of words: Speech, testimony, and intersubjectivity*. Oxford University Press.
Moss, S. (2018). Moral encroachment. *Proceedings of the Aristotelian Society, 118*(2), 177–205.
Mühlebach, D. (2022). Non-ideal philosophy of language. *Inquiry*, 1–23. https://doi.org/10.1080/0020174X.2022.2074884
Owens, D. (2006). Testimony and assertion. *Philosophical Studies, 130*(1), 105–129.
Pollock, J. (2015). Social externalism and the problem of communication. *Philosophical Studies, 172*, 3229–3251.
Pollock, J. (2023). Testimonial knowledge and content preservation. *Philosophical Studies, 180*(10), 3073–3097.
Roberts, F., & Francis, A. (2013). Identifying a temporal threshold of tolerance for silent gaps after requests. *Journal of the Acoustical Society of America, 133*(6), 471–477.
Saul, J. (2002). Speaker meaning, what is said, and what is implicated. *Noûs, 36*(2), 228–248.
Saul, J. (2010). Speaker-meaning, conversational implicature and calculability. In K. Petrus (Ed.), *Meaning and analysis: New essays on Grice* (pp. 170–183). Palgrave Macmillan.
Saul, J. (2018). Dogwhistles, political manipulation, and philosophy of language. In D. Fogal, D. Harris, & M. Moss (Eds.), *New work on speech acts* (pp. 360–384). Oxford University Press.
Schiffer, S. (1987). *Remnants of meaning*. MIT Press.
Schlegloff, E. (1982). Discourse as an interactional achievement: Some uses of 'Uh Huh' and other things that come between sentences. In D. Tannen (Ed.), *Analyzing discourse: Text and talk* (pp. 71–93). Georgetown University Press.
Schmitt, F. (2010). The assurance view of testimony. In A. Haddock, A. Millar, & D. Pritchard (Eds.), *Social epistemology: Essential readings* (pp. 216–242). Oxford University Press.
Schroeder, M. (2018). When beliefs wrong. *Philosophical Topics, 46*(1), 115–127.
Shiffrin, S. (2014). *Speech matters: Lying, morality and the law*. Princeton University Press.
Stanley, J., & Beaver, D. (2023). *The politics of language*. Princeton University Press.
Stroud, S. (2006). Epistemic partiality in friendship. *Ethics, 116*(3), 498–524.

Virtuous Arguing

Duncan Pritchard

1 Introduction

One core kind of conversation is an argument. I take it that there is a prevailing consensus that these days people argue badly (i.e., even worse than previously). The general idea is that the information age seems to have corrupted us in core respects such that we are unable to enter into the kind of good faith arguments that drive social progress, leading us instead into a kind of intellectual dead-end whereby each shouts loudly at the other from their own cultural silo. This, at any rate, is how the issue is presented by various commentators, from mainstream media to intellectuals, and I suspect there is at least some truth in it. In any case, whatever the merits of this idea that there is a particular contemporary social malaise on this front, it is surely of philosophical interest to clarify what it would mean to argue well, if only to discern what we are presently doing wrong when we argue badly.

I want to suggest that there are at least three plausible ways of evaluating good arguing. While all three are credible ways of assessing one's arguing, one of these axes of evaluation is better placed to capture what we are after when we decry contemporary argumentative practices, not least because it incorporates many of the good-making features of the other two axes of evaluation. This is what I refer to as *virtuous arguing*, which is the style of argumentation of the intellectually virtuous subject. As we will see, spelling out how the intellectual virtuous person argues will have interesting implications for how we should think of good arguing. For example, that good arguers can have genuine conviction, and thus 'stick to their guns', even while exhibiting genuine intellectual humility, and that good arguers have an intellectual obligation not only to accurately represent the views of their opponents, but also to find charitable ways to reinterpret their positions in order to make them

---

D. Pritchard (✉)
University of California, Irvine, Irvine, CA, USA
e-mail: dhpritch@uci.edu

© The Author(s), under exclusive license to Springer Nature Switzerland AG 2024
W. J. Silva-Filho (ed.), *The Epistemology of Conversation*, Philosophical Studies Series 156, https://doi.org/10.1007/978-3-031-74069-5_4

as credible as possible. If there is a malaise that afflicts the information age on this front, then cultivating intellectually virtuous subjects, and thus virtuous arguers, is a fundamental part of the solution.

2 Arguments

My interest is in a specific kind of in-person conversational exchange that concerns two subjects engaging in argument, where each subject is sincerely defending their opposing position. I take it that this is the paradigm of an argument. There can obviously be arguments involving more than two parties, though that in itself just adds further complexity to the proceedings rather than significantly changing what is taking place. Another variant from the paradigm would be a case where not all the parties are sincerely defending their position. Perhaps one of the parties is playing devil's advocate, or has other motives for defending the position they are adopting than that it is their position (such as when a lawyer is paid to defend a client). Indeed, do we even need two disputing parties for an argument, for cannot one rehearse such an argument oneself, with an imagined adversary? If so, then that would be another deviation from the paradigm case. We can also imagine more complex cases of argument where the positions in play are not opposing, but merely in tension with one another in certain respects. The nature of the argument looks very different once we move away from the paradigm case, however, given that we no longer have two people advocating for their respective, and opposing, positions. For example, one might have moral, and perhaps even intellectual, obligations to one's opponent in the paradigm case that simply don't apply when one is arguing with oneself or with someone who isn't articulating their own position.

These points loom large when we turn our attention to the kind of online arguments that characterise the contemporary digital landscape. These online disputes often involve multiple parties occupying a range of positions and hence bring with them layers of complexity. But even more significantly there is also the presence of actors in this arena who are taking positions for all sorts of reasons besides the fact that it is their sincerely held view. These motives might include the unedifying enjoyment of (anonymously) attacking someone or the desire to generate social capital. Indeed, it might even be the case that the 'actor' who represents one's dialectical opponent is not a person at all, but some sort of AI-generated bot.[1]

Focussing on the paradigm case will not only help us to keep our discussion manageable but will also offer us a template that can be applied, *mutatis mutantis*, to non-paradigm cases. Accordingly, in what follows the reader should understand arguments in terms of the paradigm case. My interest in arguments, so conceived, are the axes along which we evaluate good arguing. If we can understand what

---

[1] I've argued elsewhere that in at least some of these cases the 'disagreement' in play is, properly conceived, merely apparent, and similar points would naturally apply, *mutatis mutantis*, to treating these disputes as genuine arguments as well. See Pritchard (2018a).

constitutes good arguing in the one-on-one conversational case, then we can use that to figure out what it would look like in more complicated scenarios, such as those posed by social media.

One final point that I want to make before we proceed with our discussion is to distinguish the question of what constitutes good arguing from the more familiar epistemological discussion of disagreement. The two topics are obviously related, given that arguments involve disagreement, but they are not the same. The divergences between these topics will, I hope, become increasingly apparent as we develop our understanding of good arguing, but the core difference is that the epistemology of disagreement is a much narrower topic than the kind of analysis of good arguing that we will be attempting. There are at least two reasons why it is narrower. The first is that capturing the nature of good arguing is not merely an epistemological task (i.e., working out what stance the evidence warrants, etc.,), as it brings with it broader ethical issues about how one ought to behave, as we will see. The second, which may simply reflect an idiosyncrasy of contemporary epistemology, is that standard treatments of the epistemology of disagreement are overarchingly concerned with the question of what kind of concession, if any, one is rationally obliged to make to one's opponent's position in the context of disagreements of various kinds.[2] As will become clear, while this may be one consideration when it comes to our understanding of good arguing, it is by far not the only one (or even a particularly central concern). (Indeed, we will be arguing that there is a very good sense in which the intellectually virtuous individual can manifest their intellectual virtue in the context of argument without thereby incurring a standing obligation to downgrade their confidence in their own well-founded views).

3   Three Axes of Argumentative Evaluation

When we consider the question of what makes someone's style of argument 'good', I think there are three broad, and to some extent overlapping, types of evaluation that spring to mind. The first is probably the one that will be most natural to philosophers. This is that one is arguing in a way that is formally correct: one's reasoning is logical, one is attending to the evidence appropriately, one is not exhibiting any form of fallacious reasoning, one is correctly representing both one's own and one's opponent's position, and so on. Call this the *formal* axis of evaluation, with arguments that exhibit the features just described scoring well along this axis.[3]

---

[2] See, for example, the papers collected in two main contemporary edited collections on the epistemology of disagreement, Feldman and Warfield (2010) and Christensen and Lackey (2013).

[3] For the most part, argumentation theory—which the reader should note is a field that has a broader focus than the simple conversational arguments at issue here—has been mainly focused on what we are referring to here as the formal axis of evaluation, especially with regard to understanding the role of fallacies in bad arguments. See, for example, Hamblin (1970), Johnson and Blair (1977), Woods and Walton (1982, 1989), and Johnson (2014). See also footnote 4.

One thing that is notable about the formal style of arguing is that while it might *impress* some people (like philosophers), it is probably unlikely to be that effective at *persuading* people. Persuasion, after all, requires a different set of skills to that involved in the purely formal style of arguing. For example, one key skill in this regard is a responsiveness to the concerns of one's opponent so as to appropriately judge what kinds of consideration might make them change their opinion in your favour. One can be very good at formally structuring one's arguments without ever mastering this skill of persuasion.

With this point in mind, consider another style of argument that is focussed upon success in arguing rather than following due process in the manner of the formal axis. Call this the *strategic* axis of evaluation. Arguing well along the strategic axis of evaluation will depend on what one's goal is. The obvious goal would be persuasion, but this might not be one's only argumentative aim. Perhaps it is to browbeat the other person into submission, or to bamboozle them such that they aren't sure how to respond. For our purposes, however, I think we can reasonably restrict our attention to the core strategic goal of persuasion. The reason for this is that these other goals are clearly problematic ways to be evaluating the success of an argumentative strategy. Accordingly, insofar as we wish to identify *good* ways of arguing, then we would be wise to confine our attention to a goal like persuasion which isn't inherently problematic (even if, as we will see in a moment, it can be attained in problematic ways).[4]

Note that the strategic style of arguing needn't be opposed to using the tools of the formal style. Logical reasoning can sometimes be a useful way of persuading someone after all, and so one would expect someone who is adept along this strategic axis to employ such techniques where applicable. An argument conducted in a way that scores highly along the strategic axis of evaluation thus might also score well along the formal axis too. Given the kind of creatures that human beings are, however, it would be unrealistic to expect that we are only persuaded by good reasoning of the formal kind. Indeed, there may be cases where the strategic style of argument is best pursued by using argumentative manoeuvres that would generate a low score along the formal axis, such as by employing logical fallacies that one correctly judges will influence your adversary to regard your position in a favourable light. 'Good' arguing in the strategic sense, even when we discard inherently problematic strategic goals, might thus not be 'good' arguing in the formal sense. Since we have already noted that 'good' arguing in the formal sense is often not 'good' arguing along the strategic axis (since it is often unpersuasive), it follows that these two axes of argumentative evaluation come apart in both directions.

---

[4] One finds versions of the strategic axis of evaluation in argumentation theory, at least to the extent that there are theorists who explicitly extend their focus from purely formal features of argument (see footnote 3) to non-formal features that are nonetheless deemed important because of their persuasive powers. (We will be considering a similar combination of formal and strategic axes of argument evaluation below). See, especially, the pragma-dialectics approach to argumentation theory offered by van Eemeren & Grootendorst (e.g. 1984, 2004) and (2018). For a related proposal in this regard, see also Gilbert (1997).

Into the midst of these two distinct ways of evaluating argumentative styles, I want to introduce a third approach that blends features from both, but which is also different from the other two styles in important respects. This is a style of argumentation that is at least minimally formal, in that while it doesn't deliberately (much less strategically) involve employing formally bad argumentative manoeuvres, such as illogical reasoning or appealing to informal fallacies, it is not driven by purely formal concerns. Moreover, while it will tend to be persuasive when done well, it is also a style of argumentation that isn't at all geared towards purely strategic goals. The style of argumentation I have in mind is that employed by an intellectually virtuous subject. Call this the *virtuous* axis of evaluation. I will be suggesting that this captures a centrally important category of good arguing. In short, we should be striving to be virtuous arguers.

4 Virtuous Arguing in Outline

Let's start with virtuous intellectual character. This involves the integrated set of intellectual virtues, which are high-level cognitive traits like intellectual humility, intellectual tenacity, intellectual courage, conscientiousness, and so forth. While the intellectual virtues are cognitive skills, they are very different from many other types of cognitive skill. For example, they are reflective of one's intellectual character—they are intellectual character traits—which means that they are different from the kinds of cognitive skills that one is born with or which one naturally acquires as one matures (and which are thus not indicative of one's intellectual character). One has to consciously acquire, and then cultivate, one's intellectual virtues. Moreover, the intellectual virtues are admirable character traits, in the sense that we admire the intellectual character of someone who possesses them. This distinguishes the intellectual virtues from mere cognitive skills, as they may not be admirable (even when they are character traits). Someone might have very good memorial skills, for example, but while this might be impressive, it may not be appropriate to admire them for it. Relatedly, that they have such skills might not tell us anything about their intellectual character (perhaps they were merely born with such a capacity, for example).

Another important, and related, difference between the intellectual virtues and mere cognitive abilities is that the former is essentially truth-directed. That is, to be intellectually virtuous is to be motivated by a desire for the truth, with all that entails (e.g., a concern for accuracy rather than inaccuracy, a desire for knowledge and understanding, a respect for evidence, and so on). In particular, the intellectually virtuous person treats the truth—getting things right, broadly speaking—as a good in itself (i.e., as something that has final, and not merely instrumental, value). This is different to mere cognitive skills, which can be employed in the absence of any such motivational state on the part of the subject.[5] For example, one's perceptual faculties can be employed in the absence of any particular concern for the truth, much less a final valuing of it. Even an acquired cognitive skill, like good reasoning, can be employed for purely instrumental ends—to complete a puzzle, say—without a desire for the truth entering into the matter at all.

As just noted, we are not born with the intellectual virtues but must acquire them, usually through emulation of virtuous exemplars and via a process of habituation whereby being intellectually virtuous becomes second nature.[6] Moreover, unlike some other skills, once acquired the intellectual virtues must be continually cultivated, for otherwise they can become degraded and so lost. This feature of the intellectual virtues explains why their possession is thought to reflect one's intellectual character, specifically, in contrast to cognitive traits that one is born with or which are easily absorbed without any conscious effort as one matures.

Another way in which the intellectual virtues reflect one's character concerns their motivational component, as they reveal one's fundamental values and thus that which one cares about for its own sake. This also relates to why they are thought to be admirable character traits, as skilfully caring for the truth for its own sake in the manner exhibited by the intellectually virtuous individual is thought to be worthy of such admiration. A further way in which the intellectual virtues manifest one's intellectual character, which builds on the previous points, concerns their high-level managerial role in one's cognitive architecture. One might have lots of specific cognitive skills and know many things, but it is the intellectual virtues (or their absence) that determines whether one makes good use of these skills and this knowledge. The good intellectual character of the intellectually virtuous agent, including their final valuing of the truth, ensures this.

I do not propose to defend the intellectual virtues here but merely to articulate them.[7] My interest is rather to examine what it would mean to conceive of good arguing in terms of them. In particular, I want to suggest that the way that the intellectually virtuous subject engages in argument combines positive features of both the formal and the strategic styles of argument while also adding further positive elements of its own.

Consider first the extent to which the intellectually virtuous subject will incorporate features of the formal style of argument. Since an intellectually virtuous subject not only cares about the truth, but also skilfully seeks out the truth, we would expect them to argue in ways that at least minimally satisfy the formal rubric. The intellectually virtuous subject would not be inclined towards illogical or otherwise fallacious reasoning, they will be attentive to the evidence, keen to properly represent

---

[5] For further discussion of this motivational state that underlies the intellectual virtues, see Pritchard (2021). See also Pritchard (2022b).

[6] For further discussion of the manner in which the intellectual virtues are acquired, including the role of exemplars in this respect, see Croce and Pritchard (2022) and Pritchard (2022a).

[7] For some important contemporary treatments of the intellectual virtues, see Zagzebski (1996), Roberts and Wood (2007), and Baehr (2011a, b). See also Pritchard (2022b). For a useful survey, see Battaly (2014).

the opponent's position (and their own), and so forth. So construed, one might be tempted to think that the intellectually virtuous style of argument at least subsumes, if not completely coincides with, the formal style of argument. As we will see, however, this is not the case.

An initial point of contrast between the formal and virtuous modes of arguing is that while the former is focussed solely on one's own argumentative performance the latter has an other-regarding focus, in that it is also geared towards generating a common understanding. This follows from the truth motivation that is built into the intellectual virtues. To care about the truth, to treat it as a value, means not only striving for it oneself but being concerned to help others attain it too, as a value worth prizing.[8] This has a bearing on how one argues, as it means that it is not enough to meet formal standards of argument, which may not adequately engage with one's adversary at all, but one must go further to find points of contact with one's argumentative opponent in order to promote a common endeavour towards getting at the truth of the matter. (We will be considering some concrete examples of this point in the next section).

That the intellectually virtuous person's valuing of the truth leads them to treat argument as a collaborative enterprise also has a bearing on how the virtuous axis of argument evaluation relates to the strategic axis. There will be overlap between the two proposals on account of this collaborative dimension as it entails that the virtuous axis of argument incorporates at least some degree of concern with persuasion. Nonetheless, there are important differences between the two styles of argument. For one thing, the overarching desire for the truth that animates the virtuous style of arguing will entail not only an aspiration to persuade one's adversary if possible, but also a willingness to be persuaded if that is called for, something that is likely to be lacking from those employing the strategic mode of arguing. But the more fundamental difference is that the virtuous style of argument is not essentially strategic at all, not even with regard to its promotion of truth. For recall that on this view while the truth is prized it is not to be valued purely instrumentally, but rather to be treated as a good for its own sake. Relatedly, while the virtuous mode of arguing may tend to be persuasive, this doesn't mean that persuasion is a strategic goal of arguing on this proposal. The virtuous style of arguing thus incorporates core features of the formal and the strategic axes of argument evaluation while being importantly different from both of them.

---

[8] I think this point is often lost in discussions of intellectual virtue, in that it is assumed that to care about the truth is to try to maximize one's attainment of it for one's own ends. But that is to tacitly treat truth as an instrumental good after all—i.e., something to be prized for what it can offer you as an individual. To treat truth as a finally valuable good is to regard it as something to be promoted—if the truth is finally valuable, then one should want others to attain it just as much as one wants to attain it oneself.

5 Some Key Intellectual Virtues Manifest in Virtuous Arguing

Let's start to put some flesh on these points by considering some specific intellectual virtues and how they are manifested in intellectually virtuous arguing. I want to focus on four core intellectual virtues: curiosity, integrity, intellectual humility, and intellectual tenacity. We will take these intellectual virtues in turn.

Curiosity as an intellectual virtue is more than just the disposition to ask questions and pursue inquiries. As with all virtues, the (intellectual) virtue of curiosity lies between two opposing (intellectual) vices, a vice of excess and a vice of deficiency. The intellectual vice of deficiency is straightforward enough, as it is simply the absence of curiosity. The intellectual vice of excess is more interesting for our purposes, as it shows how the intellectual virtue of curiosity is more than just questioning. The point is that one can question, and pursue inquiries, for unvirtuous reasons, such as for frivolous reasons or simply without any wider purpose. Mere questioning, and mere inquiry, by itself is not intellectually virtuous. What makes such questioning, and such inquiry, intellectually virtuous is that it is skilfully guided by a concern for the truth.

Notice how the intellectual virtue of curiosity would impact on an argumentative scenario. To be curious, as an intellectually virtuous subject, means to be interested in the opponent's position. Why do they advocate it? What are their reasons? Why do they advance such a different position? This virtuous curiosity about their position has an impact on how they engage with the opponent, as it means that they are concerned not merely to disprove the position (as the strategic stance might demand) or merely to show that it lacks some important logical or evidential feature (as the formal stance might demand) but rather to understand why, from a truth-seeking perspective, someone might have arrived at this opposing viewpoint.

Next, consider the intellectual virtue of intellectual integrity. Integrity more broadly is concerned with appropriately acting in accordance with one's deepest values. Intellectual integrity is thus concerned with appropriately acting in accordance with one's deepest intellectual values, which means in this case one's virtuous desire for the truth. Having the virtue of intellectual integrity is more than just being honest. One can be honest in a purely strategic manner, as a lawyer might be to satisfy their professional obligations. Having the virtue of intellectual integrity means that one will go further than merely being honest in this minimal fashion by displaying a more general concern for the truth, given that the truth is one of one's deepest values. In the context of argument this will entail, for example, a genuine concern for understanding one's opponent's position. Someone with the intellectual virtue of integrity will be concerned to not merely accurately presents their own position and the position of their adversity, but will also be concerned to charitably represent the opponent's position. If one is interested in the truth, and thus is concerned to not only persuade but is also willing to be persuaded, then one will want to fully understand the opponent's position in its strongest form. One's intellectual obligations will thus extend beyond merely the accurate representation of their viewpoint to actively aiming to develop their opposing position in order to make it as compelling as possible.[9]

Consider now the twin intellectual virtues of intellectual humility and intellectual tenacity. I refer to them as 'twin' intellectual virtues because they are naturally understood in relation to one another, particularly in the context of argument. Indeed, one might antecedently think that they are in tension with one another in precisely this context, in that intellectual humility requires one to be less confident in one's opinions (and so concessive in the face of argument) while intellectual tenacity requires one to stick to one's guns in the face of argumentative opposition. Properly understood, however, these two intellectual virtues are entirely compatible with one another (just as all intellectual virtues are compatible with each other).

On any plausible rendering of intellectual humility, it doesn't demand that one should have a lower opinion of one's intellectual self—and thus one's judgements and skills—than is warranted by the evidence. In particular, it certainly doesn't demand that one should have false beliefs in this regard. The intellectual virtues are aimed at the truth, remember, and so there cannot be genuine intellectual virtues the possession of which demands inaccuracy in one's beliefs.[10] What intellectual humility does demand, properly understood, is a recognition of one's fallibility and thus an openness to the possibility of error.[11] This will manifest itself in a willingness to consider other people's opinions, particularly where they diverge from one's own, as this can be an indication that one is in error and has something to learn. Intellectual humility thus doesn't lead to an overly concessive attitude in the context of argument but rather generates an argumentative stance that is appropriate to the strength of one's supporting evidence. What it does involve, however, is an attitude to debate that is of curious engagement with the opposition rather than dogmatic commitment to one's own position. The intellectually humble person, who virtuously strives after truth, will be alert to their own intellectual failings and thus keen to learn what they can from their opponent.

---

[9] Note how manifesting the virtue of intellectual integrity means avoiding the corresponding intellectual vice of excess, which in this case would be an excessive concern for the truth. For example, this might be exhibited via a pedantic fixation on features of the argument that, while technically correct, are unimportant when it comes to gaining an understanding of what is at issue in the dispute in hand.

[10] There has been some discussion in the literature of so-called 'virtues of inaccuracy', whereby there might be particular virtues, like modesty, that require a subject to have inaccurate beliefs. See especially Driver (1989). (See also Brennan (2007), though note that the issue here is less inaccurate beliefs and more a kind of virtuous inconsistency in one's beliefs, whereby, for example, one holds oneself to standards that one would never apply to others). Such a proposal is highly contentious, however, and would be especially problematic if applied to the intellectual virtues.

[11] This aligns with the leading account of intellectual humility in the literature, which is Whitcomb et al. (2017). See also Hazlett (2012), Barrett and Church (2016), and Church (2016) for discussion of related views. Although the difference doesn't matter for our purposes, my own preference is for a subtly different account of intellectual humility which is more other-focused than the leading account. See, for example, Pritchard (2018b, 2019, 2020, 2022c). See also Roberts and Wood (2003, 2007), Priest (2016), and Tanesini (2018) for discussion of related proposals.

So construed, one can start to see how intellectual humility can be compatible with intellectual tenacity, including in the context of argument. Since the former doesn't require one to be overly concessive in one's opinions, it can be compatible with taking a view and sticking to it, even in the face of opposition, which is something that the intellectually tenacious person might be inclined to do. Note, however, that intellectual tenacity, as an intellectual virtue, is a more sophisticated character trait than simply standing one's ground in argument. Often, after all, standing one's ground can be a sign of dogmatism, and thus intellectual vice. Like all intellectual virtues, intellectual tenacity thus involves a sensitivity to relevant features of one's circumstances, in this case whether maintaining one's position in the face of opposition is appropriate or simply dogmatic. A sure sign of intellectual tenacity is that one doesn't simply abandon well-thought out opinions at the first sign of opposition. But if one continues to maintain those opinions even when the evidence against them becomes strong, much less overwhelming, then one has slipped into the corresponding intellectual vice of dogmatism.

Notice how intellectual tenacity and intellectual humility, as we are describing these intellectual character traits, are complementary rather than in tension with one another. Intellectual humility is primarily concerned with taking opposing positions seriously, in case they present relevant considerations that might expose one's own error, as opposed to making concessions at the first sign of dissent. In particular, one can manifest one's intellectual humility by giving one's opponent a careful hearing without in the process downgrading one's confidence in one's own stance (though depending on the force of the argument being presented, such downgrading might well be subsequently appropriate). Intellectual humility thus needn't prevent one being intellectually tenacious.[12] Similarly, going in the other direction, being intellectually tenacious doesn't mean being dogmatic and so it is consistent with being sensitive to the opposing considerations that one's dialectical adversary might present.

Consider now how an intellectually virtuous person, who possessed all four of these intellectual virtues, would engage in argument. They would be curious about other people's positions and why they hold them. Their intellectual integrity would entail that they are concerned to understand their opponent's position properly, where this will mean not just representing that position correctly but potentially even helping them to strengthen their argument. They would be intellectually open to the possibility of error and thereby keen to learn from their adversary, even in cases where they appropriately stick to their opinions in the face of opposition.

What underpins all of these intellectual behaviours is an overarching concern for the truth. Being intellectually humble is more than just being open-minded, for example. One can be open-minded for purely strategic reasons, for example, as when an academic keeps an open mind because it enables them to avoid forming

---

[12] I think this point has important ramifications for the epistemology of disagreement debate, where it is often taken as given that even temporarily sticking to one's opinions in the face of argumentative opposition, particularly involving an epistemic peer, is necessarily dogmatic (and thus a sign of intellectual vice). For further discussion of this point, see Pritchard (2018b, 2019, 2020, 2022c).

opinions on contentious topics that they want to stay neutral about or when a detective keeps an open mind because they think it will make their cases stand up better when they go to court. While intellectual virtues are undoubtedly practically useful, however, it is essential to them that they are not motivated in a purely instrumental fashion like this, and intellectual humility is no exception. The intellectually humble person is thus fundamentally guided by a concern to get things right, where this motivates their concern to listen to their opponent's point of view and determine whether it highlights any error on their part.[13]

6 The Three Axes of Argument Evaluation Compared

It is the overarching concern for truth that sets the intellectually virtuous style of arguing apart from the other two styles of arguing noted above. Let's start with the strategic axis of argument evaluation. While it might be a welcome result to find that one's opponent is persuaded by one's arguments, this won't be itself a goal of the argument for the intellectually virtuous subject as it is on the strategic model of argumentation. Since they care about the truth they want to get to the truth, and that is compatible with failing to convince one's opponent of the truth of one's position. Of course, in caring for the truth, they will also be concerned to help others get there too, but that doesn't mean that persuading them of one's own position is now a goal of one's arguing. What it means is rather that one argues in such a way as to make the truth available for both parties— whether that ultimately leads to persuasion will depend on one's opponent's intellectual character. In particular, the danger of making persuasion a goal of argument is that one will be tempted to employ argumentative strategies that are more likely to persuade one's opponent, even if they are not the kind of strategies that would promote the truth. For example, where one's opponent is riddled with intellectual vice, then the goal of persuasion might be best served by playing on their cognitive biases than by fairly representing the topic at hand and marshalling the relevant evidence that favours one's position.

The intellectually virtuous person's overarching concern for the truth will also set their argumentative style apart from the formal style of argumentation. As we've previously noted, the point is not that the intellectually virtuous person is inclined to argue in ways that are contrary to the formal style. Their concern for the truth will ensure that they will not embrace fallacious forms of reasoning, for example. The point is rather that their concern for the truth will entail a very different emphasis in

---

[13] Another important difference between intellectual humility and open-mindedness is that on the face of it one only needs to listen to an objection once in order to exhibit an open mind. In contrast, the intellectually humble person will be more inclined to listen to repeated statements of a counterargument in case there is something new to learn from these new presentations of the critical line. For further discussion of this point, see Pritchard (2022c). For some recent discussions of open mindedness, see Riggs (2010), Baehr (2011b), and Battaly (2018).

their manner of argumentation, one that is more driven by a desire to understand, both in terms of their own position and their opponent's position.

For example, someone employing the formal model who is satisfied that their argument is well-supported may not be particularly interested in counterarguments at all; they will essentially be just invitations to display one's supporting reasoning. In contrast, an intellectually virtuous individual in the same situation will nonetheless retain their curiosity in opposing stances and will so be motivated to explore them. Moreover, they will also be concerned to help others come to recognize the truth too, and so will have a desire to persuade that takes them beyond the formal style of arguing. Relatedly, they will also be motivated to charitably understand the opponent's position, which means helping them to improve their stance where applicable. The crux of the matter is that whereas the focus of the formal model is entirely on one's own reasoning, the focus of the virtuous model of arguing is more on a collaborative seeking of the truth.

The virtuous model of good argumentation thus diverges from both the formal and strategic models. Furthermore, I think it is clear that in both cases the divergence reveals how the virtuous model better captures what we care about when we evaluate good arguing. Persuasive argument is all well and good, but not when it trades on the intellectual vices of one's adversary. Relatedly, arguing in a formally correct way might be impressive, but it falls short of the kind of open, charitable and collaborative engagement with opponents that the virtuous model demands.

Moreover, notice that the virtuous model also fares better on this score when compared to a hybrid version of the formal and strategic models. That is, consider a combination of these two proposals whereby one argues in line with the formal model but also, in addition, has the strategic concern to persuade. Such a hybrid approach has the advantage of avoiding the concern that the strategic proposal faces of appealing to problematic forms of reasoning where they are found to be persuasive. While this hybrid proposal comes closer to the virtuous model than the two component proposals do individually, it still diverges from it in important ways. Moreover, where this is divergence, it seems that the virtuous model best captures good argumentative practice.

For example, there is nothing in such a hybrid account of good arguing that would motivate someone to have genuine interest in opposing views even where they have previously satisfied themselves of the correctness of their own positions, and yet this is entailed by the virtuous model of good arguing. Or consider the fact that the intellectually virtuous subject will be motivated to be as charitable as possible when making sense of an opponent's view, even to the extent of reformulating their position for them to strengthen it. There is nothing in the hybrid view that would entail such an approach.

7 The Proposal Applied

We began with a purported contemporary malaise associated with bad arguing, one prompted by the distinctive features of the information age, particularly in terms of its use of social media. Although many of these exchanges stretch some way from the paradigm case that we have considered, not least in terms of not involving an in-person conversation, I think we can nonetheless see how the virtuous model of argumentation would gain a purchase on understanding why these disputes can seem so problematic. For while it is true that many of these arguments on social media would count as problematic by the lights of either of the other two approaches, it is apparent that fixing the underlying problem would call for something different to what these approaches are offering.

For example, one pervasive manner of arguing on social media—one that I think many would agree is intellectually problematic—is what we might term a 'points scoring' approach. The goal is, it seems, to quickly and decisively convict the opposition of some kind of error as a means of dismissing their stance. Such an approach might well satisfy the formal and strategic models of argument (though usually it will not), in that the points being made might be formally correct and also persuasive, if not to the original party to which they were directed then at least to the wider audience of this exchange. (This is one distinctive feature of social media arguments, in that they necessarily come with a wider audience as opposed to simply being an argument between two opposing parties). Crucially, however, the intellectually virtuous arguer would never be inclined towards adopting a points scoring argument in this fashion, as it would run contrary to their desire for the truth and the manner in which this manifests itself in terms of approaching opposing positions. As we have seen, the intellectually virtuous subject will be curious about the opposing position even when they are sure it is incorrect, and also interested in engaging with their opponent on a collaborative enterprise to get to the truth; scoring points against them is not going to be an effective way of bringing such an engagement about.

Or consider another pervasive form of argument on social media, not unrelated to the points scoring approach, whereby one rigidly adopts a literal interpretation of the opponent's position in order to undermine it as opposed to seeking ways of charitably understanding what they are trying to say. People are often quite bad at representing their viewpoints, after all, so it is not generally a good approach from a truth-seeking point of view to confine one's focus only to the specific presentation that someone offers of their argument. Nonetheless, arguing in such a fashion might well satisfy the formal and strategic models of argument. The former, because one is not misrepresenting the opponent's argument. The latter, because taking this line might be a persuasive way of arguing for one's position (at least, again, where the parties to be persuaded extend beyond the target adversary to take in the wider audience for the argument). And yet, there seems to be something importantly missing in such an argumentative approach, something that is captured by the virtuous model of argumentation which would generate the seeking of a charitable reading of the opponent's position.

The crux of the matter is that if we are ever to improve our manner of arguing, and thereby deal with this contemporary malaise, then a necessary condition will be to correctly identify what captures good arguing in the sense that we want to aspire to. I have suggested that the formal and strategic approaches, despite their general merits, are not optimal proposals in this respect. Instead, what we should be seeking is the cultivation of virtuous intellectual character, and thus the development of individuals who embody the virtuous mode of arguing. This is a style of argument that incorporates the good-making features of both the formal and strategic approaches while avoiding their drawbacks.[14,15]

References

Baehr, J. (2011a). *The inquiring mind: On intellectual virtues and virtue epistemology*. Oxford University Press.
Baehr, J. (2011b). The structure of open-mindedness. *Canadian Journal of Philosophy, 41*, 191–213.
Baehr, J. (2015). *Cultivating good minds: A philosophical & practical guide to educating for intellectual virtues*. Available at: https://intellectualvirtues.org/why-should-we-educate-for-intellectual-virtues-2-2/
Baehr, J. (2019). Intellectual virtues, critical thinking, and the aims of education. In P. Graham, M. Fricker, D. Henderson, Pedersen, & J. Wyatt (Eds.), *Routledge handbook of social epistemology* (pp. 447–457). Routledge.
Baehr, J. (2021). *Deep in thought: A practical guide to teaching for intellectual virtues*. Harvard Education Press.
Barrett, J., & Church, I. (2016). Intellectual humility. In E. L. Worthington Jr., D. E. Davis, & J. N. Hook (Eds.), *Routledge handbook of humility* (pp. 62–75). Routledge.
Battaly, H. (2014). Intellectual virtues. In S. van Hooft (Ed.), *Handbook of virtue ethics* (pp. 177–187). Acumen.
Battaly, H. (2018). Can closed-mindedness be an intellectual virtue? *Royal Institute of Philosophy Supplements, 85*, 23–41.

---

[14] This way of thinking about this issue has obvious implications for our educational practices, since it suggests the importance of educating for virtuous intellectual character. I have elsewhere argued for the importance of this approach—see Pritchard (2013, 2015, 2023). For a related proposal, see Baehr (2015, 2019, 2021). Indeed, my choice of the intellectual virtues of curiosity, integrity, intellectual humility and intellectual tenacity was influenced by the fact that they are the core intellectual virtues of an applied educational project that I am engaged with at the University of California, Irvine to bring the goal of educating for virtuous intellectual character into the heart of the curriculum. See Orona and Pritchard (2021, forthcoming), Orona et al. (2023), and Pritchard (2023) for more details about this project, from both a theoretical and empirical perspective.

[15] Thanks to Waldo Silva Filho. This research was supported by the John Templeton Foundation ('Embedding the Development of Intellectual Character within a University Curriculum', #62330). This paper was written while a Senior Research Associate of the *African Centre for Epistemology and Philosophy of Science* at the University of Johannesburg.

Brennan, J. (2007). Modesty without illusion. *Philosophy and Phenomenological Research, 75*, 111–128.
Church, I. (2016). A doxastic account of intellectual humility. *Logos & Episteme, 4*, 413–433.
Christensen, D., & Lackey, J. (Eds.). (2013). *The epistemology of disagreement: New essays.* Oxford University Press.
Croce, M., & Pritchard, D. H. (2022). Education as the social cultivation of intellectual virtue'. In M. Alfano, C. Klein, & J. de Ridder (Eds.), *Social virtue epistemology* (pp. 583–601). Routledge.
Driver, J. (1989). The virtues of ignorance. *Journal of Philosophy, 86*, 373–384.
van Eemeren, F. H. (2018). *Strategic maneuvering in argumentative discourse: Extending the pragma-dialectical theory of argumentation.* John Benjamins.
van Eemeren, F. H., & Grootendorst, R. (1984). *Speech acts in argumentative discussions: A theoretical model for the analysis of discussions directed towards solving conflicts of opinion.* Foris.
van Eemeren, F. H., & Grootendorst, R. (2004). *A systematic theory of argumentation: The pragma-dialectical approach.* Cambridge University Press.
Feldman, R., & Warfield, F. (Eds.). (2010). *Disagreement.* Oxford University Press.
Gilbert, M. A. (1997). *Coalescent argumentation.* Routledge.
Hamblin, C. L. (1970). *Fallacies.* Methuen.
Hazlett, A. (2012). Higher-order epistemic attitudes and intellectual humility. *Episteme, 9*, 205–223.
Johnson, R. H. (2014). *The rise of informal logic: Essays on argumentation, critical thinking, reasoning and politics.* Windsor Studies in Argumentation.
Johnson, R. H., & Blair, J. A. (1977). *Logical self-defense.* McGraw-Hill Ryerson.
Orona, G. A., & Pritchard, D. H. (2021). Inculcating curiosity: Pilot results of an online module to enhance undergraduate intellectual virtue. *Assessment & Evaluation in Higher Education.* https://doi.org/10.1080/02602938.2021.1919988
Orona, G. A., & Pritchard, D. H. (forthcoming). Educating for virtuous intellectual character. In R. Arum, P. Courant, & A. Flaster (Eds.), *Advancing measurement of a 21st century liberal arts education.* Chicago University Press.
Orona, G. A., Pritchard, D. H., Arum, R., Eccles, J., Dang, Q.-V., Copp, D., Herrmann, D., Rushing, B., & Zitzmann, S. (2023). Epistemic virtue in higher education: Testing the mechanisms of intellectual character development. *Current Psychology.* https://doi.org/10.1007/s12144-023-05005-1
Pritchard, D. H. (2013). Epistemic virtue and the epistemology of education. *Journal of Philosophy of Education, 47*, 236–247.
Pritchard, D. H. (2015). Intellectual virtue, extended cognition, and the epistemology of education. In J. Baehr (Ed.), *Intellectual virtues and education: Essays in applied virtue epistemology* (pp. 113–127). Routledge.
Pritchard, D. H. (2018a). Disagreement, of belief and otherwise. In C. Johnson (Ed.), *Voicing dissent: The ethics and epistemology of making disagreement public* (pp. 22–39). Routledge.
Pritchard, D. H. (2018b). Intellectual humility and the epistemology of disagreement. *Synthese*, online first. https://doi.org/10.1007/s11229-018-02024-5
Pritchard, D. H. (2019). Disagreement, intellectual humility, and reflection. In W. J. Silva Filho & L. Tateo (Eds.), *Thinking about oneself: The place and value of reflection in philosophy and psychology* (pp. 59–71). Springer.
Pritchard, D. H. (2020). Educating for intellectual humility and conviction. *Journal of Philosophy of Education, 54*, 398–409.
Pritchard, D. H. (2021). Veritic desire. *Humana Mente: Journal of Philosophical Studies, 14*, 1–21.
Pritchard, D. H. (2022a). Cultivating intellectual virtues. In R. Curren (Ed.), *Routledge handbook of philosophy of education* (pp. 127–136). Routledge.
Pritchard, D. H. (2022b). Intellectual virtue and its role in epistemology. *Asian Journal of Philosophy, 1.* https://doi.org/10.1007/s44204-022-00024-4

Pritchard, D. H. (2022c). Virtuous arguing with conviction and humility. *Ethical Theory and Moral Practice*. https://doi.org/10.1007/s10677-022-10328-2

Pritchard, D. H. (2023). Educating for virtuous intellectual character and valuing truth. *Philosophies, 8*, 29. https://doi.org/10.3390/philosophies8020029

Priest, M. (2016). Intellectual virtue: An interpersonal theory. *Ergo, 4*. https://doi.org/10.3998/ergo.12405314.0004.016

Riggs, W. (2010). Open-mindedness. *Metaphilosophy, 41*, 172–188.

Roberts, R., & Wood, J. (2003). Humility and epistemic goods. In M. DePaul & L. Zagzebski (Eds.), *Intellectual virtue: Perspectives from ethics and epistemology* (pp. 257–279). Oxford University Press.

Roberts, R., & Wood, J. (2007). *Intellectual virtues: An essay in regulative epistemology*. Oxford University Press.

Tanesini, A. (2018). Intellectual humility as attitude. *Philosophy and Phenomenological Research, 96*, 399–420.

Whitcomb, D., Battaly, H., Baehr, J., & Howard-Synder, D. (2017). Intellectual humility: Owning our limitations. *Philosophy and Phenomenological Research, 94*, 509–539.

Woods, J., & Walton, D. N. (1982). *Argument: The logic of the fallacies*. McGraw-Hill Ryerson.

Woods, J., & Walton, D. N. (1989). *Fallacies: Selected papers 1972–1982*. Foris.

Zagzebski, L. T. (1996). *Virtues of the mind: An inquiry into the nature of virtue and the ethical foundations of knowledge*. Cambridge University Press.

Wit, Pomposity, Curiosity, and Justice: Some Virtues and Vices of Conversationalists

Alessandra Tanesini

1 Introduction

This chapter has two main aims. The first is to defend a virtue-theoretical characterisation of what makes a conversation good as a conversation. According to this view, excellent conversations are conversations that are carried out in the way in which virtuous conversationalists would execute them. The second is to sketch out accounts of some character traits that make a distinctive contribution to the epistemology of conversations. Two of these traits (wit and justice) are virtues that contribute to the success of conversations as vehicles for the exchange of information and to the strengthening of bonds of trust. Another trait (pomposity) is an obstacle to these kinds of conversational success. Finally, curiosity is a trait that promotes both conversational failings and successes.

This chapter consists of seven sections. In the first I provide a characterisation of conversation that distinguishes it from other speech exchanges such as a soliloquy or an interrogation. In the second section I explain what it takes for conversations to go well or badly. I argue that an informative way of capturing the distinction is by way of examining whether the interlocutors' contributions are of the kind that would be made by virtuous or vicious conversationalists. In the remainder of the chapter, I focus on the virtues of wit (Sect. 4), and justice (Sect. 5), the vice of pomposity (Sect. 6), and the mixed trait of curiosity (Sect. 7).

A. Tanesini (✉)
Cardiff University, Cardiff, UK
e-mail: tanesini@cardiff.ac.uk

© The Author(s), under exclusive license to Springer Nature Switzerland AG 2024
W. J. Silva-Filho (ed.), *The Epistemology of Conversation*, Philosophical Studies Series 156, https://doi.org/10.1007/978-3-031-74069-5_5

2 Conversations

Conversations are speech exchanges. However, given the account adopted in this chapter, not all speech exchanges are conversations. In this section I offer a characterisation of conversations primarily by distinguishing this kind of speech exchange from other ways in which we communicatively interact with others. In this respect my approach differs from the outlook commonly adopted by conversational analysists in linguistics. In their view any use of discourse in interaction with others, be it face to face or technologically mediated, is thought of as a conversation (Clayman & Gill, 2023). However, such a broad conception of conversation encompasses so many heterogenous speech exchanges that it effectively makes it impossible to offer any general evaluation of what it might take for conversations to be good or bad. Linguists who largely eschew evaluation and explanation in favour of detailed description might not be overly concerned with these limitations. However, mere descriptions cannot be sufficient, if we seek to understand what makes conversations go badly and what we might do to improve them.

That said, I agree with the main restriction on the notion of conversation imposed by practitioners of conversational analysis. Conversations are communicative interactions between interlocutors or participants. Hence, soliloquies are not conversations since they occur when agents speak aloud to themselves ignoring anyone else. It is true that one may think of a soliloquy as a conversation that one has with oneself, but if that is the case, a soliloquy is at best a parasitic form of conversation. For this reason, I shall not consider soliloquies in what follows.

I also restrict my focus to conversations that are face to face rather than technologically mediated. It is certainly true that nowadays many conversations are carried out via phone, zoom or on social media. The use of these technologies changes the dynamics of conversations in many complex ways. For example, conversations on the public channels of social media are often carried out in conditions of context-collapse where it is impossible to tailor what one says to a specific segment of one's audience (Scott, 2022, chap. 2). Thus, I doubt that we can straightforwardly generalise results about what makes for a good conversation off-line to on-line contexts. I focus on face-to-face contexts because our conventions, norms and attitudes for on-line contexts are still evolving and are likely to be influenced by current norms for off-line conversations. Hence, having a good grip on the norms for off-line contexts would be a pre-requisite for supplying an account for on-line conversations.

My characterisation of a conversation is somewhat stipulative but attempts to capture the everyday meaning of this notion. So understood, conversations are extended interactive speech exchanges. That is, a single speech act, such as an order or a warning, is not a conversation. Instead, conversations must involve several speech acts. Although some conversations might be brief, there are no clearly defined lower and upper limits in duration. Further, conversations must involve real-time back and forth between interlocutors. For this reason, conversations are generally spoken or signed rather than epistolary. Moreover, the required back and forth in conversation must take place in the main channel. Speeches that are directed at an audience are not conversations even when the audience offers some kind of feedback to the speaker by way of nodding or other signs in the so-called back channel. However, not all contributions to conversations must be spoken or signed. Instead, some of the speech acts that make up conversations might be eloquent silences (Tanesini, 2018); others might be wholly constituted by gestures such as welcoming smiles, or instances of physical humour.

Normatively speaking, the most important feature of conversations is their voluntary and cooperative nature. When engaging in conversation each party willingly offers their contribution to the outgoing discourse. When some individuals have their speech extracted from them by means of threats, manipulation, or other activities that undermine or bypass their autonomy, the resulting speech exchange might be an interrogation but it is not a conversation (McKinney, 2016). Further, conversations are at least to some extent cooperative. This is not to say that thy must be friendly or affiliative.[1] Interlocutors might strongly disagree with each other, and be forthright in conveying their disagreement, without being uncooperative.

We can define what makes a conversation cooperative by adopting Grice's *Cooperative Principle*. The principle is a prescriptive norm stating that participants in a conversation must (all else being equal) make the contribution required of them at that stage by the accepted purpose or direction of the speech exchange in which they engage (Grice, 1989, 29). There are circumstances in which one's obligation to conform to this norm is outweighed by other considerations. For instance, it is perfectly permissible to stray off the conversation to warn one's interlocutors of an immediate danger.

This defeasible norm of cooperation is constitutive of speech exchanges that are conversations. However, there are many circumstances in which a speaker is under no obligation (not even a defeasible one) to be cooperative. Under these circumstances, speech exchanges are not conversations. They might be confrontations, protests, or political stand offs. These kinds of speech exchanges are vital, but they are not governed by the constitutive norms of conversations.[2]

The prescriptive norm that embodies the *Cooperative Principle* encapsulates an overarching defeasible obligation that participants in a conversation have to each other. Any speech exchange in which, for whatever reason, participants are not subject to this obligation is not a conversation (Goldberg, 2020). It is another discursive practice with different aims, and norms. This occurs, for example, when there is no common accepted purpose or direction to the speech exchange.

Generally speaking, conversations where speakers fulfil their obligation to make suitable contributions to the conversation given its stage and agreed purpose are better conversations than those in which interlocutors get distracted, violate or flout

---

[1] Often though conversations tend to be affiliative and avoid topics that might be a source of division and of disagreement.

[2] This is a controversial claim that I am not going to defend here. Gricean pragmatics presupposes instead that all communication is cooperative. This presupposition is not shared by relevance theory which can explain communication between non-cooperative interlocutors (Sperber & Wilson, 1996).

some of the rules of thumb or maxims that regulate the suitability of conversational contributions. I shall discuss these maxims in the next section where I argue that if we wish to understand what makes conversations good, we must look at the dispositions of the interlocutors rather than try to enumerate rules or principles of conversations.

I conclude by noting that conversations are not restricted to specific purposes or directions. Grice focuses on conversation whose purpose is to exchange information. But many, ordinary conversations have different purposes other than, or additional to, the exchange of information. For this reason, conversations are often funny or amusing. They take place over food and drink in the company of friends. The ultimate purposes of these conversations are to strengthen social bonds and to have a good time. In what follows, I shall consider conversations with varied purposes rather than focus exclusively on those whose sole aim is the exchange of information.

3 The Art of Conversation

In the first section I characterised conversations as temporally extended speech exchanges involving some back and forth among two or more interlocutors that are constituted by Grice's *Cooperative Principle*. I have also indicated that conversations can have many purposes rather than being exclusively concerned with the exchange of information. In this section I aim to offer an account of what makes a conversation good as a conversation.

One may think that good conversations are simply those in which all interlocutors comply with the *Cooperative Principle*. However, since the principle is constitutive of conversations, any speech exchange that violates it is not a conversation at all. It might at best be something that purports to be a conversation, but that results in failure. Further, in those cases, interlocutors generally do not even try to be cooperative. Hence, it is preferable to think of them as being engaged in something closer to a confrontation, rather than a bad conversation. I hasten to add that even aggressive speech exchanges, including quarrels, can be conversations. A row is a conversation of sorts provided that the interlocutors take themselves to owe to each other that their contributions to the speech exchange facilitate the fulfilment of its purpose or direction.

These considerations suggest an alternative way of distinguishing good from bad conversations. A conversation that is good as a conversation is one that fulfils its purpose(s) or direction(s). A bad conversation is one that fails to fulfil its end(s). Thus, for example, a good friendly chat is one after which the interlocutors feel warm toward each other, whilst a good row is one where grievances are properly aired. This account of what makes a conversation good as a conversation presupposes that these speech exchanges have purposes or aims additional to that shared by each contributor of receiving uptake from their interlocutors (Sperber & Wilson, 1996, 161–162).

For this notion of purpose or direction to help with formulating the distinction between good conversations (as those whose end is fulfilled) from bad ones (whose purposes are not fulfilled) we need to be clearer about the nature of these purposes. A conversation might occur in the context of some practical activity. Grice supplies the examples of people mending cars or making cakes together. Here, we can imagine a speaker asking their interlocutor to pass a tool, who in response might ask where it could be found. We could thus perhaps think of the purposes of the conversation as something akin to the shared perlocutionary goals of speech exchanges. These are heterogenous. They can range from lifting the spirits, exchanging knowledge, persuading someone, sheer amusement, and strengthening bonds of friendship. According to this view then what makes a conversation good as a conversation is that it fulfils (most of) its shared perlocutionary aims.

If this is right, we can think of Grice's conversational maxims as ways in which one can be cooperative and thus contribute to the fulfilment of the purpose(s) of the on-going conversation. Although Grice (1989, 28) formulates these maxims by focusing on conversations whose goal is the exchange of information, he clearly envisages that these maxims hold also for conversations whose aims are of a different nature such as sharing a laugh or amuse. For example, the maxim of Quantity states that interlocutors' contribution should not provide more (or less) than the direction of the conversation requires. When the goal is the exchange of information, the maxim can be spelled out in terms of its amount. Interlocutors should supply all and only the required information without omitting important points or adding unnecessary details (Grice, 1989, 26). But the general maxim can also be specified in relation to the aims of friendly chats, for instance. In that case, the maxim would require that interlocutors' contributions exhibit the right amount of affiliation without displaying coldness or undue familiarity. Hence, interlocutors might use continuers (such as *uh huh*) to encourage each other, might engage in supportive emotional displays, use words that indicate support (e.g. "I feel the same way") or convey in-grouping (e.g., "us") (Lindström & Sorjonen, 2013). They would do so to the extent that is right given the pre-existing relationships among the interlocutors and the context of the current conversation. *Mutatis mutandis*, similar considerations apply to the maxims prescribing that a contribution be of good Quality, Relevant and made in the right Manner (see Grice, 1989, 28).

Gricean Maxims are not rules to be followed. A norm that prescribes that interlocutors contribute the right amount and quality to a conversation without specifying what those are offers no guidance whatsoever to the interlocutors. It is thus unfortunate that Grice formulates these maxims in the imperative. It is not very helpful to be told not to be over-informative, when one does not already know how much information is required in the current context. What these considerations suggest is that the maxims are not recipes to follow to make one's conversation go well (fulfil their purposes), the norms are abstract descriptions that vaguely characterise what skilled interlocutors do well that enables them to have good conversations.[3]

The discussion above supports the conclusion that if one wishes to provide an account of what makes conversations good as conversations one would do well to look at the skills of those who know how not to be over-informative, how not to bore their interlocutors, and how not to appear too friendly. That said, the considerations offered so far are also compatible with the claim that we can spell out what it takes for a conversation to be good irrespective of the skills and activities of the participants. One may claim that good conversations are those that fulfil their aims, even though it might take skill to figure out how one should behave so that those aims are fulfilled. If this is right the goodness of a conversation can be defined independently of the skills of interlocutors. What would make conversational partners skilled are their disposition to reliably achieve good conversations.[4]

The skills required of a good interlocutor have all the features attributed to virtues at least in Anna's (2011) prominent account. First, these skills are intelligent; they are not mere routine. Second, the skilled interlocutor can explain and justify the nature of their contribution to the conversation. Hence, their skills are not just a knack that they have picked up (Annas, 2011, 20). Good conversationalists do not only do the right thing, they also do it for the right reasons (because it is conversationally speaking the right thing). Third, those who care about having good conversations also aspire to improve and become better at this activity. Further, these skills also possess the two additional features that for Annas differentiate virtues from merely intelligent skills. They demonstrate a commitment to some values including the values of cooperativeness, fruitful exchange of information, human sympathy, and friendliness. Finally, these skills are arguably admirable in themselves. If this is right, then the skills of the good conversationalist deserve to be thought of as conversational virtues in a thick sense that goes beyond mere dispositions to reliably bring about desired effects.[5]

It might be objected that conversational skills are not admirable in themselves and as such that they cannot be virtues. Annas (2011, 5) explicitly singles out wit as a trait which is only instrumentally valuable. But this claim underestimates the importance of sociability to human flourishing. When wit is thought of as the skill required to conduct amusing conversations that foster a sense of camaraderie for the purpose of entertaining friends and acquaintances, then wit can be conceived as intrinsically valuable because of its contributory role to a flourishing community. More generally, since having good conversations is part of what makes a human life

---

[3] It should be noted, however, that interlocutors whose conversations go badly are also being cooperative. In these cases too they largely intend to comply with the maxims. They might however be unskilled at figuring out exactly what is required.

[4] See Aberdein (2010) for an articulation of a virtue theory of argumentation that develops a similar approach.

[5] In my work I have defended a motivationalist account of epistemic virtues and vices (Tanesini, 2021). The approach to virtue discussed here also has motivational components since it involves a commitment to reasons and values.

lived well, there are good reasons to conclude that the skills of the good conversationalist are ethical and/or intellectual virtues.

I have argued so far that conversations are good when they fulfil their purpose, and that the virtues of the conversationalists are those skills required to reliably carry out good conversations. This conclusion is sufficient to motivate a virtue theory of conversation. I conclude this section by taking these considerations one step further.

A good conversationalist it would seem is not merely the person who has conversations that reliably fulfil their purpose, rather they are the person who knows which conversations are worth having and when, and which purposes are fruitful for conversations to pursue in their given context. Consider for instance, a good gossiping conversation. Gossiping has an undeservedly bad reputation. It can be a conversational means used by people without much power to warn each other of the dangers posed by some individuals. Thus, for example, subordinates might engage in office gossip to alert each other of the sexually predatory behaviour of a manager (Alfano & Robinson, 2017). A good gossiper is not the person who reliably gossips well; they are the person who knows when a good gossip is appropriate.

These brief considerations suggest that what makes a good conversation good as a conversation is not the mere fact that it fulfils its conversational goals, rather what is also required is that a conversation with those goals is a good conversation to have in those circumstances. If that is so, we cannot characterise the skills of the good conversationalist in terms of an independent notion of a good conversation as one that fulfils its purposes. On the contrary, we might only be able to specify what makes a good conversation good in terms of its contribution to a good social life. That is, the notion of a good conversation is an ethical and epistemological notion that cannot be defined within the confines of theories of linguistic communication.

I hasten to add that one should not read these claims to support the view that only individuals who possess conversational virtues are able to have good conversations. Interlocutors who lack these skills could still have on occasion good conversations. When they do, they behave in the same way virtuous conversationalists would behave in those circumstances. However, since these interlocutors lack the skills and/or the motivations of virtuous conversationalists, they are extremely unlikely to engage in good conversations reliably or on a regular basis.

To summarise, because there are no rules for conversing well, knowing how to do it is a matter of skill. Conversational skills can be virtues when they are intelligent (neither routine nor a mere knack) and admirable because of the contribution they make to the good human life. If we want to provide a detailed account of good conversations, we would do well to look at the character traits and sensibilities of good interlocutors rather than focusing on theories of communication.

4 Wit and a Sense of Humour

In this, and the next three sections, I focus on some conversational virtues and vices. I only provide a few examples of character traits that have important effects on conversational dynamics to offer a flavour of the fruitfulness of a virtue-theoretic approach to understanding the normative contours of conversations. In what follows I argue that wit and justice are conversational virtues, while pomposity is a vice. I then consider curiosity, which—I argue—is a mixed trait. It can be put to both good and bad effects depending on its deployment and the circumstances.

None of these traits are manifested exclusively during conversations. For instance, a person can laugh at themself when on their own or exhibit curiosity when engaging in solitary inquiry. Nevertheless, each of these traits also makes a distinctive contribution to the way conversations are conducted. The witty person with a sense of humour amuses, consoles, teases, criticises and punctures the pretentiousness of those who take themselves too seriously. The just person gives due credit to their interlocutors and creates space for those whose voices are often ignored to contribute to the conversation. The pompous individual takes themself too seriously. They try to monopolise the floor and they bore their interlocutors. Finally, the curious person probes and peppers their conversations with questions. These are not the only character traits that have a distinctive impact on conversational dynamics. I focus on these here because they are arguably intellectual (as well as in some cases moral) character traits with a profound influence on the epistemology of conversations.

Even though Annas singles out wit as a character trait which is not a virtue, there is a small but substantive philosophical literature arguing that a sense of humour or, more narrowly, wit can be a virtue, or at least can a propaedeutic to virtue (Lippitt, 2005; Roberts, 1988). For instance, Hume claims that wit is a virtue because it is "*immediately agreeable* to others" (1978, 590 [T III.1]). Since he links wit to eloquence, Hume would seem to focus on these qualities as capacities that enliven conversations by giving pleasure to interlocutors. Wit, so understood, would be valuable because of its social function. It raises the spirits of other participants in the conversation.

Aristotle also claims that amusement is an important component of human life. Hence, he concludes that there is a virtue that governs appropriate conversational behaviour when it comes to sharing a laugh. He identifies wit as the conversational virtue to say and listen to the right jokes and jests, at the right time, for the right reasons, with the right people. In his view wit, as the disposition to tease and gently put down, is the virtuous trait that is flanked by the vices of buffoonery and boorishness (Aristotle, 1985 [NE 1128a5-b5]). Wit in this sense is not coextensive with having a good sense of humour but is identified more narrowly as a disposition to know, and make fun of, the weaknesses and foibles of one's interlocutors (Johnston, 2020). However, the witty person's enjoyment of the barbs they tell and tolerate is constrained by friendly feelings. Thus, the individual who is witty does not anger the recipient of their put downs. Instead, they are capable of engendering pleasure in their targets who can see both the truth and the funniness of the remark. Furthermore, those who are witty do not merely dish it out, they are also able to take it. That is, they are not thin-skinned.

By contrast, in Aristotle's view, the buffoon is the person whose put downs are hateful and cruel or who is not constrained in what they say by an awareness of the hurt and anger they are likely to cause in the targets of their barbs (NE 1128a34-b2). The boorish person would instead be the individual who finds a fault with everything and fails to appreciate the funniness of appropriate put downs (NE 1128b2-4).

Both Hume and Aristotle seem to focus on the social affiliative function of wit and a good sense of humour. Those who are witty give pleasure to their conversational companions and help to strengthen a sense of camaraderie and friendly feelings. In this manner humour is instrumental to building a community (Alfano et al., 2022). However, wit also makes distinctive epistemic contributions to conversations. It offers an insight into the character of the conversational partners; it builds trust; it is a means to criticise that can bypass defensiveness; it facilitates creativity and open-mindedness.

First, we have already noted that sharing a laugh can help people feel closer together (Curry & Dunbar, 2013). It is also a source of knowledge about ours, and others', character (Lippitt, 2005). For example, we can surprise ourselves by discovering that we find a distasteful joke funny. Thus, jokes can be a source of insight about aspects of our characters that we would rather not know about. In addition, humour is a cue to other people's character that is additional to the information that we might acquire from what they tell us about themselves. For Aristotle, we can understand a person's values by knowing the jokes they make and find funny (NE 1128a12) (Curzer, 2012, chap. 8). For example, we learn that a person does not really care for their interlocutors if they knowingly utter jokes that are cruel and offensive. Further, whilst it might be true, that even people who are not sexist might find some sexist jokes funny, these same people would not choose to tell these jokes and would not respond to their utterance with open laughter.

Second, precisely because sharing a laugh makes people feel closer together and is a cue to similarities in value judgments, wit and a sense of humour can contribute to building trust (Alfano et al., 2022). We trust people to whom we feel closer because we presume that they are well-disposed toward us. This presumption has an epistemic dimension. Those who have friendly feelings for each other are unlikely to deceive or mislead one another. In this way, shared witticisms, and jokes when well-judged contribute to conversations going well epistemically. When persuasion is the aim of the conversation, discovering that the other side shares our sense of humour, leads all participants to be less inclined to think that one's interlocutors might be deceptive or intentionally misleading. When consensus is the goal, witticism can create a sense of distance, making light of the seriousness of the situation (Alfano et al., 2022). This sense of perspective, especially when it is combined with a presumption of good will, is likely to facilitate the ability to compromise and thus greatly ameliorate those conversations that involve some negotiation.

Third, witticism in the form of teasing can be a palatable way of conveying hard truths. It is easier to take a criticism of one's weaknesses or foibles when it is expressed as a joke that indicates that the critic also makes light of the shortcoming (Alfano, 2019, 224). By means of their teasing, friends can both show that they are aware of our failings and at the same time signal that these are not so serious to threaten the relationship. In this manner criticism, when it is a expressed in a jocular fashion, might be especially apt at bypassing the kind of defensiveness that is characteristic of beings like us whose reasoning is often motivated by the desire to protect one's ego (Tanesini, 2021). Thus, a well-judged sense of humour brings distinctive epistemic benefits to difficult conversations among friends. It makes it more likely that interlocutors can take each other's criticisms on board and address their failings.

Fourth, witticisms require quick thinking, creativity, and imagination. The funny sarcastic comment must be delivered with timing which does not allow for much pondering. There is also a body of empirical research that links humour to creativity and innovation (Biemans & Huizingh, 2023). Thinking up of something funny often involves generating surprises and frustrating expectations so as to engender a sense of the incongruous (Olin, 2022). These are cognitive abilities that require a great deal of imagination. They also presuppose the capacity to entertain more than one point of view all at once (Morton, 2013). If this is right, a well-judged sense of humour might be a trait that facilitates the development of an open-minded attitude (Alfano et al., 2022). The adoption of such an attitude is epistemically beneficial in inquiry. It is equally helpful in conversations since when interlocutors aim to persuade each other, they are more likely to improve their epistemic standing on the matter they are considering if they listen to the opposing point of view with an open mind.

Hume and Aristotle when discussing wit are clearly concerned with civil conversations among peers. But witticism can be a valuable character trait also in the context of speech exchanges that do not count as conversations. These include verbal arguments or disputes that take place in contexts of unequal power relations among people who are not, and do not aim to be, each other's friend. In these circumstances, witticism, and a sharp sense of humour, are often important weapons in the armoury of the powerless. Humour functions in these contexts as way of insulting, disrespecting, and showing contempt for the butt of one's jokes. In this manner humour is meant to signal that one takes oneself to be superior to one's opponent from whom one's distances oneself. This kind of humour is what is known as "shade" especially in Black and queer communities. It is a form of physical or verbal satire that aims to get even, or to defeat, one's opponent.

Forms of political humour that punch up rather than down have beneficial practical and epistemic effects. Practically speaking, this form of political protest can help to create collective consciousness united in their appreciation of the weaknesses and ridiculous features of the powerful. Further, political satire is a form of knowledge. If it succeeds in puncturing the egos of persons in authority, it might be instrumental in promoting more equal and honest conversations and facilitate a better appreciation of the true nature of some political issues.

In summary, wit and a good sense of humour is an epistemic conversational virtue. It is a source of knowledge about character. It promotes trust, and thus facilitates honest conversations. It can be used to communicate hard truths during conversations in ways that are less likely to encounter resistance than direct verbal communication. It facilitates creativity and open-mindedness and thus facilitates the ability to find innovative solutions and to learn from each other in conversation. Outside conversations, witticism is also a valuable trait when it is used to express one's dissent against powerful groups and individuals.

5 Conversation Justice

Justice as a virtuous character trait of individuals comprises the ability to issue fair judgments. The just individual is fair to others by forming the right verdicts and giving to each what they are due. As such justice is a virtue that encompasses all areas of practical life. Thus understood, justice also has an epistemic dimension. Recently, Bloomfield (2021) has argued that epistemic justice is the skill of good judgment; that is, judgment that is accurate as well as fair. In what follows I restrict my concerns to the skill of doing justice to all interlocutors in a conversation.

Treating those with whom one might converse fairly has several ethico-epistemic dimensions. One such dimension has been explored by Fricker (2007) when discussing what it takes to allocate the proper level of credibility to epistemic agents with whom one engages in speech exchanges. She identifies a skilful sensibility of testimonial justice which consists in issuing accurate and fair judgements about the extent to which people, on whose testimony one depends, are credible. Fricker thinks of this skill as a corrective for systemic and widespread influences of false prejudices that are causally responsible for the prevalence of testimonial injustice. The latter occurs when individuals who are freely offering their testimony to their interlocutors are not believed because, due to prejudice, they are judged to be less competent and/or honest than they are.

The skill of good judgment in conversation goes beyond issuing accurate individual verdicts about the credibility of one's actual interlocutors. It also involves fair and accurate assessments as to whether some valuable potential contributors to the conversation have not been invited, whether some who are present are unfairly burdened or prevented from being active contributors. It comprises the skills of amplification that consist in publicly acknowledging and endorsing the contributions made to the conversation by interlocutors who are ignored due to marginalisation.

More generally, epistemic justice in conversation is a skilful sensibility required to ameliorate the effects of epistemic oppression on conversations. Epistemic oppression is a complex and heterogenous phenomenon. I have argued that it concerns the epistemic dimension of oppression as conceived in accordance with Young's (1990, chap. 2) influential framework (Tanesini, 2022). According to this view oppression occurs when structural relations among social groups are unjust. These injustices might involve the unfair distribution of goods, or forms of recognition disrespect. Young identifies five faces of oppression: exploitation, marginalisation, powerlessness, subordination, and violence.[6] These forms of oppression can be instantiated in the epistemic realm. Agents are exploited epistemically when they are coerced into doing cognitive labour for others' benefit (Berenstain, 2016). They are marginalised when their contributions are ignored or dismissed (Dotson, 2014). They are rendered powerless when their epistemic authority is undermined by being gaslit (Abramson, 2014), or treated as irrational (Cull, 2019; Tanesini, 2016). They are subordinated when they are forced to self-silence in response to others' wilful ignorance (Dotson, 2011; Pohlhaus, 2011). Finally, they are subjected to violence when they are forced to smother their own speech to avoid being threatened or insulted (Dotson, 2011).

The notion of injustice central to Young's account is political. It pertains to societies and institutions. The sort of epistemic justice I am concerned with is an individual virtue consisting in the ability to issue the right verdicts for the right reasons. It comprises fair judgments about the credibility of other epistemic subjects, accurate assessments of the validity of their arguments, proper evaluations of who, when, and to what extent, should contribute to on-going conversations. Since the injustices identified by Young are largely structural, they are unlikely to be remedied by agent-centric interventions alone. Even if every individual acquired the skills comprising epistemic justice, one would expect that many of the wrongs associated with marginalisation would persist, for instance. Marginalised subjects are often invisible to privileged individuals partly because differences in economic status create forms of spatial ghettoization. Such lack of interaction produces structural forms of ignorance that reproduce marginalization irrespective of the characters of the individuals involved (Martín, 2020).

These considerations, however, should not be taken to imply that the cultivation of epistemic justice as an individual conversational virtue is pointless or even counterproductive. Epistemic justice has the potential to be a useful corrective for ameliorating some conversations in oppressive contexts. For example, the practice of argument repair which consists in helping one's interlocutor to improve the quality of their arguments ameliorates the epistemic quality of conversations. When adopted, the practice helps to do justice to the arguments of one's conversational partners by seeking to make them the best that they can be, rather than by exploiting their weaknesses (see Hundleby, 2015). This practice offers an important corrective to the damage done by powerlessness and subordination to people's levels of self-confidence and ability to articulate their own positions.

To summarise, conversational justice is a kind of epistemic justice in the context of conversations. It comprises all the skills required to ameliorate conversations taking place within a background of oppressive relations where some participants are often exploited, marginalised, rendered powerless, subordinated, or threatened with violence. Epistemic justice is thus a virtue that enables conversations to take place in environments that are inimical to them. So understood justice requires good judgment including the ability to correct for testimonial injustice, to remedy by

---

[6] These faces of oppressions are not intended to be exhaustive or exclusive.

amplification the unfair dismissal of the contributions of the less powerful, and to address by repair some of the shortcomings of arguments especially in those cases where these shortcomings can partly be traced back to the harms caused by epistemic oppression.[7] In these ways, conversational justice promotes good conversations in structurally bad circumstances.

6 Pomposity: A Conversational Vice

Whilst wit and justice help conversations go well, pomposity is usually a hindrance to good conversations. I think of pomposity as a manifestation of pretentiousness and snobbishness. Intellectual snobs are individuals who are exceedingly concerned with their own superior social status. They base their evaluations of the epistemic merits of other agents and of their outputs not on their epistemic qualities but on their role in buttressing a hierarchy that sees the snob as occupying one of its highest ranks (Crerar, 2021). In conversation intellectual snobbishness, which involves an excessive sense of one's own importance, is manifested in a tendency to verbosity, in the use of unnecessarily obscure or technical vocabulary, a propensity to name-drop, and in an excessive concern with being regarded as part of the intellectual elite. So understood pomposity is closely associated with arrogance as superbia because it is a manifestation of a conception of one's own worth as being wholly dependent on thinking of oneself as better than other people (Roberts & West, 2017; Tanesini, 2021).

Pomposity is a conversational vice because it facilitates bad conversations. It is a vice because it is a disposition that issues from arrogant motivations and that generally causes the purposes of conversations to be frustrated. Normally, interlocutors do not engage in conversations with the goal of fanning the ego of their conversational partners. Instead, they typically wish to exchange information, pass the time, or share a laugh. These conversational goals are frustrated by pomposity and snobbishness. It is only when the pompous and the sycophant converse that their immediate purposes in conversation are met. In these instances, the pompous individual gains the recognition that they crave, whilst the sycophant might obtain the advantage that is their ulterior motive.

However, these conversations are usually bad even when the interlocutors' aims are fulfilled. These conversations do not contribute to enhancing positive social relationships since they are based on false and dishonest praise on the one side, and pretentiousness on the others. In addition, they have an overall negative epistemic effect on conversations. Since sycophants flatter, snobbish individuals are arrogant, their conversations are likely to involve the exchange of information that is often false or misleading. Moreover, these conversations do not promote trust since they

---

[7] Epistemic justice is closely related to intellectual humility. The two virtues differ in part because the former is primarily other regarding, and the latter (at least in my view), self-regarding (Tanesini, 2021).

are, at least on one side, marked by dissimulation and manipulation. These negative epistemic features of conversations taking place between pompous and sycophantic individuals indicate that pomposity is an obstacle to good conversations even when conversational partners fulfil their conversational aims.

More frequently, however, because of their tendency to verbosity, pompous individuals are generally thought to be bores. They are not concerned with directing the conversations in ways that are of mutual interest and value. Instead, their focus is on impressing their interlocutors. In this regard they often fail since others, if they are not sycophants, usually dislike being domineered by individuals with an inflated conception of their intellectual abilities. Pomposity is therefore a contrary of wit. The witty person often amuses their interlocutors. This is one reasons why wit is generally considered a valuable trait in interlocutors. The pompous individual instead tires their conversational partners because of their verbosity, obscurity, and pretentiousness.

Finally, pomposity as an aspect of snobbish arrogance is also a contrary of conversational epistemic justice. The just person is concern with fairness in conversation. They try to make sure that no one arrogates the conversational floor so that every person's contribution is given the time and space that it deserves. The pompous individual, on the contrary, is concerned with lording over their interlocutors. They are therefore likely to speak at length to demonstrate their allegedly superior taste and intelligence. In this manner, they deny their conversational partners the opportunity to make meaningful contributions to the conversation.

7 Curiosity: A Mixed Disposition

Conversations can have many ultimate ends such as strengthening social bonds or simply passing the time, but frequently even in these cases interlocutors exchange some information in the pursuit of these further goals. Often this information is solicited rather than spontaneously proffered. For these reasons, questioning is a frequent component of conversations. What questions are asked, to whom, when, and in what manner clearly depend on the context including the goals of the conversational partners. However, the personalities of the interlocutors are also likely to be relevant. In particular, one would expect that more curious individuals are disposed to ask more questions to their conversational partners. In this section I highlight psychological and philosophical considerations that speak in favour of curiosity as being a driver of both good and bad questioning in conversations. If that is right, curiosity is a mixed character trait that is neither virtuous nor vicious.

My concern in this section is with curiosity as a character trait rather than as a transient emotional state. Curiosity as an episodic emotion or passion is a trigger for inquiry. It is also a motivational force that sustains an investigation until curiosity itself wanes. Thus, understood curiosity is an epistemic emotion that would have two dimensions. First, sometimes it is an appraisal of an information gap or deprivation that triggers behaviour designed to fill it. Second, it can also be a state akin to either a sense of delight, awe or wonder in something novel that motivates a desire to explore and find out more about the source of positive affect (Haggard, 2018). Curiosity as a character trait is a disposition to seek curiosity inducing experiences. The curious individual is thus particularly interested in finding novelty and awe-inspiring situations. They are also particularly sensitive to gaps in the existing information and determined to seek out answers.

This conception of curiosity as a disposition to seek experiences that trigger feelings of curiosity as a dual episodic emotion is consistent with traditional philosophical accounts of curiosity as being something that inspires both virtuous and vicious behaviours. First, curiosity as sensitivity to information gaps can motivate a love of study and of science. However, it can also turn morbid when the desire to know is directed toward horrible events such car crashes. Moreover, when unconstrained, curiosity as a desire to fill information gaps is meddlesome and at the root of nosy behaviour, since the exceedingly curious individual often seeks information that is none of their business to find out. In doing so, they infringe other people's right to privacy (Dunnington, 2018).

Second, curiosity as a desire to experience novelty and wonder is according to Socrates, as reported by Plato in the *Theaetetus* (Plato, 1987 [155d]), and to Aristotle in the *Metaphysics* (Aristotle, 1988 [982b]) the source and foundation of all philosophising. However, this kind of curiosity can also be idle and unfocused so that the person disposed to be motivated by it is prone to distraction in the pursuit of novelty. Thus, curiosity, when idle causes individuals to possess a smattering of knowledge on many topics without mastering any of them (Gelfert, 2018). In the remainder of this section, I analyse the impact of good, morbid, meddlesome, and idle or unfocused curiosity on the activity of questioning in the context of conversations.

As Watson (2018, 2021) has convincingly argued questioning is an activity that is skilful when done well and a failing when carried out badly. For Watson the function of questions is to elicit information.[8] Questioning is done well or skilfully when, first, one is competent at eliciting information because one exhibits good judgment when deciding, when, from whom, and how to elicit information, and, second, the elicited information is worthwhile (Watson, 2018). A line of questioning is a failing when either the elicited information is not worthwhile or one is incompetent at eliciting information because one asks the wrong source and/or in the wrong way, and/or at the wrong time (Watson, 2021).

Whilst for Watson good questioning is a skill, she thinks that it is also often associated with a virtue which she labels "inquisitiveness". This would be the virtue that combines the skill of good questioning with an appropriate motivation which, for Watson (2015), consists in virtuous curiosity. I suspect that Watson identifies curiosity as an emotion of wonder which is good when it is properly directed. My focus

---

[8] The claim that the function of questions is to elicit information does not preclude that this eliciting is often in the service of further goals such as asking for forgiveness. Thus, Watson's claim is not invalidated by empirical findings that show that only rarely getting knowledge is the ultimate aims of questions in ordinary conversations (Stivers, 2010, 2776).

is instead on curiosity as the disposition to seek curiosity-triggering experiences. One might wish to distinguish a trait of virtuous curiosity from vicious tendencies of unconstrained curiosity, but there seems to be few reasons in favour of this move. First, psychologists attribute both positive and negative effects to the same trait construct (Peterson & Seligman, 2004, 134–136). Second, Western philosophical tradition also speaks in favour of thinking of curiosity as a trait that needs to be restrained (Manson, 2012). Hence, I propose that we think of curiosity as a mixed character trait that must be combined with epistemic restraint to constitute the virtue of inquisitiveness.

In conversations, the person who is inquisitive will only ask questions that should elicit information that is worthwhile whilst exhibiting the good judgment only to ask interlocutors who are likely to possess the requisite information, and to ask them at an appropriate time and in a manner that is clear, not loaded nor leading. Unbridled meddlesome, morbid, or idle curiosity are instead closely associated with bad questioning as characterised by Watson (2021).

The person who driven by curiosity that is meddlesome asks inappropriate questions. They might also ask them at inopportune times and probably in the wrong manner. This approach to questions is unlikely to competently elicit worthwhile information. People do not respond well to nosiness. They typically evade answering intrusive questions and tend to avoid engaging in conversations with people who are meddlesome. Nosy individuals are also likely to be gossips since they will attempt to elicit information about people behind their backs. Gossiping, when motivated by a desire to meddle, also fails to elicit worthwhile information.[9] These conversations often facilitate the spreading of false rumours and exaggerated claims. Such information is not worthwhile because it is inaccurate. Thus, meddlesome curiosity is a driver of bad questioning.

The person whose curiosity is morbid is fascinated horrifying events such as serious illnesses, injuries, and others' misfortunes. These individuals also ask probing questions in a manner that is unlikely to elicit worthwhile information since they might cause revulsion in their interlocutors. It is true that if all interlocutors are similarly curious, they will indulge in conversations where they satisfy their needs for thrills or titillation. Nevertheless, conversations peppered with questions designed to elicit morbid details are not conversations characterised by good questioning qua questioning. These questions are ultimately an obstacle to understanding the topic of the conversation since the focus on morbid details often derails the discussion away from the most significant information about the event at issue. For example, a morbid interest in the injury details of the victim of a car crash might cause police officers on the scene to direct their questioning of witnesses away from the causes of the accident which should be the main focus of their investigation.

Finally, one would expect the person driven by idle curiosity also to engage in bad questioning. Their tendency to distraction might lead them to pursue an

---

[9] This kind of gossiping thus differ from gossip that is motivated by a desire to warn people (Alfano & Robinson, 2017).

unstructured line of questioning often digressing away from what is salient. Hence, they would fail to ask follow-up questions even when these would be required if they are to elicit information that is worthwhile. Since these individuals have an insatiable appetite for the new, they might also be prone to repeatedly changing the subject in conversation. Thus, they might acquire a smattering of knowledge on many subjects but fail to pursue the line of questioning required to elicit the kind of information required to fully understand any topic.

To summarise, curiosity can be a trait or a dual epistemic emotion. As a trait it can, when combined with restraint, be the motivational force for good questioning which is an important skill that leads to good conversations. However, curiosity that is meddlesome or morbid motivates bad questioning since nosiness invites evasion and fascination with horrid details distracts attention from what matters. In addition, curiosity that is idle is also a motive for bad questioning since it is an obstacle to the kind of focus and perseverance that is necessary to competently elicit worthwhile information by asking questions.

In conclusion, I have first argued that if we wish to understand what makes good conversations good as conversations, we should focus on the character traits of excellent conversationalists. Second, I have offered accounts of four characters traits that make distinctive contributions to the epistemology of conversations. Wit is a source of knowledge about character and helps to strengthen bonds of trust. Epistemic justice enables good conversations in contexts that are inimical to them. Pomposity is conversational vice that is contrary to wit and to epistemic justice. Finally, curiosity is a mixed trait that promotes either good or bad questioning depending on the circumstances and the other traits of character of the conversational partners.

References

Aberdein, A. (2010). Virtue in argument. *Argumentation, 24*(2), 165–179.
Abramson, K. (2014). Turning up the lights on gaslighting. *Philosophical Perspectives, 28*, 1–30.
Alfano, M. (2019). *Nietzsche's moral psychology*. Cambridge University Press.
Alfano, M., & Robinson, B. (2017). Gossip as a burdened virtue. *Ethical Theory and Moral Practice, 20*(3), 473–487. https://doi.org/10.1007/s10677-017-9809-y
Alfano, M., Astola, M., & Urbanowicz, P. (2022). Having a sense of humor as a virtue. *Journal of Value Inquiry*. https://doi.org/10.1007/s10790-022-09918-1
Annas, J. (2011). *Intelligent virtue*. Oxford University Press.
Aristotle. (1985). *Nichomachean ethics* [NE] (T. Irwin, Trans.). Hackett Publishing Company.
Aristotle. (1988). *The metaphysics* (H. Lawson-Tancred, Trans.). Penguin.
Berenstain, N. (2016). Epistemic exploitation. *Ergo, an Open Access Journal of Philosophy, 3*(20170823). https://doi.org/10.3998/ergo.12405314.0003.022
Biemans, W. G., & Huizingh, E. K. R. E. (2023). Why so serious? The effects of humour on creativity and innovation. *Creativity and Innovation Management*. https://doi.org/10.1111/caim.12587
Bloomfield, P. (2021). The skills of justice. In E. Fridland & C. Pavese (Eds.), *The Routledge handbook of philosophy of skill and expertise* (pp. 460–475). Routledge.

Clayman, S., & Gill, V. (2023). Conversation analysis and discourse analysis. In M. Handford & J. P. Gee (Eds.), *The Routledge handbook of discourse analysis* (pp. 67–84). Routledge.

Crerar, C. (2021). Intellectual snobs. In I. J. Kidd, H. D. Battaly, & Q. Cassam (Eds.), *Vice epistemology* (pp. 208–222). Routledge.

Cull, M. J. (2019). Dismissive incomprehension: A use of purported ignorance to undermine others. *Social Epistemology, 33*(3), 262–271. https://doi.org/10.1080/02691728.2019.1625982

Curry, O. S., & Dunbar, R. I. M. (2013). Sharing a joke: The effects of a similar sense of humor on affiliation and altruism. *Evolution and Human Behavior, 34*(2), 125–129. https://doi.org/10.1016/j.evolhumbehav.2012.11.003

Curzer, H. J. (2012). *Aristotle and the virtues*. Oxford University Press.

Dotson, K. (2011). Tracking epistemic violence, tracking practices of silencing. *Hypatia, 26*(2), 236–257. https://doi.org/10.1111/j.1527-2001.2011.01177.x

Dotson, K. (2014). Conceptualizing epistemic oppression. *Social Epistemology, 28*(2), 115–138.

Dunnington, K. (2018). Pre-modern Christian perspectives on curiosity. In I. I. İnan, L. Watson, D. Whitcomb, & S. Yiğit (Eds.), *The moral psychology of curiosity* (pp. 79–96). Rowman & Littlefield International.

Fricker, M. (2007). *Epistemic injustice: Power & the ethics of knowing*. Oxford University Press.

Gelfert, A. (2018). The passion of curiosity: A human perspective. In I. I. İnan, L. Watson, D. Whitcomb, & S. Yiğit (Eds.), *The moral psychology of curiosity* (pp. 57–76). Rowman & Littlefield International.

Goldberg, S. C. (2020). *Conversational pressure*. Oxford University Press.

Grice, P. (1989). *Studies in the way of words*. Harvard University Press.

Haggard, M. (2018). Examining curiosity as psychological virtue and vice. In I. I. İnan, L. Watson, D. Whitcomb, & S. Yiğit (Eds.), *The moral psychology of curiosity* (pp. 143–155). Rowman & Littlefield International.

Hume, D. (1978). *A treatise of human nature* (2nd / with text revised and variant readings by P.H. Nidditch. ed.). Clarendon Press.

Hundleby, C. (2015). What is argument repair? https://chundleby.com/tag/repair/. Accessed 8 Mar 2024.

Johnston, R. (2020). Aristotle on wittiness. *Epoché: A Journal for the History of Philosophy, 24*(2), 323–336. https://doi.org/10.5840/epoche2020226157

Lindström, A., & Sorjonen, M.-I. (2013). Affiliation in conversation. In J. Sidnell & T. Stivers (Eds.), *The handbook of conversation analysis* (pp. 350–369). Wiley-Blackwell.

Lippitt, J. (2005). Is a sense of humour a virtue? *The Monist, 88*(1), 72–92. https://doi.org/10.5840/monist20058816

Manson, N. C. (2012). Epistemic restraint and the vice of curiosity. *Philosophy, 87*(02), 239–259. https://doi.org/10.1017/s0031819112000046

Martín, A. (2020). What is white ignorance? *The Philosophical Quarterly, 71*(4), 864–885. https://doi.org/10.1093/pq/pqaa073

McKinney, R. A. (2016). Extracted speech. *Social Theory and Practice, 42*(2), 258–284. https://doi.org/10.5840/soctheorpract201642215

Morton, A. (2013). *Emotion and imagination*. Polity.

Olin, L. (2022). The moral psychology of humor. In M. Vargas & J. Doris (Eds.), *The Oxford handbook of moral psychology* (pp. 465–494). Oxford University Press.

Peterson, C., & Seligman, M. E. P. (2004). *Character strengths and virtues: A handbook an classification*. Oxford University Press.

Plato. (1987). *Theaetetus* (R. Waterfield, Trans.). Penguin Books.

Pohlhaus, G. J. (2011). Relational knowing and epistemic injustice: Toward a theory of willful hermeneutical ignorance. *Hypatia, 27*(4), 715–735. https://doi.org/10.1111/j.1527-2001.2011.01222.x

Roberts, R. C. (1988). Humor and the virtues. *Inquiry, 31*(2), 127–149. https://doi.org/10.1080/00201748808602144

Roberts, R. C., & West, R. (2017). Jesus and the virtues of pride. In A. J. Carter & E. C. Gordon (Eds.), *The moral psychology of pride* (pp. 99–121). Rowman & Littlefield.

Scott, K. (2022). *Pragmatics online*. Routledge.
Sperber, D., & Wilson, D. (1996). *Relevance: Communication and cognition* (2nd ed.). Blackwell.
Stivers, T. (2010). An overview of the question–response system in American English conversation. *Journal of Pragmatics, 42*(10), 2772–2781. https://doi.org/10.1016/j.pragma.2010.04.011
Tanesini, A. (2016). I - 'Calm down, dear': Intellectual arrogance, silencing and ignorance. *Aristotelian Society Supplementary, 90*(1), 71–92. https://doi.org/10.1093/arisup/akw011
Tanesini, A. (2018). Eloquent silences: Silence and dissent. In C. R. Johnson (Ed.), *Voicing dissent: The ethics and epistemology of making disagreement public* (pp. 109–128). Routledge.
Tanesini, A. (2021). *The mismeasure of the self: A study in vice epistemology*. Oxford University Press.
Tanesini, A. (2022). Intellectual vices in conditions of oppression: The turn to the political in virtue epistemology. In D. Bordonaba Plou, V. C. Fernández Castro, & J. R. N. Torices Vidal (Eds.), *The political turn in analytic philosophy: Reflections on social injustice and oppression* (pp. 77–103). De Gruyter.
Watson, L. (2015). What is inquisitiveness. *American Philosophical Quarterly, 52*(3), 273–287.
Watson, L. (2018). Educating for good questioning: A tool for intellectual virtues education. *Acta Analytica, 33*(3), 353–370. https://doi.org/10.1007/s12136-018-0350-y
Watson, L. (2021). Vices of questioning in public discourse. In I. J. Kidd, H. D. Battaly, & Q. Cassam (Eds.), *Vice epistemology* (pp. 239–258). Routledge.
Young, I. M. (1990). *Justice and the politics of difference*. Princeton University Press.

Conversation and Joint Commitment

Margaret Gilbert and Maura Priest

1 Introduction

This chapter argues that *collective beliefs* as understood here play a central role in conversation. Whatever else is going on in the course of a paradigmatic conversation, the participants are negotiating the establishment of one or more collective belief on the basis of proposals made by one or another of them. This was first argued by Margaret Gilbert's in *On Social Facts*.[1] The present chapter both draws on and amplifies that discussion.[2]

The first part of the chapter introduces the relevant idea of collective belief. The second part discusses the thesis about conversation just described. The third part relates this thesis to some influential ideas about conversation, including those

---

[1] See Gilbert (1989, esp. 294–298), which covers some ground not covered here.

[2] It draws most immediately on the discussion in Gilbert and Priest (2013), whose first section discusses at greater length reasons for thinking that the concept of collective belief on Gilbert's account of it is a central everyday concept. In particular, it critically discusses a number of "summative" accounts of collective belief as understood in everyday life. See Sect. 2 here.

An earlier version of this chapter was published in French translation as "Dialogue et Engagement Conjoint" in Allouche, A. and Kunstler, R. (eds.). *Les Defis de Collectif: ontologie sociale, individualisme méthodologique et argumentation*. Hermann: Paris, 2022. It has been lightly edited and updated.

M. Gilbert (✉)
University of California, Irvine, Irvine, CA, USA
e-mail: margaret.gilbert@uci.edu

M. Priest
Arizona State University, Tempe, AZ, USA
e-mail: priest2@asu.edu

expressed in classic articles by Robert Stalnaker (1973, 1974) and David Lewis (1969, 1979).

2 Collective Belief

2.1 Everyday Collective Belief Ascriptions

In everyday language, we speak about the beliefs of individuals and also about the beliefs of groups. For example, we say things like "Victor believes that analytic philosophy is overly technical." We also say things like "The Philosophy Department believes analytic philosophy is fine as it is."

The groups in question may be of a wide variety of kinds. Thus they may be informal, transient, and have no specific name or label, like the group constituted by a couple of strangers who have just begun a conversation.[3] Participants in such cases, like those in the case of more formally constituted, long-standing, named groups such as "the Philosophy Department," may all speak of what "we" (collectively, or as a group) believe.

What provokes collective belief ascriptions? That is, what do they refer to? In short, what are *collective beliefs?* Margaret Gilbert (1987, 1989, 1994, 1996, 2004, 2023) has argued for a particular account of collective belief as fitting our everyday collective belief ascriptions.[4] What is most important for present purposes is to clarify the details of that account. In what follows, then, we introduce the account with a relatively brief indication of its relation to everyday usage.

2.2 Collective Beliefs as Potentially Disjoined from the Corresponding Individual Beliefs

We start with an example. Imagine that the University Event Committee is meeting to discuss the celebration of the University's 50th anniversary. Pauline, a member of the committee, suggests that Bob Dylan would make a great keynote speaker. Some discussion ensues, with positive comments outnumbering negative ones. After a while someone says, "So, we think that Bob Dylan would make great speaker?"

---

[3] Does such a conversational pair constitute a group as opposed to a mere plurality of persons? Perhaps not prior to the conversation; once the conversation has started, an affirmative answer is plausible. Cf. Simmel (1971, 24).

[4] There have been many responses to these discussions including Bouvier (2004), Schmitt (1994), Tollefsen (2002), Wray (2001). These responses tend to relate to questions that lie outside the concerns of the present chapter, such as whether collective belief on Gilbert's account of it is belief or a different cognitive state (on which see Gilbert (2002) and Gilbert and Pilchman (2014)), or the role of Gilbertian collective beliefs in science (on which see Gilbert (2000); Weatherall and Margaret (2016)).

Conversation and Joint Commitment 87

This time the members of the group either voice their agreement or evidence no disagreement. The matter is settled. In the opinion[5] of the Event Committee Bob Dylan would make a great speaker.

That said, it is possible that most members of the committee do not personally believe what the group believes. Perhaps most members of the Event Committee thought at the time of the discussion that Bob Dylan would be a poor speaker. Perhaps they did not speak up during the discussion out of fear of some others' disapproval. Thus they let the belief that Bob Dylan would be a great speaker become established as the group's belief. Having done so, they did not then change their own minds on the topic.

Or perhaps most members of the committee had no opinion on the matter. They may never have heard of Bob Dylan or did not feel they knew enough about him to form any personal opinion about his speaking skills. This does not prevent the Event Committee from forming the pertinent belief about Dylan's speaking skills.

Given these points, we must infer that in order for there to be a collective belief that p, as this is ordinarily understood, it is not necessary that all or even most members of the relevant population personally believe that p. One can easily go further here, and argue that not only is it not necessary to the existence of a collective belief that p that all or most members of the group in question believe that p, it is not necessary that *any* members of the group personally believe that p in order that the group believes that p.

To make this more concrete, consider again the Event Committee. One might think Pauline, who initially said that Bob Dylan was a great speaker, must have believed this. But of course she need not have. Perhaps Pauline believed Dylan was a terrible speaker and, having some grudge against him, wanted to see him make a fool of himself in front of the group. Evidently, in principle at least, the whole Event Committee scenario could have transpired without a single member of the committee personally believing what the committee came to believe about Dylan. Nor need anyone change their personal position after the collective belief was formed.

We should emphasize that the present point is not that such a radical disjunction between collective belief and the personal beliefs of members is *common*. Whether or not that is so is ultimately an empirical matter. The point is that such a radical disjunction is possible.

2.3 Collective Belief and Corresponding Rights and Obligations

Now consider a possible continuation of the Event Committee example. The committee moves on to other matters. Eventually, the meeting begins to wind down. The group is reviewing their accomplishments of the day when one member

---
[5] We use "opinion" interchangeably with "belief".

unexpectedly speaks up, "Bob Dylan will be an awful speaker." In a tone of rebuke, another member objects: "But we thought Dylan would be great!"

This brings to light an important aspect of collective belief: when one group member speaks against an established group belief, he is liable to met with a negative response from the other members, as indicated by "But...!" in the above dialogue. As indicated in that dialogue, this response is directed specifically at the speaker's contradiction of the collective belief as such. Thus the person who responds justifies his "But..." by saying "we thought".[6] As was also indicated in the above dialogue, the response in such situations may take the form of a *rebuke*. What is it to rebuke someone? Though it implies that person has done something wrong, it does more than that. One person may say to another, "You just did something wrong. Thank goodness you did! You were beginning to seem too perfect." In this case the speaker tells someone he did something wrong without rebuking him. What, then, distinguishes telling someone of his error from rebuking him or, in other terms, *telling him off?*

A rebuke is a verbal form of punitive behavior.[7] One needs a special standing or authority to punish a person—or to rebuke him.[8] In what does that standing consist?

Pursuing this question, let us return to the example. It seems that the dissenting group member could appropriately respond with an apology, perhaps accompanied by an excuse. So he might reply, "Oh, of course, you're right. I'm sorry. We agreed that Bob Dylan would be a great speaker. I was thinking of someone else." His responding apologetically would suggest that his comment was more than a simple error; it was an *offense* against his interlocutor, qua group member. His apology also suggests the aptness of a group member's *demanding* that he not speak against the group belief, should it seem that he was about to do so. As with a rebuke, a demand of the kind in question requires a special standing.

All of this suggests, again, that the group members as such were *entitled* to the absence of the action that caused the offense—that a *right* of theirs been violated by the offender. The offender had a correlative obligation *to them* not to perform the offending action. This is what puts the other members in a position to *rebuke* him for performing it.[9] Because a right of theirs was violated, the group members, as such, may engage in this form of behavior. They will thereby enforce their right, call the offender to account, and put him on notice that any similar behavior may provoke a similarly punitive reaction.

What is it about a collective belief that gives the parties the standing to rebuke one another for gainsaying the proposition in question? How does a collective belief

---

[6] For further discussion on this point see Gilbert (1987).

[7] Cf. Hart (1961, 10–11) who sees "informal reproofs" as analogous to legally imposed punishment.

[8] Such "authority-presupposing" terms often have broader senses, which can lead to confusion. See Gilbert (2006, ch. 1).

[9] Note that the obligations here are obligations *to* someone to do a certain thing. Such obligations are generally referred to as "directed" obligations. It is this type of obligation that correlates with rights of the type at issue here, referred to as "claim-rights" in rights theory (cf. Hart, 1961).

generate rights that, when violated, justify verbally punitive measures? We now present an account of collective belief that answers these questions.

2.4 *A Plural Subject Account of Collective Belief*

In everyday speech one hears frequent references not only to what we *believe,* but also to what we *are doing,* what we *prefer,* what we *intend,* and so on. Margaret Gilbert (1989, 1990, 2023) has argued elsewhere that all of these expressions refer to those who are connected in a specified manner. To use a phrase that will be explained shortly, they must be *jointly committed* in a certain way. Those who are so committed are committed *as one*. Importantly, then, a joint commitment in Gilbert's sense is not a combination of the *personal* commitments of two or more individuals.

The following discussion focuses on the *basic case* of joint commitment, in which all parties contribute directly to its creation.[10]

What does it take for a basic joint commitment to come into being? Roughly: in conditions of common knowledge, each party must have openly expressed his or her willingness for the parties *to be jointly committed* to believe some proposition, accept some goal, endorse some value, and so on, as a body.[11] This effects the relevant joint commitment of them all.

Gilbert has used her technical phrase "plural subject" to refer to those who are jointly committed with one another in some way: these people constitute a plural subject in her sense. The key to plural subject-hood, then, is joint commitment. There is no reference here to a special kind of plural, or collective *subjectivity* distinct from that of subjectivities of the individual parties to the commitment.

According to Gilbert's *plural subject account* of collective belief: A and B collectively believe that p if and only if A and B form a plural subject of the belief that p. Equivalently (and more perspicuously): A and B collectively believe that p if and only if A and B are jointly committed to believe that p as a body. Though this type of two-person case will be our focus, there would seem to be no limit in principle on how many persons can be involved (Gilbert, 2006, chap. 8). Some further amplificatory remarks are in order (Gilbert, 2006, chap. 7).

The notion of *commitment* at issue is a *normative* one: to *be committed* is to be subject to a type of normative constraint as opposed to being in a particular psychological state. A joint commitment falls into a class of commitments that may

---

[10] On basic versus non-basic cases see e.g. Gilbert (2006, ch. 7).

[11] Here "as a body" goes with "believe some proposition" etc. On *common knowledge* see Lewis (1969); also Schiffer (1972). According to one popular account: it is common knowledge in G that p if and only if (a) p; (b) everyone in G knows that p; (c) everyone in G knows that (b), and so on, *ad infinitum*. There are other accounts that do not appeal to an infinite number of knowings about knowings. See Vanderschraaf and Sillari (2009) for an overview and comparison of a variety of accounts, including the account in Gilbert (1989, chap. 4) that was introduced in discussion of acting together.

plausibly be thought of as *commitments of the will* on account of the process through which it comes into being, as described above.

A joint commitment as understood here is not an aggregate of personal commitments. A *personal* commitment is created by the person in question and unilaterally rescindable by him. Such is the commitment engendered by someone's decision. A joint commitment to which someone is subject is not created by him alone nor is it his to change.

What is required of people who are jointly committed to believe some proposition *as a body*—the kind of joint commitment at issue in the plural subject account of collective belief? The parties will fulfill this joint commitment if they speak and act as would the representatives of a single person with that belief in relevant contexts.[12]

In this connection it is important to emphasize that in order that the parties conform to their joint commitment to believe that p as a body *it is not necessary for each individual personally to believe that p*. Thus no one is committed *through the joint commitment* to himself personally believe that p.

What difference does it make to a person, normatively speaking, that he is subject to a joint commitment? We take it that he *has reason* to act accordingly, where that means roughly this: all else being equal, he must act accordingly if he is to respond appropriately to the considerations bearing on his situation.[13] Further, he must ignore his own inclinations, at least, in face of a standing commitment of this type.[14]

A *joint* commitment, however, does more than commit the individual parties in corresponding ways; *it establishes an important, many-faceted relationship between the parties*. Discussion of this here must be relatively brief.[15]

Consider the situation in which one party fails to conform to a joint commitment. It seems that, intuitively, the other party or parties have the standing to rebuke him for this failure. Again, if one party threatens not to conform, the other party is in a position to *demand* that he conform after all. As indicated in our previous discussion of the continuation of the Event Committee case, this suggests that any one party to a joint commitment has a right against each party to his conformity to the commitment, and that each party is correspondingly obligated to each party to conform. That the parties to a joint commitment, at least, have these rights and obligations will be assumed in what follows.[16]

---

[12] For the sake of brevity we omit "in relevant contexts" in what follows.

[13] As understood here, to *have reason* to do something is not necessarily to have *a reason* to do it, where having a reason implies that some good will come of one's doing it. See Gilbert (2006, chap. 2).

[14] For further discussion see e.g. Gilbert (2006, chap. 2).

[15] See e.g. Gilbert (2018b, chaps. 4 and 8) for further discussion of this relationship and its relation to joint commitment.

[16] Gilbert (2018b, chaps. 11 and 12) argues in favor of the *joint commitment conjecture*, i.e. that joint commitment is the *only* source of the rights and obligations correlative and equivalent to with a person's standing to demand some action.

Conversation and Joint Commitment

We now offer the following interpretation of what went on in the Event Committee. At the conclusion of their discussion Bob Dylan's suitability to be a keynote speaker the committee members are jointly committed to believe as a body that he will be a great speaker. Each is thus obligated to every other to act in certain ways. More precisely, each is obligated to act as though he is the representative of a single believer of the proposition that Dylan would be a great speaker. When one group member violates this obligation, the other members may appropriately rebuke him.[17]

2.5 *Concluding Remarks on Collective Belief*

We have outlined an account of collective belief in terms of a joint commitment to believe that such-and-such as a body. This account accords with many observations on everyday collective belief ascriptions, as we have shown.

In what follows, we discuss a thesis that links the dynamics of everyday conversation to the phenomenon of collective belief according to the plural subject account. If that thesis is correct, then whatever its relation to locutions common in everyday speech, the plural subject account of collective belief describes a phenomenon that cannot be ignored by theorists of conversation.

3 The Negotiation of Collective Belief Thesis

3.1 *Conversation*

We are to argue for a particular thesis relating the dynamics of everyday conversation to collective belief. This section aims to introduce that thesis and explore some of its ramifications. It does not aim to present anything like a full treatment.

We shall not attempt to characterize conversations as such. We operate, rather, with an intuitive notion. We focus on verbal interchanges that appear otherwise to have the character of conversations and that contain, *at a minimum*, an assertion made by one of the parties. The thesis at issue here can most easily be expounded in relation to assertions.

The class of verbal interchanges just described may contain all paradigmatic conversations. To say this is not to say that the thesis we shall discuss has no

---

[17] It is possible for a group member to bypass this requirement by qualifying their statement with "Well I *personally* believe..." In such a case, though the group member is not expressing the belief of the group, he makes it clear that he does not stand *entirely apart from the group*. While other group members might not be happy with such qualified statements, the qualification may be enough to avoid rebuke from fellow group members.

relevance to other classes of conversation as well. On the contrary, it surely has such relevance, though we shall not explore that here (Gilbert, 1989, 296).

Evidently, people engage in conversation for a variety of collective or individual purposes, such as becoming better informed on some topic, making plans, shooting the breeze, or increasing mutual respect. We shall not pronounce on whether or not there is some purpose, collective or individual, that characterizes all conversations as such. We do not see the thesis we discuss as dependent on any particular assumption in this regard. We do suppose that the conversations at issue are genuine, as opposed to pretend conversations such as one observes on the stage at the theater.

We shall not discuss whether conversationalists as such must collectively believe that they are having a conversation, though we take that to be a plausible idea. We are concerned with collective beliefs that emerge in the context of conversations with whatever necessary framework collective beliefs.

We are concerned with collective beliefs such that the proposition in question—the proposition that is collectively believed—has either been verbally expressed by one of the parties or implied by such verbal expression in the course of the conversation.

3.2 The Thesis

In the Event committee case a collective belief came about through a discussion among committee members of the merits of a particular proposal. Because of its relatively formal context, this discussion may not count as a paradigmatic conversation. That said, it strongly suggests that the process of everyday conversation is structured around collective belief formation. More specifically, in a paradigmatic conversation, whatever else is going on, the parties are negotiating the establishment of one or another collective belief on the basis of proposals put forward by one or another interlocutor. We shall call this the *negotiation of collective belief* thesis—the *NCB* thesis, for short.[18]

In the rest of this section we give examples of how the NCB thesis construes a variety of example conversations and conversational moves, to some extent elaborating the thesis further while doing so. In all of these cases we assume that there are no special background collective beliefs or other factors that might skew one's interpretation of what is going on.[19]

---

[18] Drawing on Gilbert's account of collective belief and her notion of joint commitment, Carassa and Colombetti (2009a) propose that, centrally, conversations involve a negotiation of *joint meaning*. We take this proposal to complement the NCB thesis. See also Carassa and Colombetti (2009b). Another discussion that suggests an "emerging" collective belief of a particular type (though it is not couched in these terms) is Brennan and Clark (1996) on what the authors refer to as "conceptual pacts". Here the envisaged pact or agreement (which we would construe as a matter of joint commitment (see *e.g.* Gilbert, 2006, chap. 10)) relates to the way in which each party is to conceptualize an object under discussion.

[19] See Gilbert (1989, chap. 5, esp. 294–298) for further pertinent discussion.

Suppose that Belle and Paul are waiting together at a bus stop on a sunny day. The two fall into conversation. "Sure is a beautiful day!" says Paul cheerfully. Belle, who prefers cool cloudy weather, replies pleasantly, "Yes, it is." According to the NCB thesis what happened, among other things, was this.

> *First*, Paul proposed for collective belief the proposition that the day in question was a beautiful day. In other terms, he made a particular *collective belief proposal*. More precisely he made what we shall refer to as an *explicit* collective belief proposal. That is, he proposed that the parties collectively believe that p by uttering a sentence that expresses proposition p.
>
> *Second*, Belle considered Paul's proposal and in spite of her personal belief to the contrary decided to go along with him and to believe the proposition in question collectively with him, indicating that she was ready to do this by her reply. In other terms, *she accepted his collective belief proposal*.
>
> *Thus*, through their conversation, Belle and Paul together established a collective belief that would persist at least through their current interaction, all else being equal.[20] We shall refer to collective beliefs that are established through the making and accepting of an explicit collective belief proposal as *explicit collective beliefs*.

In this example, Belle does not personally believe what the two collectively believe, which is fine from the point of view of the concept of collective belief. Our collectively believing that p does not entail that I personally believe that p nor does it entail that I do not personally disbelieve it. The same goes for the other person or people involved.[21]

One can imagine all kinds of variations on the first example conversation. For instance:

> Paul: "Sure is a beautiful day!"
> Belle (in a tone of doubt): "Mmm"
> Paul: "But…it is so bright and sunny!"
> Belle: "You're right: it really is a beautiful day."

Paul has to work harder here than in the previous example to establish the collective belief that it is a beautiful day. What he does in his second move in the negotiation is *give a reason* for believing the proposition originally proposed for collective belief.

Many negotiations over a given collective belief may be expected to involve such reason-giving. This may well lead to further collective beliefs, as well as the one originally proposed, to the effect that such-and-such a proposition is true *and that its truth is a reason for believing the original proposition*.

One might be inclined think that this has happened once Belle has given her second response in the above dialogue. That it has happened, however, would be clearer had Belle responded, as she might well have responded, in some such way as this.

> Belle: "True! I guess that makes it a beautiful day!"

---

[20] We shall not discuss in this paper the ways in which established collective beliefs can be amended, except to say that, absent special background understandings, such amendment requires the concurrence of the parties. Such understandings will, in effect, authorize one or another party to amend the belief. See *e.g.* Gilbert (2023, 6–7).

[21] See section I above.

Here she clearly indicates that she accepts the following propositions that Paul has proposed for collective belief. First: it is very bright and sunny. Second: If it is very bright and sunny, then it is a beautiful day. It is true that Paul does not spell out the second proposition, as he does the first. That he is indeed proposing it for collective belief, however, this is clearly indicated by his beginning with "But…"

As the first example conversation shows, "negotiating" a collective belief can be as simple as making an assertion and receiving an affirmative response. More precisely, in conditions of common knowledge you may express to your interlocutor your readiness for the two of you to be jointly committed to believing some proposition as a body, and he may immediately do likewise in response, thus ensuring that the two of you are jointly committed to believe that proposition as a body. In other words, he may promptly seal the deal.

3.3 Ways of Accepting a Collective Belief Proposal

There are many ways in which one's acceptance of a proposed collective belief might be shown. It need not involve verbal behavior. A nod of the head, for instance, might suffice, as might a smile, in the right context. If words are used a simple "Yes" may suffice, depending on its tone. Similarly, the expression "Uh-huh", said in the right way, is a form of acceptance. Something like this is presumably the most economical way to make sure one's acceptance is verbally marked. A hesitant "Ye-es" or a quizzical "Uh-huh" may lead to further discussion, and be intended so to lead. Or it may serve to indicate that the proposition in question is *not* yet collectively believed, though it has not been pushed off the table. In such a case a participant may describe the situation to one who asks what they collectively think by saying: "We've not decided *what* we think about that".

In a given context silence may rightly be taken as acceptance. For instance, suppose two friends, Emma and Adam, are out on a walk, and are engaged in conversation. Emma is doing most of the talking and it is clear that Adam is focusing closely on what she says. She may preface some of what she says with locutions like "We both know that…", "It is obvious that …" and "Everyone agrees that…" Such statements, which implicitly ascribe a particular view to the hearer, seem particularly likely to move the hearer to voice an objection if he takes them to be false, so it may be especially reasonable to take his silence as acceptance in this context.

Silence should not always be taken as acceptance, even given that one knows one has been heard. One who maintains a "stony silence" in the face of someone else's assertion may reasonably be taken to refuse to enter into a negotiation as to the truth or otherwise of that assertion.

In some contexts it may be mutually agreed that a given person's silence counts as acceptance. Thus suppose someone has been rendered temporarily or permanently incapable of speech and almost all movement, but has the ability to understand his friend's speech and tap the table with his own finger. An understanding could be established between them that, roughly, as long as he does not tap the table

Conversation and Joint Commitment 95

with his finger, he is in agreement with what is said by his friend. These two are now in a position to establish a series of collective beliefs through a series of assertions followed by silence.

3.4 Ways of Rejecting a Collective Belief Proposal

Collective belief proposals can be *rejected* in various ways such as a refusal to negotiate (as with a stony silence), or a vocal rejection of the proposal. We say something about moves of the latter kind in due course. Another thing one's interlocutor may do is, in effect, substitute for one's original proposal a related alternative.

The following short conversation involves a special type of alternative proposal:

Paul: "Sure is a beautiful day!"
Belle: "So *you* think!"

If Paul's response to Belle is of the accepting variety, the two of them have come collectively to believe not that *it is a beautiful day*, but that *Paul thinks* it is a beautiful day.

Here Belle's contribution to the negotiation is simultaneously to reject the proposition Paul proposed for collective belief and, in effect, to offer to replace it with a closely related proposition about what Paul thinks, namely: he thinks the proposition he proposed for collective belief is true.

The foregoing example makes it clear that *we* can have views about what you, on the one hand, and I, on the other, think, and so on. In other words, some collective beliefs are about the thoughts or opinions of one or more of the participants.

In some special contexts, indeed, it may be understood that the interlocutors are only interested in the subjective stance of one party. This may be the case, for instance, in certain situations involving a psychotherapist and client. As the client says such things as "I think that…", "I'm uncomfortable when…" "I'm worried that….", and the therapist responds with words indicative of acceptance of what was said, such as "I see", a series of collective beliefs about what the client thinks, feels, worries about, and so on may be established (Gilbert, 1989, 297).

3.5 A Dual Role for Certain Sentences

Even outside special contexts such as that of a psychotherapy session, a person may propose for collective belief a proposition that ascribes a propositional attitude to himself. Thus someone may say: "I think we have a good chance of winning the game".

For the sake of a label we shall refer to such sentences as *speaker propositional attitude sentences* or *SPA sentences* for short. These are tailored to ascribe a propositional attitude to the speaker. As we shall put it, they are tailored to express *SPA propositions*. In many if not most cases the proposition to which the speaker's propositional attitude is directed—what we shall call its *target*—is not itself a SPA proposition.[22] Rather, its truth or falsity is independent of the speaker's propositional attitudes. In this discussion we shall refer to such propositions as, simply, non-SPA propositions, and the sentences tailored to express them, non-SPA sentences.

We shall focus our discussion on SPA sentences expressing SPA propositions with non-SPA target propositions, such as: the sentence, said by Paul, "I think it's a beautiful day". This is a SPA sentence expressing a SPA proposition; *I, Paul, think it is a beautiful day*. The target of this proposition is a non-SPA target proposition—the proposition that *it is* a beautiful day.

Consider now the following conversation:

> Renee: "I like our chances at the World Cup"
> Arthur: "No way, our team has no depth this year"
> Caroline: "That's wrong! With Granger Jones there, we have a chance."
> Renee: "That guy could win the match himself!"
> Arthur: "So maybe we do have a chance."

Renee begins by uttering a SPA sentence. In responding as he does, however, Arthur does not address the corresponding SPA proposition, but focuses on the question of their team's chances in the upcoming game: are they good—or not? In other terms, he focuses on the non-SPA proposition that is the target of the relevant SPA proposition. Caroline continues along the same lines, as do the others in what follows. Renee, for her part, may well not take Arthur's response as a change of subject, but rather as a challenge to what she said.

Things could have gone differently. In particular, Arthur might have focused on the relevant SPA proposition, responding to Renee with, for instance: "I know you do. I don't though."

It seems, then, that not only can SPA sentences be used as vehicles for proposing SPA propositions for collective belief. They can be—and often are—used as vehicles for proposing non-SPA propositions. Indeed, it may be that with SPA sentences of the kind under discussion the default interpretation of what is going on when one of them is uttered is that both the pertinent SPA and its target non-SPA proposition is being proposed. Thus it may be that these SPA sentences are "Janus-sentences"—facing in both of two ways.[23]

A respondent, then, has a variety of options: focus on the pertinent SPA proposition, the target non-SPA proposition, or both. In the following dialogue Clara focuses on both and adds something of her own:

> Gabriel: I really hate the fact that the philosophy department is moving to another building.
> Clara: I know, so do I. It really is a shame.

---

[22] It seems that the target of a SPA proposition could be another SPA proposition. Thus consider such cases as: "I think I believe him", or "I'm not sure I really do think that".

[23] Cf. Nowell-Smith (1954, 100): "*a given word* can not only do two or more jobs at once but also *is often in the absence of counter-evidence or express withdrawal presumed to be doing two or more jobs at once*" (emphasis added). He refers to this as *the Janus principle*.

Clara's response indicates a willingness jointly to commit the two of them to at least the following collective beliefs:

1. Gabriel hates the fact that the philosophy department is moving to another building. [This is the SPA proposition expressed by the SPA sentence Gabriel uttered; affirmed by "I know".]
2. The philosophy department moving to another building is a bad thing. [This is the non-SPA target proposition associated with Gabriel's propositional attitude, affirmed by "It really is a shame".][24]
3. Clara feels as Gabriel does. [This is a new SPA proposition; indicated by "so do I".]

In light of the foregoing we now consider an actual conversation observed by one of us. The first speaker—call her Jade—felt that something had gone wrong. The pertinent part of this conversation went as follows:

> Jade: "I prefer strawberry ice-cream to any other."
> Victor: "No, no. I prefer chocolate."[25]

Why did Victor's response seem odd to Jade? This is not something one can be sure of, but suppose that, as we believe, she intended to put forward a SPA proposition—something along the lines of "I think strawberry ice-cream is the best". Then his "No, no..." would have seemed inappropriate, assuming that he had both understood her intention and that he himself intended to express a SPA proposition with his next words, that is: "I prefer chocolate". After all, *his* preferring chocolate ice-cream does not show that *she* does not prefer strawberry.

What might Victor have had in mind? One possibility is this: he was taking Jade to be intent on proposing that they collectively believe the *non-SPA* target proposition of the SPA proposition associated with her utterance, namely: *strawberry ice-cream is preferable to any other*. Wanting their collective belief about what was objectively preferable to reflect his personal preference, he therefore objected, indicating his willingness to participate in one collective belief but not another. Though it might have been more natural from the point of view of English conversational style to speak without reference to his own perspective, he couched his objection to the pertinent non-SPA proposition using a SPA sentence—perhaps because Jade herself had used such a sentence.[26]

---

[24] Note that the objective proposition in question here is not the proposition that the department is moving but the proposition that its moving is something bad—apt to be hated.

[25] Reported in Gilbert (1989, chap. 5).

[26] An alternative way of interpreting this case is offered in Gilbert (1989, 296). This too was developed in accordance with the NCB thesis and accords with it. We shall not attempt to adjudicate between these two options here.

3.6 Implicit Collective Beliefs

To what extent, if at all, can the parties to a paradigmatic conversation fail to establish one or more collective beliefs in the course of that conversation? In discussing this question we focus, as before, on the explicit collective belief proposals made in the course of a given paradigmatic conversation, the way these are handled by the protagonists, and the consequences of this handling.

Suppose that every explicit collective belief proposal put forward by one party to a conversation is rejected by the other party or parties. Here is a simple case:

Paul: "I can't wait until today is over! I hate Christmas!"
Belle: "Nonsense! You love Christmas!"

At this point in the conversation there seems to be a stalemate. Certainly it seems wrong to say either that Paul and Belle collectively believe that Paul hates Christmas, or that they collectively believe that he does not. It may seem that, indeed, the parties have failed to establish any collective belief between them.[27] It can be argued, however, that this is not so.[28]

We have so far considered only explicit collective beliefs, that is, beliefs established on the basis of a verbal expression of the proposition in question. It seems that these are not the only kind of collective beliefs that may be established in the course of a conversation. Non-explicit or *implicit* collective beliefs may also be established.

In this connection consider first the following variant on the previous example:

Paul: "I can't wait until today is over. I hate Christmas!"
Belle: "Are you crazy? It's *Easter.*"

Without attempting a definition, and intending to invoke a broad intuitive notion of implication, we shall say that Paul *implies* that they are speaking on Christmas day. We allow that what one implies may or may not be a matter of what is logically entailed by the proposition expressed by the sentence one utters. In the example, Belle ignores the details of Paul's explicit collective belief proposals and attacks a proposition that he implies, the proposition that it is Christmas day.

We return now to the first example in this section. That is:

Paul: "I can't wait until today is over! I hate Christmas!"
Belle: "Nonsense! You love Christmas!"

---

[27] Note that if even this were true, that would not refute the NCB thesis. Paul's contribution can still be viewed as a move in the negotiation of a collective belief, as can Belle's. He proposes the collective belief that he hates Christmas, and Belle rejects his proposal. The negotiation stalls, but it is still a negotiation.

[28] With respect to the discussion that follows in this section, the literature on conversation contains related ideas that do not bring collective beliefs into the picture. We compare and contrast the perspective of some classic texts in this literature with that of the NCB thesis in the fourth section of this article. To anticipate briefly: the fact that the NCB fits so well with these ideas lends support to the NCB.

Here, as in the last example, Paul implies that he and Belle are conversing on Christmas day. In this case, however, Belle does not question this implied proposition. Rather, in failing to question it, she implicitly accepts it. Indeed, it seems that she and Paul now have at least the following *implicit* collective belief: they are conversing on Christmas day, thought she has not accepted a explicit collective belief proposal to that effect, and none such has been made.

Evidently it is harder than might be thought for the parties to a paradigmatic conversation to fail to establish one or more collective beliefs. We take most such conversations to be analogous: during negotiation, interlocutors may or may not form a number of explicit collective beliefs. Even if they form no explicit collective beliefs, many implicit collective beliefs are likely to be established. When this happens, the parties establish a joint commitment to believe as a body the propositions in question.

3.7 Some Observations Regarding Conversational Collective Belief Formation

In light of the foregoing discussion, something like the following point suggests itself:

> When in the course of a conversation someone explicitly proposes a particular collective belief for the parties, he simultaneously if implicitly proposes that all of the propositions he implies in saying what he says be collectively believed as well.

We shall call this the *implication principle*.

The following related points also suggest themselves. For the sake of simplicity we assume that only two persons are involved in the conversation; a version appropriate to larger conversational groups can easily be devised.

> *First*, there is *the whole shebang principle*:
> If the hearer responds by accepting a proposed explicit collective belief without questioning any of the implied propositions, the conversationalists now collectively believe both the explicitly proposed belief and all of the implied propositions.[29]
>
> *Second*, there is *the selection principle*:
> When a speaker proposes a particular explicit collective belief for the parties, his hearer may explicitly reject that belief but still explicitly or implicitly accept one or more of the implied propositions for collective belief.

Doubtless more such points can be made, and those stated here can be made more fine-grained. If they are roughly right, however, it is indeed hard to avoid establishing one or more collective beliefs as one's conversation progresses. That is in large part because of the possibility of implicit collective beliefs.

---

[29] This implies that the individual conversationalists may not be consciously aware of the content of some of the collective beliefs of the group, in particular the implicit collective beliefs.

3.8 The Obligating Character of Implicit Collective Beliefs

We take it that implicit collective beliefs are structured similarly to explicit collective beliefs. That is, they are constituted by joint commitments implicit in whatever interchange has taken place. We take it, then, that once an implicit collective belief is in place, the group members are obligated to one another to act as if they were "of one mind" with respect to its truth.

Thus suppose that in the course of their conversation Denise and Charles have established the implicit collective belief that Harry Truman was once the President of the United States—while disagreeing on certain matters about his presidency. In their subsequent conversation they are obligated to one another not explicitly to gainsay this implicit belief or to say anything that implies its falsity. If one of them happens somehow to come up with something that says or implies that the implicit belief is false, the other has the standing to take him to task for this, as in: "What do you mean?" said in a tone of rebuke.

In contrast with this, suppose that the conversation is just beginning, and Denise starts with "Harry Truman was never President of the United States". This could well *surprise* Charles, given that the contrary is so well known. He might then raise his eyebrows and ask "What do you mean?" Failing his having some special authority relation to Denise, however, he would not be in a position to respond in the way described above—with a rebuke.

4 The Negotiation of Collective Belief Thesis Compared with Some Other Approaches to Conversation

The NCB thesis can be fruitfully aligned, contrasted, and compared with a number of existing discussions of conversation in the literature. In this section we make a beginning in this direction, without attempting anything like a complete discussion either with respect to those contributions we do discuss, or with respect to the pertinent contributions that exist.

4.1 Conversation and Obligation

The NCB thesis implies that as conversations proceed the participants will most likely accrue a set of joint commitments along with associated obligations towards one another to act as is appropriate to these commitments. Along with these obligations come authority relations consisting of the standing to demand fulfillment of the obligations, the standing to rebuke for non-fulfillment, and so on. Intuitively, obligations of joint commitment "trump" personal inclinations, at least, as far as the issue of what one ought to do is concerned. Thus, the creation of a conversational collective belief, implicit or explicit, has important normative consequences for the parties.

Though we cannot attempt that here, an extended comparison of the perspective of the literature on what have been called "discourse obligations" with that of the NCB thesis would be of considerable interest. Clearly these perspectives share the contention that obligations of some kind are part and parcel of the situation of those engaged in conversation. That said, so-called obligations are of very different kinds.

In at least some of the discourse obligations literature the type of obligation at issue is not, or not clearly, the one at issue here. In particular, it is not a matter of obligations of the kind correlated with claim-rights and the associated standings to make related demands and rebukes—as are the obligations of joint commitment. In other terms, all of which have been used in the related literature, it is not a matter of directed, relational, or bipolar obligations.

Related to this point is the following. Some discourse obligation theorists have emphasized the role of "penalties" in keeping people on the track of their obligations, as in the following quotation.

> The concept of *penalty* is employed here because of the analogy with everyday situations in which a person is threatened with concrete sanctions if he or she fails to fulfill a particular obligation (e.g. the obligation to return a library book by a certain date). In the context of dialogue, the negative consequences of failing to fulfill a discourse obligation are of course much less tangible and measurable; they include consequences such as irritation and negative judgments on the part of the dialog partner... (Jamieson and Weis 1996, 5)

It is worth observing that what the NCB thesis predicts with respect to violation of the obligations associated with the collective beliefs established in conversation is that the "penalty" in question may well take the form of something genuinely punitive—an authoritative rebuke. Such rebukes lie in the province of claim-rights and their correlative obligations. In contrast, irritation on the part of one's co-conversationalists, or their negative judgments, may not rise to the level of a punitive move.[30]

4.2 Lewis on Conversational Score and Presupposition

The NCB thesis can be brought to bear on the central theme of David Lewis's classic article "Score-Keeping in a Language Game" (Lewis, 1979). Lewis himself suggested that his discussion in that paper and in earlier papers by Robert Stalnaker might plausibly be elaborated in terms of collective belief on Margaret Gilbert's

---

[30] Thanks to Frederick Schmitt for emphasizing this point, personal communication October 24, 2011. Schmitt offers a general account of conversation and support for the NCB thesis in Schmitt (2018); see Gilbert (2018a) for a response on one point.

account of it.[31] This and the next sub-section briefly show how such an elaboration might go.

Discussing Lewis first, we are interested in the broad outlines of his ideas about conversation rather than any particular details. In particular we focus on his idea of a "conversational score" (Lewis, 1979, 347).

Consider first the following quotation, whose points are intended to apply to any "well-run conversation" (Lewis, 1979, 339). This is in the opening section of Lewis's paper:

> Presuppositions can be created or destroyed in the course of a conversation. This change is rule-governed, up to a point (…).If at time t something is said that requires presupposition P to be acceptable, and if P is not presupposed just before t, then – *ceteris paribus* and within certain limits – presupposition P comes into existence at t. (Lewis, 1979, 339–340)

Later in the same paper he recapitulates with an important addition:

> Say something that requires a missing presupposition, and straightaway that presupposition springs into existence… Or at least, that is what happens if your conversational partners tacitly acquiesce – if no one says "But France has three kings!" or "Whadda ya mean?" (Lewis, 1979, 339)

See also, later:

> Presupposition evolves according to a rule of accommodation specifying that any presuppositions that are required by what is said straightway come into existence, provided that nobody objects. (Lewis, 1979, 347)

In saying that presupposition P "springs into existence" at t, in the first quotation, Lewis is talking in terms of the idea of a "conversational score" such that "the components of a conversational score at a given stage are *abstract entities*" (Lewis, 1979, 345; emphasis added). Among these components are the presuppositions required by the said rule of accommodation.

What, one may ask, is going on between the material interlocutors as this score, abstractly conceived, develops?

Sticking to Lewis's language, let us speak now of *collective presuppositions*. Prior to fixing on an account of this particular propositional attitude in general, and without insisting that it is a form of belief, the following account of collective presupposition recommends itself.[32]

> A and B *collectively presuppose* that p if and only if A and B are jointly committed to presuppose that p as a body.

Evidently, collective presupposition is understood here along the same lines as collective belief. In particular it is understood to be constituted by an appropriate joint commitment. It does not, then, entail anything about the personal propositional

---

[31] Lewis, in the late 1980s, in Princeton: personal communication with Margaret Gilbert, after reading Gilbert (1987) around the time of its publication. Lewis acknowledges his debt to Stalnaker's work on presupposition in footnote 1 of his paper.

[32] Stalnaker (1973, 448) refers to presupposition as a propositional attitude, one that he does not equate with belief.

attitudes of the participants, nor are any facts about their personal propositional attitudes sufficient for collective presupposition—even given common knowledge of those attitudes.

We propose that Lewis's rule of accommodation for presuppositions—and a range of possible versions of it—can plausibly be rewritten in terms of collective presupposition as just defined, and incorporated within the NCB thesis. In other words, we propose and shall henceforth assume that the NCB thesis includes this point: in making an explicit collective belief proposal one at the same time implicitly proposes all of its presuppositions for collective presupposition.

4.3 Stalnaker on Presupposition

In Robert Stalnaker's classic discussions *presupposing* is something done by an individual participant in a conversation. Thus Stalnaker's analysandum in an important article is "A speaker presupposes that P at a given moment in a conversation...." (Stalnaker, 1973, 448).

As far as we can tell Stalnaker does not consider the possibility of conversationalists collectively presupposing that such-and-such, where this is distinct from each of them personally presupposing it. According to the NCB thesis, this leaves out a crucial dimension of conversation. In this section we briefly relate the notion of collective presupposition presented above to the passage from which the above quotation from Stalnaker comes.

Stalnaker writes, more fully, that "a rough definition might go something like this:"

> *A speaker presupposes that P at a given moment in conversation just in case he is disposed to act, in his linguistic behavior, as if he takes the truth of P for granted, and as if he assumes that his audience recognizes that he is doing so.* (Stalnaker, 1973, 448; emphasis in the original)

What we would like to note in relation to this is the following.

Suppose that speaker S is a member of conversational group G, and the members of G, as such, *collectively* presuppose that P. Then, roughly, while this collective presupposition remains in effect in this conversational setting, it will be incumbent upon S (and every other member of G) *to act, in his linguistic behavior, as if he takes the truth of P for granted.* Note that the italicized words are also to be found in the quotation from Stalnaker.

We say this because *acting in his linguistic behavior as if he takes the truth of P for granted* is, roughly, what a joint commitment to presuppose that P as a body dictates.[33] More precisely, with the provisos noted, he is to do his part along with the others in emulating a single body that presupposes that P. Further, this will be com-

---

[33] "Roughly": Stalnaker's discussion of the "as if" in his account is pertinent here. See Gilbert (1987, 1989, chap. 5) on the behavioral requirements of a collective belief.

mon knowledge among the parties who jointly committed themselves to presuppose as a body that P in the first place.

It seems just possible, then, that the conversational phenomenon to which Stalnaker is responding in his discussion is in fact the collective phenomenon of collective presupposition. That said, his discussion of conversation overall does not give that impression, though some of the pertinent phrases—such as "shared beliefs," "common beliefs" and "common ground"—can in principle be given a collective interpretation.

A proponent of the NCB thesis need not doubt, of course, that in the background of many conversations there are beliefs of the individual parties with the same content, beliefs about these beliefs, and so on, and that these have an important, indeed crucial, role to play in what transpires. What the NCB thesis contends is that beyond this there develops an increasingly rich cognitive profile of *collective* beliefs and presuppositions with associated expressive obligations of the parties that act as constraints on their developing conversation.

4.4 A Suggestion Derived from Lewis

Drawing on some remarks in Lewis's "Scorekeeping" article, we note that in negotiating their collective beliefs conversationalists in a broad sense may be constrained by certain collectively accepted parameters. This is something that a full development of the NCB thesis will take into account.[34]

Here is the pertinent quotation from Lewis:

> The conversationalists may conform to directives, or may simply desire, that they strive to steer certain components of the conversational score in certain directions. Their efforts may be cooperative, as when all participants in a discussion try to increase the amount that all of them willingly presuppose. Or there may be conflict, as when each of two debaters tries to get his opponent to grant him – *to join with him in presupposing* – parts of his case, and to give away parts of the contrary case. (Lewis, 1979, 345; emphasis added)

Note the words we have emphasized in the quotation. They suggest that Lewis may have been somewhat predisposed to the NCB thesis at the time he wrote this. To envisage one person's *joining with another in presupposing that such-and-such* may only be to envisage that each of them will presuppose this. That said, Lewis's choice of words fits well with a reading in terms of collective presupposition as that is understood here.

Here is a "collectivized" version of Lewis's statement that we take to be plausible, where statements about collective beliefs, acceptances, desires, and so on, are to be interpreted in terms of pertinent joint commitments of the parties. We italicize the places where we have collectivized Lewis's text.

---

[34] We interpret "collectively accepted" here in terms of a joint commitment to accept—in the relevant sense—as a body.

The conversationalists may conform to *collectively accepted* directives, or may simply *collectively desire*, that they *collectively* strive to steer certain components of their conversational score, *i.e. their conversational collective beliefs*, in certain directions. Their efforts may be cooperative, as when all participants in a discussion try to increase the amount that they *collectively* presuppose.[35] Or there may be conflict, as when each of two debaters tries to get his opponent to grant him – to join with him in collectively *presupposing* – parts of his case, and to give away parts of the contrary case, *i.e. leave these parts out of the set of collective presuppositions.*

5 Why Converse?

According to the NCB thesis, paradigmatic conversation is structured around collective belief formation. This holds off from saying anything about the purpose, function, or point of conversation, and it has not been our intent to pursue that question here. Indeed, given that different people and groups of people seek to converse for different reasons, it may not be plausible to seek for "the" point of conversation. That said, the material in this paper offers a distinctive perspective on this issue.

Someone may propose that the point of conversations generally is the exchange of information between one individual and another and, hence, an alteration in the beliefs of at least one individual. If the NCB thesis is correct, however, the personal beliefs of the pertinent individuals do not play a central role in conversation as a general practice.

Rather, the central upshot of conversations generally is this: a proposition that may or may not be a belief of an individual conversationalist comes to be collectively believed by the parties to the conversation in question. Thus it may be proposed that the point of conversation as such is the formation of one or more collective beliefs.

Of course, people may come away from a given conversation with personal knowledge or beliefs that they did not have before. If in the context of our conversation Lucas, a sensible, well-informed person, remarks to me that "Lola is going to India", and I say "Uh-huh", thus sealing our collective belief, I am likely also to come away with the personal belief that Lola is going to India. Possibly, too, Lucas's primary personal purpose in saying what he said was to produce this belief in me. Indeed, I may have inquired of him, at the outset, as to Lola's plans.

That said, someone's coming away from a situation with new personal beliefs— and, indeed, with new knowledge—is something that happens in many other instances. People come away with new personal knowledge when reading a book or newspaper, when observing the world around them, or when reflecting on their own ideas. Conversation, then, is just one potential source of new personal knowledge, something that one can in principle arrive at alone. What happens in conversations

---

[35] Here we replaced "all of them willingly" with "they collectively". The rest of the italicized material in the quotation is inserted into the text without replacing anything.

between individuals—in particular the formation of one or more collective beliefs—is not something which can be achieved by an individual alone.[36]

Crucially, the formation of a new collective belief brings both belief and related propositional attitudes *to the collective level*. This, one might argue, is what is special about conversation as such.

Perhaps it is over-bold to think of the formation of collective beliefs as *the* point of conversation as such. More modestly, then, one can argue as follows: whatever other purposes a given conversation serves, it is apt to bring the parties together precisely in the way of collective belief. This is a substantial effect, as we have argued.

It is at least somewhat plausible then to suggest that conversation can at least partly be characterized in terms of it. That is, paradigmatic *conversations are interchanges in which, at a minimum, each of two individuals express their personal willingness to be jointly committed to believe one or more propositions as a body and may thus effect one or more such a joint commitment* (cf. Gilbert, 1989, 295).

6 Conclusion

This chapter has argued for a thesis connecting paradigmatic conversations with collective beliefs—the negotiation of collective belief thesis or NCB thesis.

The chapter began by explaining the nature of collective beliefs as understood here. In the basic case, a collective belief that p is formed, in short, when in conditions of common knowledge group members express their readiness to be jointly committed *to believe that p as a body*. This can be done even if no individual group member personally believes that p. The group members are then *jointly committed* to believe that p as a body, and then, by definition, constitute a *plural subject* that believes p.

According to the NCB thesis, paradigmatic conversations are to be understood as at least in part as negotiations between the parties with respect to which propositions they will collectively believe. Absent special background understandings, when one interlocutor explicitly expresses a given proposition, he simultaneously makes a proposal that this proposition be collectively believed. The other interlocutor may refuse to negotiate; otherwise he must accept or reject it as it stands.

If he rejects it, the explicitly proposed belief does not become a collective one. Even then, other collective beliefs and cognitive states of the conversationalists are likely to come into being. These include implicit collective beliefs and collective presuppositions understood as constituted by the relevant joint commitments.

The move to understanding conversation in terms of joint commitment in the sense at issue here is a move away from the individualism of much of the existing literature on conversation, including the classic work of Stalnaker and Lewis, and important later work, such as that of Clark (1996). In referring to individualism we

---

[36] Not unless he has been granted special authority by those for whom he is entitled to opine.

have in mind that, for one thing, insofar as *commitments* are referred to by these authors these are the personal commitments of the individuals involved, albeit in combination with or in some other way related to other personal commitments.[37] Otherwise their discussions proceed in terms of the personal beliefs, goals, and so on, of the participants, including their personal beliefs about the personal beliefs of others. In our view, without recourse to the notion of joint commitment invoked in this chapter, we cannot properly articulate what is going on in conversation.

Let us understand a *collective activity* to be one that involves two or more persons who act in light of a joint commitment to pursue as a body a certain goal (cf. Gilbert, 1989, 1990). Without specifying the details, it is natural enough to see conversation as a form of collective activity. As was once tartly observed, conversation is not a monologue (Martin Gilbert, 1971, 384, 477). It takes at least two, and like the tango, it is something those two—or more—do *together*.[38]

Allowing for this important point, the NCB thesis proposes that conversation consists in large part of the development of a *collective cognitive profile*. It is *collective* as opposed to *shared* in the sense of being attributable to each of the participants as individuals, and so on.[39]

References

Bouvier, A. (2004). Individual beliefs and collective beliefs in sciences and philosophy: The plural subject and the polyphonic subject accounts. *Philosophy of the Social Sciences, 3*(3), 382–407.
Brennan, S. E., & Clark, H. H. (1996). Conceptual pacts and lexical choice in conversation. *Journal of Experimental Psychology: Learning, Memory, and Cognition, 22*, 1482–1493.
Carassa, A., & Colombetti, M. (2009a). Joint meaning. *Journal of Pragmatics, 41*, 1837–1854.
Carassa, A., & Colombetti, M. (2009b). *Situated communicative acts: A deontic approach*. 31st Annual meeting of the Cognitive Science Society (CogSci 2009), Amsterdam, pp. 1382–1387.
Clark, H. (1996). *Using language*. Cambridge University Press.
Gilbert, M. (1971). *Winston S. Churchill* (Vol. 3). Houghton Mifflin.
Gilbert, M. (1987). Modeling collective belief. *Synthese, 73*, 85–204. Reprinted in Gilbert, 1996.
Gilbert, M. (1989). *On social facts*. Routledge and Kegan Paul; 1992. Princeton University Press.

---

[37] Herbert H. Clark (1996, chap. 10) emphasizes that conversation is a "joint activity" and invokes a notion of "joint commitment". This appears to be an individualistic notion in the sense noted in the text, above, and not therefore to be the sense at issue here. Cf. Carassa and Colombetti (2009a, 1841) on Clark.

[38] On acting together generally, see e.g. Gilbert (1989, chap. 4; 1990; 2006, chaps. 6 and 7). It is there argued to have a joint commitment at its core—in this case a joint commitment to espouse as a body a certain goal.

[39] Warm thanks to Antonella Carassa, Marco Columbetti, Alison Koslow, and Frederick Schmitt for reading and commenting on earlier versions of this article. P.S. When, in this paper, we refer to what we, Margaret Gilbert and Maura Priest, believe, these collective belief ascriptions should be understood in accordance with Gilbert's account of collective belief, and therefore not logically to entail anything about what either Gilbert or Priest personally believes.

Gilbert, M. (1990). Walking together: A paradigmatic social phenomenon. *Midwest studies in philosophy*. In P. A. French, T. E. Uehling Jr., & H. K. Wettstein (Eds.), *The philosophy of the human sciences* (Vol. xv, pp. 1–14). University of Notre Dame Press. Reprinted in Gilbert, 1996.

Gilbert, M. (1994). Remarks on collective belief. In F. Schmitt (Ed.), *Socializing epistemology: The social dimensions of knowledge* (pp. 235–253). Rowman and Littlefield.

Gilbert, M. (1996). *Living together: Rationality, sociality and obligation*. Rowman and Littlefield.

Gilbert, M. (2000). *Sociality and responsibility*. Rowman and Littlefield.

Gilbert, M. (2002). Belief and acceptance as features of groups. *PRO, 16*, 35–69.

Gilbert, M. (2004). Collective epistemology. *Episteme, 1*, 95–107.

Gilbert, M. (2006). *A theory of political obligation: Membership, commitment, and the bonds of society*. Oxford University Press.

Gilbert, M. (2018a). Further reflections on the social world (2019). *PRO, 35*, 257–284.

Gilbert, M. (2018b). *Rights and demands: A foundational inquiry*. Oxford University Press.

Gilbert, M. (2023). *Life in groups: How we think, feel, and act together*. Oxford University Press.

Gilbert, M., & Pilchman, D. (2014). Belief, acceptance, and what happens in groups. In J. Lackey (Ed.), *Essays in collective epistemology*. Oxford University Press. Reprinted in Gilbert. 2023.

Gilbert, M., & Priest, M. (2013). Conversation and collective belief. In A. Capone, F. Lo Piparo, & M. Carapezza (Eds.), *Perspectives on pragmatics and philosophy* (pp. 1–34). Springer.

Hart, H. L. A. (1961). *The concept of law*. Clarendon Press.

Jameson, A., & Weis, T. (1996). How to juggle discourse obligations. *Sonderforschungsbereich 378 Ressourcenadaptive Kognitive Prozesse, 133*, 1–15.

Lewis, D. K. (1969). *Convention: A philosophical study*. Harvard University Press.

Lewis, D. K. (1979). Scorekeeping in a language game. *Journal of Philosophical Logic, 8*, 339–359.

Nowell-Smith, P. (1954). *Ethics*. Penguin Books.

Schiffer, S. (1972). *Meaning*. Oxford University Press.

Schmitt, F. (1994). The justification of group beliefs. In F. Schmitt (Ed.), *Socializing epistemology*. Rowman and Littlefield.

Schmitt, F. (2018). Remarks on conversation and negotiated collective belief. *PRO, 35*, 74–98.

Simmel, G. (1971). In D. Levine (Ed.), *Georg Simmel: On individuality and social forms*. University of Chicago Press. (First published 1908).

Stalnaker, R. (1973). Presuppositions. *Journal of Philosophic Logic, 2*, 447–457.

Stalnaker, R. (1974). Pragmatic presuppositions. In M. K. Munitz & P. K. Unger (Eds.), *Semantics and philosophy* (pp. 47–62). University Press.

Tollefsen, D. (2002). Organizations as true believers. *Journal of Social Philosophy, 33*, 395–410.

Vanderschraaf, P., & Sillari, G. (2009). Common knowledge. In E. N. Zalta (Ed.), *The Stanford encyclopedia of philosophy (Spring 2009 Edition)*, September 20th, 2011. http://plato.stanford.edu/archives/spr2009/entries/common-knowledge/

Weatherall, J., & Margaret, G. (2016). Collective belief, Kuhn, and the string theory community. In M. Brady & M. Fricker (Eds.), *The epistemic life of groups* (pp. 191–217). Oxford University Press. Reprinted in Gilbert, 2023.

Wray, K. B. (2001). Collective belief and acceptance. *Synthese, 129*, 319–333.

Group Belief and the Role of Conversation

Fernando Broncano-Berrocal

1 Introduction

Beliefs are routinely ascribed to groups such as juries, governments, committees, or even less structured groups such as markets or populations. On the other hand, conversation is a collective activity, in that it takes at least two people to have a conversation.[1] Furthermore, conversation, as a collective activity, is a natural way for groups to form their beliefs. For example, if you believe that your son shouldn't have a smartphone before the age of 16, and your partner believes the same, and you have a conversation about it and realize that you're both on the same page, you'll eventually come to believe that, not just individually, but as a couple (or as parents). Or think of a jury deliberating on the innocence or guilt of the defendant: having a conversation is the way to reach a verdict.

The aim of this paper is to shed light on the role of conversation in the formation of group beliefs. Specifically, it addresses the following questions:

> **Q1**: Is it possible for groups to form collective beliefs without communication between their members? How important is the role that conversations play in the formation of group beliefs in general?
>
> **Q2**: If conversations involve the negotiation of group beliefs, do the participants form a collective belief whenever a collective belief proposal is accepted by all?

The plan is as follows. In Sect. 2, I introduce the main debates in the literature on group belief, focusing on the debate between summativism and non summativism,

---

[1] See Schmitt (2018) for discussion of a stronger sense in which conversation is a collective activity.

F. Broncano-Berrocal (✉)
University of Barcelona, Barcelona, Spain
e-mail: f.broncano-berrocal@ub.edu

i.e., the debate about whether group beliefs are a function of the beliefs of individual group members. I pay particular attention to the most popular non-summative account in the literature, Margaret Gilbert's joint commitment account, because it fits naturally with the idea that conversations, and communication in general, play an essential role in group belief formation. In Sect. 3, I address Q1, arguing that while conversations are a natural way for many kinds of groups to form their beliefs, many other kinds of groups come to have beliefs even without prior communication between group members. Ultimately, whether conversations play a significant role in the formation of group beliefs depends heavily on what kind of groups hold the beliefs in question. I argue that while this result supports summativism, it is problematic for Gilbert's view. In Sect. 4, I introduce the negotiation of collective belief thesis, originally put forward by Gilbert and Priest (Gilbert, 1989; Gilbert & Priest, 2013) and further defended by Schmitt (2018), according to which the process of everyday conversation is structured around the formation of collective beliefs and, in particular, is geared toward the *negotiation* of collective beliefs. In Sect. 5, in response to Q2, I argue that the negotiation of collective belief thesis only makes sense in a non-summative framework, but that when specific non-summative views are combined with this thesis, the relevant non-summative views either become inapplicable or yield the wrong results. In Sect. 6, I offer some concluding remarks.

2 Philosophical Views About Group Belief

There are three main debates in the literature on group belief. One debate centers on whether group belief attributions are true. Rejectionists (e.g., Wray, 2001, 2003; Meijers, 2002, 2003; Backes, 2021), for example, hold that groups can have propositional attitudes, such as acceptances, but cannot believe propositions (*rejectionism*). Believers (e.g., Gilbert, 2002; Tollefsen, 2002, 2003), on the other hand, hold the view that groups can believe propositions (*believism*). The following discussion assumes that believism is true.

Within the logical space of believism, there are two further debates, both of which revolve around the nature of group belief. One debate is centered on the question of whether all group beliefs are of the same kind. Monists (most contributors to the literature) hold that group beliefs are of one kind and that it is in principle possible to offer a unified account of them that provides truth conditions that apply to all group belief attributions (*group belief monism*). Pluralists (Tuomela, 1992; List, 2014; Meijers, 2002), on the other hand, hold that there is more than one kind of group belief, each requiring different accounts that offer different truth conditions that apply to some but not all group belief attributions (*group belief pluralism*). Although I argue elsewhere for a pluralistic view of group belief (Broncano-Berrocal, forthcoming), I will omit the distinction between group belief monism and pluralism for the purposes of this paper.

The last debate is the most popular and revolves around the question of whether group beliefs are a function of the beliefs of individual group members (Gilbert,

1989, 239). Summativists answer this question in the affirmative. Non-summativists answer it in the negative. The clearest dividing line between *summativism* and *non-summativism* has to do with the acceptance (summativists) or rejection (non-summativists) of the following principle:

> **Correlativism**: If a group G believes that p, then at least one member of G believes that p.

That is, while non-summativists hold that it is possible for a group to believe a proposition when none of its members believe it, summativists consider this impossible.

Summativism can be formulated in different ways. A simple formulation (simple enough for present purposes) is the following:

> **Summative account**: A group G believes that p if and only if a significant percentage of the members of G believe that p.

This simple view can be reformulated in various ways to suit the insights from particular cases, e.g. by restricting the relevant set of group members to those who have sufficient authority or capacity to determine the content of the group's belief, i.e. the *operative members* of the group (cf. Tuomela, 1992), or by further requiring that there be conditions of *common knowledge* among the group members about the fact that a significant percentage of the group members believe the proposition in question (Gilbert, 1989, 264), or both (Broncano-Berrocal, forthcoming). Regardless of the correct formulation of summativism, the core idea remains that the beliefs of a group are a function of the beliefs of some of its members.

On the other hand, there are two kinds of non-summative views. First, there are views (e.g., List, 2005) that hold that group beliefs are the result of aggregation procedures (i.e., mechanisms for combining individual beliefs or votes), such as majority voting. Consider a general formulation of this kind of view:

> **Aggregationist account**: A group G believes that p if and only if an aggregation procedure of G, whose inputs are either the individual beliefs or the votes of the members of G, results in p.

The aggregationist account allows for the denial of correlativism by allowing for the possibility that a group believes the result of an aggregation procedure but no member believes it (e.g. when a group's opinion in the conclusion of an inference is reached by aggregating the majority opinions among individual members about each of the premises, leading to a conclusion that none of those members believe; see List (2005) for some examples).

According to a second type of non-summative view, group beliefs arise when (and only when) individual group members jointly accept propositions as the group's view. Joint acceptance views, the most popular being Margaret Gilbert's joint commitment account (see also Tuomela, 1992), also deny correlativism: group members may jointly accept a proposition that they individually disbelieve, for a variety of non-epistemic reasons, including compromise, externally imposed rules, or pragmatic considerations (Lackey, 2020). Here is a succinct formulation of Gilbert's view:

Joint commitment account: A group believes that p if and only if the members of G are jointly committed to accept p as the view of G.

In Gilbert's gloss, a joint commitment to accept p as the view of the group is to be understood as "an instruction to the parties to see to it that they act in such a way as to emulate as best they can a single body" (Gilbert, 2014, 33) in relation to the belief in question.[2] Such a directive leads to some group obligations (e.g. not to abandon the relevant joint commitment without reason or explanation) as well as consequences for non-compliance (e.g. rebuke by other group members). For example, politicians are usually jointly committed to the collective views of their parties, and they are reprimanded if they oppose them.

3 Group Belief Without Group Communication (and Without Common Knowledge)

According to Gilbert, "conversations, whether brief or extended, are a primary context for the formation of collective beliefs" (Gilbert, 2023, 105). Indeed, in many groups, especially small ones, conversations are the means by which group members communicate their beliefs, share their evidence and arguments, persuade others, and ultimately arrive at collective beliefs. The joint commitment account is the view that gives conversations a more significant role in the formation of group beliefs because, according to Gilbert, for group members to make a joint commitment to accept a proposition as a group, they must openly *express* their readiness to be part of that joint commitment under conditions of common knowledge (i.e., the relevant expressive behavior must be common knowledge among the involved parties). Such an open expression of readiness requires communication. In the most typical case, this communication is verbal, but not always (Gilbert offers cases where group members express their readiness to jointly commit to accept p as a group through nonverbal means, e.g. by nodding; see Gilbert (1989, 310)). Moreover, the type of communication required is *successful* communication. That is, the message (the readiness to jointly commit) expressed by the sender (i.e. a group member) with a verbal or nonverbal signal must be successfully received and processed in the right way by the corresponding receivers (the other group members).[3] If some group members do not express their readiness to jointly commit to accept p as a group, or if their expression of this readiness does not reach the other group members or is misinterpreted by them, the corresponding joint commitment does not materialize and the group does not form the corresponding group belief. In short, it follows from Gilbert's view that group beliefs are not possible without relevant successful

---

[2] Joint commitments are not personal commitments, for only the latter can be unilaterally created and rescinded. In contrast, joint commitments must be jointly created and rescinded by all parties involved.

[3] See Pagin (2008) for discussion of the notion of communicative success.

communication between group members. More generally, the joint commitment account presupposes the following thesis:

Communication thesis: A group believes that p at t only if the members of G maintain at least one communicative exchange among themselves before t that includes p as part of its content.

In what follows, I will argue that the communication thesis is false. From the fact that the members of a group do not engage in at least one communicative exchange among themselves that includes p as part of its content, it simply does not follow that the group does not believe p.

This result is only problematic for Gilbert's joint commitment view. For example, the aggregationist account is compatible with the falsity of the communication thesis. If the fact that a group believes a proposition depends on its having the right aggregation procedures, then no communication is required for the group's corresponding beliefs if these procedures do not involve communication (think of secret voting). The summative account is also consistent with the falsity of the thesis: on this view, the only thing that matters for a group to believe a proposition is that a significant percentage of its members believe it, and this may be the case even if they do not communicate that belief or talk about its content (see some examples below).

So let's look at why the communication thesis is false and how Gilbert's view runs into trouble as a result. First, consider the fact that there are many different kinds of groups. Some of them are highly organized and structured, such as governments, juries, or corporate boards. Others are less cohesive but have common goals, such as a group of people gathering for a flash mob or, more spontaneously, a mob trying to lynch a thief. Finally, there are other groups that have little or no structure or organization and are not oriented toward common goals (at least not in an obvious way), but are nevertheless considered groups because their members share a certain characteristic, such as passengers on a train, populations, billionaires, teenagers, supporters of sports clubs, artist fans or the like.

In the case of unstructured groups that have no obvious common goals, it is precisely because of their lack of structure and goal orientation that their members, who may number in the millions, do not always (probably not often) openly express their readiness to be part of joint commitments to believe propositions under conditions of common knowledge. The problem for the joint commitment view, however, is that we routinely ascribe beliefs to such groups in a meaningful way. Consider some of the many examples from the Internet: 'Teens believe that Android phones are for old people and parents only',[4] 'Americans believe that the United Kingdom is a friend of the USA'[5] or 'Nearly all Ukrainians believe they'll defeat Russia'.[6] Plausibly, the members of these groups do not tell each other (i.e., verbally express) that they are willing to believe the propositions in question jointly, nor do they do so

---

[4] https://www.phonearena.com/news/android-old-people-parents-only-say-teens_id149896/
[5] https://www.cbsnews.com/pictures/surprising-things-americans-actually-agree-on/
[6] https://www.wilsoncenter.org/blog-post/nearly-all-ukrainians-believe-theyll-defeat-russia/

through nonverbal communicative means (e.g., gestures): the majority of individuals in these groups simply believe these propositions without communicating with each other.[7]

Or take the case of the market, to which beliefs are often ascribed (e.g. about interest rate cuts or hikes, the potential growth of companies, etc.): it is not obvious that the individuals involved (i.e., investors) openly express (through direct verbal or nonverbal communication) their readiness to jointly commit to believing these propositions as a whole whenever such group beliefs are meaningfully attributed. If anything, these belief attributions are made on the basis of market behavior (e.g., stock purchases and sales), and that's it.[8]

There are some considerations that Gilbert can put forward in response to the previous objection. According to Gilbert (2014), unstructured groups such as large populations may exhibit joint commitments of various kinds and this is what makes them social groups. On Gilbert's view, the creation of a (basic) joint commitment requires at least three things: (1) the participation of all the parties to the joint commitments (*unanimity condition*), (2) their open expression of readiness to participate in those commitments (*expression condition*), and (3) common knowledge among all parties of these open expressions of readiness (*common knowledge condition*).

Let us evaluate these conditions. It is possible in principle for all members of an unstructured group to fulfill the unanimity condition. However, this will not always be the case. In large groups, there are often dissenters. Therefore, not every group member will often participate in the corresponding joint commitments. This should

---

[7] One might object that the members of unstructured groups cannot properly say, "We, collectively, believe" or make similar self-ascriptions. This would suggest that such groups do not hold beliefs. However, we naturally attribute beliefs to unstructured groups, which means that it is not a condition on group belief that group members must be able to self-ascribe collective beliefs. Not surprisingly, this property is not necessarily present in the individual case either, which means that it is not a constitutive property of belief in general. After all, biased individuals often hold beliefs that they do not ascribe to themselves. A different objection would be that some of these groups are not groups in a proper sense. While there are many different ways of individuating groups, Gilbert's preferred way (like other theorists such as Tuomela) is by their degree of social integration, so that groups with a low degree of social integration are not considered groups or collectives in a proper sense. However, as Epstein argues, this approach to collectivity risks overlooking "many groups of central interest to the social sciences—large groups, diverse groups, groups made up of colliding populations, groups with marginalized members, or groups that are created by oppression or other external circumstances collectivity or group" (Epstein, 2015, 255–256). The problem, again, is that we meaningfully attribute beliefs to such groups. Therefore, any adequate theory of group belief must account for these cases too. Many thanks to Margaret Gilbert for bringing these points to my attention.

[8] Note that the aggregationist view is unable to account for the truth conditions of some of these belief ascriptions, for although unstructured groups sometimes have procedures for aggregating individual judgments (think of a population voting in a referendum), in many cases such procedures do not exist for many such groups. It is not for nothing that the main proponent of the aggregationist view, List (2005), has opted for a pluralist view of group beliefs (List, 2014), according to which the beliefs of statistically identified groups (i.e., those who share a particular characteristic) are of a different *kind* and are best accounted for in summative terms.

not be a problem for Gilbert, as the unanimity condition can be relaxed so that not all, but only a significant percentage of group members need to participate in the relevant joint commitments.

The expression and the common knowledge conditions are less obviously fulfilled in the case of large groups. For example, if the kind of common knowledge that the common knowledge condition requires is individual common knowledge, by which is meant that everyone must know about each individual in the group that *that* person has openly expressed a readiness to participate in a joint commitment, the condition will hardly be met in the case of large groups. As argued above, it is also implausible to assume that the members of these groups communicate directly with each other, which puts pressure on the expression condition.

However, Gilbert offers a more liberal reading of the notions of 'open expression of readiness' and 'common knowledge' to make the two conditions applicable to large groups. The idea is this. First, the relevant expressions of readiness in groups such as populations need not be addressed to specific individuals (i.e., it is not necessary that the individuals expressing their readiness know or are acquainted with the recipients of these expressions), but more generally to people who fall within a particular description, e.g., 'People who live in America', 'People who live on this island', 'People who support FC Barcelona', and so on. This simply assumes that the members of the group have a certain conception of the population in question and are able to categorize people according to this conception.

Second, and relatedly, the relevant expressions of readiness need not take the form of a direct communicative exchange (verbal, e.g. in the form of a conversation, or nonverbal, e.g. through gestures): Gilbert believes that members of a population can also express their readiness in indirect ways. For example, they can publicly perform certain actions that make it clear that they are willing to participate in a joint commitment. She cites the example of people on an island who spontaneously begin to build a stone tower, so that this becomes a practice in which everyone eventually participates, even if they do not all know each other (Gilbert, 1989, 212). Even if the readiness to build the tower is not directly communicated to others verbally or nonverbally, others can easily *infer* from these public acts that the people performing them, and ultimately everyone, are willing to do so. In this way, these manifestations of willingness become what Gilbert calls *population common knowledge*, which is consistent with the fact that many people in the population do not know each other personally.

Applying these ideas to the case of group belief, the truth conditions of attributions such as 'The market believes that the Fed will raise interest rates again' can be explained analogously by the fact that there is a joint commitment among investors to believe this proposition. Crucially, this joint commitment arises not because investors directly express their readiness to jointly accept certain views about the Federal Reserve's actions, but because their public behavior (e.g., the massive selling of stocks) manifests that readiness in a way that becomes common knowledge among the population. To summarize, with this more liberal understanding of what it takes to openly express readiness and with the notion of population common knowledge in place, Gilbert may be able to explain the beliefs of large groups in terms of joint commitments.

However, Gilbert's possible response is problematic. A first problem is that it is not obvious that the fact that people's actions become publicly available evidence of their readiness to participate in joint commitments counts as a communicative exchange of such readiness. This threatens to violate the communication thesis. But perhaps on a behaviorist understanding of communication, an action that makes it clear to everyone in the group that one is willing to make a joint commitment to accept p as a group counts, if not as a communicative exchange, then at least as successful communication, so that the thesis can be formulated accordingly (e.g., a group G believes that p at t only if the members of G engage in successful communication among themselves before t that includes p as part of its content).

A more serious problem has to do with the dialectical scope of Gilbert's response. All it shows is that it is *possible* for some large groups to have joint commitments, including joint commitments to believe certain propositions. However, this does not ensure that in every case in which we meaningfully ascribe a belief to a group, the conditions described by Gilbert are met. For example, there are groups that have beliefs where the readiness to participate in the relevant joint commitments is not expressed or manifested at all, not even by their actions, e.g. because their members actively conceal this readiness from each other, so that the required common knowledge (population or otherwise) is not present. To illustrate, consider the case of a group voting anonymously on whether p, where p is a sensitive issue on which everyone actively conceals their opinion. Suppose everyone votes based on their individual beliefs (that p or that not-p) without any prior communication between group members, and everyone votes for p because they individually believe that. We can truly attribute the belief that p to the group (summativists and aggregationists will agree here). However, since the vote is anonymous and there is no prior deliberation about whether p, there are no expressions of readiness to participate in the joint commitment to accept p as a group and therefore the corresponding common knowledge. On the joint commitment view, such a group would not hold any belief because according to Gilbert (2006, 177), "there should be no attempt on the part of those who express their readiness for joint commitment with certain others to conceal this expression from the others in question" in order for the relevant joint commitments to hold.

One way out would be to argue that we should leave the voting cases aside. Another would be to explain them in terms of joint commitments.[9] But even if these

---

[9] For example, anonymous voting cases can be understood as cases in which group members jointly commit to the use of a process that does not involve communicative exchanges about its inputs. In Gilbert's terminology, group beliefs in these cases are formed through a *basic* joint commitment to believe the outcomes of the process in question (whatever those may be), which results in a *non-basic* joint commitment that arises from its implementation. However, the most common and paradigmatic cases of group belief are cases in which the relevant joint commitments involve communicative exchanges. In reply, the communication thesis can thus be restricted as follows: If the members of a group G are *not* jointly committed to a collective belief-forming process that

lines of reply were to succeed, there are plausible non-voting cases of group belief in p in which group members actively conceal their individual beliefs in p and therefore do not openly express by verbal or non-verbal communication (or openly manifest by public action) that they are willing to participate in a joint commitment to accept p as a group. For example:

> **BOARD OF DIRECTORS.** All members of the board believe that the CEO is obnoxious, but because the next promotion depends crucially on getting along with him, they all behave as if he were a nice person. Because of this behavior, everyone mistakenly believes that everyone on the board does not believe that the CEO is obnoxious. Had it not been for the promotion, everyone would have told the other members what they thought. Suspecting that the CEO is disliked by the board, one of the major shareholders of the company distributes a questionnaire to all the board members to get their opinion of the CEO, and they all write the following: "I find the CEO obnoxious, but the others find him nice". This shareholder tells the other major shareholders: "See, that's exactly what I was thinking: the board thinks the CEO is obnoxious, but for some reason it has not made an official statement about it."

Although there are no open expressions of readiness to jointly accept the proposition that the CEO is obnoxious, nor is this proposition common knowledge within the group, there is pressure to consider that the statement 'The board thinks the CEO is obnoxious' is true. This case is not anecdotal, as we often attribute beliefs to groups that we didn't know had such majority opinions after knowing the results of confidential surveys. Indeed, the widespread use of confidential surveys is explained by the fact that they are the best way to find out what a group really believes, beyond what group members publicly express or manifest (or what they jointly commit to, for that matter). And for good reason: the same pragmatic reasons that prevent joint commitments from emerging also prevent collective beliefs from being openly expressed or becoming common knowledge.[10]

So how important is the role of conversation in the formation of group beliefs? As we have seen, its importance depends on what kind of groups form the beliefs in question. For some groups, especially small groups in which members communicate with each other, conversation is a natural means of forming group beliefs. But as we have seen, group beliefs can also be formed when group members do not communicate with each other, either because there is an aggregation procedure that prevents communication (e.g. anonymous voting), or because group members do not express their views publicly for pragmatic or prudential reasons of all kinds.

---

prevents communicative exchanges involving p, then G believes that p at time t only if the members of G engage in at least one communicative exchange involving p before t.

[10] It could be argued that 'The board' in the sentence 'The board thinks the CEO is obnoxious' refers only to 'the members of the board', because the board as such has not officially commented on the matter. Had it had, it might have declared the CEO very nice. I grant that cases where there is conflicting information, e.g. an official group statement that p and information from a survey that not-p is the majority opinion among group members, may pull us in opposite directions as to whether the group believes p or not-p. However, this is not the case with BOARD OF DIRECTORS: there is no official statement contradicting the unanimous opinion that the CEO is obnoxious. In this way, this opinion can be treated as a dispositional belief of the group that has not yet been made explicit, rather than interpreting the case as the group suspending on the issue or having no attitude at all.

The summative account is the view that best does justice to this variability, precisely because it is silent on how the relevant group beliefs come about. It does not matter whether group members have been convinced of the beliefs in question by other group members in conversation, whether they have jointly committed to upholding them, or whether they have come to these beliefs themselves in private: all that matters is the end result, namely that a significant percentage of members come to believe the same proposition, however that happens. This is clearly an advantage of the summative account over more complex views such as Gilbert's.[11]

4 The Negotiation of Collective Belief Thesis

Gilbert and Priest (2013) put forward a thesis about the nature of conversation, which they motivate with the following example:

> **EVENT COMMITTEE.** The University Event committee is meeting to discuss the celebration of the University's 50th anniversary. Phyllis, a member of the committee, suggests, "J.K. Rowling would make great keynote speaker." Some discussion ensues, with positive comments outnumbering negative ones. After a while someone asks, "So we agree that Rowling would make great speaker?" This time the members of the group either voice their agreement or remain silent. The matter is settled: Rowling would make a great speaker. At this point it would be natural and appropriate for any member of the committee to make any of the following collective belief ascriptions: "We agree that Rowling would be a great speaker", "We think that...","In our opinion...", "We decided that", "Our view at this point is that...". Indeed, it seems that all of these statements are true. (Gilbert & Priest, 2013: 6)

Gilbert and Priest argue, primarily through examples, that everyday conversations are structured around collective belief formation. In EVENT COMMITTEE, for example, a proposal for a collective belief is made during the conversation (that J.K. Rowling would be a great keynote speaker) and after some negotiation, everyone agrees. According to Gilbert and Priest, the propositions that become the content of the corresponding collective beliefs are either verbally expressed by one of the participants in the course of the conversations or implied by such a verbal expression. Importantly, not all conversations involve a negotiation of collective beliefs, but only 'paradigmatic conversations', i.e. verbal exchanges between two or more people that contain at least one assertion and intuitively count as conversations, i.e. they do not think that conversations involving only non-assertoric utterances are structured around collective belief formation.[12]

---

[11] For an overview of the advantages and disadvantages of the various theories of group belief, see Broncano-Berrocal (forthcoming).

[12] Schmitt (2018) rightly points out that not all conversations that contain only assertoric utterances are centered around collective belief formation. In particular, conversations that consist exclusively of assertoric utterances expressing personal beliefs (i.e. utterances of the form 'In my personal opinion...', 'Speaking personally...') do not involve the negotiation of collective beliefs. See Gilbert and Priest (2013) for further discussion of this point.

Against this background, Gilbert and Priest formulate the negotiation of collective belief thesis as follows:

> **NCB thesis**: In a paradigmatic conversation, whatever else is going on, the parties are negotiating the establishment of one or another collective belief on the basis of proposals put forward by one or another interlocutor.[13]

Gilbert and Priest think that everyday conversation, mundane as it may be, involves such a negotiation. Here is another of their examples:

> **SUNNY DAY**. Jenny and Tom [are] waiting together at a bus stop on a sunny day. The two fall into conversation. "Sure is a beautiful day!" says Tom cheerfully. Jenny, whose actual preference is cool cloudy weather, replies, "I suppose it is." She speaks pleasantly, but without great conviction. (Gilbert & Priest, 2013, 14–15)

They reconstruct the case in the light of the NCB thesis as follows. First, Tom makes a collective belief proposal (p, the proposition that it is a beautiful day)—the proposal is that the parties collectively believe that p. Second, Jenny accepts Tom's collective belief proposal even though she is personally convinced to the contrary (she believes not p). With her reply, she shows that she is willing to accept Tom's proposal. The result is a collective belief that is maintained at least for the duration of the interaction. Gilbert and Priest understand this collective belief in terms of the joint commitment view: after their conversation, Tom and Jenny jointly commit to accept p as a group. Importantly, this involves the rejection of correlativism:

> In this example, Jenny does not personally believe what the two collectively believe, but this does not matter. Our collectively believing that p does not entail that I personally believe that p nor does it entail that I do not personally disbelieve it. The same goes for the other person or people involved. (Gilbert & Priest, 2013, 15)

Importantly, also, it can happen that the collective belief proposal of one party is rejected by the other party, e.g. if Tom claims "Sure is a beautiful day!" and Jenny replies "So *you* think". This possibility is in line with the NCB thesis, because the fact that conversation is structured around the negotiation of collective beliefs does not mean that such a negotiation must be successful and that a collective belief always emerges. However, if the collective belief proposal is accepted by all parties and the conditions of extant views of group belief apply to this proposal, the result should be that a collective belief is formed.

5 Conversation and Negotiated Group Belief

In this section, I will argue that the negotiation of collective belief thesis, including its underlying assumption that group beliefs can be negotiated, does not make sense in a summative framework, but only makes sense when interpreted in non-summative terms. However, I will also argue that when specific non-summative views are

---

[13] Schmitt (2018) also endorses the NCB thesis.

combined with the NCB thesis (namely, the aggregationist and joint commitment views), these views either become inapplicable or yield the wrong results. This not only casts doubt on the NCB thesis, but also suggests that group belief, unlike group acceptance or a group's position, is not an attitude that can be negotiated.

Any adequate theory of group belief should accommodate the fact that the clearest, most paradigmatic cases of group belief are those in which a group believes p and *all* group members believe p, i.e. cases in which the individual beliefs of group members completely match the beliefs of the group (cases of *complete doxastic match*). These cases are interpreted differently depending on which view of group belief one prefers. According to the summative view, for example, cases of complete doxastic match are simply cases in which the group and all its members believe the same proposition. On the aggregationist view, on the other hand, these are cases in which, for example, a group belief is aggregated by a majority vote and the vote results in p (i.e. the group believes p) after all members have voted for p because they believe p to be the case. Finally, according to the joint commitment view, cases of complete doxastic match are cases in which a group believes p after all members have jointly committed to accept p as a group precisely because all members individually believe p (i.e., the reason they participate in this joint commitment is that they believe p to be the case). If we regard these cases as paradigmatic, the more doxastic mismatch a case of group belief contains, the less clear it becomes *qua* case of group *belief* (though not as an instance of other group attitudes).

In this sense, according to the summative view, cases of *complete doxastic mismatch* (i.e. cases in which a group believes a proposition that all its members disbelieve) are not possible (summativists endorse correlativism).[14] At most, it tolerates cases in which there is *partial doxastic match*, i.e. where a significant percentage of group members (but not all of them) believe what the group believes. In any case, according to the summative view, the absence of complete doxastic match merely has to do with the fact that fewer than all members believe in the proposition held by the group. That is, the type of doxastic mismatch that occurs in these cases is due only to *epistemic factors* (namely, the distribution of beliefs among group members).

In contrast, non-summative views, such as the aggregationist or the joint commitment views, allow for cases of complete doxastic mismatch by introducing non-epistemic factors into the direct causes of group belief. For instance, the former allows the beliefs of groups to be determined by aggregation procedures that take individual votes as inputs. However, believing p may not be the only reason to vote for p. One can also vote for non-epistemic reasons without regard to one's beliefs about whether p. Therefore, on this view, cases of complete doxastic mismatch are possible precisely because all group members can vote for a proposition they disbelieve. In the same way, the joint commitment view holds that the beliefs of groups are determined by joint commitments to accept propositions as a group. However, believing p is only one reason for participating in a joint commitment to accept p as

---

[14] Less extreme cases of complete doxastic mismatch include cases in which the group believes p and all members either suspend on p or lack the belief in p.

Group Belief and the Role of Conversation 121

a group: group members may participate in the relevant joint commitment to accept p for many non-epistemic reasons, even if they all disbelieve p. In this way, the introduction of more complex notions such as aggregation procedures or joint commitments amounts to the introduction of *non-epistemic factors* as direct causes of group belief and thus of doxastic mismatch.

Once one opens the door to non-epistemic causes of doxastic mismatch, it is only natural to allow for the negotiation of collective beliefs—that collective beliefs can be negotiated is the key assumption of the NCB thesis. Aggregation procedures can be preceded by negotiations about what to vote on, and so can be the formation of joint commitments. However, while decisions (to vote, to join a joint commitment) can be negotiated, what one believes cannot, since negotiation implies voluntariness and beliefs cannot be adopted at will. In this sense, according to the summative view, group members cannot negotiate what the group believes: at most they can *persuade* others to adopt their own beliefs (e.g. through conversation), so that if enough members come to believe the same proposition as a result, the group can be correctly attributed a belief in that proposition. Therefore, the thesis that conversations involve the negotiation of group beliefs only makes sense in a non-summative conception of group beliefs.

The problem is that when we understand the NCB thesis in non-summative terms by combining it with specific non-summative views, these views either become inapplicable or yield the wrong results, thus offering an implausible picture of group beliefs. For example, it is unclear how the aggregationist account can be applied to the NCB thesis: even if collective belief proposals are made during conversations, conversations do not involve the kind of aggregation procedures from which collective beliefs emerge according to the aggregationist account. This leaves the joint commitment account as the most promising candidate. The expected result of combining the NCB thesis with the joint commitment account should be that whenever all participants in a conversation unanimously accept a collective belief proposal and the conditions of the joint commitment account apply to that proposal, a group belief is formed. However, as I will argue next, this combination does not yield this result, for the following five reasons.

First, negotiations are not as smooth as the kinds of interactions that Gilbert and Priest use to motivate the NCB thesis: they often involve aggressive tactics, including threats. Thus, the type of negotiation of group belief proposals that a conversation may be aimed at can also involve aggressive tactics and threats. On the other hand, group members may also participate in a joint commitment (e.g., to accept p as a group) simply because of coercion. Thus, it follows from Gilbert's view in combination with the NCB thesis that a conversation involving threats can lead to group beliefs. But in some cases, especially those in which it is common knowledge that no participant in the conversation believes the proposition in question, it is doubtful that the group composed by the participants of the conversation forms a collective belief. To illustrate, consider the following case:

> **NAKED KING**. The naked king shows up. All the members of the royal court are present. A fearsome royal guard shouts out, "Surely the king's attire is appropriate for tonight's dinner!". After looking around for a bit, one of the members shouts back, "Of course it's

appropriate." The guard looks around menacingly and asks, "Is that right?" Everyone says, "Yes!". And the guard exclaims, "Excellent, end of conversation: we all agree that the king's attire is appropriate for tonight's dinner."

It is quite obvious that all participants in the conversation, including the royal guard, and therefore the royal court disbelieve the claim that the king's attire is appropriate for tonight's dinner. That is, there is strong pressure to regard the claim "The royal court believes that the king's attire is appropriate for tonight's dinner" as false.[15] However, all the ingredients for a joint-commitment-based group belief are in place: there is a conversation, a negotiation of a group belief proposal, and a unanimous joint commitment to accept the relevant proposition as a group. At this point, one may wonder whether the resulting group attitude should be called a "belief". In this case, and in many analogous cases, there are more appropriate terms to describe the group's attitude. For example, consider the following assertions: "The official position of the royal court is that the king's attire is appropriate for tonight's dinner" or "The royal court accepts that the king's attire is appropriate for tonight's dinner". It is certainly more natural to negotiate what official position one's group will take or what will be accepted as a group than what to believe. Moreover, the previous statements are consistent with the following claim: "The royal court does not believe that the king's clothing is appropriate." For if an individual or group proclaims p as their official position, and they know that this is a lie, they do not believe p (Lackey, 2020); or if an individual or group knows that p is false, they may still accept p for prudential reasons while disbelieving it under conditions of coercion.

Furthermore, when the consequences of coercion disappear, the real group beliefs come to the surface, just as individual repressed beliefs sometimes come to the surface. In NAKED KING, for example, the members of the royal court, if they could speak freely, would surely claim (even the royal guard) that the king's attire is not appropriate (or their actions would manifest this), which would reflect the true opinion of the royal court. So it is in BOARD OF DIRECTORS, where for prudential reasons no one in the board openly expresses their opinion that the CEO is obnoxious, a group opinion that a confidential survey reveals. Indeed, if confidential surveys represent such an excellent tool for finding out what a group really thinks, it is because their confidentiality ensures that pragmatic factors such as coercion have no influence.

Second, misunderstandings can occur in negotiations just as they do in conversations. A participant in a conversation/negotiation may agree to the proposal of one of the parties and then realize that what they agreed to is not what they originally believed. For example:

COSTUME PARTY. John says, "Tonight's party will be awesome!" and Jane, his partner, replies, "Sure it will!". However, John meant the costume party tonight, while Jane interpreted John's statement as referring to tonight's wine and cheese party. Jane hates costume parties and would never think a costume party is awesome. Not wanting to disappoint John,

---

[15] If one is not convinced of this, one may consider Lackey's (2020) arguments that cases like this are paradigmatic cases of group lies and thus cases in which the group believes the opposite of what it publicly proclaims.

Jane does not give up on their joint commitment that tonight's (costume) party will be awesome. Now suppose that just before the party, when they are both already dressed up, Jane's best friend tells John that she hates costume parties. Knowing this, he abandons his belief that tonight's party will be awesome, because he believes that a party is awesome only if they both have fun, and now he has every reason to believe that Jane won't have any. John, on the other hand, thinks it's too late to cancel their plans for the evening. Consequently, he says nothing and continues to stick to their joint commitment that tonight's (costume) party will be awesome.

The result is not only a terrible party, but also a joint commitment to accept a proposition that everyone disbelieves. On Gilbert's view, the couple believes this proposition, but again, there is a strong pressure to consider the claim "The couple believes tonight's costume party will be awesome" false, at least from the perspective of someone who knows all the relevant facts. The underlying problem is that joint commitments to believe a proposition as a group can be (and often are) insensitive to changes in the beliefs of group members: group beliefs are maintained as long as the corresponding joint commitments are in place, even if these changes in the group members' beliefs lead to cases of complete doxastic mismatch and, as the case shows, intuitions of lack of group belief.

Third, negotiations can be insincere, just like conversations. One interlocutor may make a collective belief proposal and the other interlocutor may agree to this proposal, but insincerely. If one assumes that group beliefs can be negotiated through conversation (as the NCB thesis assumes), and if successfully completed negotiations can be insincere (in the sense that a proposal is unanimously accepted even if this acceptance is disingenuous by some of the parties), then the outcome of the previous situation should be a group belief. However, it is unclear whether, on Gilbert's view, a collective belief arises in this case, because the insincere party does not jointly commit to accepting the proposal in question as a group: they do so only ostensibly.

Fourth, conversations, even paradigmatic ones, are often monopolized by bullshitters, i.e. speakers who, when asserting p, are not concerned with whether p is true or false, but only with whether p serves a certain purpose, e.g. to convey a certain image of themselves, to persuade, etc. (Frankfurt, 1986). Bullshitters do not participate in any joint commitment to any collective goal, even though their interlocutors may still understand p as a request to jointly commit to accept p as a group and end up believing that they are negotiating the establishment of p as a collective view. Instead, bullshitters only make personal commitments for their own ends. For this reason, there is no negotiation at all in such cases, even if there is a conversation, which runs counter to the NCB thesis.

Finally, agreeing to a collective belief proposal may be done not in order to jointly commit to accepting a proposition as a group, but simply to end the conversation, which casts doubts on the NCB thesis. Suppose someone bothers you so much that you would agree to anything that person says just to stop hearing their voice. It is doubtful that there is a negotiation of a collective belief proposal. It is also doubtful (contrary to the prediction of the joint commitment account in combination with the NCB thesis) that a group belief arises: the bothered party commits to nothing.

To all these cases Gilbert could reply that they are not 'paradigmatic' conversations. However, according to Gilbert, 'paradigmatic' conversations are verbal exchanges between two or more people that contain at least one assertion and intuitively count as conversation. In all these cases, the verbal exchanges in question are intuitively regarded as conversations and contain at least one assertion.

Moreover, consider how naturally these cases can be understood as instances of group *acceptance* or agreement of the interlocutors to a collective *position*. In NAKED KING, for example, the royal court collectively accepts (but does not believe) the group's position that the naked king's attire is appropriate. In COSTUME PARTY, the couple collectively accepts the position that tonight's party will be awesome, even if they clearly do not believe it. Moreover, insincere interlocutors (including bullshitters) collectively accept propositions that they do not believe for various non-epistemic reasons. One can also agree to collectively accept p in order to end a conversation with someone who is bothering one, but no group belief arises. All of this suggests that group belief, unlike group acceptance or a group's position, is not an attitude that can be negotiated, against the key assumption of the NCB thesis.

6 Concluding Remarks

In this chapter, I have examined the role of conversation in the formation of group beliefs against the background of the summativism/non-summativism debate. The answers to the questions the paper has addressed (Q1 and Q2) are, first, that while conversations are a natural way for many kinds of groups to form their beliefs, many other kinds of groups form beliefs even without prior communication between group members, and that ultimately whether conversation plays an important role in the formation of group beliefs depends heavily on which kind of groups hold the beliefs in question; second, that the negotiation of collective belief thesis only makes sense in a non-summative framework, but that when specific non-summative views are combined with this thesis, such non-summative views either become inapplicable or yield the wrong results.

In contrast, summativism offers a simpler and more neutral picture of the role of conversation in group belief formation: conversations may (but need not) play an important role in the formation of group beliefs. Often, group members talk to other group members to convince them of their own beliefs, so that if enough of them come to the same belief, the group will too. Moreover, when a conversation aims to convince its interlocutors, the group consisting of the participants in the conversation also forms a group belief if enough participants become convinced of the same proposition, regardless of what the general aim of the conversation may be. In other cases, however, groups form beliefs without prior communication between their members. As we have seen, the summative account is the view that best does justice to this variability because it does not impose restrictive conditions on how groups should form their beliefs: all that matters is how individual opinions are distributed within the group.[16]

References

Backes, M. (2021). Can groups be genuine believers? The argument from interpretationism. *Synthese, 199*, 10311–10329.
Broncano-Berrocal, F. (forthcoming). Pluralistic summativism about group belief. In J. Lackey & A. McGlynn (Eds.), *Oxford handbook of social epistemology*. Oxford University Press.
Epstein, B. (2015). *The ant trap: Rebuilding the foundations of the social sciences*. Oxford University Press.
Frankfurt, H. G. (1986). *On Bullshit*. Princeton University Press.
Gilbert, M. (1989). *On social facts*. Routledge.
Gilbert, M. (2002). Belief and acceptance as features of groups. *ProtoSociology, 16*, 35–69.
Gilbert, M. (2006). *A theory of political obligation: Membership, commitment, and the bonds of society*. Oxford University Press.
Gilbert, M. (2014). *Joint commitment: How we make the social world*. Oxford University Press.
Gilbert, M. (2023). *Life in groups: How we think, feel, and act together*. Oxford University Press.
Gilbert, M., & Priest, M. (2013). Conversation and collective Belief. In A. Capone, F. Lo Piparo, & M. Carapezza (Eds.), *Perspectives on pragmatics and philosophy*. Springer.
Lackey, J. (2020). *The epistemology of groups*. Oxford University Press.
List, C. (2005). Group knowledge and group rationality: A judgment aggregation perspective. *Episteme, 2*, 25–38.
List, C. (2014). Three kinds of collective attitudes. *Erkenntnis, 79*, 1601–1622.
Meijers, A. (2002). Collective agents and cognitive attitudes. *ProtoSociology, 16*, 70–85.
Meijers, A. (2003). Why accept collective beliefs? Reply to M. Gilbert. *ProtoSociology, 18*, 377–388.
Pagin, P. (2008). What is communicative success? *Canadian Journal of Philosophy, 38*, 85–115.
Schmitt, F. F. (2018). Remarks on conversation and negotiated collective belief. *ProtoSociology, 35*, 74–98.
Tollefsen, D. (2002). Organizations as true believers. *Journal of Social Philosophy, 33*, 395–410.
Tollefsen, D. (2003). Rejecting rejectionism. *Protosociology, 18*, 389–405.
Tuomela, R. (1992). Group beliefs. *Synthese, 91*, 285–318.
Wray, K. B. (2001). Collective belief and acceptance. *Synthese, 129*, 319–333.
Wray, K. B. (2003). What really divides Gilbert and the rejectionists. *ProtoSociology, 18*, 363–376.

---

[16] Many thanks to Margaret Gilbert for her valuable comments on this paper.

Knowledge Norms and Conversation

J. Adam Carter

1 Introduction

A popular idea in epistemology holds that both thought and action are governed by epistemic norms, with *knowledge norms* being illustrative. Here are some popular contenders: knowledge norms on belief, assertion, and (non-assertoric) action.

Knowledge norm of belief: One must: believe that p only if one knows that p.[1]
Knowledge norm of assertion: One must: assert that p only if one knows that p. (Williamson, 2000, 243)
Knowledge norm of action: One must: treat the proposition that p as a reason for acting only if you know that p. (Hawthorne & Stanley, 2008, 578)

These (and other related) knowledge norms on thought and action are *distinct norms*, such that each governs a different type of thing, *viz.*, a different thought or action type. For theoretical elegance, one might be inclined to accept all sorts of knowledge norms as part of a wider 'knowledge-first' approach;[2] even so, individual knowledge norms themselves (governing various types of thought and action)

---
[1] See Williamson (2000, 255–56). As Williamson puts it: "It is plausible (…) that occurrently believing p stands to asserting p as the inner stands to the outer. If so, the knowledge rule for assertion corresponds to the norm that one should believe p only if one knows p. Given that norm, it is not reasonable to believe p when one knows that one does not know p."
[2] See Williamson (2017) for an overview of this approach. See also Ichikawa and Jenkins (2017) for some helpful discussion of how 'knowledge-first' has been associated with a cluster of claims rather than with any single claim.

J. A. Carter (✉)
University of Glasgow, Glasgow, UK
e-mail: adam.carter@glasgow.ac.uk

are typically argued for *independently*,[3] and what it is that each governs is taken to be independent from each other. If one believes that p, asserts that p, and then (non-assertorically) acts on the basis of p, in that order, then three tokenings are answerable to three separate knowledge norms, in that order.

My aim here is to consider how epistemic norms (with knowledge norms being the guiding illustrative focus), might, in some cases, apply to complex performances that involve dynamic combinations of thought and action.

I begin with a brief 'proof of concept' of this idea using practical reasoning as illustrative, and the main goal of this chapter will then be to then explore in some detail how *conversations*, or at least, a certain subset of conversations that are constitutively aimed, might themselves be knowledge governed. On the proposal I will develop, knowledge norms are applicable to aimed conversations that involve thinking *to a purpose*, practical or theoretical; aimed conversations are governed by *participatory know-how*—viz., know how to do what each interlocutor to the conversation shares a participatory intention to do. When individuals intentionally inquire together into whether p, by means of an aimed conversation X, they ought to know how to use X to find out together whether p. While participatory knowledge-how is in the above respects the norm of (aimed) conversation, satisfying it will in practice generally require interlocutors to the conversation thinking and acting in accordance with more specific knowledge norms (e.g., of assertion and inquiry). But aimed conversations are governed by know-how in a way that is not *reducible* to any concatenation of satisfying individual norms on thought and action.

2 Thought and Action

A key idea in Williamson's (2017) picture of the relationship between epistemology and action theory is that there are important structural connections (and associated analogies) between thought and action, and between the norms that govern them.

My aim here isn't to evaluate these structural analogies.[4] But rather to take Williamson's idea of the *operation of a cognitive-practical system* as illustrative of the kind of thing that can (*apart* from, and in addition to, the discrete elements of its operation) be norm governed.

A cognitive-practical system, such as human thinkers who manifest intelligence paradigmatically by reasoning and then behaving on the basis of that reasoning (*viz.*, by representing the world, then purposefully changing it), exhibit two dimensions of intelligence with opposite directions of fit, *cognitive* and *practical*, where "cognitive concerns those aspects of intelligent life which concern fitting mind to

---

[3] This is the case even when these arguments pursue similar strategy types, e.g., retraction data, lottery cases, Moore-paradoxical assertions, etc.
[4] Though see Miracchi and Carter (2022).

world, 'practical' those which concern fitting world to mind". (Williamson, 2017, 164).

On this picture, *practical reasoning* is, as Williamson puts it, the 'nexus' between the cognitive and the practical (between the mind-to-world and world-to-mind dimensions of intelligent life). On the cognitive side, we have beliefs, and, if all goes well, knowledge (the 'gold standard' in fitting mind to world). Representational attitudes such as belief and knowledge serve as *inputs* to practical reasoning, reasoning about what to do. The output of practical reasoning (which will have a world-to-mind direction of fit) isn't just another belief, but an *intention*[5] to do something, and all goes well here only if one *acts* (and not merely *intends* but fails to act).

Importantly though, a *cognitive-practical* system like us isn't, in practical reasoning, *merely* doing something that involves a mind-to-world direction of fit, or merely doing something that involves a world-to-mind direction of fit. Rather, it's—in *practical* reasoning—doing *both* kinds of things, and not in isolation from each other, but in such a way that world-to-mind intelligence is supposed to *inform* mind-to-world intelligence. As such, the operation of a practical reasoning system can fall short on *either* side, e.g., if one has an input short of knowledge or an output short of action. Here's Williamson (2017, 174):

> When all goes well in one's whole cognitive-practical system (not just one's brain), one acts on what one knows. But things often go badly. One believes that P when not P, or (perhaps as a consequence) intends to ϕ but never ϕs. In practical reasoning, the false belief plays the same local role as knowledge (it makes a premise), and the failed intention plays the same local role as action (it makes the conclusion), but they do not play the same global roles. Such malfunctions have to be understood in relation to what happens when the whole system is functioning well. (…) When the cognitive-practical system functions well, one acts on what one know.

While there are both belief-like and actional components of the operation of a cognitive-practical system, the *operation of the system*, viz., practical reasoning, itself involves a complex consisting of the beliefs and the (belief-informed) actional output. And this complex operation is itself norm-governed on Williamson's approach by a *complex* knowledge-action norm, which governs the operation of a cognitive-practical system:

Knowledge-action norm on practical reasoning (KAN): One must: reason practically only if one acts on what one knows.

A quick point of clarification. There is a crucial difference between the above 'knowledge-action' norm on practical reasoning, and what is sometimes called the 'knowledge norm of action' or alternatively the 'knowledge norm of practical reasoning' as defended by Hawthorne and Stanley (2008):

Knowledge norm of action: One must: treat the proposition that p as a reason for acting only if one knows that p.[6]

---

[5] This is the position of the updated (Williamson, 2017) analogy. See Williamson (2000, Ch. 1) for a previous statement of the analogy which holds that belief is to knowledge as desire is to action.

[6] See Hawthorne and Stanley (2008, 578).

These norms govern different types of things. Hawthorne and Stanley's knowledge norm governs *reasons treating*—viz., it governs *treating propositions as a reason to act, viz.*,—our appropriation of that *for which* we act. And possessing knowledge is the standard for doing *that*.

By contrast, KAN says knowledge *and* action, and the latter being done on the former, constitute the satisfaction of the (complex) norm for doing something else. The something else is the activity of *practical reasoning* itself.

The point of this section has been to clarify the very idea of what it would be for a knowledge-involving norm (with KAN being our example) to govern *complexes of thought and action*, even when we think that the constituent thought and action tokens that feature in the complex might be individually governed themselves by knowledge norms on thought and action types as such. Williamson's view of the operation of a cognitive practical system—practical reasoning performances— offers a precedent here.

With this precedent in view, I now want explore in what follows the idea that a *conversation* can be modelled in a way (broadly analogously to the way Williamson has modelled the operation of a practical reasoning system) such that it is plausibly constrained by a complex knowledge-implicating norm, over and above whatever knowledge norms might govern the constituent thoughts and actions that feature in a given conversation. Section 3 will take this up, beginning with several up-front clarifications and comments on scope.

3 Epistemic Norms of Conversation

What kind of thing is a conversation? Our colloquial usage is liberal here as to what would qualify. Likewise, philosophical delineations of conversations err on the side of inclusiveness. Grice's (1975) theory of conversational implicature, for example, takes a 'conversation' to be minimally "a communicative exchange", which will (typically) at least involve two interlocutors, and where at least some information is communicated through speech acts by those interlocutors.

A simple example of a conversation between interlocutors A and B might feature just two speech acts: a question (A) and an answer (B). Without knowing what that question was, or what the answer was, there is already a *trivial* sense in which a simple conversation with that {Q +A} structure might be governed by knowledge norms: one per speech act.

B's answer (whatever it was), communicated through assertion, would (on a knowledge norm of assertion) be proper only if B *knows* the answer to A's question, whatever it was. What about A's question? A recent idea, defended by Christopher Willard-Kyle (forthcoming) is that inquiring via interrogative attitudes also requires (a specific kind of) knowledge in order to be proper as an instance of inquiry, and this is the case even if we grant that we would typically have a reason to ask a question only if we were ignorant of what the answer was. On Willard-Kyle's view, there nonetheless is something defective about inquiring into something you don't *know* has a true (and direct) answer. Consider the following:

1. Why does the sun set in the east?
2. Was it Abraham Lincoln or Franklin Delano Roosevelt who was the first U.S. president?[7]
3. Is a person with 32 hairs bald?

Each of 1–3 is a defective *as* a question. (1) and (2) don't have true direct answers. And (3) is a defective question even if it did have a true direct answer so long as the individual asking this question doesn't know, when asking it, *that* it has a true direct answer. The formulation of the knowledge norm for inquiry Willard-Kyle defends, and which gets these results, holds that:

> **Knowledge Norm for Inquiry**: One ought to: inquire into (an unconditional question) Q at t only if one knows at t that Q has a true (complete, and direct) answer.

We can set aside for now what counts as a complete, true and direct answer (there is some debate here[8]), and we can also set aside whether Willard-Kyle's preferred norm is correct. While I take it to be plausible, I won't try to defend it here.

Rather, the point is just that, on a toy conversation that involves a single {Q +A} pair, we can see how that conversation would (in a trivial way) be governed by knowledge norms *in so far as* the conversation has two components (a question and an answer), where (i) the question beginning the conversation is governed by the knowledge norm for inquiry, and (ii) the answer ending the conversation is governed by the knowledge norm of assertion.

But notice that *this* sense in which a conversation might be governed by knowledge-implicating norms is not one such that the *complex* communicative exchange, qua the kind of thing *it* is (*viz.*, a *conversation*), is epistemically norm governed over and above the simple *aggregation* of the epistemic norms that govern the discrete speech acts that make the conversation up.

Even if we suppose the individual speech act components of a conversation (in the {Q +A} example above) are governed, respectively, by the knowledge norm of inquiry and the knowledge norm of assertion, is there any reason to think that conversations, *as such*, might answer to any kind of more complex, knowledge implicating norm?

Remember, conversations (taking the minimal Gricean idea as illustrative) are in essence just "communicative exchanges". The below are all conversations:

> Conversation 1 A: "France is a country." B: "I am hungry" A: "Spain is a country."
> Conversation 2 A: "Huh." B: "Eh?"
> Conversation 3 A: "How's it going?" B: "How's it going?"

These are all conversations in the sense that they are communicative exchanges. None is epistemically impressive. Is any defective *qua* conversation in a way such

---

[7] These examples in (1) and (2) are due to Willard-Kyle (forthcoming).
[8] For some discussion here, see Willard-Kyle (2023).

that, e.g., any kind of candidate knowledge norm governing conversations as such would capture this intuitive defectiveness *independent* of the aggregate sense in which the constituent speech acts might be separately knowledge governed?

We might be tempted to think so. Maybe we think that, in Conversation 1, B, simply in virtue of participating in this conversation, should have known to talk about France (or at least in some way acknowledge A's claim about it); or, perhaps A should have known to address B's hunger rather than talking about Spain.

But we actually have too little information to make this kind of assessment. For all we know, the first conversation might have occurred against a background where there was an agreement that A would continue telling B what the countries are up until the point where B mentioned their hunger twice. Similarly, for all we know, in Conversation 2, A was expressing an attitude, and B was querying the context. Without additional information about there being any *further aim* to this communicative exchange over and above the individual aims constituent in each speech acts (an attitude expression, and a question), it's not clear how there would be any overarching knowledge-implicating norm of conversation violated here. The same goes for Conversation 3. Colloquially, "How's it going" is the use of a sentence in the form of a question in order to perform the act of *greeting* someone. Conversation 3 is plausibly just a matter of two individual acts of greeting, the second in response to the first—which very plausibly might have been the (exhaustive) purpose and extent of A and B communicating at all here.

What the brief look at minimal and *prima facie* epistemically unimpressive conversations 1–3 suggests is this: without clear information about what a conversation's *purpose* is, (regardless of how such a purpose would be established—this is some thing we'll take up in the next section), we aren't in a position to work out whether any kind of knowledge-implicating norm would potentially govern particular communicative exchanges *as a conversation*. The most we can do (absent such information about conversational purpose) is normatively assess the individual speech acts featuring in the conversation relative to norms that might govern those specific acts (e.g., the knowledge norm of assertion, the knowledge norm of inquiry, etc.). And this is so even though these conversations seem to be unimpressive epistemically.

4 Conversations and Shared Intentions

Call a conversation an *aimed conversation* where the participants in the conversation have a goal that they intentionally pursue, together, by means of speech acts. Paradigmatic aimed conversations are those where interlocutors are *thinking to a purpose*, such as the purpose of, together, *figuring something out*. A conversation with this aim would involve thinking to a purpose insofar as it involves thinking to a *theoretical* purpose: a joint *inquiry*. A toy example of an aimed conversation which involves thinking to a theoretical purpose is a jury deciding together one question: whether p.

A clarification: not all joint inquiries are pursued by means of conversation, at least not in any colloquial sense. Individuals might inquire together, e.g., in cases of *distributed cognition*, where individual tasks are isolated. (Consider here Edwin Hutchins' (1995) example of a ship crew navigating to port, figuring out where to steer the ship, each by doing separate things). So joint inquiry is a wider category than aimed conversation that involves thinking to a (theoretical) purpose.

Another kind of *aimed conversation* involves thinking to a purpose that is *practical*. Here participants in the conversation have a practical goal that they *indirectly* pursue, intentionally, by means of speech acts. Such conversations function as (at least part of) the 'coordination' of coordinated action. A toy example of an aimed conversation that involves thinking to a practical purpose is a conversation in which interlocutors are communicating in order to get medical help. The goal of the conversation might be that of *getting help*.

It is *aimed conversations* that I'll defend as plausibly norm governed. Before looking squarely at what such norms would be, let's pause to clarify in some more detail what would plausibly distinguish aimed conversations (in the sense I'll be interested in, and which will matter for their being norm-governed) from conversations like 1–3 above.

There are two dimensions of such aimed conversations I want to highlight. One concerns the *intentional* character of the conversation, toward its aim, and the other concerns the *shared* dimension by which the aim is pursued by interlocutors through speech acts by which they are thinking, in aimed conversations, *together* to a purpose.

First, regarding the *intentionality* of aimed conversations. Compare the following—first, an unaimed conversation, consisting in a communicative exchange between two individuals, A and B, while waiting in a queue. They might discuss a range of topics. The speech acts through which they think together about these topics might themselves be intentional speech acts. *But*, suppose A is asked afterwards to describe the conversation had with B: A might do this by recollecting how the conversation went in much the same way as a third-party observer might do this. Relatedly: suppose prior to joining the queue and seeing B standing there, A recalls how conversations often go with B and predicts that the conversation will likely be about the weekend's gossip (which it is).

One of the epistemic hallmarks of intentional actions is that the knowledge we have of them in action is, in some important respect, *non-observational*. A famous example of Anscombe's here involves intentionally opening a window. If I intentionally open a window and in doing so happen to cast a spot of light on the wall, I know about the window-opening in a way that is not merely observational, which is how I know about the casting of light on the wall.[9] The kind of aimed conversations I am interested in are ones we'd know about, *as participants thinking together*, in a way that is like how we'd know we're opening a window when we are and not how

---

[9] For discussion of this example in relation to non-observational knowledge of intentional action, see Schwenkler (2012).

like we know it casts a spot on the wall when it does. Secondly, on the non (merely) predictive character of intentional actions. In intentionally ϕing by means ψ (say, hailing a cab by raising a hand) our knowledge of the relationship between the means and end is not merely predictive, as it might be if you observed someone raising a hand followed by a taxi approaching. In intentionally hailing a cab, you have a kind of knowledge with *means-end structure*; you know that you are ψ-ing *in order to ϕ*.[10]

Contrast now a simple jury deliberation about whether p, with our water-cooler conversation described above. The latter, we've seen, is such that our knowledge of how the conversation went would be largely observational, and if it ended up going a particular way (reaching some particular conversational conclusion), we might have predicted that, but we did not at the time know we were making conversational moves *in order to reach that point* whatsoever.

To this point I've suggested *aimed conversations* are intentional in a way that lines up with epistemic features of intentional actions. But even if the individuals each perform speech acts *intentionally* in an aimed conversation, there is also a sense in which aimed conversations (e.g., between two interlocutors) involve *shared intention*—and not merely shared in the sense that the content of each of the individual intentions of each interlocutor is the same.

The idea of a shared intention is central to most conceptions of *coordinated* activity, though its nature is a point of some theoretical debate.[11] For my purposes here, I'll at least note a few of the well-known characteristic *functional* features of shared intentions (setting aside the comparatively thornier matter of how exactly to substantively characterise the nature of such intentions), as developed influentially by Bratman (2013), and register what kind of shape these functional features take in aimed conversations specifically.

On Bratman's view, when two people (A and B) do something ϕ together, with a *shared intention*, each individual has a *participatory intention* that takes the form (on the part of A), that *A and B ϕ*. So if we take a walk together, we each intend that *we* take a walk. And our participatory intentions then structure the way we coordinate activities, plan, and bargain. To give a simple example, if A and B have a shared intention that A and B walk together, and B needs to tie B's shoe, A will stop too and wait. And A's stopping is in order that A and B walk together, etc. Likewise, if A has a strong preference which way to go on the walk, B will (ceteris paribus) agree to go that way (even if doing so is not B's individual preference apart from the participatory intention) in order for both A and B to walk together, perhaps while also expecting that A would do the same for B, for the same reason. In this way, A's and B's shared intentions structure what A and B do (in terms of executing subplans related to the shared intention), how they bargain with each other, when they take a

---

[10] For discussion of how acting intentionally characteristically involves knowledge with means-end structure, see, e.g., Anscombe (1957, §§28–9); Paul (2009, 5); Mele and Moser (1994, 63) and Pavese (2022, 375).

[11] See, along with Bratman (2013) also, e.g., Gilbert (2008, 2009) and Velleman (1997).

walk *together*, with the shared intention that they do this, rather than just walk individually near each other.

What goes for having a shared intention to do something, φ, together, goes likewise for a shared intention to *have a conversation together*. Here though a scope clarification is important. Consider two cases in which A and B share an intention to have a conversation together, and that this intention is a participatory intention in Bratman's sense. It might be that the *content* of the shared intention here is just that *we have a conversation—viz.,* that, for some conversation, X, we have X. This needn't involve any kind of thinking to any particular purpose, theoretical or practical. Compare this again with our toy example of an aimed conversation, where we (together) are trying to *figure something out*, and we use a conversation as a means towards this end. Our participatory intention here will not be that we have *any* old conversation; it is that we *figure out whether p, by means of conversation*—viz., that we have a conversation that achieves that result.

Putting the ideas in this section together, we have now got a grip on some of the key features of *aimed conversations* of the sort that will be of special interest in so far as we can construe such conversations *themselves* (and not just their individual speech act components) as governed by knowledge-implicating norms. In summary: *aimed conversations* are conversations (minimally, communicative exchanges) where participants in the conversation have a goal that they intentionally pursue, together, by means of speech acts. The goal might be theoretical or practical. Participants *intentionally* pursue the goal together in so far as they have participatory intentions that structure their behaviour (e.g., subplans, bargaining) towards that goal. And the *actions* each takes in using speech acts toward bringing about what they share a participatory intention to bring about through conversation (e.g., when thinking to a theoretical purpose, to figure out together whether p), are actions each stands to *epistemically* in a way that lines up with our epistemic position towards our intentional actions generally, in so far as this knowledge is non-observational and known by participants to have a *means-end* structure.

When conversations have the above features, and in particular—when participants have a shared intention to think together (by means of a conversation) to a particular purpose (e.g., settling a whether p question), the purpose toward which they think together intentionally is partly *constitutive* of the kind of thing they are doing by means of speech acts; their conversation is *constitutively* aimed. That the participants are using speech acts to think together toward *that* purpose distinguishes what it is they are doing together from other things they might do together with speech acts, such as have a conversation *for conversation's sake*, or, e.g., for the sake of convincing passers-by they are on friendly terms.

When we are engaged in constitutively aimed activities (chess, baseball, etc.) and someone performs in a way that doesn't accord with the rules of the game, it is appropriate to *point this out*. For instance, if we are playing baseball and a teammate lies down in the outfield to count the grass, we might say "What are you *doing*?" If they reply and tell you what they're doing (counting grass), you would appropriately rejoin with, "But that's now what *we're doing* – we're playing baseball!" The appropriateness of this kind of rebuke is explained by the fact that the shared intention of *playing baseball* together implicates the kinds of subplans, bargaining, etc., that are bound up with any genuine kind of participatory intentions, where counting grass doesn't feature in any plausible associated subplans. And what goes for constitutively aimed activities like baseball goes for constitutively (theoretically) aimed conversations, where interlocutors' participatory intentions are (by means of speech acts) to *figure out whether p*.

Compare here again with the baseball example: if you and I are trying to figure out whether either of us has ever travelled to a country with a non-extradition agreement with the United States, there are several things we need to figure out together in our communicative exchange. We need to figure out which countries actually *lack* extradition agreements with the U.S. We begin alphabetically, and work out that such countries at least include Afghanistan, Algeria, Andorra, Angola, Armenia, Azerbaijan, and Bahrain. We've not been to these, suppose, so we keep going, still unsure if either of us has been to such a country. Suppose that during this process (as we work down the alphabet), you begin telling me facts about Bahrain, given that we have after all just brought it up. I listen politely for a bit, and I'm learning a lot, e.g., that until the third century BC, it was part of the Achaemenid Empire. Although you're telling me things I'm interested in, and which you know, and I'm enjoying this, and you're enjoying this, your speech acts are still criticisable in the same way as, when playing baseball, we might ask the person lying on the ground "what are you *doing*?" Here, I might say also say, "what are you *doing*? *We're* trying to figure out whether we've been to a non-extradition country with the U.S."

Notice that the above rebuke is permissible even when your speech acts, and my speech acts, satisfy knowledge norms individually. That is, even when you know what you say about Bahrain (satisfying the knowledge norm of assertion), and even if I join you in straying from what we're doing (inquiring about U.S. non-extradition countries) by asking follow-ups about Bahrain, while knowing there is a true, complete answer to my question, etc.

With a view now as to how (constitutively) aimed conversations[12] can be norm governed *apart* from the individual speech acts that feature in them, let's turn now to a consideration of how such norms governing these conversations might be, specifically, *knowledge* norms.

5 Conversation and Zetetic Norms

When two people are engaged in a (constitutively) aimed conversation to figure out whether p, they are *inquiring* (into a question) by means of conversation. It is worth registering a point of connection between norms on *inquiry* generally, and the kind norm we'd be in the market to capture on an aimed conversation.

---

[12] That is, of the sort outlined in this section, viz., as when interlocutors think together to a (theoretical) purpose.

Knowledge Norms and Conversation 137

As Jane Friedman (2020) points out, once it's settled that what one is doing is inquiring into whether p, viz., that it is one's aim to figure out whether p, one is thereby committed, by reference to a norm of *instrumental rationality*, to take the necessary means to figuring out what one is inquiring into. Friedman calls this a *zetetic instrumental principle* (ZIP):

Zetetic Instrumental Principle (ZIP): If one wants to figure out Q, then one ought to take the necessary means to figuring out Q.

The idea developed in the previous section bears some similarities to ZIP. Consider the following principle, which codifies the idea captured by the baseball/aimed conversation analogy:

Constitutive aim/Instrumental Rationality (CAIR): When some activity one engages in intentionally has a constitutive aim, then one ought to take the necessary means to bringing about that aim.

When one intentionally goes bowling, one ought to throw at the pin.[13] The 'ought' here that applies to what one ought to do when engaged in an activity that is constitutively aim governed is an *aim relative* ought in the sense that Friedman's ZIP norm is also an instance of an aim-relative ought. Friedman's aim-relative norm on inquiry cashes out the 'aim' in terms of what one *wants* (i.e., where the aim is specifically desire-relative). CAIR is a bit different here; it gives a conditional where what suffices to make it such that one ought to take the necessary means to bringing about a given aim *is that one is intentionally engaging in an activity constitutively governed by that aim.* That, on CAIR, is taken to be sufficient for being such that one ought to take the necessary means to bring about that aim. And to reiterate the 'ought' (as with ZIP) is with CAIR not an all things considered ought, but an aim-relative ought.

CAIR is not about conversations *per se*. The special case of CAIR that will be relevant for generating knowledge norms on (constitutively) aimed *conversations* (with theoretical aims) will be more specific. A first general statement is:

Constitutive aim/Instrumental Rationality – Aimed Conversations (CAIR-AC): When individuals (A, B, ... n) intentionally inquire together into whether p, by means of an aimed conversation, then (A, B, ... n) ought to take the necessary means to figuring out whether p.

Since aimed conversations, in the sense we've characterized already, involve *shared intentions*, we can unpack CAIR-AC more fully, making explicit the connection between shared and participatory intentions.

Constitutive aim/Instrumental Rationality – Aimed Conversations (CAIR-AC*): When individuals (A, B, ... n) intentionally inquire together into whether p, by means of an aimed conversation, then (A, B, ... n) ought to take the necessary conversational means to

---

[13] Note that there are stronger versions of this norm that don't require the 'intentional' caveat. For example, Michael Lynch (2009) thinks that simply by virtue of participating in any activity that is constitutively norms governed, one is thereby committed to pursuing the value of the relevant activity's aim. This, he takes it, explains why simply being involved in the activity of inquiry commits one to the value of truth and to pursuing it.

figuring out whether p, and these means will include those structured by the *participatory intentions* (A, B, ... n) share.

Recall that when we have *participatory intentions* (e.g., I intend that *we* find out whether p, and you intend that *we* find out whether p), these structure how we negotiate, form subplans, bargain, etc., accordingly.

It is not hard to see how the requirement that participants intentionally inquiring together into whether p (by means of an aimed conversation) satisfy *individual* knowledge norms governing speech acts used (as a means to figuring out whether p) will fall out of CAIR-AC*. Consider the following further twist on our previous example case, where we are having a conversation to figure out who has been to a country without an extradition agreement with the US. Now, suppose the conversation includes this exchange:

> A: "Tajikistan is a U.S. non-extradition country, and I've not been there."
> B: "Neither have I. OK, so we still don't know if either of us has been to one. Let's think further. Have you been to Canada?"
> A: "Yes."

Note, for one thing, that interlocutors who fail a *knowledge norm of assertion* will inevitably also fall short by the lights of CAIR-AC*. Tajikistan is a U.S. non-extradition country. Suppose A is confused and *has* in fact been to Tajikistan.

On this assumption, A asserts what A doesn't know because it's false. Making such an assertion is "not" taking necessary conversational means to figuring out together whether p; on the contrary, it would be contravening the goal of figuring out together whether p (whether either has been to such a country). On the contrary, if A asserts "Tajikistan is a U.S. non-extradition country, and I've not been there" knowledgeably, that constitutes taking means necessary (working through these countries together until they figure out whether either has been to one) to figuring out whether p. So A's first assertion "Tajikistan is a U.S. non-extradition country, and I've not been there" looks like one that would constitute a speech act in alignment with CAIR-AC* only if the act itself meets the knowledge norm of assertion.

The analogous point holds with respect to a Willard-Kyle-style *knowledge norm of questioning*—though this point requires some delicacy. When B asks "Have you been to Canada?", B will of course know that this question (framed as such) has a true, direct answer. *If Canada* was not even a country, B would, through asking this question, fail the knowledge norm of questioning and by extension also (by asking a question without a true, direct answer, as would be the case if Canada wasn't a country) fail to be contributing through this speech act to the shared goal of figuring out p, as per (CAIR-AC*).

Importantly, though, in the above conversation, we know that B is (by asking *that* question) clearly *failing* CAIR-AC*, *even though* Canada is a country. So why is this? And does this mean that for one's speech acts to satisfy (CAIR-AC*) it's not enough that they satisfy knowledge norms governing individual speech acts?

The reason that B's question "Have you been to Canada" fails (CAIR-AC*) is that, since Canada *does* have an extradition treaty with the U.S., getting an answer to this question is *useless* towards the aim of figuring out the target question that A and B are pursuing. One might think though that the question asked by use of the sentence "Have you been to Canada" is actually, given the conversational context in which the sentence is used, a question expressing a false presupposition (and thus one that lacks a direct, true, answer)—namely, the question *Have you been to Canada, which is a U.S. non-extradition country?* That qualified question, if asked, actually fails the knowledge norm of inquiry given that that question lacks a true, direct answer, on account of having a false (semantic) presupposition. If the latter is the right way to think about the question asked by B about Canada, then it might seem that what goes wrong when one's speech act fails (CAIR-AC*) is going to be determined entirely by whether one satisfies *individual* knowledge norms on one's speech acts—e.g., on questions and answers.

This, however, is mistaken. To see why, we can easily imagine conversations with questions and assertions that are impeccable by the lights of knowledge norms on those particular speech act types, but which fail CAIR-AC* straightforwardly. In fact, we need just run a twist on our previous sample conversation (supposing A knows what A asserts), and change B's final question to: "Have you been to Canada, *which I know is not a US non-extradition country?*" This question is one that B *knows* admits of a true, direct answer (it lacks any false presupposition—that would be cancelled here by the added qualification)—and yet this speech act is *not* (by CAIR-AC*) actually an instance of taking necessary conversational means to figuring out whether p. It's at best chasing a red herring or stalling, at *worst* (assuming A's been to Canada) contributing to getting the wrong answer to the inquiry they're pursuing together.[14]

6 Limits of Cooperation

It might seem that the sense in which satisfying CAIR-AC* requires satisfying knowledge norms could be specified as a conjunction of satisfying (i) knowledge norms on particular speech acts used (e.g., assertion, questioning) in the aimed conversation; and (ii) Gricean cooperative norms of quantity, quality, relation, and manner. B's question "Have you been to Canada, *which I know is not a US non-extradition country?*", in the context of the conversation discussed above, satisfies the knowledge norm of inquiry while failing to be cooperative via the co-operative norm on *relation*. It is irrelevant to the conversation. So: will individuals intentionally inquiring together into whether p, by means of an aimed conversation, CAIR-AC*, take the necessary conversational means to figuring out whether p *so long as they satisfy (i) and (ii)*, viz., knowledge norms on speech acts and Gricean norms pertinent to the conversation?

---

[14] At least, it would be the wrong result if neither has in fact been to a U.S. non-extradition country. Then by thinking they had in virtue of one of them traveling to Canada, they'd conclude their inquiry incorrectly.

The answer is—for several reasons—'no', and seeing why will be instructive for getting a clearer picture of what kind of knowledge norm is best understood as governing such aimed conversations by means of which individuals inquire together.

Firstly, notice that being cooperative (as per Grice) *conditioned upon* not knowing what is in the common ground is a recipe for failing to take the necessary conversational means to figuring out whether p. Secondly, one could be well intended to be cooperative but *lack the knowledge* for how to do so, in virtue of failing to know *how* the use of speech acts such as assertions or questions could most expediently bring about the aim of figuring out *together* (with one's interlocutor) whether p.

Consider here, by way of comparison, Williamson's view of what's required for a cognitive-practical system to operate well; the gold standard here is *acting on knowledge*; mere lucky true beliefs can sometimes play the same local role in a cognitive practical system as knowledge, and yet the system as a whole still isn't operating as it should. One is acting on less than knowledge.

Likewise, consider that *even if one didn't know how to use* speech acts to bring about their shared aim, one might luckily, along with one's interlocutor, stumble upon the aim of the joint inquiry. Consider the following example inquiry (suppose A and B are pursuing this together):

> Married-Unmarried Riddle: *Alice, Bob and Charles are standing in a line. Alice is looking at Bob. Bob is looking at Charles. We know that Alice is married, while Charles is not. Is there a married person among the three who is looking at an unmarried person?*[15]

A and B are initially flummoxed. They explore (through questions and assertions) whether there is even enough information here to figure out the answer. Then A asks who Charles is looking at. B asks whether Bob is married to either Alice or Charles. These questions are all false leads, in that their answers would be useless to finding out the answer. Suppose a third interlocutor, "C", supplies A and B with a hint: "It doesn't matter whether Bob is married or unmarried." A and B don't know whether to trust C here, but they try this hint out and through a conversational back and forth stumble upon the answer—if Bob is married, he's looking at an unmarried person, Charles. If he's unmarried, a married person (Alice) is looking at him.

A and B didn't appreciate why this hint was helpful, but just blindly followed the lead. In this case, there is a sense in which even when (following the prompt) A and B begin asking questions and making assertions that not only themselves follow knowledge norms, *and* are following Gricean maxims (their answers are all cooperative/useful) they *together* are still not functioning as they should, in a way that is analogous to how a cognitive-practical system is not functioning as it should when acting on merely lucky true beliefs. Similarly, A and B didn't suffice to (as per CAIR-AC*) take the necessary conversational means to figuring out whether p: rather, it was A, B, *and C*—A and B's conversational means employed were, absent C's contribution, insufficient, despite their participatory intentions, to figure this out *together*.

---

[15] See https://codedrills.io/contests/icpc-amritapuri-2020-preliminary-round/problems/the-married-unmarried-riddle#

Moreover, notice that in the above example, A and B fall short of satisfying CAIR-AC* for an important and easily overlooked reason. They are *intentionally* inquiring together into whether p.

7 Know-How and Conversation

A hallmark of action theory holds that even when one intends to ϕ, and then ϕs, it's still an open question whether their ϕing itself qualifies as intentional; in order to do that, viz., in order to *intentionally* ϕ, one's success in ϕing must be controlled in such a way as to be suitably non-accidental. For example, I can form an intention to win an art contest, paint what is an average painting, get lucky and in fact win that art contest. But I didn't *intentionally win the art contest*. At most I intentionally painted, and submitted the art.

One idea of Anscombe's, originally dismissed due to counterexamples by Davidson (1970),[16] but which is regaining popularity, is that doing something intentionally requires knowing *that* you are doing it. This would explain why I didn't intentionally win the art contest; I knew that I was entering, but nothing I did was such that I knew I was winning when I did it. On this Anscombe-inspired way of thinking, acting intentionally is luck or accident precluding on account of the fact that acting intentionally requires acting with *propositional knowledge* and not merely with lucky belief.[17]

There's considerable debate in recent action theory about whether Anscombe's propositional knowledge condition on intentional action (or some version of it) is plausible, or whether this condition is perhaps too strong.[18] Even so, most all sides of these debates are sympathetic to a different kind of knowledge condition on intentional action, one that requires at least *know-how*:

Knowledge-How/Intentionality (KHI): If S intentionally ϕs, S knows how to ϕ.[19]

You don't intentionally pick a lock unless you know *how* to pick the lock. You don't intentionally win the lottery *because* you don't know how to actually do it, you just know how to take a means by which you might then get very lucky and win.

Of course, there is dispute over how to characterize the nature of knowledge how, whether it is propositional or dispositional—at least, that is the way that the debate is often framed. However, for the purpose I'll now explore, this contrast is (as intellectualists about know-how have pointed out) crucially misleading for the following reason: *even if* knowing how to do something is reducible to *knowing a proposition* (e.g., on the Williamson and Stanley (2001) line—this will be knowing, of some

---
[16] Though for a recent causalist approach to (luck precluding) intentional action, see Kelley (2022).
[17] For discussion, see Kearl (2023).
[18] For some recent discussion here, see Piñeros Glasscock (2020); Beddor and Pavese (2021); Paul (2009); Carter and Shepherd (2023); Shepherd and Carter (forthcoming).
[19] See Pavese (2021, §5).

way, w, for you to ϕ, *that* w is a way for you to ϕ), the *way* one has to know this proposition in order to count as knowing *how* to ϕ is special: one must know this proposition under what's called a *practical mode of presentation*.[20] To use a simple example here, consider one's knowledge how to use a pair of pliers. In order for one to know *how* to use the pair of pliers (as opposed to merely knowing how *one* uses pliers), one must be able to *think of using* the pliers as a way for oneself to use them—and in thinking this way you will be essentially disposed to, e.g., reach for them in a certain way, manipulate the handle in a certain way, to a certain purpose, etc.[21]

The matter of how to characterize practical modes of presentation within an intellectualist theory of know-how is itself a matter of dispute, though we needn't delve into this here. What matters for the present purposes is simply this: (i) KHI is almost universally held, and (ii) however one characterizes the nature of know-how in KHI (i.e., regardless of whether propositional attitudes or success-oriented dispositions are taken to be comparatively more *fundamental* in an account of knowing how to do something), we should expect that one will countenance (in one way or another) the importance of success-oriented dispositions to know-how possession.

These points give us a useful perspective to think about how *aimed conversations* themselves (regardless of how complex these are), and not just their discrete speech act components, might plausibly be governed by knowledge norms, or at least, a certain kind of knowledge norm.

The idea, to a first approximation, is that joint inquiry, by means of aimed conversation, is going as it should when and only when interlocutors *knowhow* to do what each has a participatory intention to do. In slogan form: *participatory knowhow is the norm of aimed conversation*; and in the special case of joint inquiry, interlocutors must inquire together through aimed conversation (to find out whether p) only if they actually know how to use speech acts effectively in the service of together bringing about the shared theoretical goal. That is:

> **Aimed conversations/know-how (ACK-1):** Aimed conversations are governed by participatory *know-how*.
> **Aimed conversations/know-how (ACK-2):** Individuals (A, B, ... n) must: intentionally inquire together into whether p, by means of an aimed conversation X, only if A,B,...n know how to use X to find out together whether p.

ACK-1, as a general thesis, is motivated by putting KHI together with a feature of aimed conservations, which is that their (constitutive) aim (e.g., to figure out whether something is so) is grounded in interlocutors' shared participatory intentions. ACK-2 spells out the content of ACK-1 by saying *how* aimed conversations are governed by participatory know-how in the special case of interested to us—joint inquiry by means of conversation—where the aimed conversation has the theoretical aim of (interlocutors) figuring out together whether p.

---

[20] Or, as Pavese (2015) characterizes it, a 'practical sense'.
[21] See also Stanley (2011) for an expansion of this idea.

Along with the above principled motivation for ACK-1 and ACK-2, there are also familiar linguistic data points that speak in favour of participatory know-how as governing aimed conversation. I will mention a few and then register some further payoffs that this idea has.

First, regarding linguistic data points, consider criticizability in connection with norm violation. When someone violates a norm, we expect criticism to be felicitous or appropriate. It is felicitous and appropriate to say, e.g., "But you didn't *know* that p!" if it comes to light that someone asserts that p on the basis of a guess, etc.[22] That said, suppose A and B purport to be intentionally inquiring together, by means of an aimed conversation, into whether a suspect, Mr. X, is guilty. A and B are amateur sleuths and, while they have a lot of evidence in front of them (say, a box of unsorted documents), they have no good idea where to begin, which questions to start with, what points to make salient. A and B take turns reading scattered bits of the documents out loud, making some arbitrary categorizations of what they've learned, asking questions that aren't pertinent, etc. Carrying on this way, A and B might through this conversation end up by a series of very fortunate breaks reaching the conclusion that Mr. X was innocent (which is correct). But the way they proceeded in conversation is still criticisable here. And note that this would remain so even if, towards the end of their chaotic and disorganized conversation, an expert (Sherlock) gave them reliable testimony that Mr. X was innocent, such that each individually then did *know that* Mr. X was innocent. Even so, they are criticisable on account of the fact that they didn't *know how* to do use conversation so as to take the necessary means to figuring out whether Mr. X was guilty, which is exactly what they purported to be doing, intentionally so. They *used* conversation (their scattershot speech acts met minimal conditions for a communicative exchange), and they reached that end, albeit in a way akin to how a lucky locksmith might pick a lock, the intended outcome, by giggling a pin haphazardly in a way that caused it to open.

The fact that the above inquiry via conversation, absent the relevant participatory know-how, is criticisable offers one line of linguistic data for thinking that participatory know-how is the norm of aimed conversation. Another line of linguistic data is the Moore-paradoxicality of first-person assertions that implicate norm violation. For example, it is not felicitous at all for a jury to say they are going to deliberate (via conversation) whether someone committed a crime, but then to add that they don't know *how* to use conversation to figure out such a thing — that they don't know what to say to each other or what to ask, or how talking about certain things might help them make any headway.

Setting aside these linguistic points, note that the idea that, e.g., we should use aimed conversation in the service of trying to figure out whether p only if we *know how* to use conversation to do this, fits neatly with the very idea implicit in aimed theoretical conversation *that we have a shared intention to figure out whether p.* Recall here the two epistemically relevant points that apply to intentional behaviour generally: that our knowledge of what are doing intentionally will be (by the subject

---

[22] See, e.g., Williamson (1996) and for an overview Benton (2014).

of the relevant actions) characteristically both (i) non-observational and (ii) known by participants to have a *means-end* structure.

If I didn't know how to open a window, and just made movements with my arm near the window and hoped for the best, and it happened to open, and then happened to cast light on the wall, I might learn observationally that I both opened the window and that this resulted in light cast on the wall. But, as per Anscombe, when I open the window intentionally, I know that I open the window in a way that I don't know (as I do merely observationally) that my doing so cast a light on the wall. If we are inquiring into whether p by means of a conversation where we satisfy ACK-2 we are *not* like the person who doesn't know how to open the window and learns they did so observationally; and crucially, nor are we like participants in a conversation for conversation's sake and which happens to reach unintentionally the particular denouement whereby those participants learn that Mr. X is innocent. Granted, our conversation might have, for instance, lasted longer than we'd expected, and *that* is something we'd then come to know much like one who intentionally opens the window knows (observationally) that it cast light on the wall. But we would know *non-*observationally that what we are doing is figuring out whether p. This point fits closely with the point about means/end structure: we know we are asking questions, making assertions *in order to* do what we know how to use these assertions and questions to do: to figure out p. Our epistemic position with respect to the connection between our making of these speech acts and our figuring out p isn't the same kind of epistemic position we have simply by observing empirical regularities and inferring an empirical generalisation, e.g., that the making of these kinds of speech acts tends to produce that kind of result, etc. Rather, we know we are using these speech acts as a means to do what we intend to do together (figure out p), viz., we know we are asking and saying what we are asking and saying *in order to* figure out whether p.

In a similar vein, recall the functional point about shared intention. As per Bratman, when you and I have a shared intention that *we* figure out whether p, this shared (participatory) intention is going to structure our bargaining, subplans, etc. Now, just imagine briefly how that bargaining is going if we fail to satisfy ACK-2. Even if you and I are both individually smart enough to evaluate the evidence each of us has at our disposal individually, we still might not know how to structure our conversation together in a way that would facilitate our goal. For an example that brings this point out, consider a conversation between egotistical jurors, ineffective in answering each others' questions, making false assumptions about each others' conversational backgrounds, overemphasizing particular points out of individual ego, not backing down to revisit points, etc. Even if the jurors described here desire and intend to use a conversation to figure out whether the suspect is guilty, *absent know-how* to use speech acts together such as questioning, assertion, etc. in the service of their goal, it's hard to see how their shared participatory intention is going to structure their interactions in a way that will actually lead to their intended *aim*. In this way, satisfying ACK-2 would nicely account for how interlocutors would be in a position to succeed in structuring their bargaining, formation of subplans *in line* with the participatory intention that they share.

Furthermore, consider how the know-how norm under consideration is a natural fit with CAIR-AC*. CAIR-AC* says something about what interlocutors *ought* (the ought of aim-relative, instrumental rationality) to do if intentionally inquiring together whether p by means of an aimed conversation. In particular, what they ought to do is take the necessary conversational means to figuring out whether p. This is something they'll be in a position to do only if they *know-how* to take those necessary conversational means—and so ACK-2 captures this by placing such know-how as a norm on finding out whether p together by means of conversation. In this respect, CAIR-AC* and ACK-2 are complementary normative requirements on aimed conversation, where interlocutors think together to a theoretical purpose.

Finally, consider ACK-2 in connection with individual-level knowledge norms and Gricean norms of cooperation. As the example case involving the Married-Unmarried Riddle suggested, taking the necessary conversational means to figuring out whether p together will involve more (even when individuals have excellent evidence) than just contributing to the conversation via speech acts that satisfy individual knowledge norms governing those speech acts, along with satisfying Gricean cooperative norms. In such cases, as we've seen, interlocutors might still fail to know how to take the necessary conversational means to figuring out whether p. That said, when ACK-2 *is* satisfied, we should expect that individuals will satisfy the relevant knowledge norms governing their speech acts (e.g., questions and answers) as well as Gricean norms of cooperation. Speech that fails such norms (e.g., false assertions, ill-formed questions) simply won't manifest interlocutors' knowledge how to use a conversation to figure out together the question they are inquiring into.

Putting this together: considerations about instrumental rationality, shared intentionality, the epistemology of intentional action, as well as linguistic data (including concerning criticizability and Moore-paradoxical assertions) all point in the same direction: that aimed conversations are governed by participatory know-how, and that we should intentionally inquire together into whether something is so only if we to know how to use conversational means to find out together whether p. These points are reflective of a *know-how* norm on certain kinds of conversations that plausibly entails, but is not entailed by, the satisfaction of more familiar knowledge norms applicable to conversations, and it reveals an important connection between inquiry and a kind of knowledge.

8 Conclusion

Might there be such a thing as a knowledge norm governing conversations and not just their constituent parts? Taking this question as a starting point, I began by laying out a precedent found in Williamson for a complex of thought and action to be governed by a knowledge-(implicating) norm. Sections 3 and 4 argued that a special subset of conversations—(constitutively) aimed conversations—can be norm governed *apart* from the individual speech acts that feature in them. When participants have a shared intention to think together (by means of a conversation) to a particular purpose (e.g., settling a whether p question), the purpose toward which they think together intentionally is partly *constitutive* of the kind of thing they are doing by means of speech acts. Section 5 then detailed a thesis about instrumental rationality that is applicable to interlocutors engaged in aimed conversation in the service of inquiry: when individuals (A, B, … n) intentionally inquire together into whether p, by means of a (constitutively) aimed conversation, then (A, B, … n) ought to take the necessary conversational means to figuring out whether p, and these means will include those structured by the participatory intentions (A, B, … n) share. Section 6 then showed that the above requirement on instrumental rationality of interlocutors inquiring by means of an aimed conversation won't be secured *simply* by interlocutors satisfying whatever (series of) knowledge norms govern individual speech acts in the conversation. Section 7 then defended the idea that aimed conversations are governed by know-how in a way that is not *reducible* to any concatenation of satisfying individual norms on thought and action; the view reached is that individuals (A, B, … n) must: intentionally inquire together into whether p, by means of an aimed conversation X, only if A,B,…n *know how* to use X to find out together whether p. I concluded in Sect. 7 by taking stock of both the motivations and payoffs of this particular way of thinking about the relationship between knowledge and conversation.

Funding Acknowledgement Thanks to the Arts and Humanities Research Council (Grant No. AH/W005077/1, AH/W008424/1) for supporting this research.

References

Anscombe, G. (1957). *Intention*. Harvard University Press.
Beddor, B., & Pavese, C. (2021). Practical knowledge without luminosity. *Mind, 131*, 919–936. https://doi.org/10.1093/mind/fzab041
Benton, M. A. (2014). Knowledge norms. *Internet encyclopedia of philosophy*. https://iep.utm.edu/kn-norms/
Bratman, M. E. (2013). *Shared agency: A planning theory of acting together*. Oxford University Press.
Carter, J. A., & Shepherd, J. (2023). Intentional action and knowledge-centred theories of control. *Philosophical Studies, 180*(3), 957–977.
Davidson, D. (1970). *Essays on actions and events: Philosophical essays* (Vol. 1). Clarendon Press.
Friedman, J. (2020). The epistemic and the zetetic. *Philosophical Review, 129*(4), 501–536.
Gilbert, M. (2008). Two approaches to shared intention: An essay in the philosophy of social phenomena. *Analyse & Kritik, 30*(2), 483–514. https://doi.org/10.1515/auk-2008-0208
Gilbert, M. (2009). Shared intention and personal intentions. *Philosophical Studies, 144*, 167–187.
Grice, H. P. (1975). Logic and conversation. In D. Davidson & G. Harman (Eds.), *The logic of grammar* (pp. 64–75). Dickenson Pub. Co.
Hawthorne, J., & Stanley, J. (2008). Knowledge and action. *The Journal of Philosophy, 105*(10), 571–590.

Ichikawa, J., & Jenkins, C. (2017). On putting knowledge "first". In J. Adam Carter, E. C. Gordon, & B. Jarvis (Eds.), *Knowl edge first: Approaches in epistemology and mind* (pp. 113–139). Oxford University Press.

Kearl, T. (2023). What we know when we act. *Philosophical Studies, 180*(9), 2665–2683.

Kelley, M. (2022). How to perform a nonbasic action. *Noûs.* https://doi.org/10.1111/nous.12440

Lynch, M. P. (2009). Truth, value, and epistemic expressivism. *Philosophy and Phenomenological Research, 79*(1), 76–97.

Mele, A. R., & Moser, P. K. (1994). Intentional action. *Nous, 28*(1), 39–68.

Miracchi, L., & Adam Carter, J. (2022). Refitting the mirrors: On structural analogies in epistemology and action theory. *Synthese.* https://doi.org/10.1007/s11229-022-03462-y

Paul, S. K. (2009). How we know what we're doing. *Philosophers' Imprint, 9,* 1–24.

Pavese, C. (2015). Practical senses. *Philosophers' Imprint, 15.*

Pavese, C. (2021). Knowledge how. In E. N. Zalta, & U. Nodelman (Eds.), *The Stanford encyclopedia of philosophy* (Fall 2022 Edition). https://plato.stanford.edu/archives/fall2022/entries/knowledge-how/

Pavese, C. (2022). Practical knowledge first. *Synthese, 200*(5), 375. https://doi.org/10.1007/s11229-022-03848-y

Piñeros Glasscock, J. S. (2020). Practical knowledge and luminosity. *Mind, 129*(516), 1237–1267.

Schwenkler, J. (2012). Non-observational knowledge of action. *Philosophy Compass, 7*(10), 731 740. https://doi.org/10.1111/j.1747 9991.2012.00513.x

Shepherd, J., & Adam Carter, J. (forthcoming). Knowledge, practical knowledge, and intentional action. *Ergo: An Open Access Journal of Philosophy.*

Stanley, J. (2011). *Know how.* Oxford University Press.

Velleman, J. D. (1997). How to share an intention. *Philosophy and Phenomenological Research, 57*(1), 29–50. https://doi.org/10.2307/2953776

Willard-Kyle, C. (2023). Valuable ignorance: Delayed epistemic gratification. *Philosophical Studies, 180*(1), 363–384. https://doi.org/10.1007/s11098-022-01902-6

Williamson, T. (1996). Knowing and asserting. *The Philosophical Review, 105*(4), 489–523.

Williamson, T. (2000). *Knowledge and its Limits.* Oxford: Oxford University Press.

Williamson, T. (2017). Acting on knowledge. In J. Adam Carter, E. C. Gordon, & B. Jarvis (Eds.), *Knowl edge first: Approaches in epistemology and mind* (pp. 163–181). Oxford University Press.

Williamson, T., & Stanley, J. (2001). Knowing how. *The Journal of Philosophy, 98*(8) https://ora.ox.ac.uk/objects/uuid:1fcf732b-731b-47e6-943d-aaf34905c02a

Norms of Inquiry Conversations: An Essay

Florencia Rimoldi

1 Introduction

This chapter explores the epistemic aspects of conversations, particularly Conversational Inquiries. It questions whether the epistemic norms of assertions and beliefs are the only ones that influence conversational participants and proposes that there are other epistemic norms that operate during these interactions. I argue that, when considering the common goal of the participants, many conversations could be seen as cooperative inquiries with the purpose of producing epistemic goods. Examples of such conversations include understanding disagreements, epistemic deliberations and learning from another person. Finally, I argue for a non-idealized approach to the epistemology of conversations, taking into account the social context and identities of participants to assess the validity of participation in conversations.

2 The Epistemic Aspects of Conversations: The Case of *Conversational Inquiries*

What are the epistemic norms that put pressure on agents that participate on a conversation? Epistemologists have answered this question by almost exclusively focusing on epistemically proper assertions and beliefs. This follows quite naturally from the gricean cooperative model of conversations, being that it always involves

---

F. Rimoldi (✉)
UBA/IIF-SADAF-CONICET, Buenos Aires, Argentina

contributing with relevant information.[1] Studying the epistemic norms of conversation from this perspective incorporates as theoretical resources discussions about epistemic norms of assertion, epistemology of testimony and of justified belief, of disagreement and, at least to some point, the study of epistemic injustices.[2]

Are norms of proper assertion and belief the only epistemic norms that put pressure on participants in conversations? A useful hypothesis to explore is that the answer to this question might be NO, since the agents that participate on conversations can be subjected to epistemic norms that are independent of their participation on a conversation, but still are operative while they get into it. Consider institutional or professional roles, or the epistemic norms that put pressure on agents as inquirers, such that what they can say, do, or how they should react doxastically during a conversation is required not only by their status as participants of that conversation.

A different but related question though is if the discussion given so far is exhaustive. Are epistemic norms that have been the focus of attention of epistemologists the only epistemic norms that oblige or put pressure on agents *when engaged in conversations and because of that*? The answer, I believe, has to do with the approach one takes to conversations. At the most general and idealized level, it doesn't matter which is the specific common purpose of the conversation, and thus the most heterogeneous verbal cooperations fall in the same bag: deciding on a public policy, hiring someone, conflict solving, ice-breaking, democratic deliberation, teaching, and a long list of other items. From that general perspective, the epistemic side of the conversation is most plausibly described as whatever norms stem from the Gricean Cooperativity Assumption together with the assumption that participants in conversations aim at a maximally effective exchange of information (see Grice, 1989, 28). However, if we take a look into the different types of conversations that take place in real life, one can easily see that there are more epistemic dimensions to analyze.

Silva Filho (2023) points in this direction by claiming that such a general view gives place to a mistaken image of conversations as mere transactions of epistemic goods such as true belief, knowledge and justification. Part of his motivation comes from the recognition of a productive aspect of conversations, that cannot be explained by the mutual transmission model. By addressing discussions from earlier philosophers such as Montaigne, Silva Filho argues that when we engage in conversations, in many cases we are best described as inquiring together about some issue, and therefore the correctness or incorrectness of the verbal moves that take place in those practices do not reduce to those of assertion or proper formation of

---

[1] Goldberg (2020) is probably the most salient representative of this strategy.

[2] As an example of this stance, Peter (2021) divides the epistemic norms that govern well-ordered political deliberation between substantive norms and procedural norms. Substantive norms are assimilated to epistemic norms of assertion, and procedural norms "are concerned with how political beliefs respond to higher-order evidence available in the form of contributions from other participants in political deliberation" (Peter, 2021, 402). These involve norms for proper uptake, in terms of proper responsiveness to disagreement and epistemic justice (Peter, 2021, 403–404).

beliefs. Conversations can be productive: their outcome can be new true beliefs, knowledge, or understanding, that no one had before. The interaction he has in mind is that of argumentation: a conversation that takes place in the context of a legitimate disagreement, where participants offer arguments and counterarguments, objections, challenges, and in which the conversation looks less like a transaction and more like a specific means of inquiry.

I believe that if we take this suggestion seriously, argumentation is just the tip of the iceberg. What I want to do in this chapter is to start digging into the iceberg, which implies, as a first step, moving from a highly idealized and general approach to conversations, to a less general and idealized stance, in which one can analyze certain conversations in virtue of their specific characteristics. The first and most important step is to consider conversations by taking into account the shared goal of the participants. By doing this, one can see that, just like argumentation, there are many conversations that are epistemic in a robust sense: Their common goal is epistemic. Because of this, I claim that they can be described as conversational inquiries. In this section I flesh out this idea.

2.1 Defining Conversational Inquiries: Some Examples

Many types of conversations do not have proper epistemic goals. In ice-breaking conversations, conflict solving conversations, democratic deliberations, and many others, although cooperation constrains epistemically how people can validly participate, the goal of the conversation is not truth, understanding, or any other epistemic good, but some other non-epistemic goal (gaining confidence, the resolution of a dispute, the justification of political decisions, etc.,).

On the other hand, some verbal interactions, although epistemically oriented, do not aim at *producing* an epistemic good, but to a transaction or dissemination of epistemic goods. These are typical testimonial exchanges. Ordinary ones, such as asking for directions, but also collaborative and highly sophisticated epistemic enterprises (institutionally regulated or not) in which the distribution of epistemic labor involves mere transmission of items of knowledge, such as science, law, and educative projects. In these cases, the verbal interaction is taken to be only a means for sharing information, and the epistemic "job" is done by epistemically appropriate assertions and epistemically appropriate uptakes.[3]

---

[3] This is a simplification of the epistemological approaches to testimony, that does not make justice specially to productive theories of testimony such as Lackey's (2008). However, the difference between conversations and other verbal exchanges such as testimony is also related to the difference between the nature of testimony (someone says to another person that p), as opposed to the interactional aspect of conversations. Testimonial exchanges that are the object of the most part of epistemologists or testimony are one-direction verbal transactions, and conversations cannot be reduced to a sequence of testimonies. More on this in the last part of Sect. 2.1.

Also, there are some conversations that, like argumentation, are *productive*, in the sense that because of how participants engage in them, epistemic goods are produced or discovered, such as understanding, justification and truth. I call these conversations "Inquiry Conversations":

> An *Inquiry Conversation* (IC) is a cooperative enterprise, whereby two or more participants engage in conversation with the common purpose of *producing* an epistemic good *through* that conversational engagement.

This preliminary characterization distinguishes conversations that have epistemic goals from other types of conversation, and from other epistemically oriented verbal interactions. I would say that there is no need for much argumentation for the existence of such cooperative conversational epistemic enterprises. We engage in them all the time. Aristotle's classification of arguments in *Sophistical Refutations* (1928, 165a38-b8), and specially Douglas Walton's Theory of Dialogue Types (1990, 1998) identify types of verbal engagements that can be seen as specific forms of IC.[4] What I want to do here is to show that the prototypical model of an IC, which is argumentation, is not specific or exhaustive enough in many ways that are epistemically relevant. I'll give plausibility to this idea by presenting, below, some representative (but clearly not exhaustive) cases of IC to show, on the one hand, that ICs are frequently present in our daily lives and, on the other hand, that the heterogeneity they exhibit demands a more detailed analysis about this category of conversation.[5]

Here are the examples:

(a) *Understanding disagreement*

Two people can engage in an IC after finding out that they disagree. When the disagreement is relevant for the participants, and it has no apparent explanation, then engaging in conversation in order to find out the source of disagreement is a common way to proceed. This is what Lackey (2010, 302) calls "full disclosure", and its aim is to find out why the participants disagree. This conversation might become even more challenging once they find out that they share the same evidence and arguments. It is important to notice that this is different from when two people, knowing *why* they disagree, engage in conversation for solving their differences by means of a negotiation that results in a consented decision. The former has an epistemic end (that participants understand/get a plausible explanation of a situation of disagreement) that is intended to be obtained by engaging in conversation. The latter has a practical end (deciding together what to do, given that they disagree).[6]

(b) *Epistemic deliberation*

---

[4] More on Walton in Sect. 3. I want to thank Constanza Ihnen for pointing me towards Walton's work and for very helpful discussion on this paper.

[5] I will address the epistemological relevance of these differences in Sect. 4.

[6] Argumentation takes place also after the recognition of a disagreement, but the dynamics of argumentative conversations and those that aim at understanding the source of disagreement are very different.

In many times, people that share the same evidence and arguments, cannot find a proper explanation of that evidence, or are not yet convinced of which of the alternative explanations is the right one. They might engage in conversation in order to improve their understanding of the evidence and therefore finding out a proper explanation. This can happen in ordinary situations (neighbours, friends, colleagues, etc) when people try to understand a certain relevant event, but also on medical meetings, and prototypically when juries deliberate.[7]

(c) *"Testing" someone's ideas.*

There are at least two different examples of ICs that are relevant here. In both cases, people engage in conversation so that *one of them* gets a better understanding of her own ideas. In both cases the participants pursue an epistemic good, but the epistemic good is agent-oriented. First, think of colleagues, A and B, that are discussing A's ideas so that A can clarify some, or get a better justification for them. In that case, the interaction might take a more "adversarial form". But think also of a student and a professor, engaged in a similar conversation. The assymetrical role of the participants delineates a different interaction.

(d) *Learning from someone.*

There are many examples of these ICs. Teachers and students, witnesses being interrogated, experts explaining something to a court, to legislators, or to public-policy makers, and many other examples from ordinary life. What is common to all these interactions is that the epistemic goal of the interaction is that someone (the student, the judge or jury, legislators, public-policy makers) understands (knows, or has justification for) an issue sufficiently for their purposes, and the interaction (asking and answering) is *crucial* for it to obtain.[8]

Now before theorizing on these examples, in the next section I want to motivate the idea that ICs can be really seen as inquiries and therefore that ICs are subject to a distinct type of epistemic norms.

---

[7] Actually, it is not necessary that they share the same evidence, even if there is exchange of information (and therefore testimony), as long as that is not the only purpose of the conversational engagement, sharing information can be an important aspect of some Inquiring conversations. The dynamics of this conversations is also quite different from that of argumentation, when people have already made up their mind about the issue at hand.

[8] In some specifically fruitful conversations (in therapeutic settings but not only), people can also *learn from themselves*. This happens when through interaction the person can recall some memory that was not accessible, but also when by engaging in a reinterpretation of what happened she can understand better a recollection of events. That these interactions can be epistemically assessed is crucial for some settings such as witness interrogation in legal trials and in criminal investigation. First, because (contrary to what is often assumed) the epistemic agency of an engaged witness can make a substantial difference in what she testifies. Second, and relatedly, because some interactions can be epistemically pernicious. An example of this is testimonial extraction in cross-examination (see Rimoldi & Rovatti, forthcoming), another one what has been coined the "misinformation effect" by Loftus (2005).

3 Are they Proper Inquiries? Some Motivations

Even if we recognize that ICs take place in real life, someone could put pressure on the investigative character of these conversational enterprises. Could these conversations be understood as proper inquiries? Maybe if we assume that all sorts of inquiry must somehow share some relevant procedural features with scientific inquiry, the answer would be "no".[9] However, there is a different approach, that considers that inquiries also include much more mundane attempts to find things out. This is Cassam's approach to inquiries:

> Inquiry is an activity in which we are all engaged at least some of the time. It is by inquiring that we look for answers to our questions, ranging from the trivial ('Where are my socks?') to the momentous ('What are the causes of global warming?'). Inquiry can be more or less effective, that is to say, more or less knowledge-conducive. (Cassam 2019, 7)

There are two things worth noticing here. First, inquiry is not a "success" term, so that many things can be called an inquiry without therefore implying that they are somehow epistemically appropriate. Second, and relatedly, the relevant sense of "inquiry" is quite broad. In this broader sense, we can call "inquiry" to any attempt from an epistemic agent to answer questions, and therefore gain some epistemic good by means of certain activities. So, it seems to me not stretching the word "inquiry" at all, if we say that when two people engage in a cooperative enterprise such as a conversation to obtain some epistemic good by means of that activity, they are inquiring through conversation. This will suffice for the exploratory purposes of this chapter.

In the remainder of this section, I will address the way I think Inquiry Conversations should be assessed epistemologically from a non-ideal inquiry epistemology. I will also say something about the way this assessment is related to the classic debates on epistemology of testimony and disagreement.

3.1 From Inquiry Epistemology to the Study of the Epistemic Norms of Inquiry Conversations

So if certain conversations are proper inquiries, then they are subject to epistemic evaluation in terms of how well they match their epistemic expectations. This evaluation, in terms of how effective they are in obtaining the expected epistemic good, is what has been called by many "inquiry epistemology" (Cassam, 2016, 2019; Alfano, 2012; McKeena, 2023) (See also Hookway, 2003). Here is how McKeena (2023, 14) describes it:

---

[9] In a different but related discussion, this seems to be Haack's assumption when she denies that Legal proceedings are proper inquiries (see Haack, 2009, 13).

The 'inquiry epistemologist' is interested in the activity of inquiry — in how we go about extending our knowledge. They ask questions about the mechanics of inquiry (how do we inquire?). They ask normative questions about inquiry (what is a responsible inquiry like?) and inquirers (what is a responsible inquirer like?). But they are also interested in improving inquiry. They want to make it more effective (better at reaching truth) and more responsible (better at reaching truth in the right kind of way).

Mckeena distinguishes between ideal and non-ideal versions of inquiry epistemology, depending on what aspects of specific inquiries are considered to be epistemically relevant for assessing the effectiveness of the activity as well as to provide some proposals for improvement. The non-ideal approach defended by McKeena incorporates as epistemically relevant such things as the real capacities of epistemic agents, as well as their social and political identities, the power influences that are present in epistemic interactions, the epistemic environments in which inquiries take place, and the way in which epistemic institutions such as science, education and law (among many others) are actually designed. In this chapter, I am interested in sketching how to assess ICs from the perspective of non-ideal inquiry epistemology. I believe that real life conversations have to be assessed from a perspective that does not idealize away the social context and identities of the participants involved, so as I have anticipated, I will explore here a non-ideal approach to ICs.

So how would such a project look like?

The first step would be to take a deeper look into the nature and types of IC, taking into account features that should not be idealized from the perspective of a non-ideal project, such as roles, identities and relations of power. I will briefly do that in Sect. 3. From there, we might expect to find epistemic criteria for establishing the validity of conversational participations, so that we can say that, from the perspective of the inquiry that is taking place through the conversation, a conversational move is appropriate or not. I will sketch how that might be done in Sect. 4.

What I want to stress here is that the conversational contributions that occur in ICs are subject to *distinctive* epistemic norms that emerge from the perspective of taking ICs as inquiries. This means that the epistemic agents involved in ICs are subject to epistemic norms that shall not be confused with epistemic norms of assertion, or epistemic norms of belief.

Jane Friedman (2020) has called these norms "zetetic norms", which she considers to be instrumental norms. For this reason, she called "zetetic instrumental principle" (or ZIP) and which would have the following general (and, as she points out, oversimplified) form:

ZIP If one wants to figure out $Q^?$, then one ought to take the necessary means to figuring out $Q^?$

Where "figuring out Q?" stands for the relevant inquiry-theoretic goal, be it truth, understanding, knowledge, or something else. What is important to notice here is that these norms are different from norms of proper epistemic uptake (Friedman calls them "traditional epistemic norms"), as well as from norms of assertion. One can easily see that they are different since zetetic norms comprise a wider range of actions besides coming to believe and asserting. Moreover, Friedman points out that zetic norms might clash with other epistemic norms.[10] I suspect (just as Friedman does) that a proper understanding of the different epistemic norms that put pressure on us, as real epistemic agents, would imply a different result, in which there is no clash. But, (as she does) I think that solving the problem by denying that norms of inquiry are proper epistemic norms lacks theoretical force,[11] and would clearly not do well with a non-ideal approach on inquiry epistemology which explicitly embraces an instrumental form of epistemic normativity according to which effectiveness in terms of obtaining a certain epistemic goal is reason-giving.[12] Although not thematized by Friedman, in the case of conversations, this opens the question about a potential clash between the zetetic norms of ICs and the epistemic norms of assertion. I will say something about these potential clashes in Sect. 4.

Before leaving this section, in order to get a grip on the specific approach that I am trying to delineate here, it will be useful to compare it with the well-known epistemological approaches to testimony and disagreement. Epistemology of testimony is centered on answering the question of the conditions under which a testimonial belief is justified, or, under what conditions the uptaking of a testimonial belief is epistemically appropriate. This is answered, thus, by taking into consideration the epistemic assessment of beliefs (norms of beliefs) and the epistemic assessment of assertions (the epistemic norms of assertion). As such, it is not a question of what anyone should do as an inquirer. The latter would rather imply assessing the broader range of interactions involved in conversations, and other types of acts, such as questioning, objecting to a previous assertion or remaining silent to it, etc., from the perspective of *inquiry*. It would ask, therefore, a different question: how could we, as inquirers, gain epistemic goods by having conversations with others.

A similar point can be made when taking into consideration the epistemology of disagreement, whose main concern is if, and how much, should we modify our beliefs in the face of disagreement. Again, its main interest is in the epistemic appropriateness of beliefs. When approaching a conversation in which participants disagree from an inquiry perspective, other questions become relevant, such as which conversational moves are appropriate in order to advance the epistemic goal of the conversation.

What I want to do in the following sections is to give a very general picture of how the project of theorizing on the epistemic norms of Inquiry Conversations

---

[10] Her initial example in Friedman (2020) goes like this: When you are trying to find out how many windows there are in a building, and you try to do that by counting them, then you should ignore some information and evidence that is not relevant from the perspective of your inquiry, but from the perspective of epistemic norms of belief (as are usually understood by epistemologists) you should be taking into account in order to pursue your epistemic ends as an epistemic agent (get more knowledge or more truths).

[11] See Thorstad (2022) for a challenging attempt, though.

[12] See McKeena (2023) for the details of this depiction if inquiry epistemology, which nevertheless shares a lot of familiarity with naturalist approaches to inquiry. Kukla (2021) speaks directly in terms of a naturalist-non ideal epistemology; Broughton and Leiter (2021) describe naturalist epistemology in terms quite similar to non-ideal epistemology.

would look like, so that we can assess conversational moves epistemically from the perspective of inquiry. For this, in the following section I will address the nature of ICs and the relevant conditions that need to be specified in order to assess them epistemically, from the perspective of a non-ideal inquiry epistemology.

4 The Nature of Inquiry Conversations

Lackey (2006, 2008) argues that when theorizing on testimony we should not confuse two different (but interrelated) projects, namely, that of understanding the nature of testimony and that of understanding how testimony can have epistemic import. Besides preventing epistemologists of illegitimately confusing both projects, what is of interest here is that an answer to the second question must take into account what testimony is, and this is not different in the case of the epistemology of conversation. So a natural first step in the project of understanding the epistemic aspects of ICs is to spend some time exploring the subject independently of their epistemic virtues or vices. This, of course, has been done by epistemologists as Goldberg, which takes a Gricean stance on conversations. Because of this, I will first synthetize some of the most salient features of Grice's work on conversation.[13] This is, the study of ICs as linguistic practices, and then move to what the Gricean picture makes about ICs. After this, I will consider Walton's work on Dialogue Types to understand the relevant features of ICs that should be considered from a non-ideal perspective.

4.1 A Gricean Framework

As already mentioned, the aspects of conversations that could be relevant here could be those related to cooperation and the principles that guide conversations. Grice understands conversations as a form of cooperative behavior whereby participants satisfy their interests by following principles or maxims of rational cooperation. Grice's interpretation of the general cooperation assumption ("Make your contribution such as is required...") is that it is just a means-end principle generalized to "concerted enterprises" (Grice 1989, 369). But with the informational assumption in place (the assumption that participants aim at a "maximally effective exchange of information") one can see how the principles or maxims follow. Among them are Grice's maxims of quality—further developed by Lewis (1975) into the maxim of truthfulness (and trust)—and relevance, to which Stalnaker (1978) adds a principle of informativeness:

---

[13] It is impossible to mention all relevant participants in this topic, but besides Grice, some classical works include Lewis (1979), Stalnaker (1978), and Sperber and Wilson (1995).

- Truthfulness: say what you believe to be true/have evidence for. Understand what is said as conveying what the speaker believes to be true/has evidence for.
- Relevance: address the topic under discussion.
- Informativeness: do not say what is already part of the common ground.

These three general principles or maxims enjoy a wide acceptance among the Gricean tradition, with theorists differing on the weight they carry as principles guiding competent conversations. Together they delineate what is generally considered a competent, well-run conversation. That is to say, a linguistic engagement whereby speakers make truthful, relevant and informative contributions—in terms of Lewis (1979) and Stalnaker (1978), one could say that the observance of these maxims is part of the conversational background. As such, these principles are meant to rule over most (if not all) linguistic engagements among competent speakers, especially those cooperative enterprises with the goal of solving a coordination problem (i.e., satisfying the varying interests of the parties in the conversation). It is easy to see now how the focus on the epistemic norms of conversation have tended to be in proper assertion and belief formation, that stems from the assumption that in all conversations (independently of specific common goal) there is an epistemic aim, shared by participants, which is the sharing of information.

In the case of ICs, the conversation among various participants is guided by a common epistemic interest or goal, besides the informational goal which is present in all sorts of conversations. This sets up the IC as a specific cooperative exchange, an epistemic coordination problem in search of a solution, which will implicate a new dimension of epistemic evaluation of participants and their conversational turns. But before moving forward in this direction, I want to briefly comment on the alleged incompatibility between Gricean models of cooperation and the analysis of real conversations. This has been famously called "the Non-Cooperation Problem" and is constructed on the apparent clash between the cooperation assumption and the fact that in many real conversational exchanges, we aren't best described as cooperating with each other. So how is the Gricean model supposed to account for these cases?[14]

This question is pressing in the present project, which is non-ideal, and so besides taking into account prototypical examples that, although inspired in real practices, involve cooperative and well-intentioned agents, it is important to understand how these conversations can be epistemically assessed when participants are not best described as cooperating together to get an epistemic good from engaging in conversation, but we would still consider the conversation as an epistemically oriented one. One example of this would be a case of *Learning from someone*: cross-examination. Cross examination is supposed to be the best way of getting the truth (see Wigmore 1923, §1367, 26; Ferrajoli, 1995, 138), it is a conversation, and still, should we really interpret lawyers as aiming at truth or understanding through

---

[14] Berstler (n.d.) tackles precisely this problem of non-ideal conversations. I am very thankful to Manolo García-Carpintero for directing me towards her work and for a very insightful discussion on these topics.

cross-examination? Lawyers aim at making the best case at all costs and are traditionally seen as something like wild animals in procedural cages. So, besides what they cannot do because the law forbid them to, they will and, most importantly, can *validly* do anything to fulfill their (not shared, non-cooperative) aim. So how appropriate is it to say that they are somehow subject to norms of inquiry? Another example, of *Testing Ideas*: Do colleagues in workshops always participate with the intention of helping the one presenting her ideas so that she understands them better?

As a first answer to this worry, I think it is important to understand the common epistemic goal pursued in ICs as a *cooperative* goal. According to Murphy (1993, 285–286), it would be wrong to interpret people that have cooperative goals as pursuing them individually. Cooperative goals are conceived as being promoted by working together with others. So participating in a practice with a cooperative goal does not preclude participants from pursuing individual goals such as winning the case, or embarrassing someone. In fact, that is precisely what makes a cooperative goal a case of a coordination problem. Multiple agents with multiple different interests must coordinate, achieving a common goal and thereby satisfying their individual interests—such is the case of transit and transit laws (see Lewis, 1975). So maybe some candidates to ICs that might seem uncooperative at first sight (such as a cross-examination) are cooperative if properly understood.[15] A second answer would be to emphasize that cooperating with someone does not necessarily involve that the person actually endorses the cooperative goal but that they behave accordingly, even when they both know that they both are non-cooperative.[16]

4.2 Relevant Features of ICs

Another important task would be to gain some understanding on the different types of ICs and their identity conditions. In other words: What are the factors that may affect the specific form an IC might have? In this sense, Walton's theory of dialogue types (Walton, 1989, 1990, 1998; Walton & Krabbe, 1995) is of much interest, since this theory (that has its roots in Aristotle's typologies of reasonings in dialogical contexts), offers a way of identifying dialogue types (which are conversational exchanges) according to the types of commitments that are in place (propositional

---

[15] There's more to say, of course, to understand the case of cross-examination and, in general, the part's relation to the epistemic aims of the legal process. See Marrero (2016) for a coherent explanation of their role as compatible with epistemic ends.

[16] Epistemically, this would mean that we are not assessing internal states but actions. So just as a scientist can be a good inquirer even if she thinks that science is not truth-oriented, the conversational moves of a participant of an IC can be epistemically appropriate even if he doesn't really care about the epistemic goal pursued. What is important, though, is that in all cases, they are participating as if they had the epistemic goal, and due to epistemic competence (not to some random cause). Also, see Berstler (n.d.).

or not) and, more specifically, to (i) the initial situation of the participants, (ii) the main goal of the exchange, (iii) the participants' aims and (iv) the side benefits:

> The interlocutors can, in fact, have different kinds of goal, which influence the nature of the interaction. In this conception of dialogue, we can notice that the two parties have individual goals (for instance, in a negotiation, getting the best out of the discussion), and an "interactive" goal (for instance, always in a negotiation, making a deal). The individual goals are sub-ordered to the collective goal, or purpose of the communicative interaction. A type of dialogue, in this perspective, is a normative framework in which there is an exchange of arguments between two speech partners reasoning together in turn-taking sequence aimed at a collective goal (Walton, 1998, 30).

Walton makes the relevant distinction between collective and individual goals, and one can find in his classification two dialogue types that are properly epistemic: inquiry and information seeking. Inquiry is defined as (i) starting from general ignorance; (ii) having a growth of knowledge and agreement as its main collective goal; (iii) finding a proof or destroying one as a possible individual goal, and (iv) prestige, experience and funds as possible side effects. Information seeking, on the other hand, is defined as (i) starting from personal ignorance; (ii) having spreading of knowledge and revealing positions as its main goal; (iii) gaining, passing on, or hiding personal knowledge as possible individual aims; and (iv) agreeing, venting and gaining prestige as possible side benefits (Walton & Krabbe, 1995, 66).

Although I believe his general approach is a great tool for understanding many important normative aspects of conversational moves, I see two limitations with Walton's taxonomy. Both are probably related to the fact that he was not engaged in the specific study of epistemically oriented conversations (what I have been calling ICs) and also to the fact that (as he recognizes), dialogue type theory is an idealized classification that needs further development through empirical research on real dialogues.

The first problem I find is that it is not exhaustive enough, since it leaves out many exchanges that are properly ICs.[17] If we recall the examples (a)–(d) from Sect. 1.2, *Epistemic deliberation* might be seen as an inquiry dialogue, and *Learning from someone* is clearly assimilated to information seeking. However, *Disagreement dialogues*, although they could be seen as a type of Inquiry, do not actually fit in Walton's characterization of inquiry dialogues:

> Inquiry is a collaborative investigation aimed at proving a proposition, or showing the impossibility of proving it. The focus is on propositions, not on interests such as negotiation, but the starting point is not a conflict of opinion, such as the persuasion dialogue, but an open problem. The inquiry can be successful only when all participants agree upon the same conclusion at the end. In this type of dialogue, similar to the Aristotelian demonstration, the premises of an instance of reasoning are supposed to be better established than its conclusion. The goal is not to show the plausibility or acceptability of a proposition, such as in the persuasion dialogue, but to prove that a proposition is or is not part of the established knowledge. Moreover, retraction of commitments is not generally permitted. (Walton & Macagno, 2007, 104)

---

[17] Even if we acknowledge that the basic two types involve subtypes that intend to cover different cases.

At the same time, *Testing someone's ideas* does not fit clearly in any two types. And we could imagine many other examples that are intuitively inquiry conversations that are not covered by these two basic types.

The second problem is that it does not seem to get the relevant identity conditions right. It doesn't seem that the side benefits of the conversation are a relevant variable. At the same time, whilst the expertise and knowledge of the participants are considered relevant for identifying dialogue subtypes, other asymmetrical relations, generated by institutional roles or social statuses, are not covered by his suggested criteria. He does seem to recognize as relevant that the goal might be agent-oriented (for instance, "to turn the layman into an expert himself") when analyzing subtypes. And although he does make some room for contextual considerations such as institutional restrictions, there is no consideration of environmental characteristics such as what is at stake, time limitations, and if the situation is oppressive or hostile. I am not saying that classifying and naming all these types and subtypes of ICs is worth doing. What I am saying, is that all of these factors can affect how ICs in the real world take place, and therefore we can use them to understand and explain why two conversations that share many conditions turn out to be very different at the end. Also, from a non-ideal perspective, they should not be quickly idealized away.

So here are what I believe to be the relevant factors that should be taken into account when systematizing ICs for the epistemic assessment of conversational moves and agents from the perspective of the inquiry:

Participants:	Social and political identities
	Professional or institutional roles
	Type of collaboration (Symettrical or equal/ Assymetrical or unequal)
Epistemic environment:	Methodological issues
	Dialectical issues
	Semantic issues
	Economic issues
	Degree of hostility
Epistemic Goal:	Type
	Agent-orientation

In the following section, I will describe what these parameters are and how they affect our intuitive epistemic assessment of certain conversational moves by using a few examples and discussions from related topics in epistemology. In this section I have tried to use the study of conversations as linguistic practices and the theory of dialogue types to show the importance of discussing the nature of ICs before getting into their epistemological assessment. How to understand cooperation and the principles involved in conversation, and understanding the identity conditions of different ICs is something that has to be done before trying to assess ICs and moves within them from an epistemological view.

5 The Epistemic Assessment of ICs

A good place to start sketching what would imply to apply non-ideal inquiry epistemology to ICs is to ask what sort of things might be assessed from this perspective. A standard answer would be (i) conversational moves, (ii) participants as epistemic agents/inquirers, and (iii) the conversation as a whole. In this section, I will focus on the assessment of conversational moves, hoping to expand in future work the other two types of assessments.[18] My aim here is not so much to give answers, but to show how this could be done.

This project aims to give substance to epistemic (zetetic) norms for a well-ordered IC, such as the following:

(Don't) Assert p (if and) only if…
(Don't) Make a question (if and) only if…
(Don't) Object/challenge another participant's assertion (if and) only if…
Reply to a challenge/Question only when it is (not in-)valid/legitimate

What I will do in this section is to show that our intuitive assessment of moves within conversations are sensitive to the features of conversations enumerated in the last section, in terms of participants, environment and its epistemic goal. This will give at least some motivation to pursue a non-ideal approach to ICs. To advance my strategy, I will stress, by the combination of examples and previous work on related issues, that the norms of ICs are sensitive to the roles, social and political status of participants, to some features of the environment, and to the agent-orientation of the epistemic goal pursued. I will also say something about the relevance of the recent expansion of epistemic goals. Let's begin with considering this situation:

> COLLEAGUES. Liza and Federico are colleagues. For several years they have worked on similar topics within epistemology. Federico has asked Liza to help him improve his arguments in favor of a certain view. They engage in a conversation in which Federico puts forward his main strategy and Liza tries to dig in some respects which are not so clear, or solid, by asking questions and offering challenges and objections. At the same time, she identifies good claims and offers additional reasons or ways of improving the quality of his reasoning, by making assertions and suggestions.

This is a case of *Testing Someone's Ideas*. A first step for addressing this conversation from the perspective of Inquiry Epistemology would involve identifying the relevant features signaled as relevant in the last section. At a first glance, we can see that the professional roles and status of Liza and Federico put them in a symmetrical relation. Their social and political status are left underspecified, but even if we added the information that Liza responds to she/her pronouns and Federico to he/him pronouns, we would need much more information to establish the relative social and political position of both. As to the epistemic goal, one could think that it

---

[18] Notice that conversations as a whole can not only be assessed not only in token terms but also, and more interestingly, in type terms. One could take a look at a specific interview and try to analyze how successful it was as an inquiry, but also, one can study regulated types of conversations (interviews, interrogations, cross-examinations, etc.) and try to assess the rules that guide them, eventually offering suggestions for improvement.

might be justification or understanding, and that the agent to whom those epistemic goods are oriented to is Federico, so that even if Liza gets some justification or understanding from the conversation as well, that is not constitutive of the success of the inquiry. On the other hand, if Federico fails to do so, the conversation would have not succeeded as an inquiry. I will address the status of participants and the idea of agent-oriented epistemic goals later. I will start now by considering the features of environment to which epistemic norms of IC seem to be sensitive to.

5.1 Features of the Environment

Imagine that Federico, when giving his reasons in favor of his view regarding, say, epistemic vices, asserts the following "Pragmatic encroachment is the best explanation for cases like Hannah and Sarah". Imagine also that Liza finds this claim epistemically problematic, not only because she, as a professional philosopher, knows that that there is disagreement about what is the best explanation of cases like Hannah and Sarah, but also because she actually defends that contextualism is the best explanation.

Should Liza say something? Should she object in order to set the record straight about that issue?[19] Now, in this situation, it seems quite clear that she should say something. Not only because of what she and Federico are cooperatively pursuing through conversation (i.e., that Federico gets justification or understanding) but also because it seems that for the usual informational purposes of all sorts of conversations, she is epistemically obliged to say something. There is no clash here between zetetic norms and norms of assertion.

However, we could start seeing some differences if we take into account some features of the conversational context or the environment in which the conversation takes place, to which I would like to say that zetetic norms are clearly sensitive to and leave open the question of whether norms of assertion are also sensitive in this regard. Let me explain myself.

It might be reasonable to think that when two people legitimately disagree, both acquire ipso facto the right to challenge the belief of their interlocutor, and at the same time the obligation to defend their position rationally. It may be that facing legitimate disagreement creates these normative pressures. Even if for non-epistemic reasons one should contextually refrain from objecting (not wanting to come as hostile, not having time, not wanting to loose the other person's attention, and a million other reasons) the epistemic right or duty to do it is still in place.[20] However, the effectiveness of Inquiry Conversations (their capacity of generating epistemic goods) depend crucially on how assertions, challenges, replies, and other

---

[19] Here I am taking Lackey's characterization of objections as "assertions that are added to a conversational context with the aim of correcting the record" (Lackey, 2018, 36).

[20] Lackey (2018) reacts negatively to these explanations, and claims that we don't always have the duty to object to assertions that we find epistemically problematic.

conversational participations are interlocked. If every assertion that is epistemically problematic gives the other participants ipso facto a "zetetic" right to challenge them, then maybe the conversation ends up being ineffective. In this sense, not every challenge, expression of doubt or objection will have legitimacy for the purposes of the investigative conversation, and therefore not every challenge, expression of doubt or objection will generate normative zetetic pressure, or an epistemic obligation to respond, on the addressee.

Let's illustrate this with two modifications of the context that point to different directions.

5.1.1 First Modification

What Federico asserts, in the context of supporting other theses, is "Seeing is a factive verb". Now let's imagine that Liza in fact defends, and with good reasons, the opposite, so she considers the assertion as epistemically problematic.[21] However, there is nowadays a consensus in the philosophical contemporary discussions that seeing is factive.

Even if there is a sense in which she should object, it is clearly not what she should do when considering the epistemic purpose of the conversation. Federico would not gain a better understanding of the subject matter (recall, his arguments are on epistemic vices) by engaging on a discussion with Liza about the factiveness of 'seeing'. On the other hand, if she did object Federico would be reasonably dubious on whether it is a good idea to engage with Liza in that direction. I believe Williams's contextualist matrix is quite useful for understanding the features of context that might explain this.[22]

His own view is composed of a substantive statement about the nature of epistemic facts (the denial of realism) and an explanation of the contextual matrix that allows articulating the specific form of local epistemic practices.[23] I want to separate

---

[21] Liza's situation depicts my own experience. See Rimoldi (2014). I have now learned that sometimes it is not only pointless, but also inappropriate, to make an objection every time I hear someone assert that seeing is a factive term.

[22] Williams (2007) draws interesting and subtle relationships between skepticism, traditional theories of knowledge, and relativist positions, by virtue of the recognition of theoretical assumptions that they seem to share. The commitment to the idea that the domain of epistemic facts is theoretically tractable in the same way that a natural kind is, implies the idea that the positive epistemic status (knowledge, justification, etc.) of beliefs is similar to the possession of a natural property. The abandonment of realism would not imply giving up claims to knowledge or justification, nor claims to objectivity. Rather, it would imply recognizing that there are only epistemic or justification practices (i.e., practices of giving and asking for reasons), and that only within them can there be local justification, understood as a positive epistemic status obtained by virtue of there being positive reasons to favor of what is affirmed or what is believed.

[23] He calls this position "wittgenstenian" contextualism. There is a part of this idea that seems to be exegetical: Wittgenstein in *On Certainty* could be stating something like this. But it is also a position that has its own traction and that draws on some Wittgensteinian insights to take shape. One of the ideas that we could take from Wittgenstein to understand the image that remains after the

both issues because what interests me here is to leave the substantive thesis in suspense and deploy the characteristics of the contextual matrix offered by Williams (2007) to understand the way in which the epistemic evaluation of conversational moves is subject to contextual variation.

When we think of a conversation as a cooperative investigation oriented towards an epistemic good, the matrix proposed by Williams (2007) allows us to adequately explain the dimensions of the legitimacy of conversational moves. And this (as Friedman points out) can be useful as an inquiry epistemology, regardless of whether one wants to maintain a privileged, autonomous, or invariant space for epistemic norms that regulate epistemically proper assertions (or objections) and the formation of beliefs.

To better understand what I mean, it is convenient to return to Williams' treatment of the assumption of a Claimant-challenger asymmetry:

> *Claimant-challenger asymmetry.* Whenever knowledge is claimed, the burden of justification lies with the claimant. If I represent myself as knowing that P, I invite you to ask me how I know. There is nothing you have to do, or no way that things have to be, in order for you to have the right to enter a challenge. (Williams, 2007, 99)

Williams argues that the apparent intuitive character of this principle lies in a prior commitment to epistemological realism: If you have a belief that you intend to hold, then you must exhibit what positive property it has to fall under the category of "justified" or "knowledge". This challenge is for those who have the belief or at least for the theorist of knowledge.

In opposition to this, the denial of realism allows us to understand that the affirmation of asymmetry is not intuitive. As an alternative, Williams proposes, following Brandom, a default-challenge model:

> Although it may seem plausible at first, the principle of claimant-challenger asymmetry will be false if challenges are themselves subject to justificatory constraints, so that challenges that fail to respect them are not legitimate. And if challenges are not always legitimate, there need not always be some positive property on which a claim's positive epistemic status supervenes. Maybe it is justified because, in the circumstances, there is nothing to be said against it. Globally, justification will not conform to a positive authorization model but will exhibit what Robert Brandom calls a 'default and challenge structure.' Positive authorization will be an essentially local phenomenon. Contextualism accepts this structure. But it adds that the factors influencing default justification are contextually sensitive." (Williams, 2007, 99–100)

We can use this framework to understand when a conversational move in an IC is considered zetetically legitimate or valid, and when it is considered invalid.

---

denial of epistemological realism is that of practices as a substrate of evaluations and norms, in this case epistemic. Epistemic practices take place in multiple contexts, giving rise to local epistemic assessments that, while having a family resemblance, would not be legitimate to unify into something like a general theory of justification, which would offer general rules for good reasoning, or determine once and for all the epistemic principles that say when a proposition is supported by a given set of evidence, and against which all local practices could be compared, explaining the extent to which they approach that ideal, and considering the factors "not epistemological" that explain why they move away from it (for example institutional, time, ethics, power, etc.).

According to Williams, the context is determined by everything that is presupposed in it and, therefore, will not be questioned. This is not very different from the usual characterization of conversational contexts (See Goldstein & Kirk-Giannini, 2022). The assumptions of a context may be explicit or poorly articulated, and include methodological or epistemic principles, as well as particular taken-for-granted propositions. What is interesting of this framework is that it seems to be well equipped for understanding inquiry contexts. Williams points out four types of factors that shape the context in which we are and, therefore, determine its presuppositions.

I will illustrate them for the context shared by Liza and Federico:

Semantic factors: They determine the type of questions that are intelligible for a context and which are not. The type of factors that belong to this group is very diverse. It can include mathematical truths, but also certain perceptual judgments. What distinguishes these factors is that, if they were questioned in the context determined by them, we simply would not know how to interpret that questioning. For example, it would be difficult to understand what exactly Liza would be questioning if she asked Federico "How do I know you are really Federico"?

Methodological or disciplinary factors: They determine the type of questions that are legitimate based on the research we are carrying out, and which direction it follows. The presuppositions in this case constitute those issues from which we can advance in the search for knowledge. In this sense, and as Wittgenstein (1969, §163) observed, not questioning the general legitimacy of documentary sources is a methodological necessity of, for example, historiographical research on Napoleon's last years. And in the context of Liza and Federico, both analytic philosophers, it would not be legitimate to question the general reliability of thought experiments. This would prevent the investigation regarding epistemic vices from being carried out. As Williams (2007, 102) states, "Methodological needs are presuppositions that stand in such a way that questioning them would lead us to question the entire competence of the form of research that they allow. In this sense, they determine the disciplinary meta-context of such practices...".[24]

Dialectical factors: They determine the type of questioning that is appropriate based on the current state of the discussion in the disciplinary field, the available techniques, the relevant findings and problems, etc. That is, they are all those presuppositions that are not excluded from the field of research itself, and that given its current state are not questioned, but could be questioned later. Science is full with examples of shifts in this sense. To name just one, for a long time it did not

---

[24]t is important to note that these presupossitions are not "untouchable", even within the same context. Over time, assumptions can be empirically corroborated (if research that presupposes p yields important results, then p is considered indirectly validated to some degree) and also questioned and revised on an individual basis. What cannot be done without changing context is to question all presuppositions at once.

make sense to question the idea that neurons do not regenerate once the organism is fully developed, and this was a premise of multiple research, until 1998 when new research led to the discovery of neurogenesis. In the philosophical context, I believe that this is precisely the case of seeing as factive. It's not like it has always been a settled matter, and maybe it will be challenged in the future. But right now, the current state of the discussion seems to be this one. In the specific context of the conversation, discussions that have been already settled would be another clear example.

Economic or pragmatic factors: These assumptions fundamentally (although not exclusively) determine the standards required to consider a proposition sufficiently justified, and therefore, which challenges related to this are legitimate and which are not. Time and resource considerations come into these factors. Similarly the pragmatic, ethical, and moral consequences of accepting p, and, equally important, of accepting p and being wrong about p come also into the picture. These are well-known and contested positions for epistemic norms. In the case of inquiries, however, it is quite clear that these considerations are in place.

Before moving to the next section, I want to briefly consider a different feature of the context: its epistemic hostility.[25] For this, I will make a second modification to the case of Federico and Liza a little bit, so that it depicts a very realistic situation that often takes place in philosophy departments.

5.1.2 Second Modification

As it happens, Liza and Federico are very competitive, they usually seek for the same resources, courses, and even students. The realistic turn, though, is that although competitive and sometimes even unfair to each other's ideas, they usually mean well, and respect each other enough so that they really get into the conversation cooperatively and oriented towards the same epistemic goal as before. The crucial aspect to consider is that the department in which they both work is an inhospitable epistemic environment regarding a topic which, although quite specific, is highly important to the conversation. Most members of the department are not only defendants of non-ideal epistemology but are highly prejudiced about ideal epistemology, and as a result they are misinformed about the latest discussions on ideal epistemology and have false beliefs about it. They don't care enough to be updated, and they tend to diminish the value of new discussions coming from an ideal perspective. Federico is part of the ideal epistemology minority. Now there are two situations to consider here. First, Liza is part of the majority. When Federico claims that close-mindedness is never an epistemic vice, supporting his case by an appeal to the possibility of virtues and vices being subject to pragmatic encroachment, Liza suggests emphatically that he should work much more on the case, since she thinks

---

[25] See Battaly (2018) for a depiction of hostile epistemic environments.

there is a stronger argument to be made in the opposite direction (she points to Battaly (2018) and McKeena's (2023) arguments in this topic).

Now there is a fine line to be drawn here, between good advice and stubbornness from Liza. There is a chance that she is actually making a good suggestion, and there is also a chance that she is just being stubborn and prejudiced, by not even giving a chance to Federico's arguments, partly because of their professional relation, but mostly because of the epistemic environment they are in. Without further details, one would say that Federico should suspend judgement and not take her observations very seriously (i.e. should not react epistemically to the challenge) because he is in danger of not getting what he wants from the conversation (justification or understanding), and risks loosing the support he had for his argument.[26] This judgement is specially supported by considerations of the epistemic environment they share, so that if it was not hostile (other things being equal) he should probably take Liza's suggestion into account and engage in a discussion with her on the topic.

So, besides semantic, dialectical, methodological, and economic/pragmatic factors, there are also other features about environment, such as its epistemic hostility/hospitability, to which norms of inquiry conversations appear to be sensitive to. The worst epistemic scenarios we can conceive of in terms of hostility come into mind when we take into account social and political relations of power and the identities of epistemic agents that stem from them. Let's move on to that discussion.

5.2 *Roles, Social and Political Status, and the Expansion of Epistemic Goals*

I want to briefly illustrate here how some features of the two other factors I've considered as relevant for assessing ICs, i.e. participants and epistemic goals, could get into the picture: The participant's social/political identities and roles, and the agent-orientation of epistemic goals.

Let's start with the last issue. ICs can be oriented towards understanding something (or answering questions such as "why p?") but take very different forms depending on whether participants are aiming at understanding for all of them, or just one of them. So the same discussion as COLLEAGUES, but in the context of a reading group with the purpose that everyone gets a better understanding of some philosophical discussion (in this case, Federico's ideas), might be assessed differently. For instance, maybe Federico should engage when he gets what he suspects is unfair criticism, because he is not aiming just to improving his own epistemic situation, but also Liza's. This point can be generalized to all sort of ICs, so that we can have some plausible reason to think that the assessment of conversational moves and actions is sensitive not only to the epistemic goal (justification, truth,

---

[26] This is precisely the point of Battaly (2018) and Mckeena (2023, 112–121).

understanding, or something different such as epistemic reparation) but also to its agent-orientation.[27]

When considering participants roles and social/political identities, we can add a much more robust dimension to the sort of hostile environments we can envisage (which are the most interesting and challenging ones). Also, we can see that they affect our assessment of conversational moves. Consider a different situation from that of COLLEAGUES:

> STUDENT-PROFESSOR. Ivana is working with Liza on her undergraduate thesis. They meet in Liza's office to discuss some of the main arguments Ivana wants to put forward, so that she can understand better some of her ideas and improve her justification. Ivana puts forward her main strategy and Liza tries to pick on some poijnts that are not so clear, or solid, by asking questions and offering challenges and objections. At the same time, she identifies good claims and offers additional reasons or ways of improving the quality of his reasoning, by making assertions and suggestions.

Although Federico from COLLEAGUES and Ivana from STUDENT-PROFFESSOR have the same epistemic purpose, the epistemic norms of the conversation are sensitive to the asymmetry between Ivana and Liza that stems from their academic roles and levels of expertise. Thus, Liza would do wrong in objecting to everything she finds epistemically problematic, precisely because she would put Ivana's understanding and epistemic flourishing at risk. And I am not talking here about assertions such as "Pragmatic encroachment is the best explanation for cases like Hannah and Sara", but of much more subtle points, that she would properly object to Federico, but would be off when directed to Ivana.

A different example comes from positions of power that stem not only from professional but also social standing. Consider a cross-examination of a black man who is trying to explain that he ran away from a police officer because he felt his life was in danger. When subjected to the usual "hard" questioning and tactics of control that are part of regular cross-examinations, one can see that if he remains silent after a challenge such as "why did you keep running, even when the police officer explicitly said he wouldn't harm you", it is a proper move within the context, not because he has nothing to say, and certainly not because he concedes the point. It is just that he knows that if he answers, he will probably be misunderstood and misinterpreted in a way that is contrary to the epistemic aim of the conversation.[28]

Although there is much more to say about the ways in which goals and participants affect the epistemological assessment of conversational moves in ICs, I think that for the purposes of this essay, I have sufficiently shown that they do, and why it is so.

---

[27] Lackey (2018, 2022) argues quite impeccably in favor of two related points: First, that we have epistemic duties that emerge from an interest in epistemic goods not for ourselves but for others, as individuals and as communities, and second, that the epistemic scope of evaluation is not restricted to beliefs, but also actions.

[28] Black and Brown flight is well documented as a case of hermeneutical injustice in law by Gonzales Rose (2021, 386–387).

6 Concluding Remarks

In this chap. I have tried to advance the hypothesis that there are specific conversations that can be properly understood as inquiries, what I dubbed Inquiry Conversations (ICs). I have argued that as such, they are subject to specific epistemic norms that stem from their being proper inquiries. Thus, I have tried to motivate the idea that those norms are zetetic, and that the study of those norms would be the subject of an inquiry epistemology project.

I have also tried to show how this project would look like from a non-ideal perspective, by taking into account the nature of ICs, and by showing how norms of ICs are sensitive to features of the context, the participants, and the epistemic goals pursued. I have been working with a few examples or types of ICs, that are not meant to be exhaustive nor complete. In fact, there is much more to say on every topic I have described, but the purpose of the chapter has been to motivate and generate interest in a project, much more than it has been to make substantive claims within it.

Acknowledgement This chapter was written within the framework of the research projectsUBACyT-20020170100783BA and PIP-CONICET-11220150100807CO.

References

Alfano, M. (2012). Expanding the situationist challenge to responsibilist virtue Epistemology. *The Philosophical Quarterly, 62*, 223–249.
Aristotle. (1928). *On sophistical refutations* (Loeb classical library). Harvard University Press.
Battaly, H. (2018). Can closed-mindedness be an intellectual virtue? *Royal Institute of Philosophy Supplement, 84*, 23–45.
Berstler, S. (n.d.). "The Grice is Right: Grice's Non-Cooperation Problem and the Structure of Conversation."
Broughton, G., & Leiter, B. (2021). The naturalized epistemology approach to evidence. In C. Dahlman, A. Stein, & G. Tuzet (Eds.), *Philosophical foundations of evidence law* (pp. 25–39). Oxford University Press.
Cassam, Q. (2016). Vice epistemology. *Monist, 88*, 159–80.
Cassam, Q. (2019). Vices of the mind. *From the intellectual to the political*. Oxford University Press.
Ferrajoli, L. (1995). *Derecho y Razón. Teoría del garantismo Penal* (P. A. Ibáñez, A. Ruiz Miguel, J. C. Bayón Mohino, J. Terradillos Basoco, R. Cantarero Bandrés, Trans.). Trotta.
Friedman, J. (2020). The epistemic and the zetetic. *Philosophical Review, 129*, 501–536.
Goldberg, S. (2020). *Conversational pressure: Normativity in speech exchanges*. Oxford University Press.
Goldstein, S., & Kirk-Giannini, C. D. (2022). Contextology. *Philosophical Studies, 179*, 3187–3209. https://doi.org/10.1007/s11098-022-01820-7
Gonzales Rose, J. (2021). Race, evidence, and epistemic injustice. In C. Dahlman, A. Stein, & G. Tuzet (Eds.), *Philosophical foundations of evidence law* (pp. 380–394). Oxford University Press.
Grice, H. P. (1989). *Studies in the way of words*. Harvard University Press.
Haack, S. (2009). Irreconcilable differences? The uneasy marriage of science and law. *Law and Contemporary Problems, 72*(1), 1–23.

Hookway, C. (2003). How to be a virtue epistemologist. In M. DePaul & L. Zagzebski (Eds.), *Intellectual virtue: Perspectives from ethics and Epistemology* (pp. 183–202). Oxford University Press.
Kukla, Q. (2021). Situated knowledge, purity and moral panic. In J. Lackey (Ed.), *Applied epistemology* (pp. 37–68). Oxford University Press.
Lackey, J. (2006). The nature of testimony. *Pacific Philosophical Quarterly, 87*, 177–197.
Lackey, J. (2008). *Learning from words: Testimony as a source of knowledge*. Oxford University Press.
Lackey, J. (2010). A Justificationist view of disagreement's epistemic significance. In A. Haddock, A. Millar, & D. Pritchard (Eds.), *Social epistemology* (pp. 298–325). Oxford University Press.
Lackey, J. (2018). The duty to object. *Philosophy and Phenomenological Research, 101*(1), 35–60.
Lackey, J. (2022). Epistemic reparations and the right to be known. *Proceedings and Addresses of the American Philosophical Association, 96*, 54–89.
Lewis, D. (1975). Languages and language. In *Philosophical papers volume 1* (pp. 163–188). Oxford University Press, 1983a.
Lewis, D. (1979). Scorekeeping in a language game. In *Philosophical papers volume 1* (pp. 233–249). Oxford University Press, 1983b.
Loftus, E. F. (2005). Planting misinformation in the human mind: A 30-year investigation of the malleability of memory. *Learning & Memory, 12*, 361–366.
Marrero, D. (2016). An epistemological theory of argumentation for adversarial legal proceedings. *Informal Logic, 36*(3), 288–308.
McKeena, R. (2023). *Non-ideal epistemology*. Oxford University Press.
Murphy, L. B. (1993). The demands of beneficence. *Philosophy & Public Affairs, 22*, 267–292.
Peter, F. (2021). Epistemic norms of political deliberation. In M. Hannon & J. de Ridder (Eds.), *The Routledge handbook of political epistemology* (pp. 395–406). Routledge.
Rimoldi, F. (2014). ¿Puede el conocimiento ser un estado mental? *Analisis Filosófico, XXXIV*(2), 171–201.
Rimoldi, F., & Rovatti, P. (forthcoming). Extraer la verdad del testigo adversario: ¿es el contraexamen un mecanismo epistémicamente justo? In P. Rovatti (Ed.), *La defensa penal: cuestiones fundamentales*. Centro de Estudios Constitucionales de la SCJN de México.
Silva Filho, W. J. (2023). Para uma epistemologia da conversação. In B. R. G. Santos, L. Chichoski, & L. Ruivo (Eds.), *Novos rumos da epistemologia social* (pp. 24–56). Fi.
Sperber, D., & Wilson, D. (1995). *Relevance: Communication and cognition* (2nd ed.). Blackwell.
Stalnaker, R. (1978). Assertion. In *Context and content: Essays on intentionality in speech and thought* (pp. 78–95). Oxford University Press, 1999.
Thorstad, D. (2022). There are no epistemic norms of inquiry. *Synthese, 200*. https://doi.org/10.1007/s11229-022-03896-4
Walton, D. (1989). *Informal logic*. Cambridge University Press.
Walton, D. (1990). What is reasoning? What is an argument? *Journal of Philosophy, 87*, 399–341.
Walton, D. (1998). *The new dialectic. Conversational contexts of argument*. University of Toronto Press.
Walton, D., & Krabbe, E. C. W. (1995). *Commitment in dialogue*. State University of New York Press.
Walton, D., & Macagno, F. (2007). Types of dialogue, dialectical relevance and textual congruity. *Anthropology & Philosophy, 8*(1–2), 101–119.
Wigmore, J. H. (1923). *A treatise on the Anglo-American system of evidence in trials at common law* (Vol. III). Litlle, Brown & Company.
Williams, M. (2007). Why (wittgenstenian) contextualism is not relativism. *Episteme, 4*(1), 93–114.
Wittgenstein, L. (1969). *On certainty* (D. Paul, & G. E. M. Anscombe, Trans.). Harper.

Deception Detection Research: Some Lessons for the Epistemology of Testimony

Peter J. Graham

1 Introduction

The central case of knowledge through testimony is knowledge through face-to-face conversation. There are many tasks for the social epistemology of conversation. One is to explain why it is we know and justifiably believe as much as we do through conversation. Another is to provide useful recommendations for how to do better.

Since whether we learn from another person through conversation turns, for the most part, on whether their message is sincere and competent, social epistemologists stand to learn a great deal from what social scientists have learned about the sincerity and competence of senders, on the one hand, and the abilities of receivers to judge the sincerity and competence of senders, on the other. If the extent of our knowledge through conversation and how we might do better are both empirical questions, one ought to know the relevant empirical science.

In this chapter I review some of the major discoveries from the extensive literature on *deception* and *deception detection* in the field of communication studies. I shall focus on sincerity, tabling competence for another occasion. I begin with our folk theory of deception and deception detection before showing that a few well-known social epistemologists seem to assume that our folk theory is correct and well confirmed. It turns out that it's neither. Or at least that is what the science shows.

I am not the first epistemologist to investigate this literature. Indeed, since Kourken Michealian's (2010, 2013) and Joseph Shieber's (2012) papers, the existence of this literature has become well-known. Though I admire Michaelian and Shieber's papers, I have found that readers of Michaelian and Shieber can come away without an appreciation of the nuts and bolts of the experiments, of their strengths and their limitations. I also find that they do not do as much as they could

P. J. Graham (✉)
University of California, Riverside, CA, USA
e-mail: peter.graham@ucr.edu

to show that the results of the science are ecologically valid, that what the science discovers in lab experiments really does carry over to what happens when we talk to another person outside of the lab. On both dimensions, I hope to do better.

And so, my goal in this chapter is to look closely inside some of the studies on deception detection to convey how they work and why they show what they show, with an eye towards persuading the reader that the results in the lab carry over to real life.

I then take the opportunity to apply some of the lessons learned from the literature to Elizabeth Fricker's influential work in social epistemology (see Fricker, 1994, 1995, 2004, 2006a, b, 2016, 2017a, b, 2024). If anyone has turned our folk theory of deception into a sophisticated social epistemology of conversation, it's Elizabeth Fricker. Again, I'm not the first to apply the science to Fricker's theory. But I have both a novel interpretation of her work to present, as well as what I take to be more compelling criticisms than others have offered. Though I may not be the first to apply the science to her theory, I may be the last.

The lessons learned apply not only to Fricker's work, but to any social epistemologist who relies on our folk theory. It's time for every social epistemologist to not only know of but also to understand the major findings of the last 50 years of deception detection research.

2 What Is the Folk Theory of Lying?

What is our folk theory of how senders behave when lying? And what is our folk theory of how we catch a liar?

Charles Bond led a team called The Global Research Team to answer these questions. The team surveyed 4840 subjects in 43 languages across 75 countries. The results were published in "A World of Lies" (Bond et al., 2006). The team conducted two surveys. In the first, the team asked the open-ended question "How can you tell when people are lying?" Here are the most common answers:

- Liars avert their gaze. (63.7%)
- Liars are nervous. (28%)
- Liars display incoherent speech, body movements, facial expressions, speech errors, logical inconsistencies, blushing, pauses and delayed speech. (15–25%)

Notably, fewer than 1% mentioned motivational factors by the sender ("I can tell they are lying because I know they have a motive to lie") or sender confessions of dishonesty ("I know they lied because they later confessed").

In the second study, the team then asked closed-ended questions, using some of the answers provided by the open-ended survey. Here are the most common answers:

- Liars avert their gaze. (71.5%)
- Liars shift posture more than usual, touch and scratch themselves, talk too much (66%)

- Liars act nervous (50%)

According to the results, the folk believe liars have an easily detectable dishonest demeanor. Folk wisdom then includes the idea that we reliably catch liars by observing their demeanor.

Why do people believe that liars (senders with the intent to deceive or mislead) behave like this? Because we have a folk theory of the liar's state of mind. We believe that liars know it is wrong to lie, and they fear detection (Bond et al., 2006, 70). That is why they avert their gaze. Their fear also means they will be more physiologically aroused, which causes nervous behavior. That's why they will act unusually, shift more than usual, or talk too much. Our folk theory so far then has at least these three elements:

- Lying is emotionally arousing.
- These emotions produce observable cues that the sender is lying; lying leaks and so lying well is difficult.
- Receivers use these cues to detect that the sender is lying; we reliably catch liars by detecting their deceptive demeanor.

3 Social Epistemologists Agree

Various social epistemologists agree with our folk theory. Jennifer Lackey (2008, 183) says that ordinary adults possess "ample inductive evidene" that nerviousness, lack of eye contact, and confused behavior are signs of "incompetence, insincerity, and unreliability" (Lackey (2008, 89–90, 181).

Miranda Fricker (2007, 41) says:

> …a hearer responsibly judges a speaker to be…insincere…owing to the fact that the speaker avoids looking her in the eye, frequently looks askance, and pauses self-consciously in mid-sentence as if to work out his story. The speaker's behavior justifies the hearer's judgement…as it fits an empirically reliably stereotype of testimony…an empirically reliable rule.

Sanford Goldberg (2007, 322–323) tells a story about Ralph who offers about as much false testimony about the New York Yankees as true testimony. When he asserts false beliefs, his…

> … assertions are reliably associated with characteristics, which (in other speakers) are highly correlated with false (or at least unreliable) testimony: there is a certain lack of confidence exhibited in his speech on those occasions, he can't look you in the eyes, etc. But it is also true that his assertions expressing [true] beliefs…are reliably associated with characteristics which (in other speakers) are highly correlated with true (and reliable) testimony: on these occasions he expresses himself with a good deal of confidence, he can look you in the eyes, and so forth.

Goldberg (2007, 323) then imagines Mary who "can and does discriminate the relevant features of Ralph's…testimony, and that she correctly takes them for what they are, namely, indications of the (likely) truth or falsity of his testimony". Goldberg accepts the folk theory.

Stephen Reynolds (2002, 156) says lying effectively is hard; that's how we know someone is lying: "… we can reliably tell whether someone believes what they are saying by their manner of speaking and by their facial expression. A convincingly told lie is a difficult achievement."

Elizabeth Fricker (1994, 150) agrees:

> Expert dissimulators amongst us are few, the insincerity of an utterance is very frequently betrayed in the speaker's manner, and so is susceptible of detection by [our] quasi-perceptual [deception monitoring] capacity.

How does such monitoring work? The hearer perceptually represents various behavioral cues. Certain cues are "betraying signs that…the speaker is insincere." Other cues are signs of sincerity. The perception of these cues then leads the hearer to form concious judgments about the sincerity of the speaker, e.g. "I didn't like the look of him" or "Well, she seemed perfectly normal." Such monitoring allows individuals to recognize and respond to potential signs of dishonesty or insincerity during conversations. Fricker thinks this capacity for monitoring is "usually found in ordinary hearers, at least to some extent" (cf. Fricker, 1994, 150, 2006a, 624). For Fricker, as for the folk, we detect deception by observing signs of deceit in real-time.

Elizabeth Fricker, Miranda Fricker, Sanford Goldberg, Jennifer Lackey and Steven Reynolds all accept the folk theory. And that's just a sample. I'm sure I could find many other philosophers saying the same things. Even David Hume in his essay "On Miracles" notes how we doubt testimony when delivered "with hesitation, or on the contrary, with too violent asservations" (Hume, 2007, § 7). The folk and philosophers agree. Though lying is commonplace, we reliably detect deception and thereby defeat its destructive force on testimonial uptake.

Or do we? The social psychology of lying and lie detection tells a very different story.

4 How Do Psychologists Study Deception Detection?

Social psychologists have conducted lab experiments designed to answer the following two questions:

1. Are there nonverbal and paraverbal behavioral cues to deception? Are there observable things humans do when lying that they don't do when telling the truth?
2. Can we reliably tell in real time when someone is lying or telling the truth by observing their nonverbal and paraverbal behavior? Are we good at detecting deception through observation in real time?

How do social psychologists investigate these questions? Most of the research in this area relies on controlled lab experiments. In the typical experimental paradigm, senders tell truths and lies, often to a second party (receivers). Most often the senders are college students, but not always. In most such experiments senders tell 50% truths and 50% lies–the base rate of honesty over lying in the experiments is typically 50/50–where the experimenters know when the sender was honest or lying. The senders' messages are recorded, either in writing, by audio, or by audio and video. A third group of perceivers (judges) then read, listen, or watch the sender's messages. Perceivers are told that some of the senders' messages are honest and some dishonest, but not the percentage. The perceivers then judge which are honest and which are dishonest, like taking a true/false test. Sometimes the receivers (the sender's audience) and the perceivers (the judges of honesty) are the same person. Many studies recruit professionals tasked with detecting deception, like police detectives, federal agents, or fraud investigators as judges.

When it comes to the types of lies being told, the experiments vary in several ways. Senders may tell truths and lies about their beliefs, opinions, or about personal facts. They may tell truths and lies about their personality. They may tell truths and lies about personal traumatic experiences. They may tell truths and lies about whether they are currently experiencing some physical pain. They may tell truths and lies about a movie they have just watched. They may observe a group of strangers and then tell truths and lies when describing these people. Senders may look at art they like and dislike. They may tell artists whose art they liked that they liked it, and then tell artists whose art they did not like that they liked it. They may tell truths and lies when simulating a job interview. They may participate in mock crimes and then tell truths and lies about what they did. Sometimes senders have time to plan their lies, sometimes they do not. Any number of other possible variations are possible, depending on the resources and creativity of the experimenter.

These experiments differ on whether the lie was sanctioned or motivated. In a sanctioned lie, the experiment instructs the sender to lie; the lie was "sanctioned" by the experimenter, even if not sanctioned by the receiver. In a motivated lie, the sender has a special motivation to succeed at deceiving the receiver; they want the receiver to believe their lie.

These two features (sanctioned, unmotivated) are often present or absent together in these kinds of experiments, but not always. An experimenter may sanction a lie but provide a motivation for the sender to convince their receiver. For example, an experimenter might provide the sender an additional reward for successfully deceiving the receiver.

There are also experiments without experimental subjects as senders. Instead, these studies rely on video footage of unsanctioned lies outside of experimental contexts. The videos are then shown to perceivers to judge in experimental settings. For example, perceivers watch interrogations of crime suspects, where the experimenters know from later discovered evidence whether the subject was lying or telling the truth. Or perceivers watch videos of public figures–celebrities, politicians, or even people are in the news for just a brief period–who make honest and dishonest reports, where again the experimenters know which was which. All these lies are unsanctioned and involve high stakes where the speakers are often motivated to cover up their transgressions, produced outside of the lab in "ecologically valid" conditions.

To answer the first question, social psychologists observe the ways honest and dishonest senders behave in their experiments. They then code many of the various aspects of their behavior. These aspects of their behavior are called *cues*. Some commonly studied cues include eye gaze, foot and leg movements, friendliness, head movements, involvement, nervousness, plausibility, posture shift, pupil dilation, response latency, speech errors, speech hesitations, speech rate, vocal pitch, vocal tension, and smiling. Researchers then look for correlations between these cues and honest and dishonest messages, where the cues are largely studied one at a time. Does this que or that que co-vary with honesty or deception? Just as snoring reliably correlates with being asleep, and yelping reliably correlates with being in pain, are there ways humans behave when lying but not when telling the truth, and vice versa?

To answer the second question, experiments score the accuracy rate of perceivers in their experiments when the perceivers judge the messages of senders as honest or dishonest. If we are reliable judges, based on observing the behavior, both verbal and non-verbal, of whether a sender's message is honest or dishonest, then we will judge most honest messages as honest and most dishonest messages as dishonest.

Experiments along these lines began in the 1940s and continue to this day. Sternglanz et al. (2019, 303) report over 1250 peer-reviewed articles on deception or deception detection. Fortunately, several meta-analyses of studies have been published. Meta-analyses not only summarize a larger literature—just like a literature review—but they have increased statistical power over individual studies and do not rely on a particular research team or an experimental paradigm, unlike individual studies.

5 Are We Good at Detecting Deception in Real Time?

What does the experimental literature tell us about the second question? Can we reliably detect deception in real time by observing verbal and non-verbal behavior, at least in experimental settings? The answer is no.

The most discussed meta-analysis supporting this conclusion comes from Charles Bond and Bella DePaulo (2006). According to Google Scholar as of February 2024, this paper has been cited 2686 times. Their meta-analysis covered 206 studies from 1941 to 2006. It included 6651 messages from 4435 senders judged by 24,483 perceivers. In over 75% of the studies, perceivers classified messages as lies or truths. Bond and DePaulo (2006, 230) report that the perceivers performed slightly better than chance. "Across hundreds of experiments," they conclude, "typical rates of lie-truth discriminations are slightly above 50%. For the grand mean, 54% is a reasonable estimate." Their results confirm the results of earlier meta-analyses (e.g., DePaulo, 1980; Kraut, 1980). The larger the number of participants in a study, the more likely it approaches the 54% mark, with standard deviations across studies usually being very small: overall performance for most people ranges around 54%. When classifying messages in real time in experimental settings as honest or dishonest, where perceivers are informed in advance that some of the messages are honest and others are not, where half of the messages are truths and half are lies, average accuracy is consistently slightly better than chance.

If that's the average, are there some cases where there are important exceptions? Not really. Bond and DePaulo find that the medium or modality (written, audio only, audio-visual) does not make a major difference, that sender motivation to be believed does not make a major difference, that planned versus spontaneous lies does not make a major difference, and that professional experts like police officers, detectives, secret service agents, parole officers or judges were not significantly any better than college students. The slightly better than chance result was the same result, within a percentage point or two, for all of these variables in sender, medium, and perceiver. This result even holds up when adults judge deceptive messages from children (Gongola et al., 2017).

Bond and DePaulo's conclusion has held up over time. Surveying all the meta-analyses up to 2017 in his 2020 book, Timothy Levine (2020, 40–41) finds that the 54% accuracy rate is a robust finding across variables across meta-analyses (see also Sternglanz et al., 2019). Levine (2010, 41) even remarks that "the slightly-better-than-chance accuracy finding appears to be among the most reliable, consistent, and robust findings in all of social science."

Are you confident of your own ability to detect deception in real-time? Are you sure you possess an effective monitor that would pick up on reliable cues and issue the judgment that the speaker can't be trusted on the occasion? Can you just look someone in the eye and know whether they are lying? In an earlier meta-analysis, DePaulo et al. (1996) reviewed 2972 perceivers, including college students and law enforcement personnel, and found that there is no correlation between confidence and accuracy of deception judgments.

The results provide rather strong grounds to believe that outside of an experimental setting, were a speaker to lie to you, you would not be able to reliably tell in real time based on observing their nonverbal and paraverbal behavior that they were.

Perhaps you are unconvinced. People sometimes pushback as follows:

> Sure, in the experiments the judges cannot tell who is lying and who is not. But your experiments don't reflect real life. All you have done is instructed a bunch of college students to utter sentences they don't believe (so the lies are sanctioned) in a context where there's no cost for saying something false (so the stakes are very low) where the students don't care if they are believed (so their lies are unmotivated). Indeed, the students are probably just acting, not really telling lies. You've then asked total strangers to judge whether these amateur actors are trying to mislead. How is that ecologically valid? How does that tell us anything about deception detection in real life? Just because we're no good in lab conditions like these doesn't show that we are no good in real life.[1]

As Elizabeth Fricker (2016) puts it, just because a massively deceived brain-in-a-vat never gets anything right through perception doesn't mean that you and I never get anything right when relying on perception in normal conditions; so just because we are bad in the lab doesn't show that we aren't highly effective at detecting deception

---

[1] See Frank and Feeley (2003), O'Sullivan (2008), O'Sullivan et al. (2009), and Burgoon (2015).

in real time through observing non-verbal and paraverbal cues in normal social environments.

But many of the experiments included in the meta-analyses pass such demands for ecological validity, as I've already noted. The Bond and DePaulo meta-analysis included studies for all kinds of lies. It included studies of murders' lies and lies that could harm children (Vrij & Mann, 2001); lies to lovers and deceit during criminal interrogations (Anderson et al., 1999; Davis et al., 2005); and lies in naturalistic deceptive interactions and jurors' credibility judgments (Bond & DePaulo, 2006, 232). For a more recent meta-analysis that reaches the same conclusion, see Hartwig and Bond (2014).

There's also a folk theory case against this defense of folk theory. We all know the story of Desdemona who was so nervous she would not be believed when she honestly told Othello she was not having an affair with Cassio that she looked like a liar. The story rings true because it is a common experience. Evidence from the literature backs it up. Honest people who are afraid of being disbelieved often come to resemble the stereotypical liar. "The accumulated evidence suggests that people who are motivated to be believed look deceptive whether or not they are lying." (Bond & DePaulo, 2006, 231). If motivation to be believed doesn't correlate strongly with lying, motivation doesn't ground a reliable cue for lying.

Bond and DePaulo (2006, 231) then conclude:

> Despite decades of research effort to maximize the accuracy of deception judgments, detection rates barely budge. Professionals' judgments, interactants' judgments, judgments of high-stakes lies, judgments of unsanctioned lies, judgments made by long-term acquaintances—all reveal detection rates within a few points of 50%.

Though surprising to common sense, we are just not any good at detecting lies in real-time by observing their non-verbal and paraverbal behavior.

Still not persuaded? Then read on, as I'll provide further reasons for thinking these studies really do tell us how bad we are outside the lab.

But before I do that, I want to review whether there are any valid nonverbal or paraverbal cues, cues we could use to catch a liar, if we only knew what they were and how to track them.

6 Are There Observable Cues to Deception?

If we are not any good at distinguishing truths from lies in real-time by observing the nonverbal and paraverbal behavior of senders, is that because there are no such cues to lying that are reliable, or is that because we don't pick up on the real cues? And if we don't pick up on the real cues, would training make a difference? Could we learn to become reliable detectors of deception in real time by observing aspects of the verbal and non-verbal behavior of our interlocutors. The answer to these questions is no.

Recall the #1 cue to deception according to folk theory: liars avert their gaze. Across all types of lies, is this true? Do liars reliably avert their gaze? According to a meta-analysis of cue studies by DePaulo et al. published in 2003, the clear answer is negative. Citing DePaulo et al. (2003), Levine (2020, 24) says:

> … even though avoiding eye contact is the most widely held belief about deception, it holds no actual utility as a deception cue. Its validity is zero. The amount of eye contact is unrelated to actual lying.

"The gaze aversion belief," Levine (2017, 7) concludes, "appears to be a complete myth." Similar results hold up for the other cues consistently cited by our folk theory (DePaulo et al., 2003).

Are there any reliable cues *not* mentioned by our folk theory? Are there some other cues that are the *real* cues? Levine's review of four meta-analyses of cues leads him to think there might be two: higher vocal pitch and increased pupil dilation. They are, he thinks, small but real cues to deception. However, he also notes that the pupil dilation results are based on only four studies, and the pitch findings are based on twelve, but that the effects were heterogeneous across those twelve studies. So, we have some reason to think these are real cues, but not conclusive. And even then, the results are only a statistical trend across many different senders and many different lies. When it comes to pitch, for example, lies are slightly more highly pitched than honest statements, all else being equal (Levine, 2020, 20, 306).

Perhaps the default explanation for our poor performance in detecting lies, consistent with our folk theory, is that we pay attention to the wrong cues (Miller & Stiff, 1993). If we paid attention to these valid cues, would that solve our problem?

No, for they are too weak. The effect size is just too small. Ask yourself this. Suppose you know that, on average, males are taller than females, which they are. And then you learn that two people are in a room, and one is taller than the other. Is that enough to know that the taller one is male and the shorter female? Not at all. So, suppose you learn that someone has told you something and their pupils are slightly dilated. Does that tell you they are lying? No, for the effect size for these "valid" cues is much lower than your information that males on average are taller than females. Learning that someone has dilated pupils, or a slightly higher vocal pitch doesn't tell you whether they are lying or honest (Levine, 2020, 21). It just tells you, out of a very large pool of speakers, that there is a slightly higher chance they are lying. Even when we in fact respond to "valid" cues, we still don't perform within the slightly better than chance range. Our ability to detect lies in real time is limited by the fact that valid nonverbal and paraverbal cues to deception are not very reliable (Hartwig & Bond, 2014).

What about training? Does that help? For gains in detecting deception by observing valid nonverbal and paraverbal cues in real time, the answer seems to be that the gains are moderate, at best. The results are still in slightly-better-than-chance territory.[2]

What about the ecological validity of these findings? As before, DePaulo et al. note that some of the studies involved real life criminal suspects and lies recorded

---

[2] For meta-analyses on training studies, see Frank and Feeley (2003), Driskell (2012), and Hauch et al. (2016).

in the news. It wasn't all college students. Second, DePaulo et al. note (as we will see further along in the section about the prevalence of lying), that for most lies of everyday life the sender is not motivated to succeed, nor covering up a transgression, nor entirely free to say whatever they would like. Further, for most lies of everyday life, the receiver does not challenge the sender, but either accepts the lie as truth or ignores the lie and lets the moment pass (DePaulo et al., 2003, 100). And though DePaulo et al. found a slight difference in gaze aversion for lies about transgressions from lies that were not about transgressions, so that he folk theory of lies about transgressions is not entirely in error, the effects were, in real terms, too small to make any real difference (DePaulo et al., 2003, 102, 104). Pupil dilation is a better cue. And that cue, we've just learned, won't tell you what you want to know.

7 Levine's Cheating Experiments

"No, no, no" you say, "this only shows that there are no reliable cues to deception in the lab. Outside of the lab there are plenty of valid cues. None of this is ecologically valid. Outside the lab we do just fine detecting deception in real time."

What kind of experiment would count as ecologically valid? At least for Elizabeth Fricker, it would have to involve attempts to deceive from a speaker who "deceives with bad faith, for her own gain, due to her own motives, with the attendant fear of discovery, and feelings of guilt" (Fricker, 2016, 116). Fricker here echoes some researchers in the field (Zuckerman et al., 1981; Miller & Stiff, 1993; Burgoon & Buller, 1996). The liar would have to be motivated and the stakes for the liar would have to be high (Harwood, 2014) for that is when cues to deception leak (Eckman & Friesen, 1969).

But as I have already pointed out, many of the experiments already included in the meta-analyses have these features. Just think of the experiments where experimenters took video recordings of criminal suspects during police interviews. Of those who were lying, they certainly satisfied all these criteria. But even so, judges failed to reliably detect who was lying and who was not. When it comes to motivation, for example, in the Bond and DePaulo meta-analysis (Bond & DePaulo, 2006, 2008), the average accuracy for motivated lies was 53.3% and 53.4% for unmotivated lies. Similarly for high stakes, Hartwig and Bond (2014) found no effect. Feeley and deTurk (1998) even found that sanctioned lies correlated with more speech errors and other folk cues than unsanctioned lies. It looks like ecologically valid experiments disconfirm the folk theory.

If all of this is not enough, reviewing Timothy Levine's lab experiments should seal the deal. Levine is one of the leading researchers in this field. Concerned about the ecological validity of lying experiments (Levine, 2018), he devised a sting operation that would strongly motivate the subjects to lie on their own accord to cover up a transgression (Levine et al., 2010a).

Levine had college students enter a lab for a study that they were told was federally funded, sanctioned by the university, and designed to learn about teamwork.

Deception Detection Research: Some Lessons for the Epistemology of Testimony   183

The participant was then paired with a teammate that they were told was another student, but in fact the teammate was a confederate working for the experiment. An experimenter then entered the room, and she told the students they were going to play a challenging game of trivial pursuit. For each correct answer they would receive five or ten dollars.

After the second question, another person would enter the room and tell the experimenter administering the questions that there was an emergency at home, and she needed to come right away to take a call in an office at the other side of the building. The experimenter would then run out and the students could hear three doors loudly closing in succession as the sounds of her footsteps faded away.

Once the experimenter was gone, the partner then suggested cheating. "Aren't those the answers to the questions in that folder right there? Why don't you take a look? That way we could make a lot of money. I think that would be a great idea, but I'll leave it up to you to decide. Either way I'm fine."

After the students have had enough time to look up the answers, the experimenter returns and completes the game. Then after the game, the subject is interviewed by another experimenter and asked, among other things, if the subject cheated. During the interview, all their answers were being video recorded.

There are then four possible answers:

- *Honest denial*, where the subject denies cheating and did not cheat.
- *Dishonest denial*, where the subject denies cheating but did.
- *Honest confession*, where the subject confesses cheating and did cheat.
- *Dishonest confession*, where the subject confesses cheating but did not.

Levine ran 126 students through the first version of the experiment. 96 (76%) did not cheat. When asked, they all honestly said they did not cheat. There were no dishonest confessions. 30 (24%) did cheat. Of those, 18 (60%) lied about cheating—they gave dishonest denials. 12 (40%), on the other hand, confessed.

For those who gave dishonest denials, did they have a motive to cover-up their transgressions? Certainly. They had just cheated on a federally funded experiment. The cheaters knew they were "attempting to defraud a federally funded research project for their own financial gain." (Levine et al., 2011, 382) They knew they had broken the honor code. They also had their own self-image to protect. They had reasons to fear discovery. If they lied, it was in bad faith, for their own gain, due to their own motives, with the attendant fear of discovery.

After the experiment was over, Levine asked those who had not cheated if they would re-record their interviews and falsely confess to cheating. 7 agreed. The result was taped interviews of four kinds: students honestly denying cheating; students lying that they did not cheat; students honestly confessing that they did not cheat; and students lying when confessing to cheating.

Levine then recruited 127 students to watch 27 of the recordings that involved all four kinds of responses and then judge whether the sender lied or told the truth. How accurate were the judges? For the honest confessions, they were right 95% of the time. For the false confessions, they were right 12% of the time. In other words, when people confess to transgression, we believe them, for in fact there is little reason to confess to a wrong you didn't do. So, if they are telling the truth, we get it right. But if they are lying, we get it wrong. The speaker's behavior probably has very little to do with it.

How about the denials? For the honest denials, the judges were accurate 56% of the time, and for the dishonest denials, they were accurate only 53% of the time. When it comes to sorting honest denials from dishonest denials. Performance was only slightly better than chance.

Averaging across all four kinds of messages, average accuracy came in just over 54%.

All told, Levine has run approximately 500 subjects through the game. Approximately two-thirds (approximately 335) did not cheat and honestly reported not cheating. Approximately one-third (approximately 165) cheated. Of those who cheated, about one-third (55) confessed, and two-thirds (110) denied cheating. That means about 78% were honest and 22% dishonest. In follow-up studies, when judges are asked to simply watch the videos of the senders when they deny or confess cheating without any further contextual information, accuracy continues to hover around 54%. (Levine, 2020, 266).

So much for our folk theory that when people are covering up a transgression, they will behave noticeably differently in ways that we can easily track than when they are honestly denying a transgression. If these studies get the same results as recorded by the meta-analyses, maybe our folk psychology of how liars behave really is mistaken.

A rare field study of criminal defendants interacting with police officers confirms lab results:

> In the present study, observations of real-life police-citizen interactions found the display of the "suspicious" non-verbal behaviors of frequent smiles, speech disruptions, gaze aversion, and frequent hand gestures to be ineffective and erroneous indicators of involvement in crime. The present study supported the previous literature in suggesting that individuals vary greatly in the frequency with which they display the non-verbal behaviors that police officers and other criminal justice professionals perceive as indicators of criminal suspiciousness or deception. (Johnson, 2009, 288)

Perhaps concerns about the ecological validity of the finding that we aren't any good at detecting deception in real time should now be put to rest?

8 What Really Explains Honesty Judgments?

While conducting various versions of his cheating experiment, Levine hit on a discovery anticipated first by Zuckerman et al. (1979) and then again by Bond et al. (1985). Subject to an important qualification to be made below, Levine realized that some people come off as sincere, and others do not, because of their overall demeanor, *regardless* of actual honesty or dishonesty (Levine et al., 2011).

To confirm this, Levine first ran a series of experiments where he first took his videotapes from his cheating experiments and recorded senders who were repeatedly judged honest by perceivers and those repeatedly judged dishonest by perceivers, regardless of the actual honesty of the sender's messages. He then had another group of subjects watch these videos and code aspects of the behavior of the senders into two categories. He was looking to see whether there was an overall demeanor that led a perceiver to judge that a sender's message was honest and another overall demeanor that led a perceiver to judge that the sender's message was dishonest. And that is exactly what he found. It wasn't individual nonverbal and paraverbal cues that drove judgments, but patterns of those cues: demeanors.

An honest, sincere demeanor has the following features:

- Confidence and composure
- Pleasant and friendly interaction style
- Engaged and involved interaction style
- Gives plausible explanations

And then a dishonest, insincere demeanor has the following features:

- Avoids eye contact
- Appears hesitant and slow in proving answers
- Conveys uncertainty in tone of voice
- Excessive fidgeting with hands or foot movements
- Appears tense, nervous, and anxious
- Portrays an inconsistent demeanor over the course of the interaction
- And conveys uncertainty with words

Levine thereby made explicit our folk theory of how people behave when telling the truth and how people behave when lying. And so, when someone "seems suspiciously shifty" or when we "don't like the look of him" that's because we're tracking the sender's dishonest demeanor.

To prove that sender demeanor drives perceiver judgments of honesty when we suspect dishonesty (and not the actual honesty or dishonesty of the message), Levine created four categories of videotaped interviews from his cheating experiments:

- Matched: senders who were honest and had an honest demeanor
- Mismatched: senders who were honest and had a dishonest demeanor
- Matched: senders who were dishonest and had a dishonest demeanor
- Unmatched: senders who were dishonest but had an honest demeanor.

For "matched" senders their demeanor (sincere or insincere) matches their message (sincere or insincere). Matched senders are transparent; how they seem tracks how they are. For "mismatched" senders their demeanor does not match their message. Mismatched senders are opaque; how they seem does not track how they are.

What Levine discovered is that when we are suspicious of sincerity, our judgments are largely driven by our demeanor judgments, and further that demeanor is not always correlated with underlying honesty or dishonesty. Levine was able to create tapes of matched speakers that led to very high accuracy rates by judges, and tapes of unmatched speakers that led to very low accuracy rates by judges. What causes our judgments of honesty is demeanor. That should be obvious.

What is important is that though many of us are matched senders on various occasions, many of us are not. Someone with an honest demeanor can easily fool you, and you might easily judge that someone who is telling the truth but has a dishonest demeanor is lying. A gut reaction that someone is trustworthy doesn't mean they are. And a gut reaction that someone can't be trusted doesn't mean they can't. Reporting on Levine's research in his book *Talking to Strangers*, Malcolm Gladwell (2019) tells the stories of Bernie Madoff and Amanda Knox. Bernie Madoff, who made billions in a Ponzi scheme only to eventually land in prison, had a trustworthy demeanor, and repeatedly fooled countless people, including professional investigators. Amanda Knox, on the other hand, did not have a trustworthy demeanor, especially when she was a suspect for murder, a murder with weak or no physical evidence pinning her for the murder. Because of her demeanor, the police just "knew" she was guilty. She spent over 4 years in prison before the Italian Supreme Court fully exonerated her.

Another interesting discovery in Levine's experiments is that there are a few people in the population who are really bad liars. These are people who go well beyond a dishonest demeanor. They blush bright red; they can laugh uncontrollably. Sometimes they can't even finish the sentence when they try to tell a lie; they can't keep it together. You know people like these. You don't simply suspect they are lying; you *know* they are lying. In Levine's cheating experiments, all the judges rightly catch these people as lying.

As the Madoff case illustrates, those with more honest demeanors learn they can get away with lying. Because lying is a choice and because being caught in a lie has consequences, those who are bad at lying–those that find they are easily caught–may select against telling lies, whereas those with more honest demeanors may be more likely to lie. All of this, of course, turns our folk theory on its head. People who are hard to catch by their behavior are the ones more apt to lie; they know they can get away with it. People who know they are easy to catch choose not to lie; they know it won't work. The people we can easily catch aren't as likely to lie; the people we can't easily catch are more likely to lie (Levine et al., 2010c; Serota et al., 2010). Score one more point for the ecological validity of the skeptical findings that we cannot detect deception by observing behavioral cues.

9 How Do We Really Detect Lies?

All of this, however, does not mean that we never catch people in their lies. We clearly can and do. But if we don't do it by observing behavioral cues in real time, how do we do it? Ask yourself the following five questions:

1. When was the last time you were lied to? (Where were you? What was the lie about? What exactly did the person say?)
2. How long ago did the telling of the lie take place?
3. What is the relationship between you and the person who lied to you?

4. How exactly did you discover that the person lied to you?
5. How much time has passed between the telling of the lie and your discovery that they lied?

Go ahead and take a minute and write down your answers.

Now that you have completed this exercise, what was your answer to 4? Did you appeal to your background knowledge that what they said can't be right, and know they were lying on the spot? Did you acquire additional information later that showed what they said could not be true? Did a third-party later tell you they were lying? Did they later confess to telling the lie? Or could you just see it in their eyes?

I took these five questions from a study designed by Hee-Sun Park et al. (2002). Park et al. asked 202 undergraduate students from a large Midwestern university to fill out a questionnaire with these five questions (though 8 of the students could not think of a lie they were told). When the answers to question 4 were in, the most reported methods of discovery were:

- Third-party information: 32%
- Combination of methods: 31%
- Physical evidence: 18%
- Confessions: 14%
- Behavioral cues: 2%

Most respondents were likely to say "I knew she lied when she said she was sick at home, because another friend later told me that he saw her at the county fair with her family all day" or "though he told me he quit smoking, I saw the cigarette butts in the ashtray in his car" than they were to say "she just didn't look like she was telling the truth."

Altogether seven methods were reported: third-party information; physical evidence; solicited confessions; unsolicited confessions; at-the-time nonverbal or paraverbal behavior; inconsistency with previous knowledge, and inadvertent confessions. A report of "combination of methods" would simply be a report of one or more of these methods.

Nearly all the lies were detected after they were told (around 4% in an hour; 21% in a day, 21% in less than a week, 21% in less than a month, and 17% in less than a year).

Of all the lies, only three (1.5%) were detected both at the time they were told and on the basis of verbal or nonverbal behavior. If the folk theory were true, this should be very surprising indeed. But if everything we have learned so far about how poor we are at telling whether someone is lying in real time based on behavioral cues, this should come as no surprise at all. We are terrible at detecting lies in real time from observable cues because *that is not how we detect lies*.

Park et al. (2002) understood their study wasn't representative: the students were not randomly sampled and the lies they recalled were not randomly selected either. They cautioned readers not to place much weight into the specific percentages just reported. They did conclude, however, that their results suggest that "deception judgments are often not immediate, and that they are often based on additional sources of information external to the initial message." (Park et al., 2002, 154).

Jaume Masip and Carmen Herrero (2015), in a study in Spain, sought to replicate Park et al. with a more representative group of participants. They used the same five questions as Park et al. (2002) and posed them to two groups matched for gender: 22 police officers and 22 community members. The lies told to the police officers were mostly from strangers, while the lies told to the community members were mostly from close acquaintances. Masip and Herrero added one more question at the start with the prompt "please indicate how you believe lies can be detected."

Overall, their results replicated those of Park et al. (2002): lies were less likely to be reported as detected by behavioral cues but rather by third-party information, physical evidence, confessions, or inconsistency with other knowledge, where third-party information was the most commonly reported method.

What Masip and Herrero found interesting is that both the police officers and the community members answered the initial prompt in the opposite fashion. That is, when it came to saying how they believe lies can be detected, they rated observing behavioral cues over twice as highly as the various methods of detecting lies that do not rely on behavioral information. Even when we detect deception without relying on behavioral cues, we still believe we detect lies by observing behavioral cues.

10 The Frequency of Lying

Another feature of our folk theory of lying is that it is very common. What do you think? Do you think lying is commonplace? When I have discussed this issue with other philosophers, they are inclined to say lying is commonplace. "Don't people lie all the time?" they ask rhetorically. Popular media agrees. The website for the popular TV show *Lie to Me* said "the average person tells lies three lies in ten minutes of conversation" (Fox Broadcasting Company, 2009). Pamela Meyer, the CEO of a company that trains professionals on how to detect lies, said in her TED talk "How to Spot a Liar" that "on a given day, studies show that you may have lied anywhere from 10 to 200 times" (Meyer, 2011). According to her Wikipedia page, her talk has been viewed over 31 million times, and is one of the 20 most popular of all time.

I don't know the studies that Meyer is referring to (she doesn't say), but I do know where Fox is coming from, for they cite a study by Feldman et al. (Feldman et al., 2002) entitled "Self-Presentation and Deception: Do Self-Presenters Lie More?" Does this study show that "the average person tells three lies in ten minutes of conversation"? No. The study involved undergraduates having ten-minute getting acquainted conversations with other students. The study divided the undergraduates into three groups. One third were instructed to come across as very likable. Another third was instructed to come across as extremely competent. The last third (the control group) was given no specific instructions about what impression to convey. The study was about *self-presentation*, and two of the three groups were instructed to *present themselves*. Of those two groups, 40% told no lies at all. Of the other 60% who lied, they told an average of three lies in their ten-minute conversations. If you include all the students in the treatment condition, the average was 1.75 lies per ten minutes. And then if you include the control group, the average is 0.88 lies per ten-minutes in the experimental situation. Additionally, using only undergraduates skews the results, for we have learned independently that teenagers and college students lie more on average than either young children or ordinary adults (Levine et al., 2013). The Feldman et al. study does not show that the average person tells three lies per ten minutes of conversation.

If the study Fox referred to doesn't support ringing the alarm, what do other studies say? Other studies include DePaulo et al. (1996), George and Robb (2008), Serota et al. (2010), Halevy et al. (2014), Debey et al. (2015), Serota and Levine (2015), and Serota et al. (2022). I'll take you inside the details of DePaulo et al. (1996), considered to be "the best and most cited" research on the topic (Serota et al., 2010, 3) before turning to more recent studies. The DePaulo study should be revealing.

DePaulo et al. (1996) conducted two studies. In the first they recruited 77 college students, aged 17–22. In the second, they recruited 70 community members, aged 18–71. The subjects were trained to keep a diary of their conversations throughout the day and to record their lies for a week. The participants were told to count anything as a lie—even nonverbal behavior—that was intended to mislead or deceive. The participants were encouraged to record all lies, no matter how big or small. The only exception was to exclude saying "fine" in response to the perfunctory "how are you?" questions.

Steps to encourage the reporting of all lies included allowing participants to keep the content of their lies secret if they choose; encouraging participants to include as much as they could remember about lies; telling participants if they remembered a lie from a previous day that they had not recorded to include it in later entry; and maintaining anonymity in the reporting of lies.

When a participant recorded a lie, they were asked to briefly describe the lie, the reason for the lie, and the gender of the person(s) lied to. Participants were then asked to report on a number of dimensions on 9-point scales, including:

- The intimacy of the interaction, from very superficial to very meaningful.
- The quality of the interaction, from very pleasant to very unpleasant.
- The degree of planning of the lie, from completely spontaneous to carefully planned.
- The importance of not getting caught, from very unimportant to very important.
- Their feelings before telling the lie, during, and after, from very comfortable to very uncomfortable.
- The seriousness of the lie, from very trivial to very serious.
- The recipient's reaction to the lie, from didn't believe me at all to believed me completely.

Participants were then asked two additional questions:

- How would the recipient have felt if you had told the truth instead of a lie?
- How would you have felt if you had told the truth instead of a lie?

At the end of the 7 days, participants were asked two additional questions about each lie:

- Was your lie discovered?
- If you could relive this social interaction, would you tell the lie again?

Lastly, participants were asked:

- How successful do you think you are at lying?
- How frequently do you lie in comparison with other people your age?

Once the experimenters received all the reports, they coded the lies along four dimensions:

- Content: what is the lie about? Feelings; achievements and knowledge; actions, plans and whereabouts; explanations and reasons; or facts or possessions?
- Reason: what is the reason for the lie? Self-oriented reasons to advance the interests of the liar, or other-oriented reasons to advance the interests of others?
- Type: was the lie an outright lie (a total falsehood), an exaggeration, or a subtle lie (such as telling the literal truth while omitting a relevant detail with the intention of misleading)?
- Referent: who or what was the lie about? The liar, the recipient, another person, or some object or event?

What were some of the results?

- The frequency of lies told per day: on average (the mean), the college students told 1.96 lies per day—about one lie per every three social interactions with others. And the community members, on average (the mean) told 0.97 lies per day—about one lie out of every five social interactions.
- Participants generally rated themselves as successful liars.
- Participants generally said they lied less frequently than they expected.
- Participants generally said they lied less frequently than others their age. (Our folk theory at work–we think others lie a lot.)
- Content: Most lies were about feelings; achievements, actions, plans or whereabouts.
- Reason: Most lies were self-oriented, though approximately a fourth were other-oriented. Among the self-oriented lies, however, most were for psychic rewards—to gain esteem, affection, or respect. Only a smaller number were for financial or other material gain, such as getting a better grade or a promotion.
- Types: The largest category were outright lies. For the rest, the larger group was exaggerations for the college students, but subtle lies for the community members.
- Referent: The clear majority here was a lie about the liar. But lies were also commonly about the recipient, other people, or various objects or events.

After reviewing all their findings, DePaulo et al. conclude that:

- Most lies are self-oriented. About twice as many are self-oriented than other-oriented.

Deception Detection Research: Some Lessons for the Epistemology of Testimony 191

- Most are for psychic rewards. Self-oriented lies are more for esteem or affection than for financial or material gain, and other-oriented lies are typically to protect the feelings of others.
- Lies tended to be unplanned.
- Most lies are not judged to be very serious.
- For everyday lies, most liars do not tend to worry much about being caught.
- Most liars, at the time of their lie, expect to be believed.
- And most would tell the lie again, though the percentage of lies that the liar learned were detected as lies strongly correlated with whether the liar would tell the lie again. That is, around 73% percent of college students and 82% of community members said they would lie again, and around 23% of college students and 15% of community members said the lie was discovered. This suggests that whether one would choose to lie again is a function of whether one got away with the lie.
- Though liars typically think they will be believed, they do feel a degree of distress during and after a lie. They also feel less pleasant and intimate. DePaulo et al. call these negative feelings "the smudge" associated with lying.

They concluded on a note about serious lies. The lies of everyday life are typically of little consequence. But not all lies are so little. "Serious lies, which are often deep breaches of trust, occur too, but they are far less common. They are not a fact of everyday social life." (DePaulo et al., 1996, 993).

Though I've just listed many lessons from their study that are highly relevant, the main point for now is the frequency of lying. On average, teenagers and college students lie about 2 times per day, and people who are older on average lie about once a day. That's hardly up to 200 times a day, let alone three times per every ten-minute conversation.

The main objection to studies like this is that they rely on self-reporting. There are three problems with self-report studies: participants may forget, they may fail to competently report, and they may be biased so as to make themselves look or feel good about themselves.

The main concern for this study would be the last, though there are reasons for thinking that diary studies on sensitive topics like drinking or sexual behavior will suffer from less under-reporting than simple self-report studies (Lemmens et al., 1992; Ramjee et al., 1999). DePaulo et al. (1996) did what they could to address this concern in their design of the experiment and their communications with the participants. The investigators told the participants that their role would be very important as they would be observing and recording their own behavior, and so the scientific value of the experiment would depend on the quality of their participation. The investigators explained that they neither condone nor condemn lying. The participants were encouraged to see their participation as an opportunity to learn more about themselves. Even so, the investigators believe that the actual rate of lying was somewhat higher than reported. But probably not much higher, for "...the fact that participants described about twice as many self-centered lies as other-oriented ones suggests at least some willingness to own up to selfish motives." (DePaulo et al.,

1996, 992) In a follow-up diary and lab studies, Halevy et al. (2014) found that those who lied were willing to report that they did, suggesting that concerns over self-reporting in deception studies are not as strong as one might have otherwise thought.

Hancock et al. (2004) and George and Robb (2008) replicated DePaulo et al.'s diary studies with similar results. Hancock et al. (2004) report 1.58 lies per day for college students, and George and Robb report 0.59 lies per day. The range is probably due to sample size.

Studies like DePaulo et al. (1996) on when we lie, who we lie to, what we lie about, and why we lie, provides some insight into why it is so hard to tell, when prompted, whether someone is lying: when we lie, we think it's easy:

> Our... perspective has led us to reject the view that lie telling is typically a complicated, stressful, guilt-inducing process that produces clear and strong cues. Instead, we believe that most deceptive presentations are so routinely and competently executed that they leave only faint behavioral residues.... [O]rdinary people are so practiced, so proficient, and so emotionally unfazed by the telling of untruths that they can be regarded as professional liars. (DePaulo et al., 2003, 81)

For most lies, lying is easy (McCornack, 2014). The folk stereotype of the psychology of the typical lie is a myth.

Serota et al. (2010) also performed two self-report studies, but this time with a more direct paradigm. They simply asked people how many times they lied during the day. In the first, they embedded their questions in an online commercial research tool that recruits representative samples. The survey asked 1000 American adults questions in four areas: packaged meals, cat litter products, lying behavior, and water softeners. Before the lying questions, the survey included a brief description of different kinds of lies in a non-pejorative manner with a description of the point of the questions. The subjects were then asked how many times they lied in the last 24 h using an open-ended format, "responding separately for lies to family members, friends, business contacts, acquaintances..., and total strangers." (Serota et al., 2010, 7) The results were consistent with DePaulo's results of one to two lies per day on average. They then performed a variant of the survey with 255 college students. Besides asking about the number of lies in the last 24 h, students who reported no lies in the last 24 h were also asked about the last time they told a lie: in the last 2 days, last week, last month, more than a month, or never. They also took steps to address concerns about self-reporting (Serota et al., 2010, 19).

What were the results of their surveys? For the students, the mean was 2.34 lies per day. For the survey of adult Americans, the mean was 1.65 lies per day. These results fall in line with previous results. Teenagers really do lie more on average.

In a follow-up study that surveyed just under 3000 people in the United Kingdom, the results were similar but somewhat higher: the mean was 2 lies per day (Serota and Levine (2015). All the studies I know of have similar results on the average number of lies told per day. It's not 200 lies per day.

When these studies addressed the kinds of lies told, white lies were always in the majority. There are (at least) three interesting features of white lies. First, they are socially sanctioned. We are instructed as children when to tell them, and we are criticized as adults for not telling them in certain cases: "Avoiding social ostracism, one of the most common responses to telling unpopular truths, is a powerful motivator for liars to tell polite lies" (MacKinnon, 2014, 271). Second, hearers want to hear them, at least for the most part. We're not on our guard not to be lied to about such matters, and we don't hold people to account for telling such lies. Third, it's easy to tell white lies. None of this fits with our folk theory of lying. If white lies are the majority of lies, it should be no surprise that the folk theory of lying and how we detect lies doesn't fit the facts.

One of the most interesting findings from the Serota et al. studies is that the popular reports on daily frequency of lying are misleading. The popular reports say things like "everybody lies on average N lies per day." But when Serota el al. looked closely at the individual data, they discovered a striking skew in the data. It is not that everyone is disposed to lie one or two times a day. Rather it is that most of us hardly ever lie and that a few of us lie a lot. If you have ten people and you ask how often they lie per day, and 7 say 'never' and 3 say '3-4 times a day' and then you average the data, you will conclude that on average people lie around once a day. But if you pay close attention to the data before averaging, you'll discover a skew. There are really two groups of people: those who hardly ever lie and those who lie a lot. Serota et al. discovered this skew when they reanalyzed the raw data from the DePaulo et al., 1996 diary studies and in their own survey studies, as well as the survey data from the United Kingdom. These results have also been replicated in South Korea and Japan (Park et al., 2021; Daiku et al., 2021). It's a remarkable result. A few of us are prolific liars, where most of us routinely tell the truth.

Although it is more than reasonable to wish for better studies on how we really detect lies, better studies of the frequency of lying, and better studies of the types of lies told, I think we have more than good enough studies to conclude that the folk theory about how liars behave and how we can detect lies in real time is false. Altogether, ecologically valid research (in the relevant respects) has shown that our folk theory is wrong in many respects:

- It is wrong about the frequency of lying
- It is wrong that lying well is difficult (for most of us most of the time)
- It is wrong that lying leaks reliable behavioral cues (except for a few bad liars)
- It is wrong that we can detect lies in real time by observing cues or demeanor (that's not how we catch a liar)

What should social epistemologists draw from this? On the face of it, social epistemology should not invoke what isn't true to explain how it is we come to acquire true beliefs through communication, just as social epistemology should not invoke what isn't true to explain how we might do better.

11 Fricker's Epistemology of Testimony

Based on some of the deception detection research, Michaelian (2010) and Shieber (2012) have accused Elizabeth Fricker of relying on what isn't so in her epistemology of testimony. Though I agree with their criticisms, I believe we can do deeper in expounding her view and showing just where it goes wrong. We can also take up her replies to Michaelian and Shieber. Readers should come away with a deeper appreciation of her view and its shortcomings.

I shall focus on themes from her landmark paper "Against Gullibility" (Fricker, 1994), subsequently defended, elaborated, and modified over 30 years (Fricker, 1995, 2004, 2006a, b, 2016, 2017a, 2024). Most of the replies have focused on her case for a monitoring requirement for warranted testimony-based beliefs–her argument against gullibility. Hence the title of her paper. But that wasn't the only point of her paper. As she emphasizes elsewhere (Fricker, 2006a, 620), she took the main point of her paper to argue that ordinary hearers possess adequate non-circular reasons to justify their reliance on testimony, pace so-called "anti-reductionists" who think hearers never have enough independent support to justify their reliance on testimony, (despite the title of her paper). I shall review how she makes her case for both points before turning to criticisms.

Here is her argument for her monitoring requirement:

(P1)   Lying is very common. (Folk assumption)

> "…false utterances are quite common…" (Fricker, 1994, 146); "The risks involved in trusting others are considerable… (Fricker, 2006b, 242) as "…[f]alse statements made through deceptive intent…are an intrinsic and perennial possibility… (Fricker, 2016, 92). "…it is in the nature of testimony that false testimony…is a real risk." (Fricker, 2016, 93). "[T]here is a significant possibility of false assertion…[W]e all understand how easily it can happen and all too often does happen, that a speaker lies…" (Fricker, 2017a, 268). "Our understanding of testimony is embedded in our grasp of folk psychology… [We know] there are many everyday communicative situations where the speaker has some motive to deceive, or at least conceal…We all know that human testimony…is by its nature chronically liable to inaccuracy…". (Fricker, 2024, 285–86)

(P2)   When people lie, for the most part, they know they are breaking an enforced norm against deception. (Prohibitions against lying are universal across human cultures. The knowledge (or some related) norm of assertion is constitutive of assertion and also a social norm–see Fricker (2017b).)

(P3)   So, for the most part, liars will feel guilty, and they will also be anxious as they don't want to get caught. (Knowledge of human nature.)

(P4)   These emotions, for the most part, will leak in their behavior as cues to deceptive intent. Lying well is hard. (Folk theory of the psychological effects of lying.)

> Expert dissimulators amongst us are few, the insincerity of an utterance is very frequently betrayed in the speaker's manner, and so is susceptible of detection by [our] quasi-perceptual [deception monitoring] capacity. (Fricker, 1994, 150)

(P5)   When can detect these behavioral cues: we have a (possibly subpersonal) "deception detection" mind-reading capacity that makes it easy to tell they are not trustworthy on the occasion of their utterance. We have a reliable "quasi-perceptual" competence to detect deception in real time that takes in behavioral cues or their gestalt as an input and produces a trustworthiness judgment–a demeanor judgment–

Deception Detection Research: Some Lessons for the Epistemology of Testimony 195

as its conscious output (Assumption, largely from folk psychology and introspection on anecdotal cases.)

> "[Monitoring consists in] being perceptually sensitive to betraying signs that, for instance, the speaker is lying" (Fricker, 2006a, 264). "...a hesitancy in the voice, an insincere seeming smile." (Fricker, 2004, 117). "...nervousness... or confusion..." (Fricker, 2024, 283). "Such monitoring...[is] usually found in ordinary hearers, at least to some extent....[I]ts results can generally be fished up into consciousness and expressed, albeit roughly, in words ("He seems suspiciously shifty...I don't like the look of him" (Fricker, 2006a, 624). "Well, she seemed perfectly normal". (Fricker, 1994, 150)

(P6) If we did not exercise this competence, then we would be deceived too often. Not exercising this competence is a recipe for objectionable gullibility.

> "It is a law-like general truth that testimony is not in practice a completely reliable source of belief, if accepted uncritically...[As a result, a] "recipient must...filter...[and] detect and block belief [from]...false testimony that she might easily encounter..." (Fricker, 2016, 93) For "if a significant percentage of [testimonies] are not [trustworthy]...one should not infer from [S testified that P to P]. A belief so formed is not epistemically rational". (Fricker, 1994, 146)

(C1) So as epistemologists must require hearers to exercise (and possibly improve) their quasi-perceptual capacity to detect deception in real time. We should always monitor, even if only passively, such that if there were signs of deceptive intent, we would pick them up and suspend acceptance as a result (Fricker, 1994, 145, 154, 1995, 404, 405).

> "[To avoid this] uncontroversially bad kind of gullibility" (Fricker, 2006a, 623) [a hearer must be] "disposed to pick up...tell-tale signs [of insincerity, of] symptoms of duplicity" (Fricker, 1994, 151). "Caution and canniness should govern our response to others' testimony. Unless we exercise it, we fail to maintain responsibility for our own beliefs" (Fricker, 2006b, 243). "Reliability in the process of forming belief through acceptance of testimony must be maintained in part by an effective filter at the recipient's end". (Fricker, 2016, 116)

That's Fricker's argument for her monitoring requirement. I now turn to her case for thinking hearers possess a good, non-circular reason to accept testimony, through the exercise of a reliable quasi-perceptual competence to tell that their interlocutor is trustworthy:

(P7) For a justified belief, a believer must be able to justify their belief, to provide a good reason supporting their belief. Justified belief requires the capacity for critical reflection and defense. Justification is a "standing in the space of reasons." Justified beliefs are the property of ordinary reflective adults; the beliefs of young children and non-human animals are another story. (Fricker, 1994, 126–127, 138–141, 150, 157–160, 1995, 397, 408, 2004, 114, 120–122, 2016, 89, 2017a, 276, 288, 291–292)

(P8) Some beliefs are basic in virtue of their sources, where simply describing how the beliefs are formed (citing the source) suffices to provide a good reason. For example, "I saw it" suffices to justify a perceptual belief. (Fricker, 2006a, 249, 2017a, 262–3, 266–267, 2024, 283)

(P9) Our belief that we have been told that P, formed through linguistic comprehension, is also a basic belief. Our capacity to comprehend assertive speech acts is a reliable, quasi-perceptual capacity. We do not need independent reasons to justify such beliefs. (Fricker, 2003, 2004)

(P10) But testimony-based beliefs are not basic. Simply saying "I was told that P" does not suffice to provide a good reason for a testimony-based belief (though the belief "I was told that P" counts as a basic, or quasi-basic, belief). The hearer must also justifiably believe that the speaker, on the occasion, is trustworthy. The hearer needs two justified beliefs that work in tandem to justify their testimony-based beliefs: (a) I was told that P by S on occasion O and (b) S is trustworthy on O: S would not have told me that P on O unless S knows that P. (Fricker finds this both intuitive, by the previous argument that without such a justified second premise one is likely to be fooled all too often.)

(P11) One source of the justified belief that the speaker is trustworthy would be a reliable quasi-perceptual monitoring capacity that outputs the belief that the speaker is trustworthy on the occasion. Such beliefs, like perceptual beliefs, would be basic. A hearer can then have good, non-circular reasons for their testimony-based beliefs, one from their quasi-perceptual ability to comprehend the force and content of the speech act, and another from their quasi-perceptual ability to tell that the speaker is trustworthy on the occasion.

(P12) The belief formed though such a reliable competence that the speaker is trustworthy provides a non-circular reason to believe the speaker, for it does not assume that what the speaker said is true, nor is it formed simply through taking the speaker's word for it. Our reality ability to monitor for signs of deception grounds the justified belief we need to justify our reliance on testimony.

(C2) It is then not true, as so-called anti-reductionists suppose, that hearers lack, on most (every?) occasion of a justified testimony-based belief, a non-circular justification (a good argument) in favor of the testimony-based belief.

For Fricker, our quasi-perceptual capacity to tell that a speaker is trustworthy on an occasion then kills two philosophical birds with one stone. First, it shows how a hearer can have a non-circular reason to believe a speaker on an occasion. So-called anti-reductionists who think we lack non-circular reasons to believe testimony on occasions are thus mistaken, as they have overlooked a source of justification for the belief that the speaker is trustworthy. Second, it shows, along with the assumption that lying is common, that we had better exercise this capacity, otherwise we will be deceived far too often. Our testimony-based beliefs will not only lack the good justification they require, but they will also end up riddled with errors. Once again so-called anti-reductionists are mistaken that such monitoring is not a requirement for testimonial knowledge and justification.

What should we think of these arguments? I think we have learned that (P1) is false, or at least that lying is not frequent enough, across ordinary contexts, to raise the alarm bells. "Real risk" and "significant probability" are probably exaggerations. Without (P1), the first argument is cast in doubt, as the conclusion depends on the assumption that without demeanor monitoring, we will be fooled all too often.

We can grant (P2), with the acknowledgement that white lies are an exception, or that the existence of norms for telling white lies competes with, or requires qualification of, norms of truth-telling. (P3) is probably also not true for white lies, but plausible for other types of lies, at least for some people some of the time.

Except for a few bad liars, (P4) is false. "Leakage theories" are incorrect as generalizations about human behavior. Lying is, for the most part, easy. Furthermore, as the Othello effect shows, an honest person can easily resemble a liar. The fact that demeanors in general need not correlate with honesty or dishonesty undermines the folk idea that liars fit the folk stereotype.

The evidence reviewed shows that (P5) is false. We do not possess a capacity to form demeanor judgments that are sensitive to underlying honesty or dishonesty. Since (P6) depends on (P1) and (P5), (P6) is unsupported. (P6) also assumes that there are no other ways to manage concerns regarding deception. Maybe we don't need to worry about being lied to if other facts of social life make lying less likely to occur than one might have otherwise thought. I'll return to this momentarily.

Fricker's case for (C1) and so her case against so-called anti-reductionists is not persuasive. It's an armchair argument, refuted by decades of empirical research on deception detection and the frequency and types of lies.

What about Fricker's second argument? (P7) as a thesis about knowledge or justification "deluxe" sounds fine. As a thesis about knowledge generally, it seems false. Throughout her career Fricker was aware of such a possibility (e.g. Fricker, 1994, 158, 160). In her most recent work, she grants that "justification" as "standing in the space of reasons" and knowledge through testimony might have very different requirements (Fricker, 2024, 289). That brings her close to Robert Audi's (1997) view of testimonial knowledge as less intellectually demanding than testimonial justification.

I shall pass over (P8) and (P9). (P10) dialectically depends for its plausibility on the first argument. Since several the premises in that argument are false, (P10) lacks support. On a so-called anti-reductionist view, the belief "I was told that P" might suffice to justify a testimony-based belief.

What the empirical evidence shows is that (P11) is false. We lack a capacity that reliably discriminates honest speakers from dishonest speakers by demeanor judges that respond to features of the speaker's nonverbal and paraverbal behavior. Since (P12) depends on the truth of (P11) for its truth, (P12) is false as well. Fricker has failed to show that hearers have, on every occasion of a justified testimony-based belief, an adequate non-circular reason to believe that the speaker is trustworthy that P that derives from demeanor judgments grounded in observation of the speaker's nonverbal and paraverbal behavior.

(C2), like (C1), is unsupported. The empirical science does not support Fricker's case for her so-called "local reductionism" as against so-called anti-reductionism.

In her paper "Unreliable Testimony", Fricker (2016) responds to Shieber (2012) (and mentions Michaelian (2010) in the footnotes). How did she respond to Shieber's presentation of the meta-analyses that purportedly show that we lack the ability to tell, in real time, whether someone is lying? She made three replies.

First, she denied the ecological validity of the studies. In my presentation of the research, I took pains to detail their methodology and to argue for their ecological validity. I did this because I knew Fricker's response. Fricker's concern is a reasonable one. We should always worry whether results from experiments in the lab carry over to the real world outside of the lab. But we should not assume, a priori, that they never carry over. Though reasonable, Fricker's concern is misapplied. The results of this research are ecologically valid.

Second, when it came to explaining why judgments about the speaker's trustworthiness on the occasion are justified, Fricker downplayed the emphasis on observing behavioral cues in real time and emphasized other sources of evidence that can support a hearer's judgment that a speaker's testimony is trustworthy on the occasion. We have background beliefs about the probability of the speaker's statement. That someone took an umbrella to work when the weather predicted rain is not a surprise. Why would anyone lie about that? We have knowledge of the speaker's social role and the social situation. Why would a clerk at a store lie about whether they have the size of shoe you want to buy? We often have good reason to believe that a speaker is trustworthy independent of judgments of their demeanor based on observing the nonverbal and paraverbal behavior. We have first-hand knowledge of the speaker's track-record. We have knowledge of situation specific reasons to lie.

I accept these other sources of prima facie pro tanto reasons to believe the speaker is either honest or dishonest on the occasion. What I doubt is that they can play the role Fricker needs them to play in her second argument. Though these reasons may be non-circular in the sense that they do not presuppose believing that the speaker is trustworthy on the occasion, they often depend on testimony from others. They may not be present in every case. Fricker had hoped to show that trustworthiness judgments from a demeanor monitoring capacity yielded justified basic beliefs that did not depend on testimony, available in every case. Given that we lack such a reliable capacity, we lack "basic" beliefs that the speaker is trustworthy from this route. Other routes may be possible. But the other routes may not be basic and may not be present in sufficient strength in every case, putting dialectical pressure on Fricker's reply to so-called anti-reductionists.

I also found Fricker's downplaying of the role of monitoring for behavioral cues—"telltale signs"—of deceptive intent misleading. It really is clear throughout her body of work prior to 2016 that her main case for a monitoring requirement derived from our folk theory of the frequency of lies, how liars behave, and how we can tell they are lying by observing their behavior. That's partly why I've included so many direct quotes from her writings. In a 2024 paper the emphasis on behavioral cues comes back in full force: "Such telltale giveaways might be perceived in the speaker's manner [including] nervousness [or] hesitancy…" (Fricker, 2024, 283). When it comes to worries about deception and how we know someone is not lying, Fricker's view really is the view the empirical science shows to be mistaken.

Third, Fricker reminds us that we should worry not only about deception but also incompetence. Maybe false testimony though incompetence is even the bigger concern. That may be true. But as I said at the outset, I am tabling issues of competence here. But if Fricker thinks we have a reliable quasi-perceptual capacity to issue competence judgments from observing nonverbal and paraverbal behavior, odds are she is mistaken there too.

Fricker (2024) does not mention any of the empirical research. Neither Shieber nor Michaelian are referenced. But she does hint that she might be willing to raise the white flag. She makes four interconnected remarks:

> First, she correctly says that whether we have a reliable demeanor monitoring capacity is an empirical question, not to be answered from the armchair. (Fricker, 2024, 289).
>
> Second, though she says she believes we have one, she says she will not offer any empirical evidence. (Fricker, 2024, 287) That's wise, as the available evidence shows we don't.
>
> Third, even so, she continues to insist that monitoring for demeanor, reliably so, is a normative requirement on the justification for testimony-based beliefs. (Fricker, 2024, 283, 289) No reliable monitoring, then too many false beliefs, on the one hand, and one less source for the justified belief that the speaker is trustworthy, on the other.
>
> Fourth, if humans lack such a capacity, she is then "happy" to conclude that it is "very likely so" that "people may sometimes be too credulous in their everyday reception of testimony." (Fricker, 2024, 289) She seems willing to embrace a more skeptical stance towards the extent of our justified testimony-based beliefs.

That's why I say she seems willing to raise the white flag, for she seems willing to concede that we lack the ability to detect deception in real time through monitoring the speaker's nonverbal and paraverbal behavior.[3]

I've put Fricker's work under the critical microscope, in part because she's the one social epistemologist who did the most to turn our folk epistemology into a well worked out social epistemology. But Fricker is not the only philosopher in my crosshairs: Miranda Fricker, Sanford Goldberg, Jennifer Lackey, and Steven Reynolds—not to mention all of the other philosophers I did not mention (you know who you are)—have all placed bad bets on the truth of our folk theory. No one should assume in their social epistemology of conversation that the folk theory is true. If you have placed a monitoring requirement on testimony ala Fricker, it is time to take it back. Goldberg and Henderson (2006), I'm looking at you.

12 Concluding Thoughts

Even though this chapter was long, there are still a lot of interesting issues from the literature that I have left on the table, issues central to the epistemology of testimony:

- Our default tendency to believe that others are telling the truth (the "truth bias") (Zuckerman et al., 1981; McCornack & Parks, 1986; Gilbert et al., 1990, 1993; Gilbert, 1991; Anderson et al., 1999; Levine et al., 1999; Hasson et al., 2005; Richter et al., 2009; Levine, 2014, 2022, 2023; Clare & Levine, 2019);
- The influence of the base-rate of honest over dishonest reports on the frequency of our accurate judgments of honesty over dishonest–the so-called "veracity effect" (Levine et al., 1999, 2006, 2010b, 2014b; Levine, 2019, 2020);
- Experimental evidence showing what techniques for detecting lies are much more likely to work (Hartwig et al., 2006; Granhag et al., 2007; Levine et al., 2010c, 2014a; Blair et al., 2018);

---

[3] For the exact opposite reaction, see Michaelson (2018).

- Experimental evidence of our aversion to lying despite incentives to lie (Gneezy, 2005; Lundquist et al., 2009; Ariely, 2012; Fischbacher & Föllmi-Heusi, 2013; Gneezy et al., 2013, 2018; Abeler et al., 2019);
- The role of social norms for truth-telling in explaining our aversion to lying and in otherwise supporting the reliability of testimony so that perhaps there is no need for each individual to bother with being on their guard as long as enough of us catch liars and enforce penalties (Faulkner, 2011; Graham, 2012, 2015, 2020a, b; Fricker, 2016, 2017b, 2024; Simion, 2020; Simion & Kelp, 2020; Bruner, 2024; Grodniewicz, 2024);
- Evolutionary considerations surrounding lying and lie detection (Kraut, 1980; Bond et al., 1985; Sperber, 2001, 2013; Sperber et al., 2010; Mercier & Sperber, 2011; Graham, 2015);
- and how all of the facts I covered and all of these issues that I just mentioned fit into our most plausible account of the epistemology of conversation (Graham, 2010, 2020a, b; Vesga, 2023).

Maybe I will have the opportunity to discuss further lessons for the epistemology of testimony from the deception detection research on future occasions.

But before I leave you, I want to answer an objection to my work from Mona Simion and Chris Kelp in their 2020 paper "How to be an Anti-Reductionist." They target my 2010 paper "Testimonial Entitlement and the Function of Comprehension" and argue that I should be hoisted on my own petard (though that is not how they put it). By comprehension I meant our capacity to comprehend assertive speech acts. Testimony-based beliefs are then comprehension-based beliefs, beliefs based on comprehending (as of) testimony. I then argued for the following theses:

- Epistemic warrant for a belief turns on the normal functioning of the belief-forming process when the process has forming true beliefs reliably as an etiological function.
- Comprehension of assertive speech with filtering has the etiological function of forming true beliefs reliably as a function. Filtered comprehension-based beliefs are reliable beliefs.
- Putting two and two together: beliefs formed through comprehension with filtering are (prima facie, pro tanto) warranted.

Simion and Kelp (2020) argue that I'm in trouble on the grounds that "filtering" isn't reliable. Filtering is just monitoring for behavioral cues of dishonesty, and haven't we just learned that our judgments as to whether someone is honest or dishonest based on observable nonverbal and paraverbal features of their message fail to vary reliably with whether the speaker is in fact honest or dishonest? Filtering is then, at best, an idle wheel. They cite Michaelian (2010) as providing all the relevant evidence. So if filtering is supposed to improve the reliability of beliefs formed on the basis of comprehension, it's not going to work (Simion & Kelp, 2020, 285–55; Simion, 2020; Carter & Littlejohn, 2021, 232). In effect, they are accusing me of just the mistake I accused Fricker of making. How am I going to get out of this?

By drawing a distinction. Yes, I used the word 'filtering.' And yes, Fricker uses the word 'filtering' too. But there are many possible filters, many possible ways to "screen out" unreliable testimony. When it came to the filters I discussed in my paper, I didn't include monitoring for behavioral cues to insincerity. Though at the time I didn't know the detection deception literature well, I do remember reading a presentation of some of the results in a textbook on nonverbal communication and finding myself somewhat bewildered. Since I didn't understand it, I didn't rely on it.

Instead, I relied on "filters" I understood. Like Fricker, I included information about the track-record of the speaker. Fool me once, shame on you. Fool me twice, shame on me. I included the confidence of the speaker. That may or may not have been a mistake. I included the internal coherence of the speaker's message. Like Fricker I also included external coherence of the message with our background beliefs. But unlike Fricker I did not include, and so surely did not emphasize, detecting behavioral cues to deception. So the evidence Simion and Kelp cite about the unreliability of our capacity to detect valid behavioral cues doesn't apply to me. It's not one of the filters I had in mind. Simion and Kelp in effect make the same mistake Michaelian (2013) made when he accused Sperber et al. in their 2010 paper "Epistemic Vigilance" of relying on monitoring demeanor as a means of being vigilant for misleading testimony. Just as I didn't rely on such a filter, neither did Sperber et al. (see Sperber, 2013). Maybe we should just use "demeanor judgments" for the "filter" that doesn't work and stop calling it a filter altogether.

Last question. If our folk theory is false, why is it so persistently held? Maybe it serves an important function. If people think they'll be easily caught, maybe they will be less likely to lie (Bond & The Global Detection Research Team, 2006). As always, look for the function first.[4]

References

Abeler, J., Nosenzo, D., & Raymond, C. (2019). Preferences for truth telling. *Econometrica, 87*(4), 1115–1153.
Anderson, D., Ansfield, M., & DePaulo, B. (1999). Love's best habit: Deception in the context of relationships. In P. Philippot & R. Feldman (Eds.), *Social context of nonverbal behavior* (pp. 372–409). Cambridge University Press.
Ariely, D. (2012). *The (honest) truth about dishonesty*. HarperCollins.
Audi, R. (1997). The place of testimony in the fabric of knowledge and justification. *American Philosophical Quarterly, 34*(4), 405–422.

---

[4] I am grateful to the editor for his patience and comments for improvements. I started working through this research in 2020 while visiting CONCEPT at the University of Cologne as a Humboldt Research Award winner. I had the pleasure of discussing what I was learning and its relevance to social epistemology with a number of audiences from Fall 2020 to Fall 2023 at the University of Cologne, at Southern Denmark University, at the University of Glasgow, at the inaugural meeting of the Empirical Epistemology Network, and at the Social Epistemology Network conference in Scotland. I am grateful for all of the helpful comments I received on those occasions. I recall especially helpful comments from Sven Bernecker, Elizabeth Fricker, Mikkel Gerken, Thomas Grundmann, Jack Lyons, Luis Rosa, and Cesar Shirmer dos Santos.

Blair, J., Reimer, T., & Levine, T. (2018). The role of consistency in detecting deception: The superiority of correspondence over coherence. *Communication Studies, 69*(5), 483–498.
Bond, C., & DePaulo, B. (2006). Accuracy of detection judgments. *Personality and Social Psychology Review, 10*(3), 214–234.
Bond, C., & DePaulo, B. (2008). Individual differences in judging deception: Accuracy and bias. *Psychological Bulletin, 134*(4), 477–492.
Bond, C., & The Global Detection Research Team. (2006). A world of lies. *Journal of Cross-Cultural Psychology, 37*, 60–74.
Bond, C., Kahler, K., & Paolicelli, L. (1985). The miscommunication of deception: An adaptive perspective. *Journal of Experimental Social Psychology, 21*(4), 331–345.
Bruner, J. (2024). Assertions: Deterrent or handicap? A reply to Graham (2020). *Episteme* (First View).
Burgoon, J. (2015). Rejoinder to Levine, Clare et al.'s comparison. *Human Communication Research, 41*(3), 327–349.
Burgoon, J., & Buller, D. (1996). Interpersonal deception theory. *Communication Theory, 6*, 203–242.
Carter, A., & Littlejohn, C. (2021). *This is epistemology: An introduction*. Wiley-Blackwell.
Clare, D., & Levine, T. (2019). Documenting the truth-default: The low frequency of spontaneous unprompted veracity assessments in deception detection. *Human Communication Research, 45*, 286–308.
Daiku, Y., Serota, K., & Levine, T. (2021). A few prolific liars in Japan. *PLoS One, 16*(4).
Davis, M., Markus, K., Walters, S., Virus, N., & Connors, B. (2005). Behavioral cues to deception vs. topic incriminating potential in criminal confessions. *Law and Human Behavior, 29*, 683–704.
Debey, E., De Schryver, M., Logan, G., Suchotzke, K., & Verschuere, B. (2015). From junior to senior Pinocchio: A cross-sectional lifespan investigation of deception. *Acta Psychologica, 160*, 58–68.
DePaulo, B. (1980). Humans as lie detectors. *Journal of Communication, 30*(2), 129–139.
DePaulo, B., Kashy, D., Kirkendol, S., Wyer, W., & Epstein, J. (1996). Lying in everyday life. *Journal of Personality and Social Psychology, 70*(5), 979–995.
DePaulo, B., Lindsay, J., Malone, B., Muhlenbruck, L., Charton, K., & Cooper, H. (2003). Cues to deception. *Psychological Bulletin, 129*(1), 74–118.
Driskell, J. (2012). Effectiveness of deception detection training: A meta-analysis. *Psychology, Crime & Law, 18*(8), 713–731.
Eckman, P., & Friesen, W. (1969). Nonverbal leakage cues to deception. *Psychiatry, 32*, 88–106.
Faulkner, P. (2011). *Knowledge on trust*. Oxford University Press.
Feeley, T., & deTurck, M. (1998). The behavioral correlates of sanctioned and unsanctioned deceptive communication. *Journal of Nonverbal Behavior, 22*, 189–204.
Feldman, R., Forrest, J., & Happ, B. (2002). Self-presentation and verbal deception: Do self-presenters lie more? *Basic and Applied Social Psychology, 24*(2), 163–170.
Fischbacher, U., & Föllmi-Heusi, F. (2013). Lies in disguise: An experimental study on cheating. *Journal of the European Economic Association, 11*(3), 525–547.
Frank, M., & Feeley, T. (2003). To catch a liar: Challenges for research in lie detection training. *Journal of Applied Communication Research, 31*(1), 58–75.
Fricker, E. (1994). Against gullibility. In A. Chakrabarti & B. K. Matilal (Eds.), *Knowing from words* (pp. 125–161). Kluwer Academic Publishers.
Fricker, E. (1995). Telling and trusting: Reductionism and anti-reductionism in the epistemology of testimony. *Mind, 104*(414), 393–411.
Fricker, E. (2003). Understanding and knowledge of what is said. In A. Barber (Ed.), *Epistemology of Langauge* (pp. 325–366). Oxford University Press.
Fricker, E. (2004). Testimony: Knowing through being told. In I. Niiniluoto, M. Sintonen, & J. Wolenski (Eds.), *Handbook of epistemology* (pp. 109–130). Kluwer Academic Publishers.
Fricker, E. (2006a). Varieties of anti-reductionism about testimony: A reply to Goldberg and Henderson. *Philosophy and Phenomenological Research, 72*(3), 618–628.

Fricker, E. (2006b). Testimony and epistemic autonomy. In J. Lackey & E. Sosa (Eds.), *The epistemology of testimony* (pp. 225–250). Oxford University Press.
Fricker, M. (2007). *Epistemic Injustice*. Oxford University Press.
Fricker, E. (2016). Unreliable testimony. In B. McLaughlin & H. Kornblith (Eds.), *Goldman and his critics* (pp. 88–120). Wiley.
Fricker, E. (2017a). Inference to the best explanation and the receipt of testimony: Testimonial reductionism vindicated. In K. McCain & T. Poston (Eds.), *Best explanations: New essays on inference to the best explanation* (pp. 262–294). Oxford University Press.
Fricker, E. (2017b). Norms, constitutive and social, and assertion. *American Philosophical Quarterly, 54*(4), 397–418.
Fricker, E. (2024). A defense of local reductionism about testimony. In M. Steup, B. Roeber, J. Turri, & E. Sosa (Eds.), *Contemporary debates in epistemology* (3rd ed., pp. 279–289). Wiley.
George, J., & Robb, A. (2008). Deception and computer-meditated communication in daily life. *Communication Reports, 21*(2), 92–103.
Gilbert, D. (1991). How mental systems believe. *American Psychologist, 46*, 107–119.
Gilbert, D., Krull, D., & Malone, P. (1990). Unbelieving the unbelievable: Some problems in the rejection of false information. *Journal of Personality and Social Psychology, 59*, 601–613.
Gilbert, D., Tafarodi, R., & Malone, P. (1993). You can't not believe everything you read. *Journal of Personality and Social Psychology, 65*, 221–233.
Gladwell, M. (2019). *Talking to strangers: What we should know about the people we Don't know*. Little, Brown and Company.
Gneezy, U. (2005). Deception: The role of consequences. *American Economic Review, 95*(1), 384–394.
Gneezy, U., Rockenbach, B., & Serra-Garcia, M. (2013). Measuring lying aversion. *Journal of Economic Behavior & Organization, 93*, 293–300.
Gneezy, U., Kajackaite, A., & Sobel, J. (2018). Lying aversion and the size of the lie. *American Economic Review, 108*(2), 419–453.
Goldberg, S. (2007). How lucky can you get? *Synthese, 158*(3), 315–327.
Goldberg, S., & Henderson, D. (2006). Monitoring and anti-reductionism in the epistemology of testimony. *Philosophy and Phenomenological Research, 72*(3), 600–617.
Gongola, J., Scurich, N., & Quas, J. (2017). Detecting deception in children: A meta-analysis. *Law and Human Behavior, 41*(1), 44–54.
Graham, P. J. (2010). Testimonial entitlement and the function of comprehension. In A. Millar, D. Pritchard, & A. Haddock (Eds.), *Social epistemology* (pp. 148–174). Oxford University Press.
Graham, P. J. (2012). Testimony, trust, and social norms. *Abstracta, 6*, 92–117.
Graham, P. J. (2015). Epistemic normativity and social norms. In D. Henderson & J. Greco (Eds.), *Epistemic evaluation* (pp. 247–273). Oxford University Press.
Graham, P. J. (2020a). The function of assertion and social norms. In S. Goldberg (Ed.), *The Oxford handbook of social norms* (pp. 727–748). Oxford University Press.
Graham, P. J. (2020b). Assertions, handicaps, and social norms. *Episteme, 17*, 349–363.
Granhag, P., Stromwal, L., & Hartwig, M. (2007). The sue technique: The way to interview to detect deception. *Forensic Update, 88*, 25–29.
Grodniewicz, J. (2024). Effective filtering: Language comprehension and testimonial entitlement. *The Philosophical Quarterly, 74*(1), 291–311.
Halevy, R., Shalvi, S., & Verschuere, B. (2014). Being honest about dishonesty: Correlating self-reports and actual lying. *Human Communication Research, 40*(1), 54–72.
Hancock, J. T., Thom-Santelli, J., & Ritchie, T. (2004). Deception and design: The impact of communication technology on lying behavior. *CHI Letters, 6*(1), 129–134.
Hartwig, M., & Bond, C. (2014). Why do lie-cheaters fail? A lens model meta-analysis of human lie judgments. *Psychological Bulletin, 137*(4), 643–659.
Hartwig, M., Granhag, P., Stromwall, L., & Kronsvist, O. (2006). Strategic use of evidence during police interviews: When training to detect deception works. *Law and Human Behavior, 30*, 603–619.

Harwood, J. (2014). Easy lies. *Journal of Language and Social Psychology, 33*(4), 405–410.
Hasson, U., Simmons, J., & Todorov, A. (2005). Believe it or not: On the possibility of suspending belief. *Psychological Science, 16*, 566–571.
Hauch, V., Sporer, S., Michael, S., & Meissner, C. (2016). Does training improve the detection of deception? A meta-analysis. *Communication Reports, 43*(3), 243–283.
Hume, D. (2007). *An enquiry concerning human understanding.* Edited with an introduction and notes by Peter Millican. Oxford University Press.
Johnson, R. (2009). Race and police reliance on suspicious non-verbal cues. *Policing: An International Journal of Police Strategies & Management, 30*, 277–290.
Kraut, R. (1980). Humans as lie detectors. *Journal of Communication, 30*(4), 209–218.
Lackey, J. (2008). *Learning from words.* Oxford University Press.
Lemmens, P., Tan, E. S., & Knibbe, R. A. (1992). Measuring quantity and frequency of drinking in a general population survey. *Journal of Studies on Alcohol, 53*, 476–486.
Levine, T. (2010). A few transparent liars: Explaining 54% accuracy in deception detection experiments. *Annals of the International Communication Association, 34*(1), 41–61.
Levine, T. (2014). Truth-Default Theory (TDT): A theory of human deception and deception detection. *Journal of Language and Social Psychology, 33*(4), 378–392.
Levine, T. (2017). Mysteries and myths in human deception and deception detection. *Ewha Journal of Social Sciences, 33*, 5–28.
Levine, T. (2018). Ecological validity and deception detection research design. *Communication Methods and Measures, 12*(1), 45–54.
Levine, T. (2019). An overview of detecting deceptive communication. In T. Docan-Morgan (Ed.), *The Palgrave handbook of deceptive communication* (pp. 289–299). Palgrave Macmillan.
Levine, T. (2020). *Duped: Truth-default theory and the social science of lying and deception.* University of Alabama Press.
Levine, T. (2022). Truth-default theory and the psychology of lying and deception detection. *Current Opinion in Psychology, 47*, 1–4.
Levine, T. (2023). Deception detection and question effects: Testing truth-default theory predictions in South Korea. *Human Communication Research, 49*, 448–462.
Levine, T., Park, H.-S., & McCornack, S. (1999). Accuracy in detecting truths and lies: Documenting the "veracity effect". *Communication Monographs, 66*, 125–144.
Levine, T., Kim, R., Park, H. S., & Hughes, M. (2006). Deception detection accuracy is a predictable linear function of message veracity base-rate: A formal test of Park and Levine's probability model. *Communication Monographs, 73*(3), 243–260.
Levine, T., Kim, R., & Blair, P. (2010a). (In)accuracy at detecting true and false confessions and denials: An initial test of a projected motive model of veracity judgments. *Human Communication Research, 36*, 82–102.
Levine, T., Kim, R., & Hamel, L. (2010b). People lie for a reason: Three experiments documenting the principle of veracity. *Communication Research Reports, 27*(4), 271–285.
Levine, T., Shaw, A., & Shulman, H. (2010c). Increasing deception detection accuracy with strategic questioning. *Human Communication Research, 36*, 216–231.
Levine, T., Serota, K., Shulman, H., Clare, D., Park, H.-S., Shaw, A., Shim, J.-C., & Lee, J.-H. (2011). Sender demeanor: Individual differences in sender believability have a powerful impact on deception detection judgments. *Human Communication Research, 37*, 377–403.
Levine, T., Serota, K., Carey, F., & Messer, D. (2013). Teenagers lie a lot: A further investigation into the prevalence of lying. *Communication Research Reports, 30*(3), 211–220.
Levine, T., Clare, D., Blair, J., McCornack, S., Morrison, K., & Park, H.-S. (2014a). Expertise in deception detection involves activity prompting diagnostic information rather than passive behavioral observation. *Human Communication Research, 40*(4), 442–462.
Levine, T., Clare, D., Green, T., Serota, K., & Park, H.-S. (2014b). The effects of truth-lie base rate on interactive deception detection accuracy. *Human Communication Research, 40*(3), 350–372.
Lundquist, T., Ellingsen, T., Gribbe, E., & Johannesson, M. (2009). The aversion to lying. *Journal of Economic Behavior & Organization, 70*, 81–92.

MacKinnon, S. (2014). Deception motives. In T. Levine (Ed.), *Encyclopedia of deception* (pp. 271–274). Sage.

Masip, J., & Herrero, C. (2015). Police detection of deception: Beliefs about behavioral cues to deception are strong even though contextual evidence is more useful. *Journal of Communication, 65*(1), 125–145.

McCornack, S. (2014). Difficulty of lying. In T. Levine (Ed.), *Encyclopedia of deception* (pp. 614–616). Sage.

McCornack, S., & Parks, M. (1986). Deception detection and relationship development: The other side of trust. In M. McLaughlin (Ed.), *Communication yearbook 9* (pp. 377–389). Sage.

Mercier, H., & Sperber, D. (2011). Why do humans reason? Arguments for an argumentative theory. *Behavioral and Brain Sciences, 34,* 57–111.

Meyer, P. (2011). (July). *How to spot a liar* [video]. TED conferences. https://www.ted.com/talks/pamela_meyer_how_to_spot_a_liar

Michaelian, K. (2010). In defense of gullibility: The epistemology of testimony and the psychology of deception detection. *Synthese, 176*(3), 399–427.

Michaelian, K. (2013). The evolution of testimony: Receiver vigilance, speaker honesty and the reliability of communication. *Episteme, 10*(1), 37–59.

Michaelson, E. (2018). Lying, testimony, and epistemic vigilance. In J. Meibauer (Ed.), *The Oxford handbook of lying* (pp. 215–229). Oxford University Press.

Miller, G., & Stiff, J. (1993). *Deceptive communication.* Sage.

O'Sullivan, M. (2008). Home runs and humbugs: Comments on Bond and DePaulo. *Psychological Bulletin, 134*(4), 493–497.

O'Sullivan, M., Frank, M., Hurley, C., & Tiwana, J. (2009). Police lie detection accuracy: The effect of lie scenario. *Law and Human Behavior, 33*(6), 530–538.

Park, H.-S., Levine, T., McCornack, S., Morrison, K., & Ferrara, M. (2002). How people really detect lies. *Communication Monographs, 69*(2), 144–157.

Park, H.-S., Serota, K., & Levine, T. (2021). In search of Korean outliers: "A few prolific liars" in South Korea. *Communication Research Reports, 38*(3), 206–215.

Ramjee, G., Weber, A. E., & Morar, N. S. (1999). Recording sexual behavior: Comparison of recall questionnaires with a coital diary. *Sexually Transmitted Diseases, 26,* 374–380.

Reynolds, S. (2002). Testimony, knowledge, and epistemic goals. *Philosophical Studies, 110*(2), 139–161.

Richter, T., Schroeder, S., & Wöhrmann, B. (2009). You don't have to believe everything your read: Background knowledge permits fast and efficient validation of information. *Journal of Personality and Social Psychology, 96,* 538–558.

Serota, K., & Levine, T. (2015). A few prolific liars: Variation in the prevalence of lying. *Journal of Language and Social Psychology, 34*(2), 138–157.

Serota, K., Levine, T., & Boster, F. (2010). The prevalence of lying in America: Three studies of self-reported lies. *Human Communication Research, 36,* 2–25.

Serota, K., Levine, T., & Docan-Morgan, T. (2022). Unpacking variation in lie prevalence: Prolific liars, bad lie days, or both? *Communication Monographs, 89*(3), 307–331.

Shieber, J. (2012). Against credibility. *Australasian Journal of Philosophy, 90*(1), 1–18.

Simion, M. (2020). Testimonial contractarianism: A knowledge-first social epistemology. *Nous, 55*(4), 891–916.

Simion, M., & Kelp, C. (2020). How to be an anti-reductionist. *Synthese, 197,* 2849–2866.

Sperber, D. (2001). An evolutionary perspective on testimony and argumentation. *Philosophical Topics, 29*(1–2), 401–413.

Sperber, D. (2013). Speakers are honest because hearers are vigilant: Reply to Kourken Michaelian. *Episteme, 10*(1), 61–71.

Sperber, D., Clement, F., Heintz, C., Mascaro, O., Mercier, H., & Origgi, G. (2010). Epistemic vigilance. *Mind and Language, 25*(4), 359–393.

Sternglanz, W., Morris, W., Morrow, M., & Braverman, J. (2019). A review of meta-analyses about deception detection. In T. Docan-Morgan (Ed.), *The Palgrave handbook of deceptive communication* (pp. 303–326). Palgrave Macmillan.

Vesga, A. (2023). Communicating testimonial commitment. *Ergo an Open Access Journal of Philosophy, 10*, 16.

Vrij, A., & Mann, S. (2001). Telling and detecting lies in a high-stakes situation: The case of a convicted murderer. *Applied Cognitive Psychology, 15*, 187–203.

Zuckerman, M., DeFrank, R., Hall, J., Larrance, D., & Rosenthal, R. (1979). Facial and vocal cues of deception and honesty. *Journal of Experimental Social Psychology, 15*(4), 378–396.

Zuckerman, M., DePaulo, B., & Rosenthal, R. (1981). Verbal and nonverbal communication of deception. In L. Berkowitz (Ed.), *Advances in experimental social psychology* (pp. 1–59). Academic.

Twisted Ways to Speak Our Minds, or Ways to Speak Our Twisted Minds?

Luis Rosa

1 Introduction

Cognitive dissonance is a phenomenon studied not only by psychologists, but also by philosophers.[1] There is cognitive dissonance and then there are its purported manifestations or signs, which include certain kinds of speech act. In philosophy, much attention has been paid to the latter under the name of 'Moore-paradoxical' utterances, such as a speaker's utterance of 'I am tired, but I don't believe I am'.[2]

Relatedly, philosophers have also tried to determine what, if anything, makes *akratic* mental states normatively subpar.[3] A typical example of that is a mental state where one intends to do something while believing one ought not to do it. The speech acts whereby such mental states are made manifest, of course, also signal cognitive dissonance. When a speaker utters 'I want to buy a new mattress, but I shouldn't' (in a typical conversational context), for example, she leaves her interlocutors thinking that she is somewhat at odds with herself.

In both cases, the kind of cognitive dissonance that seems to be made manifest by the speaker is a *cross-level* kind of dissonance, in that the speaker seems to either disapprove of or deny the very opinions that they are thereby expressing.

---

[1] See Festinger (1962), Elliot and Devine (1994) for how the notion of cognitive dissonance is used in psychology.
[2] See Moore (1993) and, for example, de Almeida (2001) and Williams (2015).
[3] See for example Worsnip (2018), Lasonen-Aarnio (2020) and Rosa (2022) for some of the discussion.

L. Rosa (✉)
Washington University in St. Louis, St. Louis, MO, USA

In this chapter, I am going to deal with a large class of utterances whereby speakers seem to make that kind of cognitive dissonance manifest. A mark of the utterances belonging to that class is that they all feature a step from lower- to higher-order speech: the speaker first says something (lower-order talk), and then they say something about their standing with respect to what they said before (higher-order talk). The typical Moore-paradoxical utterances are but one example of the more general phenomenon under scrutiny here, and so are utterances that seem to indicate the obtaining of akratic mental states. Those are both special cases of a more general phenomenon.

Any utterance from that large class, I claim, is either a *twisted way to speak one's mind* or a *way to speak one's twisted mind*. In the latter case, the speaker's mind harbors some kind of error or defect, and the way of talking inherits its twisted quality from the mental states it is a manifestation of. This dichotomy will reappear below. The utterances that belong to the target class include utterances of the following types (where 'p?' is an interrogative rendering of the declarative 'p'—more on this below):

(1) p, but I don't know that p.
(2) p, but it is irrational for me to believe that p.
(3) p? Though I shouldn't be in doubt about whether p.
(4) I will be there! Though it is irrational for me to intend to be there.
(5) p, but I know that $\neg p$.
(6) p, but it is rational for me to be in doubt about whether p.
(7) p? Though I know whether p.
(8) p? Though it is rational for me to believe that p.
(9) I will be there! Though I should want to be somewhere else.
(10) p, but I don't believe that p.
(11) p? Though I am not in doubt about whether p.
(12) I will be there! Though I do not intend to.
(13) p, but I believe that $\neg p$.
(14) p, but I am in doubt about whether p.
(15) p, but probably $\neg p$.
(16) p? Though I believe that p.
(17) p? Though surely p.
(18) I will be there! Though I intend to be somewhere else.

The chapter will further divide that large class of utterances into two subclasses. The utterances that belong to the first subclass, which I call 'disapprovals', are such that their higher-order bit involves the use of *normative* expressions or expressions of *evaluation* or *appraisal* (e.g., 'should', 'rational', 'know', etc.). These include the utterances of sentences of forms (1)–(9) from above. One concrete example of a disapproval is the utterance of 'God exists, but I shouldn't believe that God exists'.

The utterances that belong to the second subclass, which I call 'disavowals', are such that their higher-order bit involves *psychological* vocabulary only (e.g., the verbs 'believe', 'doubt', 'be sure', etc.) instead of normative expressions or expressions of evaluation/appraisal. These include the utterances of sentences of forms

(10)–(18) from above. One concrete example of a disavowal is a speaker's utterance of 'I have no doubt that God exists, but does he?'.

The task of the chapter will be to explain what is wrong or twisted about all of these utterances. The explanation of what is wrong about disapprovals, however, is not exactly the same as the explanation of what is wrong about disavowals. Some important commonalities aside, they are twisted in different ways. It is noted along the way that certain explanations about the wrongness or oddity of Moore-paradoxical utterances offered in the literature lack the level of generality that is needed to explain why disapprovals and disavowals in general sound so bad.

2 Expressing and Saying

Before presenting the relevant explanations, however, I need to make some of my assumptions explicit.

I will use a notion of speaker's *expressing* an attitude/its absence thereof through an utterance. I take that relation to be a three-place relation between a *speaker*, a *mental state* and an uttered sentence (a sentence *token*, including declarative, interrogative and imperative sentence tokens). Examples of that relation include a speaker's expressing her belief that *some snakes are poisonous* by uttering 'Some snakes are poisonous', a speaker's expressing her intention *to be some place* by uttering 'I will be there!', and a speaker's expressing her state of doubt or uncertainty as to whether *there are intelligent aliens* by uttering the interrogative sentence 'Are there intelligent aliens?'.

The notion of one's expressing one's attitudes/mental states through an utterance is of course crucial to expressivist theories of assent and dissent patterns of different natural language constructions.[4] Expressivists often take specific types of adjectives or verbs to play the role of helping convey some aspect of the speaker's mental life, as opposed to making a semantic contribution to how the speaker says the world is like (the world beside their mind, that is—if they do that at all). For example, the Bayesian form of expressivism put forward by Yalcin (2012, p. 125) takes it that in uttering:

(0) Allan is probably in the office,

a speaker expresses their credal state with respect to whether *Allan is in the office*, without literally *saying that* they are in that credal state. The speaker thereby makes manifest her credal state of being more confident that *Allan is in the office* than that *Allan is not in the office*, as opposed to manifesting outright belief towards a propositional content to the effect that *it is more probable that Allan is in the office than not*.

---

[4] See for example Gibbard (1990) and Schroeder (2008). For a recent expressivist proposal to diagnose Moore paradoxical phenomena, see Freitag and Yolcu (2021).

The explanation that I will offer below is *consistent* with such forms of expressivism, but it is not *committed* to them. I will assume, for example, that one can express one's belief that *p* not only by uttering '*p*', but also by uttering 'I believe that *p*', and that one can express one's certainty that *p* by uttering 'Certainly *p*', etc. (same for similar verbs/adverbs). Expression in the present sense is a relatively *cheap* phenomenon, in that there are many different linguistic means through which one can express features of one's mental states, which includes the utterance of sentences featuring propositional attitude-verbs and adverbs as a particular case. But that does not entail that the only function, or even the main function of those verbs and adverbs is to express mental states or attitudes when combined with first-person pronouns.

As already hinted at, *expressing* an attitude (or its absence thereof) is to be contrasted with *saying that* one holds (doesn't hold) that attitude. In order to say that one holds (doesn't hold) a given attitude, one must utter a sentence whose semantic value is the proposition that *one holds (doesn't hold) that attitude*. To say that one holds (doesn't hold) a given attitude is to impart that information via the utterance of a sentence that carries that very piece of information (the sentence itself is a vehicle that carries that information—think of the proposition that is the semantic value of the sentence as the information it carries).

In order for one to say that one believes in miracles, for example, one must use the verb 'believe' or some synonym/translation of it. One cannot literally say that one believes that it is raining by uttering 'It is raining'. But one can express one's belief that *it is raining* by uttering 'It is raining'. In contrast to the relation of saying, the expression of a mental state is much less tethered to linguistic form—it floats free across a multitude of linguistic expressions. One doesn't *have* to use the verb 'believe' or some synonym/translation of it in order to express one's beliefs, though one has to use such expressions in order to literally say that one has those beliefs.[5]

(For obvious reasons, the relation of expressing an attitude/its absence thereof through an utterance is to be distinguished from the expression relation that holds between a sentence and a proposition or its semantic value, as when we say that '*p*' expresses the proposition that *p*. To avoid confusion, I only use the verb 'express' in the former sense here).[6]

What is it for a speaker to express her mental states through an utterance? That is a difficult question, but minimally it involves this: in making the utterance, the speaker signals that she is in the relevant mental state to potential hearers—her utterance serves as *evidence* that she is in that state—without necessarily *saying that* she is in it. But this is not the place to try harder than that to explicate the relevant notion of expression.

---

[5] This is compatible, however, with the claim that, when it comes to speech acts (ignoring other kinds of actions), one does have to use certain kinds of verbs and adverbs in order to express other aspects of one's mental life—for example, that one has to use some device like 'probably' in order to express one's credences.

[6] See also Bar-On (2015) on this point.

3 Disapprovals

Every utterance that I will examine here is thought of as part of a single speech act, even where the sentences uttered might suggest that separate speech acts were performed (at different contexts). I adopt a convenient structuring of the target sentences, where their lower-order bit appears first and their higher-order bit appears second, reading from left to right, as in the items from the list (1)–(18) above. Thus, 'I know whether it is raining, but is it raining?' is paraphrased through 'Is it raining? Though I know whether it is raining'.

I use 'p' as a placeholder for declarative sentences, and '$p?$' as a placeholder for interrogative sentences. '$p?$' is the interrogative rendering of the declarative 'p'. For example, 'Is it raining?' is the interrogative rendering of the declarative sentence 'It is raining'.

The first group of utterances to be investigated here is the group of *disapprovals*. There are *direct* and *indirect* disapprovals. Here are some examples of direct disapprovals—think of a speaker uttering any of the following:

(1) p, but I don't know that p.
(2) p, but it is irrational for me to believe that p.
(3) $p?$ Though I shouldn't be in doubt about whether p.
(4) I will be there! Though it is irrational for me to intend to be there.

Here is a mark of direct disapprovals: the sentence used in their higher-order bit describes the mental state that the speaker expresses through their first-order bit as having some negative (deontic or epistemic) status. In the second bit of the utterance, that is, the speaker disapproves of the attitude that they have expressed in the first bit.

Consider (2), for example. When the speaker asserts that p by uttering 'p', they thereby express belief towards p—but then they go on and say that it is irrational for them to hold that very belief. In (3), the speaker asks whether p is the case by uttering '$p?$', and they thereby express a state of being in doubt about whether p is the case or not—but then they go on and say that they shouldn't be in that very state. Similarly, in the second bit of (4) the speaker says that their intention to be somewhere, which they have expressed by uttering 'I will be there!' in the first bit, is not a rational intention for them to have.

Indirect disapprovals differ from direct disapprovals in that the second bit of the former ones doesn't *directly* criticize the attitude expressed in the first bit—though some criticism of the attitude expressed in the first bit *follows* from what is said in the second bit. For example, think of a speaker uttering any of the following:

(5) p, but I know that $\neg p$.
(6) p, but it is rational for me to suspend judgment about whether p.
(7) $p?$ Though I know whether p.
(8) $p?$ Though it is rational for me to believe that p.
(9) I will be there! Though I should want to be somewhere else.

Contrast (1) and (5), for example. In (1), the second bit directly criticizes the attitude that the speaker has expressed in the first bit (a belief that is not knowledge). In contrast, the second bit of (5) makes no such direct criticism, though it *follows* from what is said in it that the belief expressed in the first bit is not knowledge: if one knows that ¬p then one does not know that p.

Similarly, it follows from what is said in the second bit of both (7) and (8) that the attitude of being in doubt about whether p, which the speaker has expressed through their first bit, is not a 100% normatively on the clear. In the case of (7), in at least one sense of 'should', it follows from the fact that one knows whether p that one shouldn't be in doubt about whether p is the case. In the case of (8), it follows from the fact that it is rational for one to believe that p that it is not rational, or at least not perfectly rational, for one to be in doubt about whether p is the case.

Some philosophers may want to dispute some of these claims—but I won't try to fix all the holes one can try to poke at the claim that (7)/(8) are disapprovals, as much as the other examples are, in that they also seem to make manifest a kind of dissonance between the speaker's attitudes and her own assessment of those attitudes.[7] If the reader doesn't want to lump these examples together with the other ones, then they are free to just think of the other ones under the label of 'disapprovals'. Still a big class of utterances is left, and many other examples besides the ones offered so far can be fleshed out.

Now why are (1)–(9) such twisted ways of talking?

4 Why Disapprovals Sound So Twisted

Any of the intensional attitudes mentioned above can be normatively subpar, or be somehow at fault or less than ideal, given the kind of attitude that it is. In holding the attitude, the cognizer fails to abide by some norm for that attitude, or that attitude falls short of its axiological (epistemic or practical) ideals.

For example, there is a norm of epistemic rationality according to which one should believe that p only if one's evidence supports p.[8] When one believes that p on the basis of insufficient evidence, one's belief is thereby normatively subpar. Another epistemic norm for belief says that one should believe that p only if one knows that p.[9] Or, at the very least, belief *at its best* is knowledge. When it isn't, it falls short of that epistemic ideal, or it is axiologically subpar (it could be better).

---

[7] Those who agree with Lewis (1982) and Stalnaker (1984) that our minds admit of different *fragments* (ways of framing things that facilitate access to different bits of information) are invited to relativize ascriptions of attitudes/expressed attitudes to *the very same* fragment. See Borgoni et al. (2021) for a recent volume on the issue of fragmentation and how it bears on a number of epistemological issues.

[8] See e.g. Feldman (2000) and Williamson (2000, chap. 8).

[9] See e.g. Smithies (2012), Littlejohn (2013).

And similarly for other intentional attitudes such as that of being in doubt about whether something is the case and that of intending that something is the case. Each of these attitudes have their own norms and axiological ideals.[10]

Now consider a speaker's sincere utterance of (1), again:

(1) *p*, but I don't know that *p*.

In uttering the first bit, the speaker *expresses* an attitude of belief that *p*. In uttering the second bit, the speaker *says that* they don't know that *p*. The reason why a speaker's utterance of (1) sounds problematic, we might think, is that *if what the speaker said* through the second bit is true, then *what the speaker expressed* through the first bit is normatively/axiologically subpar.

In sincerely uttering (1), then, the speaker is thus guaranteed to make some kind of error: either they spoke falsely in the second bit (they *do* know that *p*, even though they said they don't), or they spoke truly in the second bit, in which case the attitude that they have expressed through the first bit is normatively subpar. So *no matter how the world is like*, either the speaker's speech act is defective (in that they have asserted a falsehood) or their speech act is not that defective, but the belief that they have expressed is defective.[11]

Think of it as follows. The speaker has uttered (1) and you have heard them. Can you take their word for it? Suppose you do. So now, based on the second bit of their utterance, you conclude that they don't know that *p*. And, based on the first bit of their utterance, you conclude that they believe that *p*. Putting those two things together, then, you conclude further that they hold a belief that falls short of the ideal of knowledge.

If the speaker is right—right in what they're saying in the second bit—then the speaker is making some kind of mistake—a mistake in the attitude that they have expressed in the first bit, that is, the mistake of believing without knowing. You cannot take their word for it without finding some grounds for criticizing them (consider the criticism: 'But you don't know that!'). Otherwise, the speaker is wrong in saying what they said in the second bit. Either way, a mistake has been made by the speaker. We reach a similar conclusion with respect to a speaker's sincere utterance of (5), with only one extra step from the assumption that the speaker knows that ¬*p* to the conclusion that they don't know that *p*.

Similarly, consider a speaker's sincere utterance of (3), again:

(3) *p*? Though I shouldn't be in doubt about whether *p*.

In uttering the first bit, the speaker *expresses* a state of doubt about whether *p* is the case. In uttering the second bit, the speaker *says that* they shouldn't be in doubt

---

[10] E.g., Shah (2008) and also McHugh and Way (2018) adopt *permissibility* as a standard of correctness or fittingness for intention.

[11] I cannot quite exactly determine how this diagnosis regarding (1) is to the many purported solutions of Moore's paradox — see Green and Williams (2007) for a sample of that. It is in any case a diagnosis that generalizes to the other forms of disapproval, including those whereby the speaker asks questions and makes promises.

about whether p. The reason why a speaker's utterance of (3) sounds problematic, we might think, is that *if what the speaker said* through the second bit is true, then *what the speaker expressed* through the first bit is normatively subpar. Either that or the speaker didn't say the truth through the second bit. No matter how the world is like, again, either the speaker's speech act is defective (in that they have asserted a falsehood) or the speech act is not that defective—but then the state of uncertainty that they have expressed through the first bit is defective (they shouldn't be in it).

We reach a similar conclusion with respect to a speaker's sincere utterance of (7), with only one extra step from the assumption that the speaker knows whether p is the case to the conclusion that they shouldn't be uncertain about whether p is the case.

Summing up, regarding any disapproval: either *what the speaker says* through their second bit is false or, if it isn't, then *what the speaker expresses* through their first bit is normatively/axiologically subpar. A hearer cannot take their word for it without finding some grounds to criticize the attitudes they have expressed through their speech act. That conclusion is held, of course, under the assumption that the speaker is making a *sincere* utterance. Otherwise, if their utterance is not sincere, in that they do not hold the attitudes that they thereby express, then their speech act is problematic on that very count.

And that is why disapprovals sound so twisted. Either they are twisted ways to speak one's mind—because they are insincere, or sincere but inaccurate about the mind—or, assuming sincerity and accuracy, they are ways of speaking one's twisted mind—because the mental states thereby expressed are guaranteed to be normatively/axiologically subpar.

Notice that this explanation has the degree of generality that is needed to explain what is wrong about *all* of (1)–(9). In this it contrasts with other explanations of the absurdity of Moore-paradoxical utterances in the literature—for example, ones using the unknowability of (1) plus a knowledge norm of assertion (as in Williamson, 2000, chap. 11). Sure enough, it is impossible for one to know that p and know at the same time that *one doesn't know that p*. But how does that explain what is wrong about (3), for example? (A state of doubt is not a state of belief, therefore it is not the kind of state that is in the game to become knowledge).

Similarly, Whitcomb (2017) explains the incoherence of what he calls 'Mooreparadoxical questions', such as a speaker's utterance of 'I know it is snowing, but is it snowing?' and 'Am I the only omniscient being?' by appealing to a constitutive norm of inquiry, namely, that one should inquire into a given question only if one doesn't already know what the true answer to that question is. But how does that very explanation tell us what is wrong with (1)? Some explanations explain the twisted-ness of (1) without explaining the twisted-ness of (3), others explain the twisted-ness of (3) without explaining the twisted-ness of (1). And here I am offering an explanation that explains the twisted-ness of all of (1)–(9) at the same time.

5 The Mental Counterparts of Disapprovals

What about the 'purely mental' counterparts of (1)–(9)? That does *not* mean: Why is it problematic for one to *believe* each of (1)–(9)? So understood, the question is ill-formed. There isn't such a thing, for example, as believing that *p? Though I know whether p*. Since one cannot believe a question, one cannot believe the conjunction or concatenation of a question and a proposition.

A better sense of the initial question is made as follows. Let '(n)' be a variable ranging over all of (1)–(9). There seems to be a problem with a total intensional state that is constituted by both, the attitude that is *expressed* through the first bit of an utterance of (n) and the attitude that is *expressed* through the second bit of an utterance of (n). For example, regarding (1), when the speaker utters '*p*' they thereby express belief that *p*, and when they utter 'I don't know that *p*' they thereby express belief that *they don't know that p*. Now the question is: what is wrong with a person's doxastic state when they believe that *p* and they believe at the same time that *they don't know that p*? And, regarding (3), what is wrong with a person's doxastic state when they are in doubt about whether *p* and they believe at the same time that *they shouldn't be in doubt about whether p*? And, regarding (4), what is wrong with a person's intensional state when they intend to be somewhere and they believe at the same time that *it is irrational for them to intend to be there*? Etc.

Now the twisted ways of *talking*—the twisted utterances—are out of the picture, and we just have to determine what is twisted about the mind that harbors the relevant combinations of intentional attitudes. But the considerations from above already provide us with a ready answer to the question of what makes them so: it is *impossible* for all of the attitudes of such combinations to simultaneously abide by their respective norms or live up to their axiological ideals (norms and ideals for belief, intension, doubt, etc.). At least one of the relevant attitudes is *guaranteed* to be normatively/axiologically subpar, assuming that the other one isn't.

Consider for example believing that *p* while at the same time believing that *one doesn't know that p* (doxastic analog of (1)). Assume that the latter belief is *not* in any way normatively or axiologically subpar. Then one knows that *one doesn't know that p*. So one doesn't know that *p*, because knowledge is factive. But that entails that their belief that *p* is axiologically subpar (it doesn't constitute knowledge). Or consider being in doubt about whether *p* while at the same time believing that *one shouldn't be in doubt about whether p* (doxastic analog of (3)). Assume that the latter belief is not axiologically subpar. Then one knows that *one shouldn't be in doubt about whether p*. So one shouldn't be in doubt about whether *p*. But that entails that their state of doubt about whether *p* is normatively subpar (they shouldn't be in that state).

And so on. The same kind of explanation can be given about why any of the doxastic analogues of each of (1)–(9) are problematic.

6 Disavowals

In Sect. 4 I have offered an explanation of why *disapprovals* sound so twisted. They are either *twisted ways to speak our minds*—because they are insincere, or rather sincere but inaccurate—or they are *ways of speaking our twisted minds*—because the mental states they express are guaranteed to be normatively/axiologically subpar. Now it is time to tackle disavowals, the second big group of twisted utterances investigated here.

As I mentioned in Sect. 1, the explanation of what is so twisted about disapprovals is not exactly the same as the explanation of what is so twisted about disavowals. Similarly to disapprovals, however, disavowals also come in *direct* and *indirect* versions. Here are some examples of direct disavowals—think of a speaker sincerely uttering:

(10) *p*, but I don't believe that *p*.
(11) *p*? Though I am not in doubt about whether *p*.
(12) I will be there! Though I do not intend to.

A speaker making any of these utterances in the context of a conversation is bound to leave their interlocutors confused. Does the speaker of (10) believe that *p* or not? Is the speaker of (11) in doubt about whether *p* or not? Etc. They all sound like they are a bit mixed, ambivalent.

Here is a mark of direct disavowals: the sentence used in the second bit *say that* the speaker does not hold the attitude that they have expressed through the first bit. Another way of putting it: the sentence used in the second bit *denies that* the speaker holds the attitude that they have expressed through the first bit. And it is exactly here where the difference between direct and indirect disavowals lies, for the sentence used in the second bit of *indirect* disavowals does *not* itself deny that the speaker has the attitude that they have expressed through the first bit. Consider some examples of indirect disavowals:

(13) *p*, but I believe that $\neg p$.
(14) *p*, but I am in doubt about whether *p*.
(15) *p*, but probably $\neg p$.
(16) *p*? Though I believe that *p*.
(17) *p*? Though surely *p*.
(18) I will be there! Though I intend to be somewhere else.

For example, neither (13) nor (14) directly deny that the speaker believes that *p*, which is the attitude they have expressed by asserting that *p* in their first bit—though it might be argued that it *follows* from what is said in their second bit that the speaker does not believe that *p* (in case it is *impossible* for one to believe that *p* and believe that $\neg p$ at the same time, impossible for one to believe that *p* and be in doubt about whether *p* at the same time). This particular issue need not be addressed here, however, for the explanation that I will offer for the twisted-ness of indirect disavowals is not committed to the claim that such entailment relations in fact hold.

Now notice that there is an important difference between (15) and (17), on the one hand, and the remaining disavowals from that list, on the other. (15) and (17) feature *adverbs,* as opposed to intentional attitude *verbs* that connect the grammatical subject 'I' to some complex construction (such as a declarative sentence), as in the other examples of disavowals.

Given the presence of such examples, we cannot capture what is common to all disavowals as follows: the sentence in the second bit *says that* the speaker holds such-and-such attitude, which is not the same as the attitude that they have expressed through the first bit. The sentence 'probably ¬p' from (15), for example, does not *say that* the speaker is more confident that ¬p than she is that p, or something along these lines. Neither does the sentence 'surely p' *say that* the speaker is sure that p in (17).

This makes the task of fleshing out a general explanation of the twisted-ness of disavowals all the more difficult. Difficult, but not impossible.

7 Why Direct Disavowals Sound So Twisted

Even though the speaker who utters (15) does not thereby *say that* they are confident that ¬p, they do thereby *express* high confidence that ¬p. And, even though the speaker who utters (17) does not thereby *say that* they are sure that p, they do thereby *express* certainty that p. So expression is the more general relation to capture how the second bit of a disavowal (of any kind) relates to its first bit. Let us see how that works for the case of the direct disavowals (10)–(12), as well as the remaining indirect disavowals (13), (14), (16) and (18).

As remarked in Sect. 2, the expression of a mental state is a relatively cheap phenomenon. For there are many different speech acts, involving a variety of verbal forms, through which a speaker can express some mental state (which minimally involves, again, their signaling that they are in the relevant mental state to potential hearers—their utterance serves as *evidence* that they are in that state). In particular, the utterance of 'I don't believe that p' is not only a means of *saying that* the speaker doesn't believe that p (because that is the very bit of information that the target declarative sentence conveys) but also a means of *expressing* the state of not believing that p.[12] Similarly, 'I am in doubt about whether p' is a means of expressing doubt about whether p, and so on. The difference between 'surely p' and 'I am sure that p' is that the speaker *says that* they are sure that p by uttering the latter, not by uttering the former. But *both* of them express the speaker's state of being sure that p.

Intentional attitude verbs have this special feature, namely, that when a speaker uses the singular first-person pronoun to relate themselves to a proposition or question through that verb, they end up not only *saying that* they have/do not have

---
[12] On this point, see also Williams (1998), Marek (2011) and Freitag and Yolcu (2021).

such-and-such intentional attitude, but also *expressing* that very attitude/its absence to their hearers. 'I intend to be there' is an expression of one's intention to be there, 'I do not intend to be there' an expression of one's lack of intention to be there — even though both of them also *say* things *about* the speaker's mental state (in contrast to 'You bet!', for example).

In uttering an disavowal, then, the speaker (i) expresses one kind of attitude or mental condition through the first bit of the utterance, and (ii) they express a different kind of attitude or mental condition through the second bit, sometimes using a sentence that also *says that* the speaker has that attitude or satisfies that condition, other times using a sentence that features adverbs such as 'probably' and 'surely'— and one that does *not* say that the speaker has that attitude or satisfies that condition.

Now notice that, given the general characterization in (i) and (ii), we cannot expect to account for the twisted-ness of disavowals in the same manner that we have accounted for the twisted-ness of disapprovals above (Sect. 4). That is, we cannot explain the twisted-ness of a disavowal starting as follows: assuming sincerity on the part of the speaker, either what is said in the second bit is false, or blah-blah-blah (something about the first bit). For now we cannot simply assume that there is something that is *said* in the second bit of disavowals to begin with, over and above the fact that the speaker expresses some aspect of their mental life through it.

Rather, the relevant explanation should go as follows. Assume that a speaker utters a disavowal. According to our characterization from above, then, the speaker has thereby expressed two different intentional attitudes or conditions in the course of their utterance. The problematic character of disavowals stems from the fact that it is *either* impossible for the utterance to be sincere, in that it is impossible for all of those attitudes or conditions to simultaneously obtain *or*, even if it is possible for them to simultaneously obtain, it is still impossible for all of the attitudes thereby expressed to simultaneously abide by their respective norms or to simultaneously live up to their ideals. In the latter case, again, at least one of the relevant attitudes is guaranteed to be normatively/axiologically subpar, assuming that the other one isn't. Let us examine some concrete examples of this kind of explanation now.

Suppose again the speaker utters (10):

(10) p, but I do not believe that p.

In uttering the first bit, the speaker expresses an attitude of believing that p. In uttering the second bit, the speaker expresses a mental state of non-belief that p, signaling that she does *not* believe that p. The reason why a speaker's utterance of (1) sounds so twisted is that the speaker cannot satisfy both of these conditions at the same time: they cannot believe that p and not believe that p at the same time (at least not relative to the same 'fragment' — see Fn. 7). That means, in effect, that it is impossible for the speaker to *sincerely* utter (10). For, in order for them to sincerely utter (10), they would have to believe that p (so as to sincerely utter the first bit), and they would also have to *not* believe that p (so as to sincerely utter the second bit).

A similar explanation holds for the twisted-ness of (11) and (12), since it is impossible for one to be in doubt about whether p (a condition expressed by a speaker's sincere utterance of the interrogative '*p?*') and at the same time not be in doubt about whether *p* (a condition expressed by a speaker's sincere utterance of 'I am not in doubt about whether *p*'), and it is impossible for one to intend to be somewhere (a condition expressed by a speaker's sincere utterance of 'I will be there!') and at the same time not to intend to be there (a condition expressed by a speaker's sincere utterance 'I do not intend to be there').

So the twisted-ness of *direct* disavowals stems from the impossibility that the speaker is and is not in a certain mental state at the same time. In the case of *indirect* disavowals, however, the story is a bit different, at least assuming that it is *not* impossible for one to have mutually contradictory beliefs, or to be in doubt about whether *p* while at the same time believing that *p*, or to intend to bring about mutually incompatible scenarios. I turn to that now.

8 Why Indirect Disavowals Sound So Twisted

Even assuming that the attitudes that a speaker expresses through an indirect disavowal are compossible, the twisted-ness of their utterance still stems from a certain kind of impossibility, namely, the impossibility that all of those attitudes simultaneously abide by their norms or live up to their ideals. One of the attitudes is guaranteed to be normatively/axiologically subpar, assuming that the other one isn't.

Suppose, for example, that the speaker utters (14):

(14) *p*, but I am in doubt about whether *p*.

In uttering the first bit, the speaker expresses an attitude of believing that *p*. In uttering the second bit, the speaker expresses an attitude of being in doubt about whether *p*. The reason why an utterance of (14) sounds so twisted is that, even if it is possible for the speaker to believe that *p* and be in doubt about whether *p* at the same time, these two attitudes cannot both be at their epistemic bests or abide by their norms at the same time. For one is rationally required not to believe that *p* and be in doubt about whether *p*.[13] And, if one knows that *p*, then one is not justified in being in doubt about whether *p*.

That very same explanation is the one that explains why an utterance of (16) sounds so twisted, again:

(16) *p?* Though I believe that *p*.

For, in uttering the first bit, the speaker expresses an attitude of doubt about whether *p* and, in uttering the second bit, they express an attitude of belief that *p*.

What about indirect disavowals that do not feature intentional attitude verbs, but rather adverbs, in their second bit? Let us consider an utterance of (15), again:

(15) *p*, but probably ¬*p*.

---

[13] This (wide scope) rational requirement is a meant here as a requirement of *coherence*.

In uttering the first bit, again, the speaker expresses an attitude of believing that p. In uttering the second bit, however, the speaker expresses more confidence in $\neg p$ than in p, or high credence that $\neg p$ (higher than 0.5, using the unit interval). The reason why an utterance of (15) sounds so twisted is that, even if it is possible for the speaker to believe that p and be confident that $\neg p$ at the same time, these two attitudes cannot both be at their epistemic bests or abide by their norms at the same time. For one is rationally required not to believe that p and be confident that $\neg p$. And, if one knows that p, then one is not justified in being confident that $\neg p$.

Or consider an utterance of (17), again:

(17) p? Though surely p.

In raising the question in the first bit, the speaker expresses an attitude of being in doubt about whether p. In uttering the second bit, however, they express an attitude of being sure that p. But one of these attitudes is guaranteed to be normatively/axiologically subpar, given that the other one isn't.

So the explanation of the twisted-ness of indirect disavowals—namely, that in uttering them the speaker expresses attitudes that cannot be normatively on the clear or at their bests at the same time—is essentially the same for disavowals that involve intentional attitude verbs and for disavowals that involve adverbs such as 'probably' and 'certainly'.

9   A Sum-Up of Everything

The overarching explanation of the twisted-ness of disavowals of both kinds goes as follows, then. Either they are *twisted ways to speak one's mind*—because they must be insincere, on account of it being impossible for the speaker to hold all of the attitudes that they thereby express—or, even assuming sincerity, they are *ways of speaking one's twisted mind*—because the attitudes that are thereby expressed are guaranteed to be normatively/axiologically subpar.

Notice that this explanation has the degree of generality that is needed to explain what is wrong about *all* of (10)–(18). Notice, furthermore, that the explanation already contains a diagnosis of what would be wrong with the 'purely mental' counterparts of (10)–(18), *if any such mental counterparts could there be*.

The mental counterpart of a disavowal would be a mental state where one holds all the attitudes or satisfies all the mental conditions expressed by the utterance of that disavowal. But in the case of the direct disavowals (10)–(12) and their ilk, as we saw, it is not even in principle possible for a subject to be in a mental state of believing p and *not* be in a mental state of believing that p, to be in a mental state of doubt about whether p and *not* be in a mental state of doubt about whether p, etc. So the question concerning the twisted-ness of the purely mental counterparts of direct disavowals doesn't even get off the ground—for *there aren't* such purely mental counterparts to begin with.

Where the purely mental counterpart of a disavowal is even so much as possible, however, the explanation of their twisted-ness is already contained in what was said above: it is impossible for all of the attitudes that make up such counterparts to abide by their norms, or to be at their bests/satisfy their respective ideals at the same time. Where the question about the purely mental counterpart of a disavowal *does* get off the ground, then, the answer to it can be borrowed directly from the very explanation of the twisted-ness of the *speech act* of uttering that disavowal offered above.

Disapprovals and disavowals are two ways of talking that seem to make manifest some kind of cross-level cognitive dissonance on the part of the speaker, and they constitute a large, comprehensive class of utterances. They are unified by the fact that they feature a step from lower- to higher-order speech: the speaker first says something, and then they say something about their standing with respect to what they said before. I have tried to explain why *any* member of that large class sounds so twisted in a way that works for both disapprovals and disavowals: they are either twisted ways of speaking our minds (because insincere or inaccurate about our minds) or they are ways to speak our twisted minds (because they express mental states that are guaranteed to fall short of their normative standards or ideals).

Whether this attempted explanation will withstand further critical scrutiny, however, is left for future investigation.

References

Bar-On, D. (2015). Expression: Acts, products, and meaning. In S. Gross, N. Tebben, & M. Williams (Eds.), *Meaning without representation: Essays on truth, expression, normativity, and naturalism* (pp. 180–209). Oxford University Press.

Borgoni, C., Kindermann, D., & Onofri, A. (2021). *The fragmented mind*. Oxford University Press.

de Almeida, C. (2001). What Moore's paradox is about. *Philosophy and Phenomenological Research, 62*(1), 33–58.

Elliot, A. J., & Devine, P. G. (1994). On the motivational nature of cognitive dissonance: Dissonance as psychological discomfort. *Journal of Personality and Social Psychology, 67*(3), 382–394.

Feldman, R. (2000). The ethics of belief. *Philosophy and Phenomenological Research, 60*(3), 667–695.

Festinger, L. (1962). Cognitive Dissonance. *Scientific American, 207*(4), 93–106.

Freitag, W., & Yolcu, N.-M. (2021). An expressivist solution to Moorean paradoxes. *Synthese, 199*(1–2), 5001–5024.

Gibbard, A. (1990). *Wise choices, apt feelings: A theory of normative judgment*. Harvard University Press.

Green, M., & Williams, J. N. (Eds.). (2007). *Moore's paradox: New essays on belief, rationality and the first person*. Clarendon Press.

Lasonen-Aarnio, M. (2020). Enkrasia or evidentialism? Learning to love mismatch. *Philosophical Studies, 177*(3), 597–632.

Lewis, D. (1982). Logic for equivocators. *Noûs, 16*(3), 431–441.

Littlejohn, C. (2013). The Russellian retreat. *Proceedings of the Aristotelian Society, 113*(3), 293–320.

Marek, J. C. (2011). Expressing and describing experiences: A case of showing versus saying. *Acta Analytica, 26*(1), 53–61.

McHugh, C., & Way, J. (2018). What is good reasoning. *Philosophy and Phenomenological Research, 96*(1), 153–174.
Moore, G. E. (1993). Moore's paradox. In T. Baldwin (Ed.), *G. E. Moore: Selected writings*. Routledge.
Rosa, L. (2022). Coherence and Knowability. *The Philosophical Quarterly, 72*(4), 960–978.
Schroeder, M. (2008). *Being for: Evaluating the semantic program of expressivism*. Oxford University Press.
Shah, N. (2008). How action governs intention. *Philosophers' Imprint, 8*, 1–19.
Smithies, D. (2012). The normative role of knowledge. *Noûs, 46*(2), 265–288.
Stalnaker, R. (1984). *Inquiry*. MIT Press.
Whitcomb, D. (2017). One kind of asking. *The Philosophical Quarterly, 67*(266), 148–168.
Williams, J. N. (1998). Wittgensteinian accounts of Moorean absurdity. *Philosophical Studies, 92*(3), 283–306.
Williams, J. N. (2015). Moore's paradox in thought. *Philosophy Compass, 10*(1), 24–37.
Williamson, T. (2000). *Knowledge and its limits*. Oxford University Press.
Worship, A. (2018). The conflict of evidence and coherence. *Philosophy and Phenomenological Research, 96*(1), 3–44.
Yalcin, S. (2012). Bayesian expressivism. *Proceedings of the Aristotelian Society, 112*, 123–160.

Aesthetic Disagreement, Aesthetic Testimony, and Defeat

Mona Simion and Christoph Kelp

1 Introduction

The phenomenon of defeat is hot in epistemology. However, surprisingly little attention has been paid to defeat in the semantics of aesthetic discourse and aesthetic epistemology.[1] We think that this is a lack that needs supplying. Here, we first argue for a conditional claim: if epistemic defeat about aesthetic matters—what we will call, for convenience, aesthetic defeat—exists, this gives us (*pro tanto*) reason to worry about several views in the semantics of aesthetic discourse—to wit, contextualism and relativism—and one major player in the epistemology of aesthetic testimony—i.e. pessimism about the capacity of aesthetic testimony to generate knowledge. None of these can straightforwardly accommodate aesthetic defeat. The alternative is to endorse scepticism about aesthetic defeat; however, there is reason to believe the latter move is highly implausible. We conclude that the theorist of aesthetic discourse is faced with a choice between either being a realist about the semantics and an optimist about the epistemology, or coming up with a thorough defence of defeat scepticism.

---

[1] The epistemology of aesthetic testimony has mostly focused on whether one can gain knowledge about aesthetic matters on the mere say-so of others. Aesthetic testimony optimism (e.g. Robson, 2023) answers 'yes.' Pessimism (see e.g. Hopkins (2000) and Whiting (2015)) disagrees. The kind of pessimism we are discussing here is also known as unavailability pessimism. It is distinguished from unusability pessimism (e.g. Hills, 2002), which we won't discuss here, and according to which testimony can generate knowledge of aesthetic matters in hearers, but knowledge on mere say-so has a lesser normative status, in that it cannot e.g. justify action or assertion.

M. Simion (✉) · C. Kelp
Cogito Epistemology Research Centre, University of Glasgow, Glasgow, UK
e-mail: mona.simion@glasgow.ac.uk; christoph.kelp@glasgow.ac.uk

Why does this matter? If we're right, the epistemology of conversation about aesthetic matters has major implications for the semantics aesthetic discourse, as well as for the epistemologies of warranted aesthetic assertion, warranted testimonial belief about aesthetic matters, as well as the metaphysics of aesthetic acts.

Here is the game plan: We start by motivating the claim that scepticism about aesthetic defeat is implausible (Sect. 1). Further on, we discuss consequences for the semantics of aesthetic discourse and the epistemology of aesthetic disagreement and testimony (Sects. 2 and 3). Last, we show how a view that combines realism in semantics with optimism in epistemology has all the resources we need to accommodate the data on the ground, in that it can explain both aesthetic defeat and different levels of faultlessness on the side of the disagreeing parties.

2 Aesthetic Defeat

Consider the following exchange between a traditionalist about fashion and her avant-garde friend:

Veggie Hat §1
Ann: Wow, sorry to say, Mary, but that hat you're wearing is exceptionally ugly. What got into you to buy such a thing? Really? Velvet aubergines on felt?
Mary: I love it, it's gorgeous! You're just a bit of a traditionalist, Ann, I didn't quite expect you to like it anyway, to be honest.
Ann: Dearest Mary, ever so avant-garde. I guess we can just agree to disagree.

Whatever we might think about veggie hats ourselves, one thing is clear: we are not convinced that Mary is doing something terribly wrong in dismissing Ann's testimony in this case. Indeed, knowing Ann to be such a traditionalist, Mary seems right to hold steadfast in her aesthetic beliefs about avant-garde fashion in spite of Ann's assertion, and vice versa.

Contrast the conversation in Veggie Hat §1 with the following exchange between Mary and her friends who, like Mary, are also avant-garde fashionistas:

Veggie Hat §2
Mary: Folks, check out what a gorgeous hat I found at the boutique down the street! So avant-garde!
Mary's entire group of friends: Wow, sorry to say, but that's one ugly hat, Mary! Really? Velvet aubergines on felt? There's avant-garde, and then there are fashion car crashes!

Finally, consider the following case:

Veggie Hat §3
Mary just bought a new hat from the boutique down the street, which she finds fabulous and very avant-garde. It's a felt hat featuring velvet aubergines. Upon arriving home, she googles the model only to find out that the hat in question won the award for the ugliest hat of the year at the most recent expert poll by fashion.com. Indeed, unprecedentedly, fashion experts interviewed unanimously agreed that the hat was spectacularly unsightly.

Our intuition is that, in contrast to Veggie Hat §1, in Veggie Hat §2 and Veggie Hat §3, Mary should seriously consider taking that hat back. We are not wedded to this intuition, though; maybe she could defensibly hold on to it for a bit longer and investigate the issue further; maybe she could even try to launch a new trend; we can get ourselves to think either way. One datum that we take to be very robust, however—bordering on truism—is the following fact: *Mary should be less confident that the hat is pretty in Veggie Hat §2 and §3 than in Veggie Hat §1 (henceforth also 'the defeat datum').*

Why do we call this datum 'the defeat datum'? To answer this question, we'd like to briefly say a few words about defeat. For present purposes, we will be working with what we take to be a fairly lightweight characterisation of defeat as having a reason against. While defeat is a phenomenon that can be found in all normative domains, here we will focus on epistemic defeat, and, to be more precise, on defeat for having various doxastic attitudes such as beliefs, degrees of confidence, and so on.

To get a better handle on defeat, it may be worth looking at a paradigm case. First, suppose that I tell you that I will be away from work tomorrow. You come to justifiably believe with a high degree of confidence that I will not be at work tomorrow based on my testimony. When you arrive at work the next day, you are told by a colleague that I am in my office with a client. Your colleague's testimony that I am in the office with a client is a reason against believing with so high a degree of confidence that I will be away from work today and so constitutes a defeater for your high degree of confidence.

A key feature of defeaters for doxastic attitudes is that defeat affects justification of doxastic attitudes negatively. If, in the case above, you hold on to your high confidence that I am not at work, you will at least be less justified in your doxastic attitude. Your justification has been undermined or defeated.[2]

With these points in play, we can now see why we call the above datum 'the defeat datum'. After all, what the datum indicates is that there is such a thing as epistemic defeat about aesthetic matters. Here is why. By stipulation, Mary starts off with the same degree of justified confidence in all three cases. Crucially, by the defeat datum, in Veggie Hat §2 and §3, she ends up in a situation in which she should be less confident that the veggie hat is pretty than in Veggie Hat §1. But, of course, if Mary should be less confident in Veggie Hat §2 and §3 than in §1, it must be that her justification for believing that the hat is pretty has been affected differentially. In particular, it must be that she has less justification for believing that the hat is pretty in §2 and §3 than in §1. That's why she should have a lower degree of confidence in §2 and §3 than in §1. But, of course, if Mary's justification for believing that the hat is pretty has been affected differentially in this way, it follows that her justification underwent aesthetic defeat in §2 and §3, but not (or less so) in §1.

Note that defeaters can work in different ways. Most importantly for present purposes, defeaters can negatively affect one's justification for believing p by providing one with a reason for believing not-p. Defeaters that work in this way are known as 'rebutting' defeaters (e.g. Pollock, 1986). The case in which you believe

---

[2] For more on defeat see e.g. (Pollock, 1986) and the contributions to (Brown & Simion, 2021).

that I will not be at work and the next day a colleague tells you that you are in a meeting with a client is a case of rebutting defeat. The colleague's testimony negatively affects your justification for believing that I am not at work today by providing you with a reason for believing that I am at work today. Crucially, the defeaters Mary acquires in Veggie Hat §2 and §3 are also rebutting defeaters. Just as your colleague's testimony negatively affects your justification for believing that I am not at work today by providing you with a reason for believing that I am at work today, so the testimony of the friends/experts in Veggie Hat §2 and §3 negatively affect Mary's justification for believing that her hat is pretty by providing a reason for believing that it is not pretty.[3]

Can on deny the defeat datum? Since our first ambition here is merely to defend a conditional claim—i.e., if aesthetic defeat, then realism about the semantics and optimism about the epistemology—, and due to lack of space, we will not explore all possible ways to defend scepticism about aesthetic defeat. However, here are three reasons to think a defence of aesthetic defeat scepticism will not be a trivial endeavour:

Consider, first, an error theoretic response to the cases above: what we take to be 'the defeat datum' is not a normative, but a descriptive datum: the intuition does not track a 'should'—i.e. that Mary *should* be more confident in one case than in the other that he hat is pretty—but rather a psychological datum—that Mary *would* be more confident in one case than in the other. Compatibly, on this view: Mary doesn't have to hold these different degrees of confidence in the two cases, in virtue of the fact that there is no such thing as aesthetic defeat. One desideratum on a view like this would, of course, be to explain why, even though she shouldn't, we intuit that Mary would be more confident in the first case than in the other two cases. Perhaps one can blame peer pressure as the culprit in the first case, and prestige bias in the second. One problem with this reply, however, is that it overgeneralizes to all cases of defeat—i.e. to cases about non-aesthetic defeat as well.

Another, even more serious problem is that we don't need an epistemic obligation for our argument to go through: a permission to hold different levels of confidence will do. To see this, note that, if aesthetic defeat is not an actual phenomenon, Mary's evidential situation doesn't change from one case to another, so changing her levels of confidence would be unwarranted, and thereby epistemically impermissible. But that result seems even more problematic in terms of extensional adequacy: surely, even if we get ourselves in a mindset to reject the obligation claim, Mary is at least permitted to be less confident that the hat is pretty when there she overwhelming testimony to this effect.

Third: It is plausibly a desideratum on any theory of the aesthetic to accommodate the phenomenon of aesthetic expertise. Insofar as experts exist in the aesthetic domain, though, we need to accept that everyday folk will be more justified to form beliefs based on their testimony about aesthetic matters, than based on layman

---

[3] Defeaters can also negatively affect one's justification for believing that p by providing one with a reason to believe that one's basis for believing that p is not in good working order (aka undercutting defeaters) (e.g. Pollock, 1986).

testimony. Indeed, without this assumption in play, it seems as though the existence of the institution of the aesthetic expert itself remains unmotivated. This difference in justification, in turn, can be in justification to believe that a particular item x is pretty, or in the denial of this claim. In turn, justification in favour of believing the denial of 'x is pretty' will also be justification against believing that it is pretty—i.e. it will constitute a defeater for believing that x is pretty. In a nutshell, then, the phenomenon of aesthetic expertise, together with the plausible claim that one should be more confident in what an expert says than in what a layman says, implies that there is such a thing as aesthetic defeat: when an expert asserts that x is ugly one has less justification to believe that x is pretty than when a layman asserts the same proposition. This is precisely the defeat datum we started from. As such, it would seem, denying the defeat datum would commit the contextualist and the relativist to either denying that there is such a thing as expertise in the aesthetic domain, or denying that one should be more confident in what an expert says than in what a layman says—in which case the very existence of institution of the aesthetic expert remains unmotivated. We take it that these are heavy costs. This is why we worry about the prospects of an aesthetic defeat scepticism.

That being said, not much rests on this for our purposes: again, our concern here is merely to defend a conditional claim: As we are about to argue, the defeat datum provides reason for optimism about both the capacity of aesthetic testimony to generate knowledge, and the prospects of a realist semantics for aesthetic discourse.

3 Semantics

Notable views in the semantics of aesthetic discourse aim to explain why, in cases like Veggie Hat §1, it is intuitive that (1) Ann and Mary disagree (henceforth, the disagreement intuition), and (2) they do so faultlessly—in a sense to be further specified (the faultlessness intuition).

3.1 Contextualism and Defeat

Very roughly, a contextualist semantics for a certain term holds that the term can have different contents in different contexts. As a result, sentences featuring context sensitive terms can have different contents, i.e. they express different propositions, in different contexts also. Contextualist approaches[4] to aesthetic disagreement venture to explain the intuitions about aesthetic disagreement by appealing to a contextualist semantics for aesthetic terms. Contextualist approaches to aesthetic disagreement excel when it comes to handling the faultlessness intuition. For

---

[4] For recent defences see e.g. Sundell (2011), Plunkett and Sundell (2013).

instance, in the Veggie Hat cases, if 'pretty' affords a contextualist semantics, the sentence 'The hat is pretty' may express different propositions depending on whether it is uttered in Mary's context or in Ann's context. In this way, contextualism can allow that Mary's assertion that the hat is pretty and Ann's assertion that it is not pretty are both true, in the relevant contexts. Contextualism promises to accommodate the faultlessness intuition in a straightforward way.

The bad news for contextualist approaches to aesthetic disagreements is that they struggle to also accommodate the disagreement intuition.[5] After all, if 'The hat is pretty' expresses different propositions in Mary's and Ann's contexts, the contents of their assertions and beliefs are different as well. What's more, if both of these propositions can simultaneously be true, then they are entirely compatible. In that case, it is hard to see how there could still be a genuine disagreement between Mary and Ann.

Most importantly for our purposes, in virtue of struggling to predict that there is a genuine disagreement in these cases, contextualism also struggles to explain the defeat datum that we put forth in the previous section. If Ann in Veggie Hat §1, Mary's friends in Veggie Hat §2 and the experts in Veggie Hat §3 alike are all merely asserting propositions that are perfectly compatible with the proposition that Mary asserts, why is it that Mary should be less confident in §2 and §3 than in §1? After all, the content of Ann's friends' assertion that the hat isn't pretty is that the hat isn't pretty-according-to-Ann's- friends'-context (or something similar). But clearly, if that's what Ann's friends' assertion amounts to, it's not the case that Mary should now lower her confidence in her belief that the hat is pretty. After all, what this belief amounts to is that the hat is pretty-according-to-Mary's-context (or something similar).

One popular way to go about accommodating the disagreement intuition within a contextualist framework is to appeal to metalinguistic disagreements: according to one prominent view, due to David Plunkett and Tim Sundell (2013), what is going on in the Veggie Hat cases is a disagreement about whether the veggie hat *should* be included in the extension of 'pretty hat' or not at the context. Now the main reason this is relevant for present purposes is that if contextualists can successfully accommodate the disagreement intuition, then they might also be able to handle the defeat datum. More specifically, in Veggie Hat §2 and §3, the assertions by her fashionista friends/the fashion expert may still provide a defeater for Mary's belief that the veggie hat should be included in the extension of 'pretty hat'.

One problem that this view faces concerns inter-contextual disagreements. Suppose Ann believes the hat is ugly, whilst being in her house in Leeds and Mary believes it's pretty, whilst at work in Bristol. Suppose, further, that they don't even know about each other. In this case, they would still count as disagreeing about whether the hat is pretty or not—although not sharing a context of assessment that the metalinguistic disagreement could pick out. Since they don't share a context of

---

[5] This point has been pressed forcefully especially by champions of relativism e.g. Kölbel (2002) and MacFarlane (2014).

assessment, it's hard to see how it can be that they disagree about what should be included under the extension of 'pretty hat' at a particular context of assessment.

Even if we set this problem aside, there are remaining difficulties. To see the first, note that small children can have aesthetic disagreements. For instance, two three-year-olds may disagree on whether a certain dress featuring a unicorn is pretty. Arguably, however, they don't disagree on whether the dress in question should be in the extension of the term 'pretty'. They don't have the intellectual sophistication required to form beliefs about matters as complex as this.

Another question that arises concerns the type of should at issue in the metalinguistic disagreement in question. One way to go would be to take the should in question to be an all-things-considered should. However, it seems as though we can easily imagine cases in which Mary and Ann agree that the veggie hat should—all things considered—be included in the extension of 'pretty hat'—say, because they both have a gun to their head, in which case prudential considerations override aesthetic considerations. However, even in a case like this, it seems like they would still be in disagreement as to whether the veggie hat actually is pretty or not.

According to a more plausible alternative, the 'should' at stake is an aesthetic should. Unfortunately, this suggestion does not fare much better, for at least two reasons. First, consider the question as to what, if anything, grounds this aesthetic should. The intuitively most plausible answer is that it is the aesthetic truths on the ground. For instance, what explains why Mary's veggie hat should (aesthetically) fall under 'pretty hat' is that it is pretty. However, this answer isn't available for champions of the present proposal. After all, this leads us right back into the territory of first order aesthetic disagreement, which is what we needed to explain in the first place. What's more, it is particularly hard to see how learning about the metalinguistic disagreement could still provide a genuine defeater for the first order belief. For instance, if what Mary learns in her exchange with her fashionista friend is that they think that the veggie hat should not be included in the extension of 'pretty', it's not clear that she should lower her confidence that the hat is pretty, given that it is true at her context that it is pretty and given that whether the hat should fall in the extension of 'pretty' turns on the first-order truths on the ground. But, of course, since it cannot be aesthetic truths on the ground that explain the aesthetic should under consideration, the question arises as to what does.

Let's move on to the second reason why the metalinguistic view remains problematic. If the 'should' at stake here is indeed an aesthetic should, then it is plausible that something aesthetically should fall in the extension of aesthetic term 'F' if and only if it is F. For instance, Mary's veggie hat aesthetically should fall in the extension of 'pretty' if and only if it is pretty.[6] But now note that since according to contextualists aesthetic terms such as 'pretty' are context sensitive, then 'aesthetically should fall in the extension of "pretty"' must be context sensitive also. Otherwise, it couldn't be that something aesthetically should fall in the extension of 'pretty' *if and only if* it is pretty. But of course, once we are clear that 'aesthetically should fall

---

[6] Note that this leaves open the question as to what the direction of explanation is here.

in the extension of "pretty"' is context sensitive in this way, it is easy to see that the exact same problem that we encountered at the first order will resurface at the metalinguistic level. In particular, if 'The veggie hat is pretty' means something different when uttered by Mary than when uttered by Ann, then so does 'The veggie hat aesthetically should fall in the extension of "pretty"'. But if so, we don't have a disagreement at the metalinguistic level either. Finally, it goes without saying that the problem with defeat will resurface also.

3.2 Relativism and Defeat

What we saw above is that this allowed contextualists to accommodate the faultlessness intuition but not the disagreement intuition. Relativist approaches (e.g. Kölbel, 2002; MacFarlane, 2014) aim to improve on contextualism by avoiding the idea that aesthetic terms are context sensitive. As a result, sentences featuring them will express the same proposition across all contexts. For instance, 'The veggie hat is pretty' expresses the same proposition no matter whether Mary or Ann utters it, i.e. the proposition that the veggie hat is pretty. Relativists accommodate the disagreement intuition in this way.

This leaves the question of the faultlessness intuition. How can it be that, for instance, Mary and Ann are both faultless given that they are genuinely disagreeing on one and the same proposition, i.e. that the veggie hat is pretty? To answer this question, relativists distinguish between context and circumstance of evaluation. The circumstance of evaluation includes a range of parameters that determine the truth value of the proposition determined at the context. Standard views include worlds and times in the circumstance of evaluation.

With these points in play, here is how the relativist explains the faultlessness intuition. To return to our familiar example, while the sentence 'The veggie hat is pretty' expresses the same proposition no matter whether Mary or Ann utters it, whether it is true or not will turn in addition on who is the judge in question. And the thought is that when Mary is the judge, the proposition comes out true, while when Ann is the judge, it comes out false. In this way, relativism promises to improve on contextualism.

Is the view also, thereby, going to fare better on the defeat datum? Unfortunately, there is reason to think that the answer is no: relativism does no better than contextualism. To see this recall that a defeater for a doxastic attitude that p provides a reason against believing p. More specifically, a rebutting defeater for believing p provides a reason against believing p by providing a reason to believe that not-p, and thereby that one's belief that p is false. That's why one should lower one's degrees of confidence in the face of defeat. The trouble is that, on relativist approaches to aesthetic disagreement, when one believes that p, an assertion that not-p cannot provide a defeater for one's belief that p. This is because the assertion that not-p simply doesn't give one a reason to believe that one's belief that p is false. After all, whether one's belief that p is false turns on who fills the judge parameter.

And the fact that if the judge parameter is filled by a different person means that the proposition one believes comes out false is no reason to think that one's own belief is false, given that the truth of one's own belief turns on a different judge parameter. To return to the case of Mary and the veggie hat, on a relativist view, when Mary discovers that her fashionista friends/the fashion experts believe that her hat is not pretty, this gives her no reason to believe that her belief that the hat is pretty is false. After all, whether her belief is true turns on whether its content is true relative to her circumstance of evaluation, at which she, Mary, fills the judge parameter. The fact that the content of Mary's belief is false relative to some other circumstance of evaluation, at which someone else, e.g. her fashionista friends or the fashion experts, fill the judge parameter, is of no consequence.[7] This is why relativists cannot accommodate the defeat datum.

3.3 Realism and Defeat

According to realist views, there is no semantic mystery about aesthetic disagreements such as the Veggie Hat cases: one of the two parties is right, and the other one is wrong. On this view, short of occasional cases of indeterminacy, disagreements about aesthetic matters are garden variety factual disagreements: there is a fact of the matter as to whether the veggie hat is pretty or not, and thereby one of the parties to the disagreement is making a mistake. Unsurprisingly, realists will have no problem at all accommodating the defeat datum: since, according to realists, aesthetic matters are merely garden variety matters of fact, aesthetic beliefs and their justification are the proper target of epistemic defeat. According to the realist, then, the difference between Veggie Hat §1 on the one hand, and Veggie Hat §2 and §3 on the other, lies in degrees of justification: Mary gets more epistemic support for the denial of 'the hat is pretty' from a large number of peers and, respectively, from fashion experts, than she gets from one disagreeing party of no special aesthetic expertise.

Defenders of realism are, however, hard pressed to explain the intuition that, as opposed to non-aesthetic factual disagreements, it feels to us as though neither Mary nor Ann made any mistake in forming the beliefs they formed and, furthermore, that it wouldn't be an outrage to hold on to their beliefs even post-disagreement.

We believe this datum does not constitute a problem for the realist at all. After all, Ann and Mary's 'faultlessness' need not imply that none of our characters is asserting

---

[7] One might wonder whether this isn't that too strong. Doesn't Mary know that the standards of taste of her fashionista friends/experts are very similar to her own? In that case, won't their judgement defeat her own? No. To see why not, note that we may suppose that Mary doesn't know that the standards of taste are thus similar. One may now wonder whether in that case the defeat intuition isn't significantly weakened. Even if we allow this in the case of her fashionista friends, it clearly won't work for the case where the disagreement is with fashion experts. After all, clearly we can get the defeat intuition without assuming that Mary knows that the fashion experts have very similar standards of taste to her own.

a falsehood[8]: one can make mistakes faultlessly, after all, in all walks of life. To see this, consider, first, an internalist dogmatism about justification, according to which one is prima facie justified in believing that p if it seems to one that p (e.g. Huemer, 2007). Straightforwardly, this view delivers the result that both women are justified in their beliefs about the veggie hat, since they have the corresponding seemings. Compatibly, of course, one of them is wrong: seemings can sometimes lead us astray.

Here is, also, alternatively, how a mainstream externalist theory of justification can explain what is going on in Veggie Hat §1: both women employ their reliable aesthetic belief formation processes in forming their respective beliefs about the veggie hat (e.g. Goldman, 1979). Reliability, though, need not imply infallibility. As such, it is hardly surprising that one of them ends up being right, and the other one wrong: it is just an instance in which the otherwise reliable aesthetic beliefs formation process of one of them is failing. What if we stipulate that e.g. Ann is not, in fact, reliable about aesthetic matters; in fact, she gets it wrong all the time? Isn't it true that the intuition of faultlessness survives this stipulation, while the explanation in terms of reliability justification does not? It may. Crucially, however, when it does, this is just a garden variety case of blameless deception for the reliabilist, in the same category with brains in vats. Since this problem and its solution are not specific to cases of aesthetic false belief, but rather to seemings-sourced deception more generally, we take it that the epistemic reliabilist that likes semantic realism about aesthetic discourse is just as well positioned as the epistemic reliabilist simpliciter to accommodate these cases. Finally, note that should we stipulate that Ann is not blameless epistemically for forming her false belief—say that Ann knows about herself that she has pretty poor taste in fashion, and she gets it wrong all the time—the intuition of faultless disagreement is lost as well: Ann should be more hesitant in forming outright beliefs and making outright assertions in this field.

We will not run through more theories of epistemic justification on the market to make our point. Unless we adopt a factive view of justification, it is open to the realist to say that one of Mary and Ann has a false, albeit justified belief about the veggie hat, and that it is justification that explains the faultlessness intuition. And even if one endorses a factive view of justification, the explanation in terms of blamelessness remains available.

How about the intuition that it is open to the two women to hold steadfast even post-disagreement? Can realism accommodate this datum? We think the answer is yes, and furthermore, that it can do a better job at explaining subtle differences between different ways of thinking about the case. Here is why.

To begin with, suppose that learning about a disagreement on p gives one a defeater for one's belief that p. If so, it may now seem more difficult than ever to accommodate the intuition that Mary and Ann may hold steadfast in §1. After all, they do learn about a disagreement. On the present view, this means that they do get defeaters for their beliefs on whether the hat is pretty. The crucial point, however, is that defeaters are themselves defeasible. And, in §1, both Mary and Ann have the relevant defeater defeaters. Mary knows Ann to be a traditionalist and so expects her

---

[8] Pace Kölbel (2002).

to think that her hat is not pretty. In this way she has a standing defeater for Ann's testimony that the hat is not pretty. And, similarly, Ann knows Mary to be an avant-gardist and so expects her to think that the hat is pretty. In this way, she has a standing defeater for Mary's testimony that the hat is pretty. In light of this, both can justifiably dismiss the other's view and remain steadfast. Note also that, in §2 and §3, Mary does not have a defeater defeater. Here the defeater retains its force. As a result, Mary cannot permissibly remain steadfast.[9]

Interestingly, note that these subtleties are not available to the contextualist and the relativist, precisely because they cannot accommodate aesthetic defeat. For them, then, there can be no difference between the case described as a disagreement between known peers, and one where the two don't trust each other's taste one bit. Realism scores another point on this front.

4 Aesthetic Testimony

Pessimists about the epistemic import of aesthetic testimony think that, as opposed to garden variety matters of fact, we cannot acquire epistemic justification and knowledge of aesthetic matters from the mere say-so of others.[10] Going back to Kant (1952), this view usually takes it that perception needs to be involved in the acquisition of justification about aesthetic matters (henceforth aesthetic justification, for convenience).

Pessimists are mainly motivated by some or all of the following set of data: (1) we tend to be less open to accepting the testimony of others about aesthetic matters than about garden variety factual matters (the psychological steadfast datum henceforth); (2) it seems epistemically permissible to be less open to accepting testimony of others about aesthetic matters than about garden variety factual matters (the epistemic steadfast datum) (3) aesthetic beliefs based on mere say-so seem to provide us with less affordances: e.g., it seems we are less warranted to assert, to admire objects, or to make decisions on aesthetic beliefs based on mere say-so than on garden-variety testimonial beliefs (the affordance datum); (4) wide-spread disagreement about the aesthetic makes the epistemic environment non-fertile for acquiring knowledge (the disagreement datum).

---

[9] There is a large literature on peer disagreement. The leadings views are conciliationism (e.g. Christensen, 2007; Feldman, 2006), which holds that agents need to revise their doxastic attitude in these cases, and their steadfast rivals, according to which it's permissible to remain steadfast (e.g. Kelly, 2005; Lackey, 2008). Note that our view does not commit us to a steadfast view, or at least not to an implausible version of it. The reason for this is that it can grant a key conciliationist principle, i.e. that disagreement generates defeat, and then go on to explain why Mary and Ann are nonetheless entitled to remain steadfast in §1, by appealing to defeat defeat. As a result, our treatment of the case is compatible with conciliationist treatment of the bulk of cases in the literature that are thought to favour conciliationism.

[10] For defences of pessimism see e.g. Hopkins (2000) and Whiting (2015). The kind of pessimism we are discussing here is also known as unavailability pessimism. It is distinguished from unusability pessimism (e.g. Hills, 2002), which we won't discuss here.

4.1 Justification

We believe testimony about aesthetic matters can generate justification (and knowledge). While space does not permit us thorough responses to all challenges above, here are a few reasons to be an optimist:[11] first, concerning the psychological datum (see Robson, 2014), we are sceptical about its empirical plausibility. We are in general resistant to accepting the testimony of others when it outright conflicts with our own perceptually formed beliefs. Go ahead and tell us that there's no computer in front of us while we're writing this chapter, see if it goes down well. We also strongly disagree that we should be less open to aesthetic than to garden variety testimony: as we have just seen in the previous section, there are cases of aesthethic testimony in which we are equally resistant; §1 be our prime exhibit here.

Third, concerning various affordances: as one of us (and others) has argued extensively in previous work (Simion 2016), the heard impropriety of aesthetic assertions based on mere say-so is readily explained by Gricean pragmatics: when I assert 'The movie is good!', I trigger a conventional conversational implicature— i.e. an implicature carried by the meaning with which the sentence is commonly used—that I've seen the movie (see Robson, 2015).[12] For the rest, we strongly disagree that aesthetic testimony cannot provide us with reasons to act: in §2 and §3 above, the testimony by Mary's fashionista friends/the fashion experts that the hat is ugly may provide her with reason to return it, or at least, not to wear it.[13] We also disagree with the intuition that aesthetic testimony cannot ever provide one with reasons for aesthetic admiration. To see this, we'd like to turn the focus away from individual works of art to more lofty objects of aesthetic admiration, such as oeuvres. We want to say that we know from experts that Picasso's oeuvre is among the most beautiful in the world. Surely that gives us reason to admire it, even if we have not had the chance to experience it ourselves (perhaps no individual other than Picasso himself has because it is too large and scattered).[14]

Finally, we take the disagreement datum seriously and we agree that when widespread disagreement is present, due to defeat, knowledge might not be ubiquitous. We agree, then, that knowledge will not be readily available about hotly disputed aesthetic facts—just like it is not widely available about hotly disputed facts of any

---

[11] For other defences of optimism, see e.g. (Lord, 2016; Meskin, 2004; Robson, 2023).

[12] Note, also, that the implicature is perfectly cancellable: 'This movie is good—at least that's what I heard from all of my friends'.

[13] Might pessimists not hold that the real reason to act is that the hat is considered to be ugly? Not plausibly. Suppose that the hat is indeed ugly. In this case, the pessimist claim would have to be an impossibility claim: that it cannot be that Mary is returning the hat because it's ugly, that it has to be that she does so because other people think it is. This is a very strong and, we think, implausible claim.

[14] Compatibly, it may be thought that testimony from a friend about the Mona Lisa's aesthetic qualities cannot give me reason to admire it. We disagree; but even if our objector is right, note that it is compatible with the thesis that aesthetic testimony can generate aesthetic justification that the particular variety of justification required for admiration is of perceptual variety.

other sort. We do, however, disagree with the empirical assumption that disagreement is widely spread about all aesthetic facts, or about aesthetic facts par excellence: we might often disagree about whether avant-garde hats are beautiful. We disagree less about many other aesthetic facts, such as the beauty of flowers, or mountains, or the sunset, or Robert Redford, or Marilyn Monroe. In cases like this,[15] knowledge is readily available.

Most importantly though, and leaving the empirical datum aside, the fact that a domain features widely spread disagreement, and as a result knowledge is less ubiquitous than in calmer epistemic waters, does not tell against the capacity of testimony to generate knowledge in that field. After all, capacities are dispositions (e.g. redacted, Sosa, 2015), and dispositions can be masked: vases maintain their fragility in rooms filled with pillows. It just can't manifest itself.

Furthermore, as we are about to argue, if the defeat datum is correct, not only does this not speak against the capacity of aesthetic testimony to generate knowledge, but, to the contrary, it implies that aesthetic testimony has this capacity.

To see this, note that the mechanism by which environments with widely spread disagreement come to be lacking in knowledge is the mechanism of defeat. If there is widely spread disagreement about what the best political system is, we all lack knowledge about what the best political system is—even those of us who started off knowledgeable. We should lower our confidence in whatever position we started with until further investigation. Similarly, if all of us disagree about whether the veggie hat is pretty or not, all else equal (e.g. absent reasons to believe some of us are less reliable than others), we all lack knowledge on this matter—even those who started off knowledgeable.

Again, though, the very possibility of testimonial aesthetic defeat implies that there is such a thing as testimonial justification about aesthetic matters of fact. After all, what we have in these cases is rebutting defeat.[16] By definition, rebutting defeat for one's justification to believe p is, at the same time, justification to believe not-p (or, in other words, evidence against p). As such, it follows from the fact that testimony is capable to generate rebutting aesthetic defeat that testimony can generate aesthetic justification.

---

[15] These cases are discussed in the literature on aesthetic testimony under the label 'aesthetic common knowledge'. See Robson (2012).

[16] Couldn't pessimists agree with Christensen and Feldman that cases of (aesthetic) disagreement are cases in which the belief is defeated because the supporting reasons are bracketed or that they involve undercutting defeat? No. Suppose we are at the theatre. I can see the play that's on but can't hear it because my ears are blocked. You can hear the play but not see it because your eyes are shut. I believe it was beautiful because the costumes and the acting were excellent. You think it wasn't because the dialogue was terrible. We tell each other about this and find out that we disagree. In this case, we should both be less confident in our beliefs than we were before discovering the disagreement. This means that there is defeat in this case. At the same time, the reasons for our beliefs are not bracketed nor is the justification undercut. Rather, my reasons provide evidence that the play was beautiful that, once in the balance with your reasons for thinking it was not, require you to decrease your degree of confidence. And, of course, the same holds, mutatis mutandis, for me. But this means that the defeat at issue here must be rebutting.

What if one denies the disagreement datum? Again, this will not hurt the optimist much. First, going back to the veggie hat: the intuitive difference between Veggie Hat §1 on one hand, and Veggie Hat §2 and §3 gives us independent reason to believe that rebutting aesthetic defeat exists, as does the possibility of aesthetic expertise, in conjunction with the plausible claim that we should trust the word of experts more than that of laymen in the aesthetic domain.

4.2 Knowledge

What about testimonial knowledge? Can't the pessimist withdraw to the weaker claim that even though aesthetic testimony can generate (some) justification, it cannot generate knowledge (call this 'weak pessimism' henceforth)? We think she can't. To see why not, we'd like to start with a clarification. We agree that testimony that x is not pretty from one person and one person alone, about whom we don't know that they're an expert on the matter, might not generate enough epistemic support to defeat our current perceptual justification for a belief that x is pretty. Crucially, again, that will be the case with most perceptual beliefs about garden variety medium-sized dry goods. What we do believe, though, and what we take the Veggie Hat cases to show, is that testimony, indeed, can generate some amount of justification. Insofar as that is true, it will be hard, on theoretical grounds, to hold that aesthetic testimony can't generate knowledge, given the available views on the relation between knowledge and justification. There are two main positions available on the market: one can have a knowledge-first view—according to which justification is to be unpacked in terms of knowledge, or a justification-first view—who takes the analysis to go the other way around.

On a non-traditionalist, knowledge-first view of justification, on which justification is to be unpacked in terms of knowledge (e.g. Williamson, forthcoming), it follows trivially that if aesthetic testimony can generate justification, it can generate knowledge as well. Since it cannot be that justification is present but knowledge is not, we take it that it's clear that the optimist will have no trouble moving from the argument in favour of aesthetic testimony having the capacity to generate the former to its capacity to generate the latter. What if the pessimist wants to take an even stronger stance, and argue that outright justification cannot be generated by aesthetic testimony, but rather only degrees of justification? The problem reappears: since on knowledge-first views degrees of justification (or evidence, or warrant) are commonly (and, arguably, of pain of internal theoretical incoherence, should be) unpacked in terms of knowledge as well, it will be difficult, if not impossible, to combine weak pessimism with a knowledge-first view of the relation between knowledge and justification.

On the vast majority of traditional, justification-first view, *ceteris praesentibus* (i.e. granted that properly based non-Getteirized belief and truth are present), degrees of justification aggregate to generate knowledge. If this is so, enough reliable testifiers—or, alternatively, high degrees of expertise—will aggregate enough testimonial justification for the hearer to come to know based on mere say-so. Thus, granted that aesthetic testimony can generate some justification, it can generate knowledge as well.

How about a view on which knowledge-level justification from aesthetic testimony is a qualitative rather than a quantitative affair? On such a view, some kinds of justification are such that degrees thereof never aggregate to generate knowledge-level justification. One classical example is merely probabilistic justification: most epistemologists agree that we can never come to know based on statistical evidence alone. Couldn't the weak pessimist take aesthetic testimony to fall in the same category? Couldn't she maybe say that what we can gain from the testimony of others is knowledge that it is likely that e.g. the veggie hat is pretty (the more testifiers—or the higher the expertise—the higher the likelihood), but never knowledge that the hat is pretty?

We think that this is implausible, for one key reason, having to do, again, with the phenomenon of defeat. Consider the following case of comparative aesthetic beliefs: I think my drawing is the most beautiful masterpiece in the world, followed closely by Picasso's Guernica. All experts I consult, however, tell me my drawing is rather mediocre. In light of their testimony, while I continue to think my drawing is great, I now come to believe Guernica is better. What is going on in this case? For one, note that I now know (based partially on perception, and partially on expert aesthetic testimony) that the comparative claim: 'Guernica is more beautiful than my drawing' is true. Note, though, that in order to know the comparative claim, it needs be that I know that my drawing is not the most beautiful masterpiece. Since the only justification I have for believing that my drawing is not the most beautiful masterpiece is the expert testimony I have just received, it seems to follow that I came to know that my drawing is not the most beautiful masterpiece based on expert aesthetic testimony. The phenomenon of aesthetic defeat suggests that aesthetic testimony can generate knowledge.

In a nutshell, then, what we have seen is that if testimonial aesthetic defeat exists, then so does testimonial aesthetic justification, and if the latter exists, aesthetic testimony can generate knowledge of aesthetic matters.

5 Conclusion

This chapter has investigated the relation between the epistemology of conversation about aesthetic matters, aesthetic disagreement, defeat, and the semantics of aesthetic discourse. We have argued for a conditional claim: that aesthetic defeat provides support for realism about aesthetic discourse. This is because rival views, such as contextualism and invariantism, cannot accommodate the phenomenon of aesthetic defeat. What's more, aesthetic defeat also supports optimism about aesthetic testimony. The reason for this is that testimony about aesthetic claims can provide defeat for aesthetic beliefs only if it can provide justification for them also. In sum, then, if we like aesthetic defeat, there is reason for us to be realists about aesthetic discourse and optimists about aesthetic testimony.

References

Brown, J., & Simion, M. (Eds.). (2021). *Reasons, justification, and defeat*. Oxford University Press.

Christensen, D. (2007). Epistemology of disagreement: The good news. *Philosophical Review, 116*, 187–218.

Feldman, R. (2006). Epistemological puzzles about disagreement. In S. Hetherington (Ed.), *Epistemic futures* (pp. 216–236). Oxford University Press.

Goldman, A. (1979). What is justified belief? In G. Pappas (Ed.), *Justification and knowledge: New studies in epistemology* (pp. 1–25). Reidel.

Hills (2002). Aesthetic testimony, understanding and virtue. Nous, 56(1), 21–39.

Hopkins, R. (2000). Beauty and testimony. In A. O'Hear (Ed.), *Philosophy, the good, the true and the beautiful* (pp. 209–236). Cambridge University Press.

Huemer, M. (2007). Compassionate phenomenal conservatism. *Philosophy and Phenomenological Research, 74*, 30–55.

Kant, I. (1952). *Critique of judgment* (J. C. Meredith, Trans.). Oxford University Press.

Kelly, T. (2005). The epistemic significance of disagreement. In T. Szabo Gendler & J. Hawthorne (Eds.), *Oxford studies in epistemology* (Vol. 1, pp. 167–196). Oxford University Press.

Kölbel, M. (2002). *Truth without objectivity*. Routledge.

Lackey, J. (2008). What should we do when we disagree? In T. Szabo Gendler & J. Hawthorne (Eds.), *Oxford studies in epistemology* (Vol. 3, pp. 274–293). Oxford University Press.

Lord, E. (2016). On the rational power of aesthetic testimony. *British Journal of Aesthetics, 56*, 1–13.

MacFarlane, J. (2014). *Assessment sensitivity: Relative truth and its applications*. Oxford University Press.

Meskin, A. (2004). Aesthetic testimony. *Philosophy and Phenomenological Research, 69*, 65–91.

Plunkett, D., & Sundell, T. (2013). Disagreement and the semantics of normative and evaluative terms. *Philosophers' Imprint, 13*(23), 1–37.

Pollock, J. (1986). *Contemporary theories of knowledge*. Rowman and Littlefield.

Robson, J. (2012). Aesthetic testimony. *Philosophy Compass, 7*(1), 1–10.

Robson, J. (2014). Aesthetic autonomy and self-aggradisement. *Royal Institute of Philosophy Supplement, 75*, 3–28.

Robson, J. (2015). Norms of belief and norms of assertion in aesthetics. *Philosopher's Imprint, 15*(6), 1–19.

Robson, J. (2023). *Aesthetic testimony: An optimistic approach*. Oxford University Press.

Sosa, E. (2015). *Judgment and agency*. Oxford University Press.

Sundell, T. (2011). Disagreements about taste. *Philosophical Studies, 155*(2), 267–288.

Whiting, D. (2015). The glass is half empty: A new argument for pessimism about aesthetic testimony. *British Journal of Aesthetics, 55*, 91–107.

Williamson, T. (forthcoming). Justifications, excuses, and sceptical scenarios. In J. Dutant & F. Dorsch (Eds.), *The new evil demon*. Oxford University Press.

Critical Social Epistemology and the Liberating Power of Dialogue

Solmu Anttila and Catarina Dutilh Novaes

1 Introduction

In recent years, in particular since the publication of Miranda Fricker's *Epistemic Injustice: Power and the Ethics of Knowing* in 2007 (Fricker, 2007), analytic philosophers (working broadly in the field of social epistemology) have been reflecting more systematically on moral and political wrongs and harms occurring in epistemic processes, and more generally on the intersections between political and epistemic phenomena.[1] Through the notion of *testimonial injustice* in particular, they have been investigating how epistemic injustices can occur in conversational situations, for example when a speaker is given less credibility than is appropriate in view of her actual expertise on the topic in question.

But conversation and dialogue can also be the locus for *resistance and liberation from oppression*, not just for injustice. This is one of the main insights in the work of Brazilian educator and scholar Paulo Freire (1921–1997), who investigated the role of dialogical forms of education for the empowerment of traditionally oppressed groups. Indeed, Freire's work contains valuable ideas that, in our opinion, should be included in the debates on epistemic injustice and related topics. Our goal with this contribution is to present some aspects of his thought that are relevant for these

---

[1] Naturally, in other intellectual traditions, this general topic has received sustained attention for much longer. These include, but are not limited to, black feminism (Collins, Walker, hooks, Davis, Lorde, Barkley Brown), various social theories throughout the twentieth century (DuBois, Foucault, Mannheim, Bourdieu, Berger, Luckmann), radical philosophy, critical race theory, feminist theory, Marxist theory, and critical theory.

S. Anttila · C. D. Novaes (✉)
Vrije Universiteit Amsterdam, Amsterdam, The Netherlands
e-mail: c.dutilhnovaes@vu.nl

debates, thus showing that social epistemologists have much to benefit from engaging with Freire's work. Given the centrality of *dialogue* for Freire, it is fitting that this contribution should appear in a volume dedicated to the epistemology of conversation.

Freire has been extremely influential in his primary field, education studies, but also more broadly in the humanities and social sciences.[2] By contrast, his work is scarcely engaged with by philosophers: tellingly, only five entries of the *Stanford Encyclopedia of Philosophy* refer to him.[3] And yet, his writings are deeply philosophical, reflecting on general topics such as the human condition, the significance of dialogue in epistemic processes, relationships between power and knowledge, and between the self and the world. Importantly, while Freire's work is theoretically rich, it is also deeply embedded in concrete conditions of (post-)colonialism and his work as an educator; indeed, theory and praxis are never sharply distinguished for him.

The paper proceeds as follows. Section 2 provides Freire's historical background (characterized by oppressive colonial power relations), which is likely to be unfamiliar to most interested readers, and yet is crucial for a deeper understanding of his ideas. Section 3 discusses some key aspects of Freire's educational vision, which essentially revolves around *dialogue*. He emphasizes the prior knowledge of learners, the absence of strong hierarchies between learners and educators, and the significance of dialogical education for values of freedom and humanity. Section 4 discusses how Freire orients his educational vision towards the struggle for liberation from oppression: dialogical education helps learners to develop a critical stance towards prevailing social conditions, their own place in society, and the causes of their downtroddenness. This process is called "*conscientização*" (often translated as "critical consciousness"). With what we see as Freire's key contributions to (critical) social epistemology in place, Section 5 hones in on the more precise meanings of some of the key concepts that arise in the previous two sections: oppression, liberation, the oppressed, and the oppressors. This gives us the necessary ingredients to discuss, in Sect. 6, connections, overlaps, and distinctions between Freire's work and a selection of topics from recent critical social epistemology, which directly invoke themes and concepts similar to Freire's: epistemic injustice (Fricker, 2007), the epistemology of resistance (Medina, 2013), and epistemic oppression (Dotson, 2012, 2014).

---

[2] As of writing, his total number of citations according to Google Scholar is 551.035.
[3] Surprisingly, the entry on philosophy of education is not one of them.

2 Freire in Context

Freire engaged with and was influenced by various intellectual traditions throughout his life, such as phenomenology, existentialism, Marxism, radical Catholicism (in particular liberation theology), critical theory, and decolonial thinking (among others). In his work, he sought to systematize and apply insights from these various traditions. At the same time, Freire remained involved hands-on with educational practice throughout his life, in particular with adult education and literacy programs.

For decades, Freire worked on developing (and applying) an account of literacy acquisition, and of education more generally, as a learner-centered process, departing from the learner's own (experiential, if not formal) knowledge, and marked by a horizontal, dialogical relationship between learner and educator. He consistently used the term 'educando' to refer to learners, which roughly means 'capable of education': a potentiality to be actualized that, according to Freire, every human has. (Latinists will recognize the gerundive construction).[4]

During Freire's lifetime, Brazil was (and remains to this day) an extremely stratified society, where inherited colonial power structures were perpetuated by elites who exploited the vast working masses. While officially abolished in 1888, the marks of slavery were still everywhere to be seen: in the marginalization of Afro-Brazilians, the descendants of the enslaved; in the extractivist approach to labor by the elites; and in the overall contempt of the latter for the lower classes. Illiteracy was very widespread, especially among impoverished farmworkers, and this had significant implications for inequality; due to their inability to read and write, large swaths of Brazilians were effectively excluded from societal and political processes. Crucially, illiterate adults were not allowed to vote, a provision that served the interests of powerful elites in perpetuating the disfranchisement of the poor and their marginal social and political position.

In 1963, Freire conducted a groundbreaking adult literacy program in the city of Angicos (in the poor hindland of the Brazilian Northeast), which went on to become a reference in adult education for decades to come. Through the program, 300 farmworkers acquired the ability to read and write within only 45 days of instruction. Following the success of this program, Freire was invited by the government of progressive president João Goulart to lead a nation-wide adult literacy program, where the method deployed in Angicos was to be applied in more than 20.000 municipalities.

In virtue of this and other measures, president João Goulart was increasingly seen as *too* progressive, including by the US government who was deeply concerned with the possible spread of communism in Latin America after the success of the Cuban Revolution in 1959. Soon after inviting Freire to lead the new national

---

[4] In the present contribution, we use the terms 'educator' and 'learner' to translate Freire's 'educador' and 'educando', respectively. The standard translation of *Pedagogy of the Oppressed* uses 'teacher' and 'student', which are not suitable choices in the context of the views articulated by Freire.

literacy program, Goulart was ousted by a military coup in 1964 (Patto Sá Motta, 2022), with the support of the US government (Pereira, 2018), a month before the official launch of the literacy program. In this new, oppressive political climate, Freire was viewed as a 'subversive individual', a 'communist', in particular due to his commitment to the empowerment of the poor and the marginalized through education. Under 'treason' accusations, he was incarcerated for 70 days, and then had to go into exile in 1964; he remained in exile until 1980, when it became possible for him to return to Brazil safely after the Amnesty Law of 1979.[5]

Freire first went to Bolivia and then to Chile, where he lived for 5 years and remained actively involved with adult literacy programs (in collaboration with UNESCO) and agrarian reform programs. It is in Chile that he wrote *Pedagogy of the Oppressed*, which was concluded in 1968, published in Spanish in the same year, and in English in 1970.[6] The book went on to become immeasurably influential, and is said to be the third most cited book in the social sciences (Green, 2016). While he continued to develop and refine his views and to publish several other books, *Pedagogy of the Oppressed* remains Freire's *opus magnum*. In what follows, we draw primarily on *Pedagogy of the Oppressed*, using the 30th anniversary edition (Freire, 2000).

In recent years, with a surge of right-wing extremism in Brazil (culminating in the election of Jair Bolsonaro as president in 2018), Paulo Freire became again prominent in public debates, but now accused of representing everything that is amiss with left-wing, 'ideological' education (the Brazilian version of the so-called 'cultural wars'). It thus became critical to clarify and defend his legacy against baseless, ill-informed attacks, leading to renewed interest in his thought. But the importance of revisiting Freire's legacy is not restricted to (Brazilian) cultural wars; for social epistemologists, it is high time to recognize the philosophical significance of Freire's work for many of the current debates that address the complex relationships between power and knowledge. As previously noted, with the present contribution, we hope to introduce his thought to a wider philosophical audience, showing that there is much to be learned from him that is relevant for these contemporary debates.

---

[5] Most of his years in exile were spent in Geneva, where he was to remain for 10 years working as a consultant for various international humanitarian organizations. In particular, in the second half of the 1970s, he became actively involved with education reform programs in Portuguese-speaking African countries (former colonies of Portugal), where he helped develop decolonial approaches to education in these newly independent countries.

[6] It was only published in Brazil in 1974, as Freire's work was censured by the military government. Before that, it was published in the original Portuguese version in Portugal in 1972, and in Italian, German and French translations.

3 Education as Dialogue

As a scholar, Freire is known primarily for his specific approach to education, *critical pedagogy*, which he developed in particular based on his practical experiences with literacy programs and adult education. *Pedagogy of the Oppressed* is an account of Freire's theoretical reflections on these activities. At the same time, in what follows, we will argue that his theory of dialogical education contains significant *epistemic* insights, and thus offers an important contribution to the epistemology of conversation.

The practical conditions from which Freire's pedagogy stems involve concrete circumstances such as poverty, hunger,[7] and, naturally, illiteracy, in addition to what Freire takes to be more abstract practical conditions, such as the learners' unfreedom, oppression, and their dividedness. Freire suggests that education, if suitably practiced, can offer learners the tools to take control of their world and lives, thus paving the way for liberation from oppression. This educational approach starts from a recognition of the learners' existing (experiential, if not formal) knowledge (despite often not realizing themselves that they too have valuable knowledge (Freire, 2000, chap. 2)), their common sense, their personal experiences of the world, and hands authority over their learning process to themselves. The role of the educator, thus, is to facilitate the learning process rather than to 'preach' to students.

While he emphasized the importance of practical aspects and conditions for education, for Freire, praxis and theoretical reflection are mutually supportive.[8] A key result of Freire's interplay of praxis and theory is a specific vision of the human condition. As aptly described the foreword of the original edition of *Pedagogy of the Oppressed* by theologian Richard Shaull, Freire "operates on one basic assumption: that man's ontological vocation (as he calls it) is to be a Subject who acts upon and transforms his world, and in so doing moves toward ever new possibilities of a fuller and richer life individually and collectively." (Shaull, 2000, 32) Inspired by existentialist ideas and interpretations of the Christian faith centered on liberation (which found their most worked-out versions in liberation theology), Freire emphasized *freedom* as a fundamental feature of human existence, and, conversely, oppression as theft of that freedom. According to Freire, all humans aspire to flourish and thrive as active subjects, and have the potential to do so if given the necessary conditions. Freire introduces the technical term *ser mais* ('to be more')[9] to capture the potential

---

[7] Despite coming from a middle-class background, Freire himself experienced hunger in his youth, when his family faced financial difficulties for a few years. The experience of hunger was extremely formative; Freire dedicated his adult life to improving the life conditions of the impoverished and the oppressed, a commitment that he explicitly associated with his early experience of poverty and hunger (Macedo, 2000).

[8] Freire (2000, 125) quotes Vladimir Lenin: "Without a revolutionary theory there can be no revolutionary movement".

[9] As pointed out in Rocha (2018), "*ser mais*" is not accurately translated in the English translation of *Pedagogy of the Oppressed*. "*Ser mais*" is translated as "more fully human", and the italicized emphasis in the original (which suggests that *ser mais* is a technical term for Freire) is lost in the

for self-determination and flourishing as a central feature of the human ontological vocation.

At the same time, whether and how this potential is actualized will depend on various contingent factors of concrete situations. Indeed, Freire rejects what he describes as "fatalistic positions": fatalists on the right seek to "domesticate the present" so that the status quo prevails, while fatalists on the left view the future as pre-ordained and inexorable (he is here referring to Marxist historical determinism). They "both develop forms of action that negate freedom" (Freire, 2000, 38). In reality, the future is open and malleable; humans can act upon and transform the world around them and their own lives.[10] "Freire contended that human nature is expressed through intentional, reflective, meaningful activity situated within dynamic historical and cultural contexts that shape and set limits on that activity." (Glass, 2001, 16)

An important condition to be able to transform one's world, and in particular to resist oppression, is the development of a *critical stance*, which consists in a grasp of one's personal, social and material conditions that does not simply take them for granted; it is the refusal of a static conception of this reality as immutable. "This can be done only by means of the praxis: reflection and action upon the world in order to transform it." (Freire, 2000, 51) This critical stance is created primarily by means of *dialogical encounters*:

> [E]very human being, no matter how 'ignorant' … he or she may be, is capable of looking critically at the world in a dialogical encounter with others. Provided with the proper tools for such encounters, the individual can gradually perceive personal and social reality as well as the contradictions in it, become conscious of his or her own perception of that reality, and deal critically with it… "People educate each other through the mediation of the world." (Shaull, 2000, 32)

These dialogical encounters are of various kinds, and Freire is particularly interested in how the broader conception of education as empowerment through dialogue can be implemented in formal educational settings. However, what he identifies in traditional educational methods is in fact a complete disregard for the learner's agency, in what he famously described as the 'banking conception of education'.

> Education thus becomes an act of depositing, in which the students are the depositories and the teacher is the depositor. Instead of communicating, the teacher issues communiqués and makes deposits which the students patiently receive, memorize, and repeat. This is the "banking" concept of education, in which the scope of action allowed to the students extends only as far as receiving, filing, and storing the deposits. They do, it is true, have the opportunity to become collectors or cataloguers of the things they store. But in the last

---

translation. More generally, the standard English translation has a number of significant shortcomings, as indeed we discovered when discussing the book in seminars where some of the participants (including one of the present authors) were reading the book in the original Portuguese version and others in the English translation.

[10] A similar conception of critical agency was articulated recently in (Srinivasan, 2019), where Srinivasan speaks of the 'worldmaking' potential of critical genealogies. Freire also shares with genealogical approaches the stress on contingency and historicity (Dutilh Novaes, 2023).

analysis, it is the people themselves who are filed away through the lack of creativity, transformation, and knowledge in this (at best) misguided system. (Freire, 2000, 72)

In the banking model (based on mechanical memorization and rote learning), only the teacher plays an active role, while the student has little to no room to exercise her curiosity and creativity. The relation between teacher and student is entirely asymmetric and hierarchical, and the specific epistemic and social positionalities of students are completely disregarded (i.e., the process is depersonalized (Rocha, 2018)). There is no room for dialogue, as the primary mode of communication is the *monologue* from the teacher to the student. Such practices quench rather than stimulate the learner's curiosity, epistemic agency, and critical stance. Crucially, the banking model is not only inefficient as an instrument for learning: it is in fact one of the institutional instruments for the perpetuation of oppression and inequality in stratified societies.[11]

In opposition to the banking model, Freire formulates a conception of education aligned with his vision of the human ontological vocation, based on freedom and on fostering a critical stance.[12] The starting point is the situated knowledge of the learner: what she already knows from her lived experiences and skills in engaging with the world. Formal education must start from what the learner already knows. This means that standardized learning methods, e.g., textbooks, are inadequate. For example, when tutoring learners on how to read and write, it makes no sense to start with words for objects that are not part of the learners' experiences; more concretely, it makes no sense to start with the word 'apple' when the learners themselves have never eaten or even seen an apple.[13] Instead, the educator must adapt the learning process to the learners' perceived reality (their "historicity"). More generally, human beings in their epistemic processes can never be separated from *social* processes.

Freire describes this alternative model as "problem-posing education". In problem-posing education, the question of 'why' is central: learners investigate together themes that they pick out from their own experiences with the world (this is the "generative" component of the process). For example, educator and learners may talk about who knows how to build a house, what it takes to build a house, why some people have comfortable houses and others do not etc. The words 'brick' or 'house' can then be used for literacy instruction.[14] A very concrete element of the

---

[11] Compare Foucault's analysis of institutions, including formal education, as disciplinary instruments (Foucault, 1995).

[12] This general point had been made earlier by thinkers such as Rousseau and Dewey. In the twentieth century, Jean Piaget and Maria Montessori also developed learner-centered approaches to education.

[13] In practice, Freire's method is syllabic, and takes as a starting point words that are familiar to the learners from their lived experiences. Given the phonetic and orthographic properties of Portuguese, a syllabic method is very appropriate, but for other languages such as English this is not necessarily the case.

[14] Freire's focus on literacy has two paradoxical implications. Firstly, if the epistemic practice *par excellence* is dialogue, why focus so much specifically on *writing*? Secondly, from a decolonial

lived experiences of learners thus serves as a starting point for critical engagement with reality.[15]

Problem-posing education differs from the banking model because learners investigate *together* through dialogue. This requires a horizontal relational scheme between educator and learner (as opposed to the verticality of the banking model). Properly speaking, the educator does not 'teach' the learners; the educator does not 'explain' or 'narrate' the material to the learners in a one-directional way. Instead, educators and learners form a joint process where everyone is a learner who learns from one another: education is a learning process for the educator as much as it is for the learner, and the learners are also educators for each other.

> The educator is no longer merely the-one-who-educates, but one who is himself educated in dialogue with the learners, who in turn while being educated also educate. They become jointly responsible for a process in which all grow… Here, no one educates another, nor is anyone self-educated. People educate each other, mediated by the world, by the cognizable objects which in banking education are 'owned' by the teacher. (Freire, 2000, 80; translation modified)

The key element in the horizontal relation between educator and learner is, of course, *dialogue*, understood as a process wherein educator and learner truly interact to reflect critically on their shared reality. Dialogue is integral to the human ontological vocation, as it is through dialogue that a person truly realizes the human potential for communication, for critical engagement with reality, and for transformation (of the world and of themselves). In a theoretical sense, this is achieved because dialogue corresponds to an interplay between objectivity and subjectivity: "the subjective aspect exists only in relation to the objective aspect (the concrete reality, which is the object of analysis). Subjectivity and objectivity thus join in a dialectical unity producing knowledge in solidarity with action, and vice versa." (Freire, 2000, 38). This is a process which cannot be undertaken in a solitary manner: "people educate each other" and "learners are active co-investigators". As noted by Freire,

> …dialogue characterizes an epistemological relationship. Thus, in this sense, dialogue is a way of knowing and should never be viewed as a mere tactic to involve students in a particular task. We have to make this point very clear. I engage in dialogue not necessarily because I like the other person. I engage in dialogue because I recognize the social and not merely individualistic character of the process of knowing. In this sense, dialogue presents itself as an indispensable component of the process of both learning and knowing. (Freire & Macedo, 1995, 379)

---

perspective, isn't the focus on literacy a reaffirmation of Eurocentric knowledge as 'superior' (given that writing is an imported technology)? These two aspects deserve further investigation, but will not be addressed here for reasons of space.

[15] The edited collection Shor (1987) contains various essays discussing concrete implementations of problem-posing education, and has become an important reference for this approach since its publication.

One may be reminded here of John Stuart Mill, for whom discussion is essential for the rectification of mistakes.[16] But Freire's conception of dialogue is not primarily focused on truth-conduciveness: instead, it is through dialogue that one's *critical agency* truly comes into being, understood not only as a mere passive relation of coming to know one's reality but also as the capacity to *transform* one's reality (Dutilh Novaes, 2023; Srinivasan, 2019). Thus, Freire's understanding of epistemic processes goes much beyond the acquisition of 'justified true beliefs'.[17] Indeed, dialogue and education are practices of *freedom and liberation*, seeking to strengthen the learner's capacity for *critical agency*. Importantly, this transformation is not only a goal for individuals: a core strength of dialogical education as a practice of freedom is that it is simultaneously a way for people to organize themselves and coalesce socially, politically, and epistemically.

> For apart from inquiry, apart from the praxis, individuals cannot be truly human. Knowledge emerges only through invention and re-invention, through the restless, impatient, continuing, hopeful inquiry human beings pursue in the world, with the world, and with each other. (Freire, 2000, 72)

In the next section, we further discuss the liberating, empowering potential of education and dialogue, in particular in oppressive contexts such as those scarred by a history of colonialism.

4 *"Conscientização"*: Critical Agency and Resistance

The considerations above apply generally, and in various educational settings.[18] But of course, Freire's main inspiration comes from his experiences with education of the *oppressed*, as suggested by the title of his *opus magnum*: the illiterate poor in Brazil, then in Chile, and later through his involvement in designing educational policies in former Portuguese colonies in Africa, in the 1970s. What these countries all have in common is that they are former colonies of European colonial powers, where colonial relations still persist. While Freire himself does not explicitly formu-

---

[16] "[Man] is capable of rectifying his mistakes, by discussion and experience. Not by experience alone. There must be discussion, to show how experience is to be interpreted. Wrong opinions and practices gradually yield to fact and argument; but facts and arguments, to produce any effect on the mind, must be brought before it." (Mill, 1999, p. 41)

[17] There are also interesting parallels with Socratic dialogue. In the *Theaetetus*, Socrates describes himself as the 'midwife' who assists his interlocutor in 'giving birth' to the knowledge she already has, thus playing a facilitating role for the learner to do most of the cognitive work herself. Freire uses the childbirth metaphor to refer to *liberation* (from oppression): "Liberation is thus a childbirth, and a painful one." (Freire, 2000, 42) See Fernández-Aballí Altamirano (2020) and Morrow and Torres (2019) for insightful presentations of other epistemological aspects of Freire's thought.

[18] Indeed, the recent concept of *flipped learning* in higher education (Talbert, 2017) is very much in the spirit of Freirean pedagogy: activating students' prior knowledge and letting students play an active role in the process where they also learn from each other, with the instructor primarily having a facilitating role.

late his discussion in terms of the concept of *decoloniality* (a term which was to be coined only in the 1990s by the Peruvian sociologist Aníbal Quijano (2007)), it is clear that he belongs to the broader movement of reflection on the lasting effects of colonialism in the twentieth century, famously associated with authors such as Aimé Césaire and Frantz Fanon, both from the French colony of Martinique (more on Fanon shortly). Indeed, as vividly described by Macedo, Freire's ideas immediately resonate with readers from colonized countries (in particular in Latin America and Africa). Macedo, a linguist, literacy expert and frequent collaborator of Freire's, describes his first contact with Freire's ideas in the following terms:

> I remember vividly my first encounter with *Pedagogy of the Oppressed*, as a colonized young man from Cape Verde who had been struggling with significant questions of cultural identity, yearning to break away from the yoke of Portuguese colonialism. Reading *Pedagogy of the Oppressed* gave me a language to critically understand the tensions, contradictions, fears, doubts, hopes, and 'deferred' dreams that are part and parcel of living a borrowed and colonized cultural existence. Reading *Pedagogy of the Oppressed* also gave me the inner strength to begin the arduous process of transcending a colonial existence that is almost culturally schizophrenic: being present and yet not visible, being visible and yet not present. (Macedo, 2000, 11).

Freire's oppressed are Fanon's "wretched of the Earth",[19] those who have been subjected to the dehumanizing effects of colonization and slavery, which are felt both individually and collectively. Colonization deprives individuals and nations from a sense of dignity and self-worth, making them literally mentally unhealthy; hence Fanon's psychoanalytic approach in his 1961 groundbreaking book *The Wretched of the Earth* (Fanon, 2001), which Freire cites (2000, 62). Freire identifies patterns of the colonizer-colonized relations in the relations of the elites vis-à-vis the poor also in countries that had formally ceased to be colonies (Brazil became officially independent from Portugal in 1822), in particular in narratives of the intrinsic inferiority of the poor/colonized.

> Self-depreciation is another characteristic of the oppressed, which derives from their internalization of the opinion the oppressors hold of them. So often do they hear that they are good for nothing, know nothing and are incapable of learning anything—that they are sick, lazy, and unproductive—that in the end they become convinced of their own unfitness. (Freire, 2000, 63)

The oppressed so deeply internalize the opinions that the oppressors hold of them that they start believing themselves that they are lazy and incompetent (compare Du Bois' notion of double consciousness, also taken up by Fanon).[20] Educational expe-

---

[19] Puzzlingly, the exact phrase "wretched of the earth" ("condenados da terra", a translation of the French "damnés de la terre") appears in the original version in Freire's description of the oppressed at the beginning of Chapter 1, but not in the English translation, which uses "rejects of life" (Freire, 2000, 45). "Wretched of the earth" does appear on page 133 of the English translation.

[20] See Freire's idea that the oppressor is 'housed' inside the oppressed discussed in *Pedagogy of the Oppressed*. Another interesting parallel here is with the Civil Rights Movement in the USA, in particular Martin Luther King Jr.'s focus on non-violent resistance as a path towards *empowerment*, both individual and collective: as a way for African-Americans to regain a sense of dignity, humanity and agency (Nojeim, 2004). It is not a coincidence that Freire and King were both deeply

riences can create the conditions for them to develop a critical stance and to come to realize that these are simply false narratives. Freire's educational praxis thus consists in much more than teaching illiterate adults how to read and write; the larger goal is to support them in developing the conditions to 'be more' (*ser mais*), to develop their full potential as humans who can come to understand and transform their realities. As described by Shaull (2000, 34):

> When an illiterate peasant participates in this sort of educational experience, he or she comes to a new awareness of self, has a new sense of dignity, and is stirred by a new hope... When this happens in the process of learning to read, men and women discover that they are creators of culture, and that all their work can be creative. "I work, and working I transform the world."

Thus seen, education is a deeply subversive force, indeed a tool for resisting oppression, which partially explains why Freire was viewed as an imminent threat by the military regime that took power in Brazil in 1964 (leading to his incarceration and exile). Freire uses the semi-technical term *conscientização* (which remains untranslated in the English translation of *Pedagogy of the Oppressed*) to refer to processes whereby individuals and groups come to perceive social, political and economic contradictions, and acquire skills to take action against the oppressive elements of reality. (Compare the Marxist notion of overcoming *false consciousness*.) "[B]y making it possible for people to enter the historical process as responsible Subjects, *conscientização* enrolls them in the search for self-affirmation." (Freire, 2000, 36) *Conscientização* is the process "by means of which the people, through a true praxis, leave behind the status of *objects* to assume the status of historical *Subjects*" (Freire, 2000, 160). Dialogue is an essential component of the process, as *conscientização* is not an individual but rather a collective process, where individuals are simultaneously learners and educators of each other.

Indeed, *conscientização* is fundamentally an *epistemic* process whereby humans (and in the pedagogical context, learners) develop a sense of critical agency through epistemic empowerment. In a short book published in 1979 in Portuguese (based on lectures that he had given over the years), Freire emphasizes the indissoluble unity of action and critical reflection. There, he describes the path corresponding *conscientização* in the following terms:

> Initially, reality does not present itself to humans as an object that they can cognize through critical conscience. In other words, in the spontaneous human approximation to the world, the fundamental, normal position is not a critical one but rather a naive position. At this spontaneous level, when approaching reality, the person simply has an experience of the reality where she finds herself and looks for. (...) *Conscientização* thus implies that we overcome the spontaneous sphere of apprehension of reality so as to arrive at a critical sphere where reality presents itself as a cognizable object, where the person assumes an epistemological position. (Freire, 1979, 15)

Crucially, this epistemological position is not merely theoretical, it is also deeply practical: it is thanks to a critical stance that a person can *understand* her reality,

---

influenced by Christian humanistic ideas, and were both reacting to the enduring consequences of slavery in their respective countries.

question what is otherwise presented as 'natural' and immutable, and thus acquire the means to *transform* this reality. Provided that a critical, dialogical, problem-posing orientation is followed (rather than the banking model), educational settings offer favorable conditions for the process of *conscientização*: indeed, *conscientização* must be the guiding principle of *any* educational intervention.

5 Oppression and Liberation

The previous two sections have discussed two key features of Freire's critical pedagogy: dialogical education and *conscientização*. Both of these features describe concrete actions that must occur in Freire's vision for practices of education; accordingly, we have deliberately chosen to discuss them first given Freire's emphasis on praxis. This section discusses Freire's conceptualization of the broader framing of these practices in the context of oppression, the goal of liberation, and the key characters, the oppressed and the oppressors, within this context (In the next section, we elaborate on similarities and differences between Freire's ideas and the work of Fricker, Medina, and Dotson respectively).

It is important to note that Freire's strategy in accounting for these concepts, while rigorous, does not begin from abstraction, but instead from his experiences of colonial oppression and domestic class-based oppression in educational action, and a quasi-empirical, social diagnosis point of view. In Freire's thought, no clear distinction is drawn between a universalistic conception of 'oppression' in theory, and how oppression occurs and can be described to work by experiencing it (in this case, primarily mid-twentieth century South America).

Oppression For Freire, again drawing on his personal and pedagogical experiences, the crux of oppression is a relationship of continued and extensive control by one social group (the oppressors) over another (or multiple other) social group(s) (the oppressed) because of a stark inequality of social, political, and economic power between social groups. Crucially, inequalities in social, political, and economic power have vital downstream epistemic effects, and in turn are also further maintained by oppressive epistemic practices such as 'banking education', in a feedback loop.

The control practiced by the oppressors amounts to the elimination of any real freedom for the oppressed, which in turn forces them, not only practically but also cognitively, to conform to the will of the oppressors. For Freire, this cognitive conformity robs the oppressed of their humanity, who cannot live their own authentic lives. In Freirean terminology, this is called "adhesion" to the oppressors by the oppressed (Freire, 2000, 163).[21] While adhesion, unfreedom, and dehumanization seem to be among the core moral wrongs of oppression for Freire, they also create

---

[21] Adhesion is notably close to the concept of false consciousness.

stability for oppression: when the oppressed are convinced to conform to the oppressors, oppression can easily go unchallenged, in which case it has the effect of strengthening the power imbalance between the groups and even greater opportunities for control by the oppressors. The epistemic effects of oppression, in this sense, also help maintain and perpetuate oppression, in a feedback loop. The power imbalance is strengthened by tactics against the interests of the oppressed like divide and rule (Freire, 2000, 146), manipulation (Freire, 2000, 60), and false charity (Freire, 2000, 45). All of these tactics are intended to keep the oppressed from mounting any real challenge to oppressive power. Because Freire believes that this challenge must essentially be made through dialogical action (and critical consciousness, created through dialogical action), Freire describes oppression as "anti-dialogical" (Freire, 2000, chap. 4).

The Oppressed The oppressed are not a single, monolithic group, but they are generally characterized as victims of the violence and dehumanization of oppression. Here again it is important to keep in mind that Freire is reflecting on the basis of concrete social and political situations, primarily in post-colonial South America (Brazil and Chile), against the background of the history of massive enslavement of Africans and their descendants. While slavery in Brazil had been officially abolished in 1888, the elites' extractivist relation towards the working masses was still the norm. The 'wretched of the earth' in this context were primarily the Afro-Brazilian descendants of the enslaved,[22] who, while nominally free, were still by and large functionally treated as enslaved (in many senses resembling Jim Crow in the United States, even if not based on explicit segregation laws). In this context, liberation is not just a metaphorical way of speaking: the working masses had in practice still not been freed from slavery. Freire's conception of the oppressed is thus relevantly different from the Marxist distinction between proletariat and bourgeoisie in virtue of the slavery background (as well as Freire's primary focus on farm workers rather than factory workers). It is however conceptually related to Hegel's master-slave dialectic, where the two categories (master and slave, oppressor and oppressed) are ontologically defined by their relation to one another.

Living under oppression and adhesion, the oppressed are divided and unfree; they endure inauthentic lives. The everyday effects of adhesion for the oppressed manifest as attempts to culturally, socially, and ideologically mimic the oppressors and internalized negative self-images. Interestingly, for Freire, adhesion does not entail that the oppressed learn to ignore that they are downtrodden, but that the appropriate response to any downtroddenness they experience is not social resistance and dialogue but even more adhesion. Because adhesion corresponds to the oppressive ideology, it never prescribes any kind of dialogical action that might suggest liberation; part of the narrative is that there is an intrinsic relation of

---

[22] Colonial violence had already virtually decimated the Brazilian indigenous population at the time of Freire's writing, so purely in terms of numbers, the largest group of dispossessed were the descendants of the African enslaved. In a 2022 census, less than 1% of Brazilians classified themselves as indigenous, while over 55% classified themselves as black or mixed race black.

inferiority at play (especially among different races), thus justifying and naturalizing the status quo of extreme inequality. This is how adhesion takes on the form of oppression itself and how the oppressed can learn to oppress themselves and each other as "sub-oppressors". In a turn of phrase evoking Foucault, Freire describes how the oppressed often do not even need bosses, as the "boss is 'inside' them" (Freire, 2000, 64).

As we saw previously, collective knowledge creation among the oppressed happens through specific kinds of dialogue. In dialogue, the oppressed come to see the world around them differently: they learn to recognize the real causes of their downtroddenness, their oppression, and how they really relate to the world as humans. Through dialogue, the oppressed are literally recovering their lost humanity. However, for real liberation, not only must the oppressed liberate themselves, but in fact *also* the oppressors, who also suffer from (a different kind of) dehumanization. In conditions of oppression, neither the oppressed nor the oppressed can actualize their potential to 'be more', '*ser mais*'.

In addition to the oppressors and the oppressed, Freire also speaks of "radicals", who are the oppressed who are dedicated to liberation, "leaders", who are radicals who must only act as coordinators and not amass all decision power in the liberatory movement (which would be anti-dialogical), and "sectarians", who are oppressed who lack solidarity with other oppressed groups and thus are a threat to liberation.

Liberation Liberation is the conceptual counterpoint to oppression, and the goal of Freirean critical pedagogy, dialogical education, and *conscientização*. Freire emphasizes that striving toward liberation involves a blend of reflection and practical action: it is both simultaneously epistemic and practical, just as oppression involves epistemic components and practical components. This blend occurs perfectly when the oppressed collectively and cooperatively create knowledge together, and learn to use that knowledge against their oppression. (Very concretely, learning how to read and write meant in the context of mid-twentieth century Brazil being allowed to vote at elections.) As mentioned above, there are different oppressed social groups, and in liberation they can, do, and ultimately must come together in solidarity. Although the oppressors have a specific kind of role in achieving liberation (as we discuss below), it is only the oppressed who can liberate: "Only power that springs from the weakness of the oppressed will be sufficiently strong to free both [the oppressors and the oppressed]." (Freire, 2000, 44).

Dialogue for liberation is an extreme challenge. Freire likens liberation to childbirth, as it is as if a new person is 'born' from the process (and the process is itself typically quite painful). One of the key obstacles for liberation that Freire discusses at length is the oppressed's potential "fear of freedom". Liberation is risky, and does not succeed if the unity and solidarity between the oppressed is insufficient. This creates what might be thought of as a collective action problem, as those who fear too much may not join the struggle for freedom, creating more risk and fear in those who would otherwise be willing to join the struggle for freedom. "The oppressed, having internalized the image of the oppressor and adopted his guidelines, are fearful of freedom. Freedom would require them to eject this image and replace it with autonomy and responsibility." (Freire, 2000, 47)

The Oppressors The oppressors are those who have amassed enough power to exercise violence, abuse, and to exploit other social groups. (In the context of colonial histories, this power was initially the prerogative of the colonizer, and later of the local elites who reproduced colonial power relations.) The oppressors are the core of oppressive ideology, and actively "prescribe" adhesion to the oppressed. The oppressors think about the world primarily in terms of possession: for them, "to be is to have". While in one sense they are the beneficiaries of oppression, Freire emphasizes that in oppression, the oppressors also forgo liberation for themselves; they cannot fully actualize their ontological vocation of *ser mais* as long as they oppress. The oppressors, like the oppressed who experience adhesion, are also affected by a kind of ignorance; because of the cognitive distortion that oppression also has on them, the oppressors struggle to recognize their true, human, authentic interest in liberation as well. For Freire, liberation is not a zero-sum game: both oppressors and oppressed will 'win'—they will 'be more'—through liberation.

However, Freire emphasizes that the oppressors cannot not "gift" liberation to the oppressed (Freire, 2000, 47). Ontologically speaking, the process of liberation *must* be led by the oppressed. The oppressors do, however, have a fundamental role in liberation: the oppressors must intentionally choose to be on the side of the oppressed, and trust the oppressed's struggle for liberation.

6 Freire and Critical Social Epistemology

In the previous sections, we have discussed key components of Freire's epistemology, which is rooted in liberatory, primarily dialogical praxis. Given the recent interest in the intersections of justice, liberation, and epistemology also in analytic epistemology (which until recently had been traditionally averse to interpreting epistemological issues as also political), one might think it appropriate to include Freire, a monumental figure on these topics, in these investigations. Such has not been the case yet. In this section, we briefly discuss overlaps and distinctions between Freire's views and some key topics in the recent literature on critical social epistemology. These are *epistemic injustice*, *the epistemology of resistance*, and *epistemic oppression*, in the works of, respectively, Miranda Fricker, José Medina, and Kristie Dotson. There are undoubtedly connections between Freire and other philosophical authors and frameworks—Charles Mills, Linda Alcoff, Patricia Hill Collins, standpoint theory (among others)—that should also be explored. For reasons of space, however, we leave these explorations for future research.

6.1 Epistemic Injustice

Epistemic injustice occurs when epistemic agents are morally wronged in an epistemic capacity, for example because they are ascribed an unfairly low level of credibility when trying to testify to a claim (testimonial injustice), or because the conceptual tools they have at their disposal are unfairly distorted, inhibiting the epistemic agent from making sense of their world and experiences (hermeneutical injustice) (Fricker, 2007). Unfair credibility ascriptions and distortions in collective conceptual tools occur primarily because of prejudices towards social identities.

While the concept of epistemic injustice has received plenty of uptake in social epistemology, a perhaps slightly overlooked aspect in Fricker's account is *why* she thinks epistemic injustices are extremely grave moral wrongs. Fricker is very clear that, in violating agents with regard to their epistemic capabilities, epistemic injustices violate epistemic agents in precisely the capacities that makes them *human*. For Fricker, the capacity to give credible testimony to one's experience is "essential to human value". Capacity for testimony is one aspect of the more general category of the capacity to reason, which, Fricker observes, has been routinely identified throughout the history of philosophy as "lending humanity its distinctive value". Specifically, being denied the capacity for testimony and reason by others can "cramp self-development, so that a person may be, quite literally, prevented from becoming who they are, and forego participation in "the very activity that steadies the mind and forges an essential aspect of identity" (Fricker, 2007, 5).

From the perspective of perpetrators of epistemic injustices, the ability of epistemic injustices to undermine the humanity of groups of epistemic agents is precisely what provides the motivation for them to commit epistemic injustices (or presumably let them emerge in the case of hermeneutical injustices), even if this happens without conscious endorsement. For Fricker, this method of oppression is a version of Fanon's 'psychic alienation',[23] in which oppression occurs through the separation of some essential attribute of personhood from oppressed persons; according to her, one essential attribute is testimony, i.e., the ability to credibly participate in communicating knowledge to others.

Freire's analysis undoubtedly shares two important features with Fricker's. They both i) aim to describe how people are morally wronged as agents who have epistemic capacities, which they are barred from fully utilizing, and ii) share the view that the epistemic is strongly connected with the human. Oppressive practices and structures that interfere with the epistemic aspects of people's lives, in particular what they can say and how they think about their experiences, are unjust because in doing so they interfere with their humanity.

However, it is already on *how* the epistemic is connected to the human that the two authors diverge. For Freire, the connection between humanity (and specifically *ser mais*) and knowledge is articulated in two dimensions: dialogue and epistemic freedom from the world-view of the oppressor. Fricker's emphasis on the ability to

---

[23] Fricker (2007, 58) cites Fanon through Sandra Lee Bartky.

provide testimony and the ability to reason is at most indirectly related to the Freirean ideas, that is, if we understand testimony to be a part of liberatory dialogue and the collective interpretive resources as a reflection of the oppressors' worldview. Freire does not distinguish the testimonial dimensions of this form of oppression from the kinds of conceptual tools that people have to make sense of their oppression *per se*. Arguably, the epistemic aspects of oppression for him are closer to the idea of hermeneutical injustice in the sense that he, like Fricker, discusses how people can and cannot make sense conceptually of their experiences of the world. However, even on this understanding it seems that, for Freire, it is not that there are *gaps* in the collective interpretive resources, but that the oppressed have the entirely wrong ones insofar as they have internalized the oppressor's ideology (an idea that Freire explicates with the metaphor of the oppressor 'living inside' the oppressed).

In the testimonial, interpersonal case, the relevant characters who are engaging in epistemic exchange also illuminate a stark difference between Fricker's and Freire's perspectives. Fricker seems to be mostly interested in interactions between the oppressors and the oppressed, and how moral wrongs occur when people attempt or desire to be good informants to others. By contrast, Freire is less interested in interactions between oppressor and oppressed where the oppressed attempt to be informants; rather, he is primarily interested in how the oppressed can resist by interacting and learning about the world *together*. In other words, unlike Fricker, Freire's goal is not to make these punctual interactions between oppressor and oppressed (instances of testimony) more just. Consequently, Freire's analyses go beyond credibility ascriptions and prejudice, because he is not trying to describe and address a set of moral wrongs that have to do with receiving little credibility (although he of course also problematizes the contempt, epistemic and otherwise, that the oppressor typically has *vis-à-vis* the oppressed). Instead, Freire is describing a more general political strategy for resisting oppression; this strategy is epistemic because, for Freire, structural oppression itself *is* epistemic (i.e., it has a significant epistemic component). The relevant actions for addressing the epistemic aspects of oppression are strategies (in his case, pedagogical, cooperative ones) that help the oppressed see the world in a critical, liberatory way.

This distinction is also reflected in how the two authors describe their moral goals. Fricker's goal is perhaps best characterized in terms of *inclusion*: wrongs of testimonial injustice occur for example when its victims are "excluded from trustful conversation" (Fricker, 2007, 53), and the wrong of hermeneutical injustices is that the interpretive tools the marginalized would need to make sense of their experiences are not included in the dominant set of interpretive resources. By contrast, Freire isn't really thinking about the issue in terms of inclusion/exclusion: for him, the oppressors' circle is not one that is valuable to be included in. Freire's goal is not for the oppressed to be included in the dominant epistemology, but that the oppressed (and oppressors) are liberated from oppressive structures by dismantling the worldview of the oppressor.

Consequently, the two also have different prescriptions of how to address epistemic moral wrongs. Fricker's prescription is toward the perpetrators of injustices:

she suggests that people ought to try to foster virtues of epistemic justice to help address internal prejudices.[24] By contrast, and recalling from Sect. 5, Freire does not think it is possible for effective solutions to moral epistemic wrongs to come from the oppressors; they must come from empowerment of the oppressed. Empowerment thus understood is an important component that is arguably missing in much (though not all) of the recent discussions on epistemic injustice. Overall, Freire proposes interventions that are much more radical and fundamental than the ones proposed by Fricker.

6.2 *Epistemology of Resistance*

José Medina's epistemology of resistance explores the character and normative significance of resistance for the cultivation of democracy through a theory of epistemic interaction (Medina, 2013). Epistemic interaction, for Medina, occurs when diverse resources, life experiences, and imaginations are brought together, compared, and contrasted. Epistemic perspectives can and often are mutually incompatible, thus creating conflict; however, these contrasts can be productive and give rise to 'epistemic friction' (the concept of 'friction' is inspired by Wittgenstein). Epistemic interactions are epistemic in the sense that they might change people's sensibilities, but they are also practical, in the sense that they may change people's practices and habits.

Medina suggests that social and political contestation and resistance are generally epistemic, and feature epistemic interaction and epistemic friction: in epistemic resistance, marginalized agents attempt to collectively challenge and change the oppressive, epistemic status quo, which heavily features willful elite group ignorance about the practical conditions of oppression (Mills, 2007). This happens through epistemic interactions with each other and other groups with diverse life experiences. Medina observes that willful elite group ignorance can be cashed out in terms of *epistemic vices*, i.e., corrupted epistemic dispositions that get in the way of knowledge. Conversely, epistemic interactions oriented towards epistemic resistance help develop *epistemic virtues*, which are dispositions that provide epistemic advantages to the agent and those that interact with her. Epistemic resistance, for Medina, is not only epistemically productive for its own sake, but also beneficial for democracy and necessary to address widespread injustice, epistemic and otherwise.

In framing resistance through its political benefits, Medina identifies his account as following 'resistance models of democracy', also found in the democratic theories of John Dewey, Elizabeth Anderson, and Iris Marion Young (though Medina's

---

[24] Fricker has been criticized for adopting the perspective of the perpetrators in preventing and addressing epistemic injustices; critics are skeptical about the potential and effectiveness of this approach (Alcoff, 2010; Doan, 2018; Langton, 2010). A Freirean perspective on epistemic injustice, centering those on the receiving end of epistemic harms, offers a valuable counterpoint to Fricker's focus on the perpetrator.

account naturally places great emphasis on epistemic aspects and the nature of contestation). Only by making room for contestation, epistemic resistance, and diversity in democratic communication can we expect existing social practices and institutions to reflect the diversity of the society in which they exist, which appears as a key political goal in Medina's project. Indeed, Medina suggests that this part of his account is akin to an epistemic version of Anderson's 'imperative of integration' (Anderson, 2013). Some rules for the 'imperative of epistemic interaction' involve an *expressibility requirement*, according to which social groups must have opportunities to "coalesce in a public with expressive capacities, so that they can articulate their shared experiences and perspectives" and a *responsiveness requirement*, according to which "the social and epistemic conditions of communication and interaction be such that the expressions of a public have the proper uptake by other publics and by society as a whole" (Medina, 2013, 9).

Medina and Freire share the views that resistance to oppression is importantly epistemic, and that communication, especially across differences, is simultaneously epistemically and politically productive. However, this may be the extent of their similarity. While Medina emphasizes the significance of conflict in creating productive epistemic friction, which also occurs between oppressor and oppressed (as we saw with Fricker), this emphasis is not present in Freire, who instead approaches communication primarily as a cooperative joint effort between communities of oppressed groups who create epistemic power for themselves together in identifying the conditions and causes of their oppression. While Freire recognizes that conflict may occur and differences appear in dialogue, conflict is not the central driving force of epistemic production and the creation of new worldviews. (This being said, Freire emphasizes the imperative of *critical* dialogue, not merely the uncritical juxtaposition of experiences, as pointed out in (Macedo, 2000).)

By adopting a virtue perspective, Medina highlights how epistemic interaction, and in particular epistemic friction, fosters character traits, virtues, habits, and sensibilities. Moreover, Medina does not speak of epistemic interaction as a kind of learning, but instead as a kind of discourse through which pre-existing epistemic positions of epistemic agents are compared and contrasted. As we've seen, for Freire, the transformation that takes place in achieving critical consciousness is one of worldviews, when the individual comes to understand the causes of her oppression and to perceive paths towards overcoming it. But for Freire too, as for Medina, epistemic interaction may lead to *personal transformation*, in particular as it offers possibilities of *empowerment* for those who were told they were inherently inferior all their lives. While Medina is interested in the practical aspects of epistemic interaction as changes in habits and dispositions, Freire is arguably practical in a more concrete way in the sense that there is a concrete location—educational institutions such as adult education and literacy programs—and a concrete method—critical pedagogy—through which his version of epistemic resistance is implemented.

Lastly, in *Epistemology of Resistance,* Medina's political goals seem to be primarily those of making liberal democracy as it exists function better, more inclusively, and in an 'integrated' way. By contrast, Freire seems to be less interested in how the oppressors and the oppressed could become 'integrated' with each other;

instead, the goal, as previously mentioned, is collective liberation by the oppressed for everyone—in other words, a real *transformation* of age-old oppressive political structures. While Medina takes liberal democracy as the status quo to be largely maintained (even if improved upon), Freire aims for a rehaul of colonial power structures.[25] Thus, Freire articulates a conception of epistemic resistance for contexts of *extreme oppression and inequality*, something that Medina arguably does not offer.[26]

6.3 Epistemic Oppression

Kristie Dotson was one of the first authors to point out limitations in Fricker's treatment of epistemic injustice, arguing that the issue requires a problematization not only of injustice but of the more systemic, structural phenomenon of *oppression*. The key idea is that epistemic oppression occurs when epistemic agents are excluded from the production of knowledge (Dotson, 2014). Given that they both center oppression in their analyses, Dotson and Freire share many commonalities, and a 'dialogue' between them can shed light on both positions. The gist of Dotson's articulation of epistemic oppression is aptly summarized thus:

> Dotson's account of epistemic oppression is both self-consciously Black feminist and fundamentally structural in that it recognizes that the injustice of epistemic injustice is not the exception but the rule in colonial epistemologies. The injustice goes all the way down in the systems that produce it – and it does so, for the most part, by design. (Berenstain et al., 2022, 284)

In this passage, we recognize clear echoes of Freire's diagnosis of the 'colonial epistemology' of the oppressor, at heart consisting of a collection of strategies to dehumanize the oppressed. In recent work, Dotson has been engaging specifically with the concept of colonial epistemologies, as shown for example in her contribution to (Berenstain et al., 2022). But her earlier work on epistemic oppression, presented as an expansion and reformulation of Fricker's notion of epistemic injustice, already contains the seeds of a decolonial approach that brings her closer to Freire than the two authors previously discussed (Fricker and Medina). In Dotson (2012), she discusses Fricker's notion of 'epistemic bad luck', understood as cases of epistemic harm to knowers that result from 'innocent errors' that are presumed to be accidental or historically incidental. She identifies in Fricker "the inclination to believe that epistemic injustice cannot be conceptualized so that it is too easy to commit." (Dotson, 2012, 37) Dotson argues that epistemic injustice is in fact very

---

[25] Recall that Freire himself had been exiled by a non-democratic military government. Significantly, the 1964 coup had ousted a progressive president who had ascended to office through legitimate democratic institutions. Thus, Freire knew from personal experience how fragile liberal democracies can be when pitted against entrenched political interests.

[26] In his recent work on carceral epistemic injustice and collective resistance (Medina, 2021), Medina seems to come closer to a Freirean perspective on resistance.

easy to commit; specifically, she identifies in the concept of epistemic bad luck the risk of narrowing the responsibilities that members of an epistemic community may have to avoid perpetrating injustices. In sum, according to Dotson, Fricker fails to recognize the pervasiveness of epistemic injustice and, by extension, of epistemic oppression.

Dotson further critiques Fricker for suggesting that there is just *one* set of collective hermeneutical resources that everyone depends upon. She suggests instead (echoing an observation familiar to readers of Foucault) that there are various "alternative epistemologies, countermythologies, and hidden transcripts that exist in hermeneutically marginalized communities *among themselves*" (Dotson, 2012, 31). (We recognize here Freire's emphasis on the valuable bodies of knowledge of the oppressed, even if they initially do not sufficiently recognize themselves as knowledgeable.) Dotson also notes that the concepts of testimonial and hermeneutical injustice do not cover epistemic injustices that do not emerge from credibility deficits or gaps in collective interpretive resources. To remedy this limitation, she introduces a third category of epistemic injustice: *contributory injustice*. Contributory injustices occur when epistemic agents (intentionally) utilize structurally prejudiced interpretive resources, thereby causing harm to other knowers. In Freirean terms, contributory injustice pertains to how oppressors impose their worldviews on the oppressed, which results (among other things) in crushing their capacity to recognize themselves as knowers and to understand their experiences in their own terms.

For Dotson, epistemic oppression is fundamentally structural, but is not universally reducible to political oppression; this observation motivates the conceptual distinction between 'reducible epistemic oppression' and 'irreducible epistemic oppression' (Dotson, 2014). What distinguishes these two kinds of epistemic oppression are the different responses they require to be addressed. Reducible epistemic oppression can be addressed merely with corrective changes to the epistemic resources that we already have, while irreducible epistemic oppression cannot. In addressing reducible epistemic oppression, we need to either apply correctives to the existing epistemic resources so they no longer function to exclude agents (Dotson calls this a 'first-order change') or, in cases where some required epistemic resources are missing entirely, introduce those new resources (while potentially phasing out others) (this is a 'second-order change', similar to Fricker's description of hermeneutical injustice). By contrast, in addressing irreducible epistemic oppression ('third-order change'), we need to "throw into question the relevance of a given community's overall dominant resources in light of the knowledge production activities in question" (Dotson, 2014, 129). This latter kind of oppression is very hard to identify, because identification needs to occur *outside* the epistemic resources of the dominant epistemological system. On the one hand, oppression is resilient because those who experience it the most have the most challenging position to communicate it to others. On the other hand, in Freire's terms, it is precisely for this reason that liberation from oppression must come from the oppressed, as they are better placed to engage critically with the dominant worldview of the oppressor (through *conscientização*), and thus to develop alternative, non-oppressive epistemic resources by means of dialogical praxis.

In sum, both Freire and Dotson recognize the pervasiveness of epistemic oppression and its entanglement with colonial power structures, especially in contexts such as the United States and Brazil. Both also recognize that the oppressed have valuable knowledge. The liberation of the oppressed for Freire will come about not through the absorption of the epistemic resources of the oppressor, but through the development of their own critical stance and further articulation (by means of critical dialogue) of the epistemic resources that they already possess. In fact, for Freire as well as for Dotson, it seems that *only* third-order change can lead to truly overcoming epistemic oppression. Thus, the practice of Freire's critical pedagogy can be seen as addressing contributory injustice as conceptualized by Dotson. Clearly, those interested in Dotson's analysis of epistemic oppression have much to gain from engaging with Freire's ideas.

7 Conclusion

In this contribution, we presented some of the key components of Paulo Freire's dialogical approach to education and pedagogy. He highlights the liberating power of dialogue, in educational settings and beyond, for humans to actualize their ontological vocation to 'be more': to engage critically with the world and with each other in processes where knowledge and praxis are inherently intertwined. Especially for those whose sense of human dignity and critical agency have been crushed by oppression, dialogical education offers possibilities for empowerment and liberation.

We also argued that Freire's investigations on critical pedagogy offer important insights for social epistemology, and for the epistemology of conversation in particular. For him, the epistemic is not merely theoretical, and the political is not merely praxis. In our opinion, this entanglement of the epistemic, the political, the theoretical and the practical means that epistemology must be approached also through education. When considering issues of (political and social) epistemology, it is imperative to take into account the practical contexts in which knowledge is created and exchanged, and this applies in particular to educational settings. And yet, with very few exceptions, social epistemologists have so far had limited engagement with philosophy of education and education more generally. We hope that the 'conversation' between epistemologists and Freire presented here will also pave the way for a more sustained engagement with philosophy of education within social epistemology.

Acknowledgments This research was generously supported by the European Research Council with grant ERC–2017–CoG 771074 for the project 'The Social Epistemology of Argumentation'. The two authors were equally involved in the design and writing of this piece. Thanks to Hugo Mota, Natalie Ashton, and Waldomiro J. Silva Filho for comments on previous drafts.

References

Alcoff, L. M. (2010). Epistemic Identities. *Episteme, 7*(2), 128–137. https://doi.org/10.3366/epi.2010.0003

Anderson, E. (2013). *The imperative of integration* (First paperback printing). Princeton University Press.

Berenstain, N., Dotson, K., Paredes, J., Ruíz, E., & Silva, N. K. (2022). Epistemic oppression, resistance, and resurgence. *Contemporary Political Theory, 21*(2), 283–314. https://doi.org/10.1057/s41296-021-00483-z

Doan, M. (2018). Resisting Structural Epistemic Injustice. *Feminist Philosophy Quarterly, 4*(4). https://doi.org/10.5206/fpq/2018.4.6230

Dotson, K. (2012). A cautionary tale: On limiting epistemic oppression. *Frontiers: A Journal of Women Studies, 33*(1), 24–47. https://doi.org/10.1353/fro.2012.a472779

Dotson, K. (2014). Conceptualizing epistemic oppression. *Social Epistemology, 28*, 115–138.

Dutilh Novaes, C. (2023). Should we be genealogically anxious? From anxiety to epistemic agency and critical resistance. *Midwest Studies in Philosophy, 47*, 103–133. https://doi.org/10.5840/msp2023103142

Fanon, F. (2001). *The wretched of the Earth* (C. Farrington, Trans.). Penguin Books.

Fernández-Aballí Altamirano, A. (2020). The importance of Paulo Freire to communication for development and social change. In J. Servaes (Ed.), *Handbook of communication for development and social change* (pp. 309–327). Springer. https://doi.org/10.1007/978-981-15-2014-3_76

Foucault, M. (1995). *Discipline and punish: The birth of the prison* (2nd Vintage Books ed., A. Sheridan, Trans.). Vintage Books.

Freire, P. (1979). *Conscientização: Teoria e prática da libertação*. Cortez & Moraes.

Freire, P. (2000). *Pedagogy of the oppressed* (M. B. Ramos, Trans.). Bloomsbury.

Freire, P., & Macedo, D. (1995). A dialogue: Culture, language, and race. *Harvard Educational Review, 65*(3), 377–402.

Fricker, M. (2007). *Epistemic injustice: Power and the ethics of knowing*. Oxford University Press.

Glass, R. D. (2001). On Paulo Freire's philosophy of praxis and the foundations of liberation education. *Educational Researcher, 30*(2), 15–25. https://doi.org/10.3102/0013189X030002015

Green, E. D. (2016). *What are the most-cited publications in the social sciences (According to Google scholar)?* Impact of Social Sciences Blog. http://blogs.lse.ac.uk/impactofsocialsciences/

Langton, R. (2010). Review of Miranda Fricker's epistemic injustice: Power and the ethics of knowing. *Hypatia, 25*(2), 459–464. https://doi.org/10.1111/j.1527-2001.2010.01098.x

Macedo, D. (2000). Introduction of the anniversary edition. In P. Freire (Ed.), *Pedagogy of the oppressed* (pp. 11–28). Bloomsbury.

Medina, J. (2013). *The epistemology of resistance: Gender and racial oppression, epistemic injustice, and resistant imaginations*. Oxford University Press.

Medina, J. (2021). Agential epistemic injustice and collective epistemic resistance in the criminal justice system. *Social Epistemology, 35*(2), 185–196. https://doi.org/10.1080/02691728.2020.1839594

Mill, J. S. (1999). *On liberty*. Broadview Press.

Mills, C. (2007). White Ignorance. In Sullivan S., & Tuana, N. (eds.), *Race and epistemologies of ignorance* (pp. 11–38). State University of New York Press.

Morrow, R. A., & Torres, C. A. (2019). Rereading Freire and Habermas: Philosophical anthropology and reframing critical pedagogy and educational research in the neoliberal Anthropocene. In C. A. Torres (Ed.), *The Wiley handbook of Paulo Freire* (pp. 239–274). Wiley. https://doi.org/10.1002/9781119236788.ch13

Nojeim, M. J. (2004). *Gandhi and King: The power of nonviolent resistance*. Praeger.

Patto Sá Motta, R. (2022). *A present past: The Brazilian military dictatorship and the 1964 coup*. Liverpool University Press.

Pereira, A. W. (2018). The US role in the 1964 coup in Brazil: A reassessment. *Bulletin of Latin American Research, 37*(1), 5–17. https://doi.org/10.1111/blar.12518

Quijano, A. (2007). Coloniality and modernity/rationality. *Cultural Studies, 21*(2–3), 168–178. https://doi.org/10.1080/09502380601164353

Rocha, S. D. (2018). "Ser Mais": The Personalism of Paulo Freire. *Philosophy of Education, 2018*(1), 371–384.

Shaull, R. (2000). Foreword. In P. Freire (Ed.), *Pedagogy of the oppressed* (pp. 29–34). Bloomsbury.

Shor, I. (Ed.). (1987). *Freire for the classroom: A sourcebook for liberatory teaching*. Boynton/Cook.

Srinivasan, A. (2019). Genealogy, epistemology and Worldmaking. *Proceedings of the Aristotelian Society, 119*(2), 127–156. https://doi.org/10.1093/arisoc/aoz009

Talbert, R. (2017). *Flipped learning: A guide for higher education faculty*. Stylus Publishing, LLC.

Epistemology of Conversation: General References

The work on the Epistemology of Conversation is not yet organized as a field of Social Epistemology, as is the case with the Epistemology of Testimony or Political Epistemology. For this reason, research in this area generally discusses references from various fields of Epistemology, Moral Philosophy and Philosophy of Language, among others. Below is a broad, but not exhaustive, list of articles and books that are often referred to in literature on the epistemic aspects of conversation.

References

Abeler, J., Nosenzo, D., & Raymond, C. (2019). Preferences for truth-telling. *Econometrica, 87*(4), 1115–1153.
Aberdein, A. (2010). Virtue in argument. *Argumentation, 24*(2), 165–179.
Alcoff, L. (2001). On judging epistemic credibility: Is social identity relevant? In N. Tuana & S. Morgen (Eds.), *Engendering rationalities* (pp. 53–80). State University of New York Press.
Alfano, M. (2012). Expanding the situationist challenge to responsibilist virtue epistemology. *The Philosophical Quarterly, 62*, 223–249.
Alfano, M., & Robinson, B. (2017). Gossip as a burdened virtue. *Ethical Theory and Moral Practice, 20*(3), 473–487. https://doi.org/10.1007/s10677-017-9809-y
Alfano, M., Klein, C., & de Ridder, J. (Eds.). (2022). *Social virtue epistemology*. Routledge.
Anderson, E. (2013). *The imperative of integration*. Princeton University Press.
Anderson, L., & Lepore, E. (2013). What did you call me? Slurs as prohibited words. *Analytic Philosophy, 54*(3), 350–363.
Anscombe, G. (1957). *Intention*. Harvard University Press.
Anscombe, E. (1979). What is it to believe someone? In C. F. Delaney (Ed.), *Rationality and religious belief*. University of Notre Dame Press.
Ariely, D. (2012). *The (honest) truth about dishonesty*. HarperCollins.
Audi, R. (1997). The place of testimony in the fabric of knowledge and justification. *American Philosophical Quarterly, 34*(4), 405–422.
Austin, J. L. (1962). *How to do things with words*. Oxford University Press.
Bach, K., & Harnish, M. (1979). *Linguistic communication and speech acts*. MIT Press.
Backes, M. (2021). Can groups be genuine believers? The argument from interpretationism. *Synthese, 199*, 10311–10329.
Baehr, J. (2011a). *The inquiring mind. On intellectual virtues and virtue epistemology*. Oxford University Press.
Baehr, J. (2011b). The structure of open-mindedness. *Canadian Journal of Philosophy, 41*, 191–213.
Baehr, J. (2019). Intellectual virtues, critical thinking, and the aims of education. In P. Graham, M. Fricker, D. Henderson, Pedersen, & J. Wyatt (Eds.), *Routledge handbook of social epistemology* (pp. 447–457). Routledge.
Baehr, J. (2021). *Deep in thought: A practical guide to teaching for intellectual virtues*. Harvard Education Press.
Baier, A. (1986). Trust and antitrust. *Ethics, 96*, 231–260.
Baker, J. (1987). Trust and rationality. *Pacific Philosophical Quarterly, 68*, 1–13.

Bar-On, D. (2015). Expression: Acts, products, and meaning. In S. Gross, N. Tebben, & M. Williams (Eds.), *Meaning without representation: Essays on truth, expression, normativity, and naturalism* (pp. 180–209). Oxford University Press.

Basu, R., & Schroeder, M. (2019). Doxastic wronging. In B. Kim & M. McGrath (Eds.), *Pragmatic encroachment in epistemology* (pp. 181–205). Routledge.

Battaly, H. (2014). Intellectual Virtues. In S. van Hooft (Ed.), *Handbook of virtue ethics* (pp. 177–187). Acumen.

Battaly, H. (2018). Can closed-mindedness be an intellectual virtue? *Royal Institute of Philosophy Supplements, 85*, 23–41.

Battaly, H. (2021). Closed-mindedness and arrogance. In A. Tanesini & M. O. Lynch (Eds.), *Polarisation, arrogance, and dogmatism: Philosophical perspectives* (pp. 53–70). Routledge.

Bavelas, J., Coates, L., & Johnson, T. (2000). Listeners as co-narrators. *Journal of Personality and Social Psychology, 78*(6), 941–952.

Benson, J. (2023). Democracy and the epistemic problems of political polarization. In *American political science review* (pp. 1–14). https://doi.org/10.1017/S0003055423001089

Berenstain, N., Dotson, K., Paredes, J., Ruíz, E., & Silva, N. K. (2022). Epistemic oppression, resistance, and resurgence. *Contemporary Political Theory, 21*(2), 283–314.

Bird, A. (2002). Illocutionary silencing. *Pacific Philosophical Quarterly, 83*(1), 1–15.

Bond, C., & DePaulo, B. (2006). Accuracy of detection judgments. *Personality and Social Psychology Review, 10*(3), 214–234.

Bond, C., & DePaulo, B. (2008). Individual differences in judging deception: Accuracy and bias. *Psychological Bulletin, 134*(4), 477–492.

Bond, C., Kahler, K., & Paolicelli, L. (1985). The miscommunication of deception: An adaptive perspective. *Journal of Experimental Social Psychology, 21*(4), 331–345.

Bordonaba Plou, D., Fernández Castro, V. C., & Torices Vidal, J. R. N. (Eds.). (2022). *The political turn in analytic philosophy: Reflections On social injustice and oppression*. De Gruyter.

Bratman, M. E. (2013). *Shared agency: A planning theory of acting together*. Oxford University Press.

Brennan, J. (2007). Modesty without illusion. *Philosophy and Phenomenological Research, 75*, 111–128.

Brennan, S. E., & Clark, H. H. (1996). Conceptual pacts and lexical choice in conversation. *Journal of Experimental Psychology: Learning, Memory, and Cognition, 22*, 1482–1493.

Broncano-Berrocal, F., & Carter, J. A. (Eds.). (2021). *The epistemology of group disagreement*. Routledge.

Broughton, G., & Leiter, B. (2021). The naturalized epistemology approach to evidence. In C. Dahlman, A. Stein, & G. Tuzet (Eds.), *Philosophical foundations of evidence law* (pp. 25–39). Oxford University Press.

Brown, J. (2010). Knowledge and assertion. *Philosophy and Phenomenological Research, 81*, 549–566.

Brown, J., & Cappelen, H. (Eds.). (2010). *Assertion: New philosophical essays*. Oxford University Press.

Brown, J., & Simion, M. (Eds.). (2021). *Reasons, justification, and defeat*. Oxford University Press.

Burge, T. (1993). Content preservation. *Philosophical Review, 102*(4), 457–488.

Burgoon, J., & Buller, D. (1996). Interpersonal deception theory. *Communication Theory, 6*, 203–242.

Campbell, T., & Sadurski, W. (Eds.). (1994). *Freedom of communication*. Dartmouth.

Carassa, A., & Colombetti, M. (2009). Joint meaning. *Journal of Pragmatics, 41*, 1837–1854.

Carassa, A., & Columbetti, M. (2009). Situated communicative acts: A deontic approach. In *Proceedings of the CogSi* (pp. 1382–1387).

Carter, A., & Littlejohn, C. (2021). *This is epistemology: An introduction*. Wiley-Blackwell.

Chakrabarti, A., & Matilal, B. K. (Eds.). (1994). *Knowing from words*. Kluwer Academic Publishers.

Christensen, D. (2007). Epistemology of disagreement: The good news. *Philosophical Review, 116*, 187–218.

Christensen, D., & Lackey, J. (Eds.). (2013). *The epistemology of disagreement: New essays*. Oxford University Press.

Clark, H. H. (1996). *Using Language*. Cambridge University Press.

Clark, H. H., & Brennan, S. A. (1991). Grounding in communication. In L. B. Resnick, J. M. Levine, & S. D. Teasley (Eds.), *Perspectives on socially shared cognition* (pp. 127–149). APA Books.

Clayman, S., & Gill, V. (2023). Conversation analysis and discourse analysis. In M. Handford & J. P. Gee (Eds.), *The Routledge handbook of discourse analysis* (pp. 67–84). Routledge.

Coady, C. A. J. (1992). *Testimony: A philosophical study*. Oxford University Press.

Craig, E. (1999). *Knowledge and the state of nature: An essay in conceptual synthesis*. Oxford University Press.

Cull, M. J. (2019). Dismissive incomprehension: A use of purported ignorance to undermine others. *Social Epistemology, 33*(3), 262–271. https://doi.org/10.1080/02691728.2019.1625982

Cuneo, T. (2014). *Speech and morality: On the metaethical implications of speaking*. Oxford University Press.

Darwall, S. (2006). *The second-person standpoint: Respect, morality, and accountability*. Harvard University Press.

Davidson, D. (1992). The second person. In *Subjective, intersubjective, objective* (pp. 107–121). Oxford University Press, 2001.

Davidson, D. (1994). Dialectic and dialogue. In G. Preyer et al. (Eds.), *Language, mind, and epistemology* (pp. 429–437). Kluwer Academic Publishers.

Davis, W. (1988). *Implicature: Intention, convention, and principle in the failure of Gricean theory*. Cambridge University Press.

DePaulo, B. (1980). Humans as lie detectors. *Journal of Communication, 30*(2), 129–139.

Dotson, K. (2011). Tracking epistemic violence, tracking practices of silencing. *Hypatia, 26*(2), 236–257. https://doi.org/10.1111/j.1527-2001.2011.01177.x

Dotson, K. (2014). Conceptualizing epistemic oppression. *Social Epistemology, 28*(2), 115–138.

Driver, J. (1989). The virtues of ignorance. *Journal of Philosophy, 86*, 373–384.

Edenberg, E., & Hannon, M. (Eds.). (2021). *Political epistemology*. Oxford University Press.

Ellefsen, G. (2021). Conversational cooperation revisited. *The Southern Journal of Philosophy, 59*(4), 545–571.

Enfield, N. (2017). *How we talk: The inner workings of conversation*. Basic Books.

Farkas, D., & Bruce, K. (2009). On reacting to assertions and polar questions. *Journal of Semantics, 27*, 81–118.

Faulkner, P. (2011). *Knowledge on trust*. Oxford University Press.

Faulkner, P., & Simpson, T. (Eds.). (2017). *The philosophy of trust*. Oxford University Press.

Feldman, R. (2000). The ethics of belief. *Philosophy and Phenomenological Research, 60*(3), 667–695.

Feldman, R., & Warfield, T. (Eds.). (2010). *Disagreement*. Oxford University Press.

Feldman, R., Forrest, J., & Happ, B. (2002). Self-presentation and verbal deception: Do self-presenters lie more? *Basic and Applied Social Psychology, 24*(2), 163–170.

Filmore, C. (1981). Pragmatics and the description of discourse. In P. Cole (Ed.), *Radical pragmatics* (pp. 143–166). Academic.

Fogal, D., Harris, D., & Moss, M. (Eds.). (2018). *New work on speech acts*. Oxford University Press.

Foley, R. (2001). *Intellectual trust in oneself and others*. Cambridge University Press.

Frankfurt, H. G. (1986). *On bullshit*. Princeton University Press.

Fricker, E. (1994). Against gullibility. In A. Chakrabarti & B. K. Matilal (Eds.), *Knowing from words* (pp. 125–161). Kluwer Academic Publishers.

Fricker, E. (1995). Telling and trusting: Reductionism and anti-reductionism in the epistemology of testimony. *Mind, 104*(414), 393–411.

Fricker, E. (2003). Understanding and knowledge of what is said. In A. Barber (Ed.), *Epistemology of langauge* (pp. 325–366). Oxford University Press.

Fricker, E. (2004). Testimony: Knowing through being told. In I. Niiniluoto, M. Sintonen, & J. Wolenski (Eds.), *Handbook of epistemology* (pp. 109–130). Kluwer Academic Publishers.

Fricker, E. (2006). Second-hand knowledge. *Philosophy and Phenomenological Research, 73*, 592–618.

Fricker, M. (2007). *Epistemic injustice: Power and the ethics of knowing*. Oxford University Press.

Fricker, E. (2017). Norms, constitutive and social, and assertion. *American Philosophical Quarterly, 54*(4), 397–418.

Fridland, E., & Pavese, C. (Eds.). (2021). *The Routledge handbook of philosophy of skill and expertise* (pp. 460–475). Routledge.

Friedman, J. (2020). The epistemic and the zetetic. *Philosophical Review, 129*(4), 501–536.

Garcia-Carpintero, M. (2004). Assertion and the semantics of force-markers. In C. Bianchi (Ed.), *The semantics/pragmatics distinction* (pp. 133–166). CSLI/Stanford University Press.

Gauker, C. (2001). Situated inference versus conversational implicature. *Noûs, 35*(2), 163–189.

George, J., & Robb, A. (2008). Deception and computer-meditated communication in daily life. *Communication Reports, 21*(2), 92–103.

Gibbard, A. (1990). *Wise choices, apt feelings: A theory of normative judgment*. Harvard University Press.

Gilbert, M. (1990). Walking together: A paradigmatic social phenomenon. *Midwest Studies in Philosophy, 15*(1), 1–14.

Gilbert, M. (2004). Collective epistemology. *Episteme, 1*, 95–107.

Gilbert, M. (2008). Two approaches to shared intention: An essay in the philosophy of social phenomena. *Analyse & Kritik, 30*(2), 483–514. https://doi.org/10.1515/auk-2008-0208

Gilbert, M. (2009). Shared intention and personal intentions. *Philosophical Studies, 144*, 167–187.

Gilbert, M. (2014). *Joint commitment: How we make the social world*. Oxford University Press.

Gilbert, M. (2023). *Life in groups: How we think, feel, and act together*. Oxford University Press.

Gilbert, M., & Priest, M. (2013). Conversation and collective belief. In A. Capone, F. Lo Piparo, & M. Carapezza (Eds.), *Perspectives on pragmatics and philosophy* (pp. 1–34). Springer.

Gilbert, D., Krull, D., & Malone, P. (1990). Unbelieving the unbelievable: Some problems in the rejection of false information. *Journal of Personality and Social Psychology, 59*, 601–613.

Ginzburg, J. (1996). Dynamics and the semantics of dialogue. In J. Seligman & D. Westerstahl (Eds.), *Language, logic, and computation* (pp. 221–237). CSLI Lecture Notes.

Ginzburg, J. (2012). *The interactive stance: Meaning for conversation*. Oxford University Press.

Gladwell, M. (2019). *Talking to strangers: What we should know about the people we don't know*. Little, Brown and Company.

Gneezy, U., Kajackaite, A., & Sobel, J. (2018). Lying aversion and the size of the lie. *American Economic Review, 108*(2), 419–453.

Goldberg, S. C. (Ed.). (2002). *The Oxford handbook of assertion*. Oxford University Press.

Goldberg, S. C. (2010). *Relying on others: Essay in epistemology*. Oxford University Press.

Goldberg, S. C. (2014). Interpersonal epistemic entitlements. *Philosophical Issues, 24*(1), 159–183.

Goldberg, S. C. (2015). *Assertion: On the philosophical significance of assertoric speech*. Oxford University Press.

Goldberg, S. C. (2020). *Conversational pressure: Normativity in speech exchanges*. Oxford University Press.

Goldberg, S. C. (2022). What is a speaker owed? *Philosophy and Public Affairs, 50*(3), 375–407.

Goldman, A. (2001). Experts: Which ones should you trust? *Philosophy and Phenomenological Research, 63*, 85–110.

Goodwin, C. (1995). The negotiation of coherence within conversation. In G. A. Gernsbacher & T. Givon (Eds.), *Coherence in spontaneous text* (pp. 117–137). Benjamins.

Graham, P. (2010). Testimonial entitlement and the function of comprehension. In D. Pritchard, A. Millar, & A. Haddock (Eds.), *Social epistemology* (pp. 148–174). Oxford University Press.

Graham, P. (2016). Testimonial knowledge: A unified account. *Philosophical Issues, 26*(1), 172–186.

Graham, P. J. (2020). Assertions, handicaps, and social norms. *Episteme, 17*, 349–363.

Greco, J. (2010). *Achieving knowledge: A virtue-theoretic account of epistemic normativity*. Cambridge University Press.
Greco, J. (2020). *The transmission of knowledge*. Cambridge University Press.
Greco, J. (2021). What is social epistemic dependence? *Philosophical Topics, 49*(2), 113–132.
Grice, H. P. (1957). Meaning. *Philosophical Review, 66*, 377–388.
Grice, H. P. (1975). Logic and conversation. *Syntax and Semantics, 3*(Speech arts), 41–58.
Grice, H. P. (1989). *Studies in the way of words*. Harvard University Press.
Halevy, R., Shalvi, S., & Verschuere, B. (2014). Being honest about dishonesty: Correlating self-reports and actual lying. *Human Communication Research, 40*(1), 54–72.
Hamblin, C. L. (1970). *Fallacies*. Methuen.
Hancock, J. T., Thom-Santelli, J., & Ritchie, T. (2004). Deception and design: The impact of communication technology on lying behavior. *CHI Letters, 6*(1), 129–134.
Hannon, M., & de Ridder, J. (Eds.). (2021). *The Routledge handbook of political epistemology*. Routledge.
Hardwig, J. (1985). Epistemic dependence. *Journal of Philosophy, 82*, 335–349.
Hardwig, J. (1991). The role of trust in knowledge. *The Journal of Philospyhy, 88*(12), 693–708.
Harwood, J. (2014). Easy lies. *Journal of Language and Social Psychology, 33*(4), 405–410.
Hawley, K. (2014a). Partiality and prejudice in trusting. *Synthese, 191*, 2029–2045.
Hawley, K. (2014b). Trust, distrust, and commitment. *Noûs, 48*(1), 1–20.
Hinchman, E. (2005). Telling as inviting to trust. *Philosophy and Phenomenological Research, 70*(3), 562–587.
Hinchman, E. S. (2013). Assertion, sincerity, and knowledge. *Noûs, 47*(4), 613–646.
Hinchman, E. S. (2014). Assurance and warrant. *Philosopher's Imprint, 14*, 17.
Holton, R. (1994). Deciding to trust, coming to believe. *Australasian Journal of Philosophy, 72*, 63–76.
Jameson, A., & Weis, T. (1996). How to juggle discourse obligations. *Sonderforschungsbereich 378 Ressourcenadaptive Kognitive Prozesse, 133*, 1–15.
Johnson, R. H. (2014). *The rise of informal logic: Essays on argumentation, critical thinking, reasoning and politics*. Windsor Studies. in Argumentation.
Johnson, C. R. (Ed.). (2018). *Voicing dissent: The ethics and epistemology of making disagreement public*. Routledge.
Johnson, R. H., & Blair, J. A. (1977). *Logical self-defense*. McGraw-Hill Ryerson.
Jones, K. (2002). The politics of credibility. In L. Antony & C. Witt (Eds.), *A mind of one's own: Feminist essays on reason and objectivity* (pp. 154–176). Westview.
Ke, W., & Li, Z. (2017). Critical voices against the cooperative principle. *Canadian Social Science, 13*(10), 15–21.
Keller, S. (2004). Friendship and belief. *Philosophical Papers, 33*(3), 329–351.
Kelly, T. (2005). The epistemic significance of disagreement. In T. Szabo Gendler & J. Hawthorne (Eds.), *Oxford studies in epistemology* (Vol. 1, pp. 167–196). Oxford University Press.
Kelp, C., & Simion, M. (2022). *Sharing knowledge: A functionalist account of assertion*. Cambridge University Press.
Khoo, J., & Sterken, R. (Eds.). (2021). *The Routledge handbook of social and political philosophy of language*. Routledge.
Kidd, I. J., Battaly, H. D., & Cassam, Q. (Eds.). (2021). *Vice epistemology*. Routledge.
Kölbel, M. (2002). *Truth without objectivity*. Routledge.
Lackey, J. (2008a). *Learning from words: Testimony as a source of knowledge*. Oxford University Press.
Lackey, J. (2008b). What should we do when we disagree? In S. T. Gendler & J. Hawthorne (Eds.), *Oxford studies in epistemology* (Vol. 3, pp. 274–293). Oxford University Press.
Lackey, J. (Ed.). (2014). *Essays in collective epistemology*. Oxford University Press. Reprinted in Gilbert, 2023.
Lackey, J. (2020a). *The epistemology of groups*. Oxford University Press.
Lackey, J. (2020b). The duty to object. *Philosophy and Phenomenological Research, 101*(1), 35–60.

Langton, R., & Hornsby, J. (1998). Free speech and illocution. *Legal Theory, 4*(1), 21–37.
Leonard, N. (2016). Testimony, evidence and interpersonal reasons. *Philosophical Studies, 173*(9), 2333–2352.
Lepore, E., & Stone, M. (2015). *Imagination and convention: Distinguishing grammar and inference in language*. Oxford University Press.
Lewis, D. K. (1969). *Convention: A philosophical study*. Harvard University Press.
Lewis, D. K. (1975). Languages and language. In *Philosophical papers volume 1* (pp. 163–188). Oxford University Press, 1983.
Lewis, D. K. (1982). Logic for equivocators. *Noûs, 16*(3), 431–441.
Lewis, D. K. (1996). Elusive knowledge. *Australasian Journal of Philosophy, 74*(4), 549–567.
List, C. (2005). Group knowledge and group rationality: A judgment aggregation perspective. *Episteme, 2*, 25–38.
List, C. (2014). Three kinds of collective attitudes. *Erkenntnis, 79*, 1601–1622.
MacFarlane, J. (2014). *Assessment sensitivity: Relative truth and its applications*. Oxford University Press.
Maitra, I. (2009). Silencing speech. *Canadian Journal of Philosophy, 39*(2), 309–338.
Martín, A. (2020). What is white ignorance? *The Philosophical Quarterly, 71*(4), 864–885. https://doi.org/10.1093/pq/pqaa073
Matira, I., & McGowan, M. K. (Eds.). (2012). *Speech and harm: Controversies over free speech*. Oxford University Press.
McGowan, M. K. (2009). Oppressive speech. *Australasian Journal of Philosophy, 87*(3), 389–407.
McKeena, R. (2023). *Non-ideal epistemology*. Oxford University Press.
McKenna, M. (2012). *Conversation and responsibility*. Oxford University Press.
McKinney, R. A. (2016). Extracted speech. *Social Theory and Practice, 42*(2), 258–284. https://doi.org/10.5840/soctheorpract201642215
McMyler, B. (2007). Knowing at second hand. *Inquiry, 50*, 511–540.
McMyler, B. (2011). *Testimony, trust, and authority*. Oxford University Press.
McMyler, B. (2013). The epistemic significance of address. *Synthese, 190*, 1059–1078.
Medina, J. (2013). *The epistemology of resistance: Gender and racial oppression, epistemic injustice, and resistant imaginations*. Oxford University Press.
Meibauer, J. (Ed.). (2018). *The Oxford handbook of lying*. Oxford University Press.
Meijers, A. (2002). Collective agents and cognitive attitudes. *ProtoSociology, 16*, 70–85.
Mercier, H., & Sperber, D. (2011). Why do humans reason? Arguments for an argumentative theory. *Behavioral and Brain Sciences, 34*, 57–111.
Mercier, H., & Sperber, D. (2017). *The enigma of reason: A new theory of human understanding*. Penguin.
Miller, G., & Stiff, J. (1993). *Deceptive communication*. Sage.
Moran, R. (2005). Getting told and being believed. *Philosopher's Imprint, 5*, 1–29.
Moran, R. (2018). *The exchange of words: Speech, testimony, and intersubjectivity*. Oxford University Press.
Mühlebach, D. (2022). Non-ideal philosophy of language. *Inquiry*, 1–23. https://doi.org/10.1080/0020174X.2022.2074884
Munitz, M. K., & Unger, P. K. (Eds.). (1974). *Semantics and philosophy*. University Press.
Olson, K. (2011). Legitimate speech and hegemonic idiom: The limits of deliberative democracy in the diversity of its voices. *Political Studies, 59*(3), 527–546.
Owens, D. (2006). Testimony and assertion. *Philosophical Studies, 130*(1), 105–129.
Pagin, P. (2008). What is communicative success? *Canadian Journal of Philosophy, 38*, 85–115.
Pollock, J. (2015). Social externalism and the problem of communication. *Philosophical Studies, 172*, 3229–3251.
Pollock, J. (2023). Testimonial knowledge and content preservation. *Philosophical Studies, 180*(10), 3073–3097.
Priest, M. (2016). Intellectual virtue: An interpersonal theory. *Ergo, 4*. https://doi.org/10.3998/ergo.12405314.0004.016

Pritchard, D. H. (2022a). Cultivating intellectual virtues. In R. Curren (Ed.), *Routledge handbook of philosophy of education* (pp. 127–136). Routledge.

Pritchard, D. H. (2022b). Virtuous arguing with conviction and humility. *Ethical Theory and Moral Practice*. https://doi.org/10.1007/s10677-022-10328-2

Recanati, F. (1986). On defining communicative intentions. *Mind and Language, 1*, 213–242.

Resnick, L. B., Levine, J. M., & Teasley, S. D. (Eds.). (1991). *Perspectives on socially shared cognition*. APA Books.

Riggs, W. (2010). Open-mindedness. *Metaphilosophy, 41*, 172–188.

Roberts, R. C., & Wood, J. (2007). *Intellectual virtues: An essay in regulative epistemology*. Oxford University Press.

Ross, A. (1986). Why do we believe what we are told? *Ratio, 28*(1), 69–88.

Saul, J. (2002). Speaker meaning, what is said, and what is implicated. *Noûs, 36*(2), 228–248.

Saul, J. (2010). Speaker-meaning, conversational implicature and calculability. In K. Petrus (Ed.), *Meaning and analysis: New essays on Grice* (pp. 170–183). Palgrave Macmillan.

Sbisà, M. (2002). Speech acts in context. *Language & Communication, 22*, 421–436.

Schiffer, S. (1972). *Meaning*. Oxford University Press.

Schiffer, S. (1987). *Remnants of meaning*. MIT Press.

Schmitt, F. (Ed.). (1994). *Socializing epistemology: The social dimensions of knowledge*. Rowman and Littlefield.

Schmitt, F. F. (2018). Remarks on conversation and negotiated collective belief. *ProtoSociology, 35*, 74–98.

Schroeder, M. (2008). *Being for: Evaluating the semantic program of expressivism*. Oxford University Press.

Shieber, J. (2012). Against credibility. *Australasian Journal of Philosophy, 90*(1), 1–18.

Shiffrin, S. (2014). *Speech matters: Lying, morality and the law*. Princeton University Press.

Sidnell, J., & Stivers, T. (Eds.). (2013). *The handbook of conversation analysis*. Wiley-Blackwell.

Silva Filho, W. J., & Tateo, L. (Eds.). (2019). *Thinking about oneself: The place and value of reflection in philosophy and psychology*. Springer.

Simon, J. (Ed.). (2020). *The Routledge handbook of trust and philosophy*. Routledge.

Smithies, D. (2012). The normative role of knowledge. *Noûs, 46*(2), 265–288.

Sosa, E. (2015). *Judgment and agency*. Oxford University Press.

Sperber, D. (2013). Speakers are honest because hearers are vigilant: Reply to Kourken Michaelian. *Episteme, 10*(1), 61–71.

Sperber, D., & Wilson, D. (1995). *Relevance: Communication and cognition* (2nd ed.). Blackwell.

Stalnaker, R. (1973). Presuppositions. *Journal of Philosophic Logic, 2*, 447–457.

Stalnaker, R. C. (1978). Assertion. *Syntax and Semantics, 9*, 315–332.

Stalnaker, R. (1984). *Inquiry*. MIT Press.

Stanley, J. (2011). *Know how*. Oxford University Press.

Stanley, J., & Beaver, D. (2023). *The politics of language*. Princeton University Press.

Stivers, T. (2010). An overview of the question–response system in American English conversation. *Journal of Pragmatics, 42*(10), 2772–2781. https://doi.org/10.1016/j.pragma.2010.04.011

Strosetzki, C. (Ed.). (2023). *The value of conversation: Perspectives from antiquity to modernity*. Springer.

Stroud, S. (2006). Epistemic partiality in friendship. *Ethics, 116*(3), 498–524.

Sweet, K. (2022). *Collaborative inquiry: An epistemological account of inquiring together*. Dissertation, Saint Louis University, St. Louis, MO.

Tanesini, A. (2018a). Eloquent silences: Silence and dissent. In C. R. Johnson (Ed.), *Voicing dissent: The ethics and epistemology of making disagreement public* (pp. 109–128). Routledge.

Tanesini, A. (2018b). Intellectual humility as attitude. *Philosophy and Phenomenological Research, 96*, 399–420.

Tanesini, A. (2021). *The mismeasure of the self: A study in vice epistemology*. Oxford University Press.

Tanesini, A., & Lynch, M. P. (Eds.). (2021). *Polarisation, arrogance, and dogmatism: Philosophical perspectives*. Routledge.
Tannen, D. (Ed.). (1982). *Analyzing discourse: Text and talk* (pp. 71–93). Georgetown University Press.
Tuomela, R. (1992). Group beliefs. *Synthese, 91*, 285–318.
van Eemeren, F. H., & Grootendorst, R. (1984). *Speech acts in argumentative discussions: A theoretical model for the analysis of discussions directed towards solving conflicts of opinion*. Foris.
van Eemeren, F. H., & Grootendorst, R. (2004). *A systematic theory of argumentation: The pragma-dialectical approach*. Cambridge University Press.
Velleman, J. D. (1997). How to share an intention. *Philosophy and Phenomeno- logical Research, 57*(1), 29–50.
Vesga, A. (2023). Communicating testimonial commitment. *Ergo an Open Access Journal of Philosophy, 10*, 16.
Walton, D. N. (1992). *Plausible argument in everyday conversation*. SUNY Press.
Walton, D. N. (1998). *The new dialectic. Conversational contexts of argument*. University of Toronto Press.
Walton, D. N., & Krabbe, E. C. W. (1995). *Commitment in dialogue*. State University of New York Press.
Watson, L. (2015). What is inquisitiveness. *American Philosophical Quarterly, 52*(3), 273–287.
Whitcomb, D. (2017). One kind of asking. *The Philosophical Quarterly, 67*(266), 148–168.
Whitcomb, D., Battaly, H., Baehr, J., & Howard-Synder, D. (2017). Intellectual humility: Owning our limitations. *Philosophy and Phenomenological Research, 94*, 509–539.
Williamson, T. (1996). Knowing and asserting. *The Philosophical Review, 105*(4), 489–523.
Williamson, T. (2000). *Knowledge and its limits*. Oxford University Press.
Wittgenstein, L. (1969). *On certainty* (D. Paul, & G. E. M. Anscombe, Trans.). Harper.
Woods, J., & Walton, D. N. (1982). *Argument: The logic of the fallacies*. McGraw-Hill Ryerson.
Woods, J., & Walton, D. N. (1989). *Fallacies: Selected papers 1972–1982*. Foris.
Worthington, E. L., Jr., Davis, D. E., & Hook, J. N. (Eds.). (2016). *Routledge handbook of humility*. Routledge.
Wray, K. B. (2001). Collective belief and acceptance. *Synthese, 129*, 319–333.
Zeldin, T. (1998). *Conversation: How talk can change our lives*. Harvill.